SRI LALITA DEVI

THE THOUSAND NAMES of the DIVINE MOTHER

Śrī Lalitā Sahasranāma

WITH COMMENTARY
by
T.V. Narayana Menon

Edited by
Prof. K.V. Dev

Translated into English by
Dr. M.N. Namboodiri

MATA AMRITANANDAMAYI CENTER
San Ramon, California

THE THOUSAND NAMES OF THE DIVINE MOTHER
Sri Lalita Sahasranama

PUBLISHED BY:
Mata Amritanandamayi Center
P.O. Box 613
San Ramon, CA 94583-0613
Tel: (510) 537-9417

Printed in the United States of America

FIRST PRINTING May 1996

ALSO AVAILABLE FROM:
Mata Amritanandamayi Mission Trust
Amritapuri P.O., Kollam Dt., Kerala
INDIA 690525

ISBN 1-879410-67-2

This Book Is Humbly Dedicated To

SRI SRI MATA AMRITANANDAMAYI

The Embodiment of the Divine Mother, Śri Lalitā Devī

Sā-jayati-śaktirādyā-nijasukhamayanirupamākārā |
Bhāvicarācarabhījam-śivarūpavimarśanirmalādarsaḥ | |

She, the Primordial Śakti who excels all and who, in Her own true nature, is eternal, limitless Bliss, is the seed of all the moving and motionless things which are to be, and is the Pure Mirror in which Śiva, the Absolute, experiences Himself.

KĀMA KALĀ VILĀSA
Verse 2

CONTENTS

NOTES

ABOUT THE COMMENTATOR: TIRUVALI VALLIKKATTU NARAYANA MENON

Mr. Narayana Menon was born in 1855 in Mancheri in Kerala, and was a great devotee of Devi. He worshipped Devi daily, on a Śrī Cakra made of gold, through *Lalitā Sahasranāma arcana*. As a result of his untiring efforts, he had the good fortune to complete a commentary on *Lalitā Sahasranāma* in Malayalam before his death at the age of seventy-two.

After the death of Mr. Menon, the commentary came into the hands of his daughter Meenakshi Amma who was also a devotee of Devi. From her, the manuscript passed to her daughter Kalyanikkutty Amma and son-in-law Dr. K.P.N. Menon. Dr. Menon, who was the president of the Shornur branch of the Mata Amritanandamayi Seva Samiti, placed this distinguished commentary by his wife's grandfather at the holy feet of Mother for publication in 1988. As instructed by Mother, Prof. K.V. Dev expanded and edited the manuscript to suit the present age. The first edition of the commentary in Malayalam was published in 1994.

COMMENTARIES ON LALITĀ SAHASRANĀMA

The best known and most authoritative of the commentaries on *Lalitā Sahasranāma* is *Saubhāgya Bhāskara* written in Sanskrit by Śrī Bhāskararāya (Bhāsurānanda) who lived in the eighteenth century. Bhāskararāya was a great scholar who practiced Śrī Vidyā worship and worked to propagate Śākta doctrine. It is believed that his commentary was written in 1785. The other prominent early commentators of the *Sahasranāma* are Vimarśanānandanātha, Vidyāraṇya Muni and Bhaṭṭanārāyaṇa.

The present commentary is based mainly on the work by Bhāskararāya. Also included are the new interpretations that originated in the mind of the commentator as a result of his deep devotion for Devi. In addition, relevant ideas contained in several other available commentaries have also been adopted as necessary.

THE ENGLISH TRANSLATION

The present translation of the Malayalam original into English has been done by Dr. M.N. Namboodiri, who is a scientist engaged in nuclear research originally in India and now in the U.S. Born in Kerala, he now lives with his wife near Mother's Aśram in San Ramon, California.

PREFACE

Our ancestors declared to the world ages ago: "There is only one Truth. The men of wisdom say that the paths to It are many." The root of all the confrontation and violence in the name of religion and ideology is the insistence that "My way is the only right way; all others should turn to it." This is what fuels all drives for religious conversion. This is the cry of conflict and hatred. The voice of India is gentle: "Let whatever be the path; it should lead to Truth." That voice is full of tolerance; it is the voice of friendship and accommodation. But where is tolerance or accommodation when one loudly proclaims universal brotherhood and in the same breath fights to push forward one's own parochial view?

Our prayer is,

Sarve bhavantu sukhinaḥ
Sarve santu nirāmayāḥ
Sarve bhadrāni paśyantu
Mā kaschid duhkhabhagbhavet

Let everyone be happy! Let there be no sickness! Let us see the good in all! Let not grief be anyone's lot!

'Let everyone be happy.' But where is happiness for someone who may not have at least two meals a day, a change of clothes, and a shelter to sleep without fear? Everyone should have at least the bare essentials in life; luxuries can wait.

All are prone to diseases and need the help of medicine. Dhanvantari's (the founder of Ayurveda) incarnation was for that. What is the real meaning of the prayer, 'Let there be no sickness?' There will always be sickness, but we wish that medical care reaches everyone. Today, even basic medical care is a form of luxury. Essential care should reach everyone. Only then, will everyone be *anāmaya*, free of afflictions.

But even when this much is guaranteed, there is an inherent fault in man: jealousy. This drives him to find fault in others. This is a danger to society. This is at the root of religious conflicts also. What is the cure for this?

'Let us see the good in all!' God is in everything. Therefore, the spark of goodness will be in everything, however hidden. We have to try to open our eyes to this from childhood. When we can see goodness everywhere and in everything, there is no more conflict, no more hatred. It will purify even animal tendencies. 'Sarve bhadrāni pasyantu!' Let us see the good in all!

When such a stage is reached, no one will be a victim of sorrow. Only then the prayer

Lokāḥ samastāḥ sukhino bhavantu
May the whole world be happy!

will have any meaning.

This vision that India has does not belong to any particular religion; it may be called the vision of a universal religion. It is acceptable to any civilized society. Thus it is valid through the ages, it is eternal. It is for this reason that the philosophy that includes such ideals was called *sanātana dharma*, the eternal code of life.

'Live and let live' is the foundation of this philosophy. This code is not practical for animals. Even an animal that spares its own kind, kills members of other species. Killing and death are everywhere in the animal world. No one grieves over this. But it is very regrettable when man sinks to that level. That is why murder deserves punishment - in humans, though not in animals.

'May we live for a hundred years!' - *Jivema śarad śatam*. Our ancestors had made this prayer come true. Thus, they were said to live a human life span. What is the condition today? How numerous are the lives destroyed even before reaching the prime of youth because of hatred, jealousy and intolerance! Foreseeing this danger, the sages of India, and thousands of years later, the great souls of other lands, established the connection between life and religion, between life and God.

A question arises here. Is it not possible for man to live without religion and God? Yes, it is. But even there, he has to adopt certain values as the basis of his life, as his articles of faith. It is when they are lacking that he slides into a life of evil, even as his tongue is professing great ideals. Faith is the light of life. It is the core of everything. Without the light of faith, man will falter in darkness, fall into the ditch. When one's sense of values are connected to God, then it will be a house built on rock. Otherwise, its foundation will crumble in course of time.

God is the light of consciousness. It is present in everything, hidden from view. The declaration by the sages, "*Īśavasyamidam sarvam*," "All this is covered by God," is a scientific one.

We cannot indicate our entire face by touching it at one place. Wherever we touch is only a part of the face - the eye, the forehead, cheeks, lips, chin and so on. Still we don't conclude that there is no such thing as the face. Take the axis of the earth. Where is it? Who has seen it? In the sense that it is a force that guides the rotation of the earth, no one will deny its presence. Amma says, "Just as the tree is contained in the seed, butter in the milk, ice in the water, God fills the entire universe. The mother points out the father to the child. Similarly, Nature points to God. Even one who disobeys the father cannot deny the existence of that father!"

According to the ancient wisdom, the cloud is born from the sun, food from the cloud, the seed of life from the food, and each living being from that seed. Each being starts the search for happiness, from the moment he is born. He carries happiness within as as a dormant bud and he starts life's journey in search of ways to make it blossom.

The goal of the journey may be very near, but if the way is not known, one may wander for a long time without reaching that goal. One may ask for directions. But only those who know the way can help. Following the directions given by those who don't know, one may roam for a long time and may end up very far from the goal.

This is where the Satguru comes in. He is called Īśvara, God. Īśvara or Īśa is one who protects. And Īśo (Jesus) is none other than Īśa, the protector. Īśa is, indeed, Śiva who is bliss. Those who know this subtle truth will not fight over God. But our eyes are not on the subtle; alas, they are always on what is gross! That is the cause of all the problems. We are like the blind men who encounter the elephant. Or, we are like those who fuss with the fiber and shell on the outside of a coconut, ignoring the pulp inside.

India, Bhārata, is not the land of blindness. It is the land of light; it is the land that rejoices in light (*bhā:* light, *rata:* delighted in). The light here is the light of the knowledge of the Self. The happiness here is the Bliss of the Self. And reaching that is the ultimate goal of life. To reach that goal, one searches for a Guru who has reached there. Bhārata is the land of such Gurus. Billionaires are forgotten here, but Gurus are revered. The history of this land is not one of kings; it is one of the *rishis*. That is why India is known as *ārshabhūmi* - the land of the *rishis*.

Who is a *rishi*? None other than the Guru. Guru is God. If there is a state beyond God, Guru is that. That is why it is said, "Guru is Brahmā, Guru is Viṣṇu, Guru is Maheśvara. Guru is verily the Supreme Brahman. Salutations to that holy Guru!"

Amma says, "One who is learned might say he is the same as God; but even he will not say he is the same as his Guru." That is the greatness of the Guru.

There is a mantra that has been chanted for ages: 'Matru devo bhava'. Mother is none other than God. Even Śri Śankarāchārya who proclaimed, "I have no God other than Hari, Lord Viṣṇu," says in the *Saundarya Lahari:*

"When Śiva joins You, O Śakti, He is able to engage in His cosmic tasks; otherwise He cannot even move about! That is why Brahmā, Viṣṇu, Maheśvara and all the other divinities worship You. How can one who has not accrued any merit be capable of bowing to You or extolling Your glory?"

It has been believed through the ages that just a benevolent glance from that Ādi Parāśakti, the Original Cosmic Power, will sever all the knots in our lives and bring happiness and strength. And it is a belief based on actual experience. That is how the *Lalita Sahasranāma* became an anchor in the devotional life of millions. When the boat of life is threatened by gathering storms, that anchor protects it from disaster.

Amma's spiritual odysseys are bringing worldwide renown to the *Sahasranāma*. Wherever She goes, the *archana* using this hymn appeals to the hearts of devotees increasingly, in the East and West, regardless of caste or creed.

The sacred *Lalita Sahasranāma* is a part of the second canto of *Brahmāṇḍa Purāṇa*. There, Hayagriva tells the sage Agastya that only devotees of abiding faith should be initiated into this hymn. This mantra of secret import, directed towards Devi, should never be revealed to anyone who lacks devotion. 'It should never be given to those who are deceitful, evil-minded or faithless.' It is laid down that 'this hymn of a thousand names should be given only to a pure-minded *upāsaka* (worshipper) who is full of devotion for the Divine Mother and who is intent on the regal Śrīvidya worship.'

The *Lalita Sahasranāma* is meant to be chanted daily. It will take about an hour. Amma often says, "Those who chant the *Lalita Sahasranāma* daily with devotion will never lack food or clothes. Along with material progress, they will be blessed with spiritual advancement."

It is believed that Devi's presence will always be felt in a house where the Thousand Names are chanted daily. Poverty will not enter there. People vouch from their own experience that even severe diseases are cured through the daily practice of this hymn with complete surrender. It is astonishing that man who has faith in machines *(yantras)* created by the mind lacks faith in mantras which are also the products of the mind. *Tantraśāstra* (the tantric scriptures) refers to *chakras* and symbols such as Śrī Chakra by the name *yantras*. Mantras are no less fruitful than *yantras* - mechanical creations. And the mantras in this hymn bear fruits promptly according to the learned opinion.

Each being born in this universe is whole in itself. From the tree that is whole is born the seedling that is also whole. From the cow that is whole, is born the calf that is whole as well. This is the general nature of creation. There may be some exceptions which are not natural and there may be special reasons for them.

Each such offspring has to have a mother. Thus even Brahmā, Viṣṇu and Śiva must have a mother. That mother is called Lalitāmbika. It is another way we refer to the Ultimate Truth, the Supreme Brahman. That is none other than the Ādi Parāśakti.

This is a realm which the intellect can not penetrate. The ultimate Truth is realized in a realm of personal experience that is born from worship, beyond the sphere of the intellect. What we must do is to believe the words of the great sages who attained that realization. We are prepared to believe reporters, who write stories for a living, stories that may just as well be false as true. Yet we consider the truthful words of the great *rishis*, who spoke only for the good of the world, as unbelievable! Even the Vedas take the stand that the 'words of the rishis are the words of God.'

The Universal Mother is Ādiparāśakti, the Primeval Cosmic Power. No one who takes refuge in Her remains without protection. There may be children who forsake their mother, but there is no mother who forsakes her child. If there is, then the word 'mother' has no meaning there. For the Mother of the Universe, the good and the bad are equally Her children.

And the wicked will become good also. It may take a little time. It may even take a few births. But we need not doubt the fact that the wicked will regain his goodness. Because, he is the son of the Mother of the Universe. He is nothing but the Truth.

Amma has prescribed how we should picture that Divine Mother and how we should worship Her through the chanting of Her names. (Her words are given elsewhere in this book) We should follow those words with faith and attention. Practice is more important than knowledge. As Amma says, "If the seed is left in the granary, it may become food for the mice, but if the seed goes under the soil, then what is inessential - *asat* - in it will rot and the essence - *sat* - will sprout and emerge above the soil and grow. It will lead to countless new seeds." That is the greatness of constant practice.

The child who plays with toys will cry for its mother when it gets bored, or when the toys are taken away by someone or when it is hungry. The child who gets lost in the fair grounds will also cry for its mother. The sights at the fair are not amusing any more; getting back to the mother is the only thing that the child wants. All the objects of pleasure that we can get in this world are mere toys, even our spouses and children. There is a limit to the delight that a jiva can derive from them. When that limit is reached he will cry for his mother. Even when the mother hurts him through punishment, he would cry only for her. The father comes only after the mother. Even a child who is normally more attached to the father will get tired of him when it is away from the mother for a long time; but no one gets tired of the mother. This is an experience that evokes our wonder. Even when immersed in worldly affairs and pleasures, we secretly yearn to cling to the hem of our mothers' dress.

The mother who gives birth, however rich she is, may not be able to satisfy all the desires of her children. And however loving she is, after a certain point she will be forced to leave the children to fend for themselves. But the Mother of the World who is Parāśakti - Amma - always holds Her childrens' hands and leads them on the right path. There is no question of the childrens' age here.

And the right path is the path towards Liberation. 'Where there is attachment to pleasures, there is no Liberation at all. And where there is yearning for Liberation, there is no trace of the desire for the pleasures of the senses. But where there are persons intent on the worship of Lalitambika, there physical pleasures and Liberation are both at hand.' The *Lalita Sahasranāma* is thus the golden chain that links the material and the spiritual realms.

Prof. K.V. Dev

INTRODUCTION

"O Mother, for the ignorant, the dust of Your holy feet is the island city of the sun, which dispels the darkness from their minds; for the dull-witted, it is the stream of honey from a flower-bunch that is Pure Consciousness; for the poor, it is a collection of cintāmaṇi gems that yield all wishes; and for those who are submerged in the ocean of samsāra, it is the tusk of the Boar incarnation of Lord Viṣṇu."

Saundarya Lahari, v.3

What is the greatest boon God has given to all living beings including man? We can answer without any doubt that it is a mother's love. The bond between mother and child is that sacred. "What is to be done in time of danger?" The universally accepted answer to this question is, "Remember the feet of the Mother of the Universe!" Mother is the embodiment of forgiveness, who pardons all mistakes and showers Her love on Her children again and again. "There may be wicked children, but there will never be a wicked mother," says Śri Śaṇkarācārya. The closeness and freedom that a son feels in the relationship to his mother is not seen in any other relationship. The sense of security that children enjoy in the cool shade of mother's protection is indescribable. Indeed, there is no other love that is as pure, selfless, warm and constant as the love of a mother for her child. But this love of a biological mother is only a tiny fraction of the love of the Mother of the Universe. If the mother who bears us into this world protects us to some extent from the struggles in this life, the Mother of the Universe protects us in all our births. She nourishes everything in the universe with Her milk that is the eternal nectar of love.

The tradition of worshipping God as Mother is well established in India. This tradition of worshipping the Divine Power as feminine and as Mother was prevalent also in Egypt, Greece, Rome and Japan. When we refer to God as Mother, the question may indeed arise as to whether there is a form or a male-female distinction for God. Even though God is a concept that is beyond the reach of thought and speech, man always prefers to see God in an individual form. The Supreme in its ultimate essence may be attributeless, formless and actionless; but in the plane where we speak of the *Paramātman* and the *jīvātman*, God is one who has attributes, form and actions. The devotee needs, for his worship, a form that is close to his heart. The *Gītā* also points out that the worship of the unmanifested, attributeless Brahman is extremely difficult. Because of the taste that is diverse and distinct from individual to individual, the custom of worshipping the transcendent, all-pervading Supreme in different forms and attributes became widespread in various regions of the world. It is in *sanātana dharma* (the eternal code of life laid down in the scriptures of ancient India) that the individual's freedom to worship God in any form that appeals to his heart was always recognized. In *sanātana dharma*, He is worshipped in manifold forms such as Śiva, Viśṇu, Śakti, Kumāra, mother, father and lover. The devotee sees his chosen deity as the Supreme Lord and all other divinities as His parts and as contained within Him. This is not a doctrine that accepts more than one God. In this worship of many forms, there is no room for conflicts or strife. It is a broad view that sees that "Lord, You are within all, You are all-pervading; all are Your forms; You are the source of all; You are the soul of all." (*Viṣṇu Purāṇa*) The name and form of the worshipped deity are not a hindrance to the realization of the Supreme. The devotee, who is initially attracted to the infinite divine qualities of his chosen deity, meditates constantly on those qualities; in the end the worshipper and the object of worship become one, and the devotee merges into the Absolute Truth that is without name or form.

It must be due to the unparalleled quality of the mother-child relation that the worship of God as Mother became widespread. The worship of Śakti started in prehistoric times in India. In the *Vedas*, the concept of Devī arises as the Goddess of Dawn, who is the weaver of Time, the foundation of Truth, and the remover of *tamas* (darkness). That concept expands to include Mother Earth who is all-forbearing (*sarvamsahā*), the Goddess of Speech who is the embodiment of sound and Night, who is the embodiment of Time. In *Kena Upaniṣad*, Devī Umāmaheśvarī is pictured as the Guru who imparts knowledge of the Self. In the *Vedas*, the worship of Devī is enriched through various hymns such as *Devīsūkta*, *Lakṣmīsūkta* and *Durgāsūkta*. In time various *Upaniṣads* devoted to Devī also took shape, such as *Ehāvana Upaniṣad*, *Tripura Upaniṣad*, *Bhahvrija Upaniṣad*, *Kaula Upaniṣad* and *Tripuratāpini Upaniṣad*. In *Rāmāyaṇa* we see Rāma worshipping Durgā Devī for success in battle and in *Mahābhārata* we see the Pāṇḍavas doing the same at the instance of Kṛṣṇa. In the *Bhāgavata*, we see the *gopis* praying to Devī: "O Kātyāyanī, Thou who art Mahāmāya, the great Yoginī and Mistress of all! Deign to make the son of Nanda (Kṛṣṇa) my husband! Prostrations to You!" The picture of Devī blossoms in the various *Purāṇas* such as *Brahmāṇḍa Purāṇa*, *Mārkanḍeya Purāṇa*, *Devī Purāṇa*, *Devī Bhāgavata* and *Kālika Purāṇa* in which She is portrayed as causing the creation, maintenance and dissolution of the universe and as ruling over the Trinity of Brahmā, Viṣṇu and Śiva. It is in the *Tantric* texts that the picture of Śakti and Her worship as the Supreme Principle and as the embodiment of Consciousness which is identical to Brahman gain their fullness. The *Lalitā Sahasranāma* (from *Brahmāṇḍa Purāṇa*), *Devī Mahātmya* (from *Mārkānḍeya Purāṇa*) and *Saundarya Lahari* believed to be written by Śaṇkarācārya are priceless gems in the tradition of Śakti worship.

As the worship of Devī became widespread, certain individual aspects of Devī became important. The worship of Devī as Gayatrī, the mother of the *Vedas* and the embodiment of *Vedas*, as Lakṣmī, the abode of beauty and prosperity, as Sarasvatī, the presiding deity of all knowledge and arts, as Durgā, the Śakti who consolidates *dharma* and bestows victory, as Mahākālī, the Mother who is the embodiment of Nature and who confers Liberation, as Lalitā Tripurasundarī who is the embodiment of Śiva and Śakti in one, all became prevalent. Even though She is worshipped throughout India as Durgā, Lakṣmī and Sarasvatī during the festival of *Navarātri,* each part of the country considers a different aspect of Devī as important. Thus She is worshipped as Umā in the Himālayas, as Ambā in Kashmir, as Kāmākhya in Assam, as Bhavānī in Maharashtra, as Mīnākṣī and Kanyākumāri in Tamil Nadu, as Chāmuṇḍeśvari and Śāradā in Karnataka, as Bhagavatī in Kerala, as Durgā and Kālī in Bengal, as Bhadrakālī in the villages of southern India, and as Lalitā Tripurasundarī all over India, especially in the south. Fifty-one abodes of Śakti (*Śaktipīṭhas*) became famous throughout India as centers of pilgrimage (*tīrthas*). These centers are believed to represent the fifty-one letters of the alphabet or the fifty-one Śakti principles.

"O Devī, Thou who art the consort of Supreme Brahman! Those who know the essence of the Vedas call Thee the Goddess of Speech, the consort of Lord Brahmā. Thou art also known as Lakṣmī, the queen of Lord Viṣṇu and as Pārvatī, the companion of Lord Śiva. But Thou really art Turīyā, and one who possesses infinite glories beyond our comprehension and the Mahāmāyā who deludes the entire universe!"

Saundarya Lahari, v.97

THE PHILOSOPHY OF ŚAKTI WORSHIP

According to *Śākteya* (pertaining to Śakti) philosophy, the Supreme Truth and the ultimate cause of the universe are Śiva-Śakti. Śiva and Śakti are not distinct from each other. The Śiva principle is the Essence of Consciousness devoid of attributes, without parts, actionless. Śakti is the power of action latent in that Consciousness. If Śiva is Consciousness (*Cit*), Śakti is its embodiment. If Śiva is *prakāśa*, the undivided Consciousness, Śakti is *vimarśa* that engenders awareness in Śiva of His own existence. Śakti is inseparable from Śiva as burning power from fire and light from the sun.

The creation of the universe starts when Śakti emerges from Śiva on its own. Śakti is all-pervading and dwells in everything. The *Śākteya* doctrine states that Śiva, Śakti, the *jīva* and the universe are intrinsically one and the same. In this doctrine, the universe is the true manifestation of the Supreme Principle.

The *Śākteya* doctrine describes thirty-six *tattvas*, principles, as the basis of creation. The cause of creation is the evolution of five forms of power, those of consciousness, bliss, will, knowledge and action (*cit*, *ānanda*, *icchā*, *jñāna* and *kriyā*). Of the thirty-six principles, the first five are considered as pure, the next seven as mixed (pure-impure) and the last twenty-four as impure. The first five are Śiva, Śakti, Sadāśiva, Īśvara and Śuddhavidya. When Śakti is latent in Śiva, She is *citśakti*, the *śakti* of consciousness. In the first stage of manifestation, Śakti appears distinct from Śiva, as *ānandaśakti*, the *śakti* of bliss. This is the second principle. In the same way, the power of will (*icchāśakti*) appears in Sadāśiva, the power of knowledge (*jñānaśakti*) in Īśvara and the power of action (*kriyāśakti*) in Śuddhavidya. The term *nāda* is sometimes used instead of the Sadāśiva *tattva*, and *bindu* instead of Īśvara. The next seven *tattvas* of creation are *māyā*, *kāla*, *niyati*, *rāga*, *vidyā*, *kāla*, *puruṣa* or *jīva*. Of these, *māyā* is the power that conceals the *jīva's* knowledge; the next five *tattvas* are the sheaths that bind the *jīva*, the seventh. The next twenty-four *tattvas*, considered impure, are nature (*prakṛti*), intellect (*buddhi*), ego-sense (*ahamkāra*), mind (*manas*), the five sense organs, the five organs of actions, the five *tanmātras* (subtle elements) and the five elements; this list is in accordance with that given by the *Samkhya* philosophy. All these arise from *māyā*. The *Śākteyas* consider *māyā* as the womb of Śakti. Sometimes fifty-one *tattvas* are mentioned which include the three guṇas (the principles of purity, activity and inertia), the five vital airs (*prāṇas*) and the seven ingredients of the body (*dhātus*), in addition to the thirty-six mentioned above. The list of *tattvas* differ slightly from text to text. In addition to this description of creation based on meaning, a description based on sound is also seen in *Śākteya* philosophy. This is discussed in the commentary on *mantra* 366 (*para*) in the *Sahasranāma*.

SĀDHANA AND MOKṢA

According to the *Śākteya* doctrine, *jīvas* are of three kinds: *paśu, vīra and divya.* The *jīva* in bondage starts his spiritual evolution through the observances of *paśu* rites. Subsequently, through *vira* rites, he attains the state of Rudra and finally through *divya* rites, he unites with Śakti. Liberation (*mokṣa*) is the knowledge of the oneness of Śiva and Śakti. In the fullness of bliss, the *jīva* experiences the merger of Śiva and Śakti. As in the *Śaiva* method, the four paths of worship, *cārya*, *kriyā*, *yoga* and *jñāna* are adopted in the *Śākteya* method also. *Cārya* consists of actions performed with a sense of surrender to God. *Kriyā* consists of worship using *mantras*, *mudras* (special finger and hand poses used in worship) and *prāṇāyāma* (breath control). *Yoga* includes *kuṇḍalinī* meditation and other meditations. *Jñāna* is nothing but the knowledge of the oneness of Śiva and Śakti. *Tantric* texts such as *Kulārṇavatantra* describe the following seven ascending stages of *sādhana: vedācāra*, *vaiṣṇavācāra*, *śaivācāra*, *dakṣiṇācāra*, *vāmācāra*, *siddhāntācāra* and *kaulācāra*. *Vedācāra* can be compared to the path of action, *vaiṣṇavācāra* to the path of devotion and *śaivācāra* to the first steps in the path of knowledge. These first three *ācāras* belong to the *paśu* classification, *dakṣiṇācāra* and *vāmācāra* belong to the *vira* classification and *siddhāntācāra* and *kaulācāra* to the *divya* category. In *divyācāra*, the *jīva*, who is free from *vāsanas* (inherent tendencies), recognizes more and more completely the unity of Śiva and Śakti and thus attains divine status. In the *Śākteya* doctrine, it is Śakti who presides over the evolution of nature and the orderly upward growth of the *jīva*. It is Śakti that the devotee should worship; or, in other words, Śakti is none other than the Śiva principle which is worthy of worship and which is capable of being experienced. *Śākteyas* stress the need for a Guru. They accept the Guru as the human manifestation Śiva-Śakti, the Supreme Guru. They consider the entire universe to be divine and see everything as the purposeful working of Śakti.

TANTRAS

Tantras are the texts of the practical science of *sādhana* that describe the principles and practice of Śakti worship. According to the definition, this science is *tantra*, because it states and explains the meaning of the principles with the accompaniment of *mantras* and leads to liberation from *samsāra* (*tan*: to extend, to propagate; *trai*: to protect, to save from). *Śākteya tantras* fall into three groups: *samaya*, *kaula* and *miśra*. Knowledge (*jñāna*) is stressed in *samaya*, upliftment through *mantras* is stressed in *kaula* and both are stressed in *miśra*. There are eight *tantras* in the *samaya* group, sixty- four in *kaula* and eight in *miśra*. Methods of *sādhana* such as the *ṣoḍaśopacāras* (sixteen prescribed rites), worship using *yantras*, *mantras* and *mudras* and meditation on *kuṇḍalinī* are treated in *tantric* texts.

SAMAYA AND KAULA DOCTRINES

Samaya and *Kaula* are two principal divisions of Śakti worship. *Samaya* follows the path of the *Vedas*, while *Kaula* is relatively independent of the *Vedic* path. *Samaya* doctrine considers Śakti to be important during creation and Śiva as important during dissolution. Followers of the *Kaula* path believe that Śakti is paramount at all times. While *Samaya* followers assert that Śakti is latent in Śiva, *Kaula* followers maintain that Śiva is latent in Śakti. *Samaya* doctrine says that the seeker reaches his goal when the *kuṇḍalinī* reaches the *sahasrāra cakra* where the union of Śiva and Śakti takes place. *Kaula* doctrine believes that the *kuṇḍalinī* returns to the *mūlādhāra* after the seeker attains bliss at the union of Śiva and Śakti. Dakṣiṇāmurti is the sage of the *Samaya* path and Kameśvara and Kameśvarī are the deities. Bhairava is the sage of the *Kaula* path and Ānandabhairava and Ānandabhairavi are the deities. The main treatise of *Samaya* is *Śubhāgamapañcaka* which contains the teachings of the sages Sanaka, Sanatkumāra, Sananda, Śuka and Vasiṣṭha. The main treatises of *Kaula* are *Paraśurāmakalpa Sutra* and the sixty-four *tantras*.

DAKṢIṆĀCĀRA AND VĀMĀCĀRA

Śākteya doctrine also describes the two paths, *Dakṣiṇācāra* and *Vāmācara*. The former is in accord with the *Vedas* and is associated with *Samaya* doctrine. The latter is independent of the *Vedas* and is close to the *Kaula* doctrine.

ŚRĪ VIDYĀ WORSHIP

Śrī Vidyā worship is the worship of Devī as Lalitā Mahātripurasundarī, who is the union of Śiva and Śakti, the embodiment of *prakāśa* and *vimarśa*, and the cause of creation, maintenance and dissolution. The chief ingredients of this are *mantra*, *yantra* and *kuṇḍalinī yoga*. The *yantra* in Śrī Vidyā worship is Śrī Cakra (and Śrī Yantra) and the *mantra* is the fifteen-syllabled *mantra*, *pancadaśākṣari*. Adding the syllable Śrī to that *mantra*, one gets the sixteen-syllabled *mantra*, the *ṣoḍaśākṣari*. Śrī Cakra is said to represent the gross form of Devī and the *pancadaśākṣari mantra* Her subtle form. The Śrī Cakra is also the symbol of the three *tattvas*, the individual soul, the universe and Śakti. The seeker who starts with *yantra* worship gives, in course of time, more importance to mental worship of Devī and meditation. The height of Śrī Vidyā worship is to dedicate all actions and motions to Devī and to meditate on them as different manifestations of Consciousness, *citśakti*. *Brahmāṇḍa Purāṇa* prescribes *Lalitā Sahasranāma* as an essential ingredient of Śrī Vidyā worship.

AMMA AND LALITĀ SAHASRANĀMA

Generally, human life is full of sorrow. Sorrow, misfortunes, desires and disappointments plague man from birth to death. Philosophers describe this world and the life here as 'perishable, sorrowful,' 'the abode of grief, transient,' and so on. *Lalitā Sahasranāma* worship, in large groups and as a daily routine, is one of the most important practical methods for the removal of human suffering and for spiritual growth prescribed and popularized by Mother who has listened to the sorrows of millions of people and has dedicated Her life to the alleviation of their pain. As a result of Her untiring efforts, *Sahasranāma arcana* and chanting have become widespread even among the general public. The big *Sahasranāma yajñas* that She organizes regularly in India and abroad are a proof of the wish to strengthen that which is cherished by Mother whose only desire is the happiness of the world.

Amma says this about the importance of the worship of the Mother of the Universe and *Lalitā Sahasranāma arcana* at the present time: "In the present age, the instincts of the heart and the motherly instinct have been lost. Motherhood is the symbol of love, compassion and forbearance. Feminine qualities like compassion and love should become stronger in men and masculine qualities like steadiness and courage should grow in women. Rapid progress will then become possible in both worldly and spiritual life. The worship of the Divine Mother is ideal for enhancing these good qualities. Worship (*arcana*) using *Lalitā Sahasranāma* is of the utmost value for the prosperity of the family and for peace in the world. There will never be shortage of food or clothing in the home where *Lalitā Sahasranāma* is chanted daily. In olden days, when giving Kṛṣṇa or Viṣṇu *mantras* to their disciples, gurus usually instructed them to do *arcana* with *Lalitā Sahasranāma* as well."

THE RELEVANCE OF UPĀSANA

Even though human life is full of sorrow, man's real nature is one of bliss. Sorrow and bondage of mind and body arise from the conviction, "I am this body, I am limited." By strengthening, step by step through spiritual practice, the awareness that "I am Brahman," one can get release from sorrow and attain eternal bliss. This is the goal of human life. Without recognizing his own inherent fullness, however, man nurtures various desires and engages in actions that do not lead to the goal. Most of the misfortunes in life arise as results of such actions done earlier. One who knows the essential truth, recognizes that the phenomena in nature do not affect the *ātman* and accepts, with an evenness of mind, the joys and sorrow which constitute his *prārabdha*. But this is not easy for an ordinary person or even for a spiritual seeker. This is where worship - *upāsana* - becomes relevant. By worshipping the Supreme in the form and disposition dear to one's heart, one puts an end to sorrow and attains success in life and spiritual progress at the same time. In this way, gradually an attitude of loving devotion (*premabhakti*) and surrender become strong in the seeker and he will be able to live happily accepting joy and sorrow as the will of God and to merge with the deity of his worship before long.

THE UNIQUE GREATNESS OF LALITĀ SAHASRANĀMA

Mother has chosen *Lalitā Sahasranāma arcana* (and chanting) as a daily practice for relief from the perils in life and for spiritual progress, as She is fully aware of the unparalleled greatness of this hymn which is full of the power of *mantras* and is capable of fulfilling all desires. Among the many hymns, *mantras* and devotional songs available, this *Sahasranāma* is specially suitable for worship in the morning and gives results quickly. While *Sahasranāmas* which give material well-being and salvation are prescribed for all castes and in all stages of life, *Lalitā Sahasranāma* is especially suitable for householders.

Lalitā Sahasranāma is an unequalled composition in which the profound import of *mantras*, poetic beauty and musical quality combine in a captivating manner. With this hymn, one worships Lalitā Mahātripurasundarī who is the Supreme Goddess, the union of Śiva and Śakti, through a thousand names arranged in a metrical framework. Each name is a *mantra*. The entire hymn can be considered also as a single *mantra*. The names shed light on Devī's form, attributes, abode, the stories of Her incarnations and on Her gross, subtle, and supreme nature. Of the numerous *Sahasranāmas* that extoll the greatness of *Parāśakti*, the Supreme Power, ten are most important; and among them, the most exalted is the *Lalitā Sahasranāma* according to scholars in the science of *mantras*. The *Brahmāṇḍa Purāṇa* says that among *mantras*, Śrī Vidyā, among deities Lalitāmbika and among cities Śri Pura are the most exalted. In the *Lalitā Sahasranāma*, we see the beautiful confluence of the highest ideals, methods of *sādhana* and concepts of the *mantras*, *tantras* and *yantras* of both *Śaiva* and *Śākteya* doctrines. Also, we see the merger, on an equal footing, of the *Kaula* and *Samaya* branches of *Śākteya* worship through choice of names from both branches such as Kaulinī, Kulayoginī, *Kaula*mārgatatparā, Samayācārā, Samayāntasthā and Samayācāratatparā. Thus, it is seen that the *Lalitā Sahasranāma* is, in all respects, the ripe fruit of thousands of years of Śakti worship.

THE LALITĀ DEVĪ OF THE LALITĀ SAHASRANĀMA

Lalitā, literally, is one who is engaged in *līlā* (sport) or is amusing herself in play. Her sport is nothing but the creation, maintenance, destruction, total dissolution and blessing of the universe (These five divine functions are described in *mantras* 264 - 274).

Even though Devī transcends everything, the *Lalitā Sahasranāma* portrays Her as the abode of endless, auspicious attributes, full of all human qualities and easily accessible to all devotees. The very first name introduces Devī as the Mother full of love. Following that, it is made clear that She who is the Queen of the universe has incarnated from the fire-pit of knowledge, for the establishment of *dharma* (righteousness, justice). The picture that we get from the *Sahasranāma* is of a Lalitā Devī, always of pleasant countenance, who possesses the radiance of a thousand rising suns, the coolness of a thousand full moons, who holds in Her hands a sugar-cane bow that is the mind, a goad that is anger, a rope that is love and arrows that are the five *tanmātras* (subtle elements), who sits in the lap of Śiva Kāmeśvara on a cushion that is Sadāśiva, spread on a cot whose legs are Brahmā, Viṣṇu, Rudra and Īśana. This Kāmeśvara-Kāmeśvarī image placed higher than the motionless Sadāśiva image is noteworthy. The description from head to toe of the Devī who is the treasure-house of beauty unfolds through epithets brimming with poetic charm. She is one who immerses the entire universe in Her red effulgence. She is the Lakṣmī - the queen of prosperity - of Kāmeśvara's house of matrimony. Her eyes are like fish that swim about in the lake of beauty that is Her face. Devī's ear ornaments are the sun and the moon and the rows of Her teeth are the buds of pure knowledge. Her voice is sweeter than the sound of Sarasvatī's *vīna*. After describing Devī's form through such poetic imagery to facilitate meditation by devotees, the *līlās* of Her incarnation, and Her great qualities and glories are described. Devī who is fond of flowers, likes especially the flowers of *campaka*, *aśoka* and many other blossoms. She nurtures poetry, dance, music and other arts. She is one who rejoices at the meritorious acts of Her devotees. In the descriptions of Devī who transcends everything, we see the gross and the subtle coming together beautifully and also that which has form and that which is formless. This is to remind the devotee of the true nature of Devī even as Her human aspect is being described. It is asserted that the Devī who is described earlier as the treasure house of supreme beauty is of the essence of Existence-Consciousness-Bliss, that She is Pure Consciousness, Pure Intelligence and one without names and forms. She is the embodiment of Brahmā, Viṣṇu and Śiva. She is the soul of all *mantras*, *tantras* and *yantras*. She is the abode of all knowledge, all scriptures and all arts. She who is of the nature of liberation and the bestower of liberation is also the embodiment of desires and one who fulfills desires. She who strengthens virtue is also beyond the concepts of virtue and vice. She who is fond of Her devotees is the embodiment of love, the ocean of compassion and quick to be pleased. Devī is the hurricane that drives away the wisps of cotton that are the misfortunes of the devotees. She is the radiance of the sun that dispels the darkness of their disease of *samsāra*. She is the shower of nectar that puts out the wild fire of *samsāra*. She is the pearl enclosed in the shell made of all the scriptures. She is the axe that cuts down the tree of death. She is the moonlight that raises tides in the ocean of good fortune of Her devotees. The *Sahasranāma* depicts the glories and sports of Devī through such picturesque images. Here we see the merger of the paths of *karma*, devotion, *yoga* and knowledge, of the paths of worship according to *Samaya*, *Kaula*, *Dakṣiṇa* and *Vāma* doctrines, of all knowledge. Here we see the unfolding of the path of *sādhana* that starts with rituals, grows through actions, matures through *yoga* and reaches fullness in *jñāna*.

PURĀṆIC BACKGROUND

Lalitā Sahasranāma appears in the 36th chapter of *Lalitopākhyāna* which itself is contained in *Brahmāṇḍa Purāṇa*. It is presented in the form of instruction imparted to the sage Agastya by Hayagriva who is an incarnation of Viṣṇu. It has three parts; the first is the background leading to the hymn, the middle part is the collection of *mantras* forming the hymn, and the last is the statement of benefits accruing from its chanting. The background story is summarized below.

Hayagriva tells Agastya the story of the incarnation of Lalitā Devī and describes Her sports. He then describes the city of Śrī Pura, Her abode, the greatness of Her *mantra*, the *panchadaśākṣari*, the essential oneness of Śrī Yantra, Śrī Vidyā, Lalitāmbika and Śrī Guru, and initiates Agastya into the *Sahasranāmas* of Devī's attendant deities. But Hayagriva does not mention the *Lalitā Sahasranāma*. When Agastya asks for it, he points out that the *Sahasranāma* is highly secret, highly potent and exalted and that these are the reasons why he did not impart it in the first place. He then proceeds to describe the genesis of *Lalitā Sahasranāma*.

Once Lalitā Devī addressed Vāśini and the other *vāgdevatas* (goddesses of speech) and told them: "I command you who know the secrets of Śrī Cakra and of Śrī Vidyā and other *mantras* to compose a hymn of a thousand names that reveal My greatness. Let My devotees obtain My grace by chanting it!" Accordingly, Vāśini and the other deities of speech composed the *Lalitā Sahasranāma* consisting of the most secret *mantras*. Subsequently, one day, Devī sitting on Her throne gave the opportunity of Her *darśan* to all those present in court, including countless Brahmīs, countless Viṣṇus, Rudras and Śaktis such as Mantrinī, Daṇḍinī, and the inhabitants of heaven. She gave them all the opportunity to worship Her. As everyone took their seats, Lalitā Devī gave Vāśini and the other deities a signal with the corner of Her eye. They stood up with their palms joined in devotion and sang the *Lalitā Sahasranāma* in Her praise. Everyone was immersed in wonder and bliss. Devī was pleased and spoke these words: "Children, this hymn has been composed by Vāśini and the other deities of speech, for the good of the world, according to My wish. Chant this hymn, which is dearest to Me, daily to obtain My favor. Those who chant it are dearest to Me. I will grant all their wishes through this."

THE STORY OF THE INCARNATION INDICATED IN THE SAHASRANĀMA

Lalitopākhyāna describes the story of Lalitā Devī's incarnation. During the time of the earlier incarnation of Śakti, Kāmadeva, the god of love, became the subject of Śiva's wrath and was burnt to ashes by the fire from His eye. An attendant of Śiva, by the name Citrakāma, drew the figure of a man with the ashes. When Śiva glanced at the picture, the figure came to life. This new being praised Śiva singing the *śatarudrīya* hymn. Śiva was pleased by this and gave him the boon of the lordship of heaven for sixty-thousand years. He became famous by the name of Bhaṇḍāsura. He harassed the *devas* and brought about the decay of righteousness. Nārada advised the unhappy *devas* to perform a sacrifice and to worship Parāśakti. From the sacrificial fire Devī arose at the center of Śrī Cakra. Since Bhaṇḍāsura could not be killed by a maiden, Devī throws into the air a garland with which to choose a mate. The garland falls on the neck of Śiva Kameśvara and Devī weds Him. In the ensuing battle that lasted for four days, Devī destroys Bhaṇḍāsura and his followers. Afterwards, Devī brings Kāma back to life according to the wishes of the *devas*. She then goes to Śrī Pura, a city built by Māyā and Viśvakarma on the peak of Mount Meru, and resides there with Lord Kameśvara in a mansion of *cintāmaṇi* (wish-fulfilling stone).

LALITĀ SAHASRANĀMA AND OTHER SAHASRANĀMAS

The practice of worshipping the chosen deity through a thousand names started after the time of the *Vedas*, during the period of the epics. Compositions such as the *Rudrādhyāya* of *Yajur Veda* may have inspired this. It is believed that among these hymns of a thousand names, the earliest is *Viṣṇu Sahasranāma* to which Yudhiṣṭhira is initiated by Bhīṣma in the Anuśāsana Parva of Mahābhārata. The advent of *Lalitā Sahasranāma* took place later, after a period of time during which the sciences of *mantras* and *tantras* evolved.

In *Viṣṇu Sahasranāma*, abstract, formless ideas have predominance. There are only a few *mantras* that depict the human aspect of Viṣṇu. But in the *Lalitā Sahasranāma* special importance is given to the human aspects of Devī like Her habits, form, abode, ornaments, and the stories of Her incarnation, along with *mantras* that point to Her subtle and supreme essence. This is to make worship easier by strengthening the image of Devī in the mind of the devotee.

Another special feature of *Lalitā Sahasranāma* is that its language is beyond reproach. There is no repetition of *mantras* in this hymn. In *Viṣṇu Sahasranāma*, seventy-six names are repeated twice, thirteen names thrice and two names four times. But in *Lalitā Sahasranāma* not a single name is repeated. Similarly, filler words like *ca*, *api* (meaning *and*) are used frequently in other *Sahasranāmas*. In *Lalitā Sahasranāma*, however, compliance with metrical rules and fullness of the power of *mantras* are achieved in charmingly poetical language without the use of such fillers even when very long compound words are employed. It is a marvel that this has been achieved without the loss of the potency of *mantras* and the grace of the language. This unequalled purity must be due to the fact that the authors were the goddesses of speech.

The superiority of *Lalitā Sahasranāma* is also indicated by the high frequency of names which are many syllables long. The distribution of the lengths of names in *Lalitā* and *Viṣṇu Sahasranāmas* are given below for comparison.

	Lalitā Sahasranāma	Viṣṇu Sahasranāma
Mantras of		
one syllable	3	3
two syllables	72	228
three syllables	138	338
four syllables	280	273
five syllables	122	106
six syllables	57	34
seven syllables	2	-
eight syllables	241	18
ten syllables	7	-
eleven syllables	3	-
twelve syllables	2	-
sixteen syllables	73	-
Number of verses	182½	107

There is a special *mantric* import attached to each name in the *Sahasranāma*. Chanting of the hymn or performing *arcana* name by name confers the benefits of the *mantra*. Along with the beauty and perfection of the language, the arrangement of potent *mantras* and the exposition of deep spiritual principles are achieved at the same time. From all this it is seen that *Lalitā Sahasranāma* is a *stotra* (hymn) of great distinction.

THE PRACTICE OF WORSHIP USING THE SAHASRANĀMA

Worship of Śrī Cakra, chanting the fifteen-syllabled *mantra* (*pancadaśākṣari*), and chanting the *Lalitā Sahasranāma* are three main ingredients of Śakti worship. While the *Sahasranāma* is indispensable for those who do Śrī Cakra *puja* and chant the *pancadaśākṣari*, the *Sahasranāma* can be chanted by itself. *Brahmāṇḍa Purāṇa* says that chanting the *Sahasranāma* gives the benefits of the other two observances. The best time for chanting the *Sahasranāma* is in the morning, right after a bath.While daily practice is the best, certain special days are prescribed for those who cannot do it daily (days of *samkrama* i.e. the first of the month, the ninth and fourteenth lunar days, full moon days, Fridays, birthdays of family members and times of eclipse).

Chanting the *Sahasranāma* is a spiritual practice that strengthens devotion and can be followed by everyone, man or woman, young or old, at any time. It is desirable to set apart a fixed time for daily chanting or *arcana*. If that time is missed, it is important to maintain the daily observance by doing it as soon as possible afterwards. Although it is important to strive for clarity in pronunciation while chanting, it is not necessary to give up the *arcana* if one finds it hard to pronounce the names. God is one who understands our heart. Mother reminds us that the father knows that the baby is calling him and feels love for it whether it says 'ccha' or 'accha' (father). In the same way, devotion and concentration are more important than *nyāsa* and other rituals or lamps, or incense. There is no need to interrupt the daily practice because of difficulty in obtaining materials of worship such as flowers or food offering. All such materials are only props for concentration or symbols of surrender. Purity of heart and one- pointedness of mind are most important. That is why Mother says that mental worship - *mānasa puja* - is the most exalted form of worship.

Even though many different benefits are indicated to accrue from the *Sahasranāma*, it is best to do the worship just for obtaining love of God, wisdom and dispassion. Worship with no desire for results will actually bring an end to the struggles arising from *prārabdha* and result in all desirable benefits. The Mother of the Universe who is full of love for those who take refuge in Her will never forsake anyone coming to Her with unwavering devotion. What higher good fortune is there than being able to be the object of the kindness of the Mother whose heart is always melting with compassion and to enjoy the nectar of Her motherly love as an innocent child in Her lap?

Brahmachari Brahmāmrita Chaitanya

PHALAŚRUTI

(STATEMENT OF BENEFITS)

The aim of the *Vedas* and other scriptural texts is to inspire the love of God and dispassion in human beings and to raise them step by step to the realization of the Self. The object of the *phalaśruti* - the description of the benefits accruing from a certain form of worship - is to strengthen the sense of devotion in people and to make them qualified for higher forms of *sādhana*, by pointing out the way to remove the hardships of life and to gain prosperity. The main items in the *phalaśruti* on *Lalitā Sahasranāma* given in the *Brahmāṇḍa Purāṇa* are summarized below.

1. This *Sahasranāma*, which is most secret, is most pleasing to Lalitā Parameśvarī. There is nothing to equal this in the *Vedas* or *Tantras*.

2. The daily chanting of this hymn gives the same merit as that obtained from bathing in holy rivers and giving gifts of wealth, food, land and cows.

3. All the faults arising from not completing *puja* rituals or from not observing various rites on time are removed by the chanting of this hymn. This hymn may be chanted instead of various expiatory rituals.

4. Chanting this prevents untimely death and grants long life and good health. Relief from fever is obtained if this hymn is chanted with a hand held on the head of the one who is suffering. The person who is suffering can do this himself. Depending on the severity of the disease, it may be necessary to chant the hymn several times. The holy ash used for *Sahasranāma arcana* brings immediate relief from all diseases.

5. Relief from afflictions due to the influence of planets or evil spirits can be removed by chanting the *Sahasranāma* while holding some water and then pouring that water over the head.

6. If this hymn is chanted while picturing Lalitā Devī as residing in the ocean of nectar, one obtains relief from the effects of poison.

7. Barren women get the gift of children by taking *ghee* that has been made potent by chanting *Lalitā Sahasranāma.*

8. By daily chanting of the *Sahasranāma*, the effects of evil spells are removed.

9. Devī protects those who chant this hymn daily from dangers and from attacks by enemies. Victory in battle is gained through the chanting.

10. Daily chanting of the *Sahasranāma* augments prosperity, eloquence and fame. Chanting on Fridays is especially good for prosperity.

11. The *Sahasranāma* may be chanted by those who are in any of the four stages of life (*brahmacārya*, *gṛhastha*, *vānaprastha* and *sannyāsa*). Chanting it while wishing fame brings fame and wishing wealth brings wealth. Chanting this hymn with love and without any desire brings the knowledge of Brahman.

12. One name of Śiva is equal to a thousand names of Viṣṇu. One name of Devī is equal to a thousand names of Śiva. Of a thousand *Sahasranāmas* dedicated to Devī, *Lalitā Sahasranāma* is the most exalted.

13. By holding *yajñas* of *Lalitā Sahasranāma* (worship in large groups) the consolidation of *dharma* becomes possible in the age of Kali. Chanting this hymn is most beneficial for individuals also, for eliminating the ill effects of Kali Yuga. There is no barrier of country, caste or religion in this regard.

14. It is difficult to please Devī without the chanting of *Lalitā Sahasranāma*. Through this hymn, the sins accrued in many births are removed.

15. There are many *Sahasranāmas* dedicated to Devī. The following ten are the chief among these: *Gangāstava*, *Bhavānīstava*, *Gāyatrīstava*, *Kālīstava*, *Lakṣmīstava*, *Sarasvatīstava*, *Rājarājeśvarīstava*, *Bālāstava*, *Śyāmalāstava* and *Lalitāstava*. Of these, the most exalted is the last one, *Lalitā Sahasranāma*.

ŚRĪ CAKRA

ŚRĪ LALITĀ SAHASRANĀMA

THE THOUSAND NAMES
OF THE
DIVINE MOTHER

Original Commentary in Malayalam by
Thiruvallikkattu Nārāyaṇa Menon

Edited by Professor K.V. Dev

Translated into English by
Dr. M. Neelakantan Namboodiri

Śrī Lalitā Sahasranāma
Meditation Verses

The ancient sages have adopted four verses as Meditation Verses (*Dhyānaślokas*) for *Lalitā Sahasranāma.*

सिन्दूरारुणविग्रहां त्रिनयनां माणिक्यमौलिस्फुरत्
तारानायकशेखरां स्मितमुखीमापीनवक्षोरुहाम्.
पाणिभ्यामलिपूर्णरत्नचषकं रक्तोत्पलं बिभ्रतीं
सौम्यां रत्नघटस्थरक्तचरणां ध्यायेत्परामम्बिकाम्..

sindūrāruṇa vigrahām trinayanām
māṇikya mauli sphurat
tārānāyaka śekharām smita mukhīm
āpīna vakṣoruhām
pāṇibhyām alipūrṇa ratna caṣakam
raktotpalam bibhratīm
saumyām ratna ghaṭastha rakta caraṇām
dhyāyet parām ambikām

O Mother, I meditate on Your resplendent red form with three sacred eyes, wearing a sparkling crown jewel and the crescent moon and displaying a sweet smile! I meditate on You, Mother of the Universe, with Your large breasts brimming with motherly love, holding in each hand jewel-studded vessels decked with red lotus flowers which are encircled by bees, and with Your red lotus feet resting on a golden jar filled with jewels!

ध्यायेत् पद्मासनस्थां विकसितवदनां पद्मपत्रायताक्षीं
हेमाभां पीतवस्त्रां करकलितलसद्धेमपद्मां वराङ्गीम्.

सर्वालङ्कारयुक्तां सततमभयदां भक्तनम्रां भवानीं
श्रीविद्यां शान्तमूर्तिं सकलसुरनुतां सर्वसम्पत्प्रदात्रीम्..

dhyāyet padmāsanasthām
vikasita vadanām padma patrāyatākṣīm
hemābhām pīta vastrām karakalitalasad
hemapadmām varāṅgīm
sarvālaṅkāra yuktām satatam abhayadām
bhaktanamrām bhavānīm
śrī vidyām śānta mūrtīm sakala suranutām
sarva sampat pradātrīm

O Mother Bhavānī, let me meditate on Your beautiful form with the color of gold, with a beaming face and large lotus eyes, sitting in the lotus flower wearing a yellow garment and resplendent with all the ornaments, holding a golden lotus in Your hand, worshipped by the bowing devotees and always giving refuge! Let me meditate on You, O Śrī Vidyā, embodiment of peace, the object of worship by all the devas, *and the bestower of all the riches!*

सकुङ्कुमविलेपनामलिकचुम्बिकस्तूरिकां
समन्दहसितेक्षणां सशरचापपाशांकुशाम्.
अशेषजनमोहिनीमरुणमाल्यभूषोज्ज्वलां
जपाकुसुमभासुरां जपविधौ स्मरेदम्बिकाम्..

sakuṅkuma vilepanā malika cumbi kastūrikām
samanda hasitekṣaṇām saśara cāpa pāśām kuśām
aśeṣa jana mohinīm aruṇa mālya bhūṣojvalām
japā kusuma bhāsurām japavidhau smaredambikām

O Mother of the Universe, as I sit for japa, *let me remember Your form with the beauty of the hibiscus flower, wearing a red garland and sparkling ornaments, smeared with red saffron, shining with a mark of musk on Your forehead whose fragrance is attracting the bees, holding in Your hands the bow and the arrow, the noose and the goad, and displaying a gentle smile, throwing sweet glances around, and beguiling everyone!*

अरुणां करुणातरङ्गिताक्षीं धृतपाशाङ्कुशपुष्पबाणचापाम्.
अणिमादिभिरावृतां मयूखैरहमित्येव विभावये महेशीम्..

aruṇām karuṇā taraṅgitākṣīm dhṛta pāśāṅkuśa
puṣpa bāṇa cāpām
aṇimā dibhirāvṛtām mayūkhai
rahamityeva vibhāvaye maheśīm

O Great Goddess, let me imagine that I am one with Your glorious red form, surrounded by the golden rays from anima *and the other eight divine glories, holding the noose and the goad the bow and the arrows of flowers, with eyes in which rise waves of compassion!*

COMMENTARY

Om

It is said that long ago, before the Universe was born, two sounds emerged from Lord Brahmā's throat: *Om* and *atha* (*atha* literally means here, now). These two sounds came to be celebrated as propitious or benedictory. It is also well-known that *Śrī* is such an auspicious word. Prosperity in this world and Liberation (*mokṣa*) in the world beyond are connoted by the word *Śrī*. Everyone hopes for these; thus it is an ancient belief that it is auspicious to begin a book with one of these three words.

1. श्री माता

Śrī mātā

She who is the auspicious Mother.

The sacred *Lalitā Sahasranāma* starts with this name which has several different meanings.

It is the Indian tradition to honor womanhood. The *ardhanārīśvara* (the half-female, half-male god) concept of Śiva is an excellent example of this. The presiding deities of power, knowledge and wealth are also female: Parāśakti, Sarasvatī and Lakṣmī. Everything in the universe needs a mother; it is that Universal Mother who this first *mantra* invokes.

Śrī, the Mother who is full of glory, can be both Lakṣmī and Sarasvatī, the Mother of prosperity and knowledge. In addition, *Śrī* signifies earth, tribe, victory, beauty, ornament, high position, royal grandeur and intellect according to various lexicons. Devī Lalitā is Mother to all these.

The word *Śrī* also means first or premier, and antidote. She is the Mother who was the Primal Pulse, the Cause of the universe, and to Lord Śiva who ate poison, Devī became the antidote.

The sages say that sense objects are more harmful than poison. The objects experienced by the senses are even stronger in their evil than the poison of the cobra. "Poison kills the one who absorbs it, but the sense objects even kill the one who only looks at them," according to Śaṅkara. (*Viveka Cudāmaṇi*, verse79) Devī, on the other hand, is the Destroyer of poison, the embodiment of eternity.

Mā means to measure, to limit. *Mātā* is one who measures or sets limits. *Śrī Mātā* becomes one who has the power to limit *Śrī* (Lakṣmī). To possess glory that exceeds that of Lakṣmī means true Liberation; Liberation that is unbroken, solid Bliss. *Śrī Mātā* is the embodiment of that Liberation.

Another view is that *Śrī* means the immortal *Vedas*. *Śrī Mātā* is then the Mother of the *Vedas*. According to the *Purāṇas*, it is Parāśakti who imparted the essence of the three *Vedas* to Lord Brahmā. If *Śrī* stands for the *Vedas*, then Devī becomes one who measured and delineated the *Vedas*, the one who incarnated in the form of Vyāsa.

Everything that is to be honored is qualified by adding *Śrī* - Śrī Nārāyaṇa, Śrī Kṛṣṇa, Śrī Rāma. *Śrī Mātā* is the Mother who is honored by all.

Śrī may mean a *cakra*, a cycle or wheel. *Śrī*, prosperity, does not linger anywhere. It revolves constantly like a cycle, a *cakra*. We say "the cycle of the universe," "the cycle of life," so *Śrī Mātā*, then, would be the Mother of *cakras*. The Mother of all *cakras* is *Śrī Vidyā* or *Śrīcakra*. We may take the most auspicious *cakra* to be *Śrīcakra* and *Śrī Mātā* to be the Mother of that *cakra*. *Śrī* also means the universe. Then the name implies the Universal Mother.

Śivaśaktyaikyarūpiṇī - one who is the union of Śiva and Śakti, is the 999th name in the *Sahasranāma*. This union is the secret of *Śrīcakra*. We referred to *Śrīcakra* also as *Śrī Mātā*. The name *Śrī Mātā* is a *mantra* which contains several *bījākṣaras* or seed syllables. The 1000th name is the Divine Mother's own name, *Lalitāmbika*. Thus we can view this *mantra*, *Śrī Mātā*, as the essence of all the *mantras* in the *Sahasranāma*.

2. श्री महा राज्ञी

Śrī mahā rājñī

She who is the Empress of the Universe.

Śaṅkarācārya describes the universe as full of the unimaginable splendor of creation. Devī is the Mistress of this Universal Empire.

The first part of this *mantra* contains the letters *m,a,h,a. Ha* is Śakti and is called *vimarśa* or "the word." A stands for Lord Śiva and is called *prakāśa* or "meaning" - thus the word and its meaning. The great poet Kālidāsa starts his *Raghuvamśa* by remembering these Divine Parents of the universe who are as inseparable as word and meaning. Moreover, A and *ha* come together in *aham*, meaning "I," the self, none other than Devī, who is the embodiment of the Self.

The text *Saṅketapaddhati* discusses *prakāśa* and *vimarśa*: "A, the first of all letters, is *prakāśa*, the Supreme Śiva; *ha* the last letter, stands for *kalā* and is renowned as *vimarśa*." *Kalā* is none other than Devī.

3. श्रीमत् सिंहासनेश्वरी

Śrīmat simhāsaneśvarī

She who is the queen of the most glorious throne.

The throne is the foremost seat. Naturally, Devī, who governs the universe continuously, deserves the highest throne. All other thrones are swept away by the flow of time. Devī's throne is indestructible, eternal; that is why it is called the most glorious throne. Other thrones are subject to an order of succession. Devī's throne cannot be claimed by anyone else.

Śrīmat simhāsaneśvarī also means the Goddess who is seated on the most celebrated lion (*simha*). Devī's mount cannot be an ordinary lion, hence the use of the term *Śrīmat* (glorious) for this lion. The virgin Devī, seated on Her lion, kills the demon Mahiśāsura, according to the *Devī Purāṇa*. If we transpose the word *himsa* (killing), we get *simha*. *Āsana* means throwing away. *Simhāsana* may be the transposed form of *himsāsana*, meaning killing and casting away, a total destruction. Devī is the Goddess presiding over this destruction. Devī is that final state, as the *Śruti* (scripture) says, "... in which everything finally redissolves."

Viśa means man. When transposed, this word becomes Śiva. Man becomes Śiva, worthy of worship, when he turns around, or looks inward and finds his real nature.

Śrīmat simhāsana is the throne associated with deities (*Śrīs*). The book *Jñānārṇava* states that this *mantra* contains eight other *simhāsana mantras*, starting with *Caitanyabhairavi* and *Sampadpradabhairavi*. Devī is the presiding deity of these *mantras*, hence the name.

As we see thus far, the first name celebrates Devī as the Creator, the second as the Ruler of the universe and the third as Goddess in control of Destruction. The succeeding names up to the 999th describe the scope, diversity and richness of the sphere of Her *līlā* (sport), concluding with the 1000th name which pays homage to the Goddess with Her own name, *Lalitāmbika*.

4. चिद् अग्नि कुण्ड संभूता

Cid agni kuṇḍa sambhūtā

She who was born in the fire-pit of Pure Consciousness.

The nature of *Brahman* is *sat-cit-ānanda*. Cit is the undivided *Brahman*, the ultimate Source of everything. It is *jñānagni*, the fire of knowledge that burns away worldly attachments. Devī is one who came out of that fire. The undivided *Brahman* is attributeless and actionless and of that *Brahman*, Devī is the form with attributes, engaged in action.

The *devas* (gods) prepared the sacrificial fire and began worshipping the Parāśakti with the aim of destroying the demon Bhaṇḍāsura. According to the *Lalitopākhyana*, Parāśakti emerged from that fire.

The heart (*cit*) of a *sādhak* or spiritual seeker is also a sacrificial fire-pit. Note that spiritual pursuit is called *tapas* (heat, fire). It is from that sacrificial fire that Devī arises with the radiance of a thousand suns.

Fire is pictured as knowledge because it removes darkness or ignorance. It is the experience of sages that the effulgent Devī appears in the midst of the fire of knowledge to wipe out the darkness of ignorance.

One may ask why the attributeless, formless *Brahman* assumes qualities and form. The answer lies in the next *mantra.*

5. देव कार्य समुद्यता

Deva kārya samudyatā

She who is intent on fulfilling the wishes of the gods.

In the *Bhagavad Gītā* (IV-7), Lord Kṛṣṇa makes the promise: "Whenever there is a decline of righteousness and rise of unrighteousness, O Bhārata, I manifest Myself." This resolve by the Lord is very significant. It is an irrefutable fact that whenever oppression of righteousness is ascendant, the Divine Power incarnates to quell it. Devī's incarnation was for the protection of the *devas* who were defeated and tortured by the conquering Bhaṇḍāsura.

There are *devas* and *asuras* (demons) in all ages and lands. The *Gītā* (XVI, 1-6) says, "There are two types of beings created in this world - the *devas*, those with divine attributes; and the *asuras*, those with diabolical attributes. Fearlessness, purity of mind, steadfastness in knowledge and concentration, charity, self-control and sacrifice, study of scriptures, austerity and uprightness, non-violence, truth, freedom from anger, renunciation, tranquility, aversion to fault finding, compassion to living beings, freedom from covetousness, gentleness, modesty, absence of fickleness, vigor, forgiveness, fortitude, purity, freedom from excessive pride are the innate qualities of those who are born with a divine nature.

On the other hand, ostentation, arrogance, excessive pride, anger, hardness and ignorance are the innate attributes of those with a demonic nature."

The war between the *devas* and the *asuras* took place in the distant past, yet it still takes place today and will in the future, as well. Thus, in order to protect those with inborn divine qualities from those evil souls born with demonic temperaments, Devī manifests Herself wherever and whenever needed.

6. उद्यद् भानु सहस्राभा

Udyad bhānu sahasrābhā

She who has the radiance of a thousand rising suns.

Devī is Parāśakti and is the embodiment of *prakāśa*, radiance. This radiance is red and white in color, and so can be compared to the sun.

Devī's form is to be understood at three levels, similar to our own bodies: gross, subtle and causal. The gross form is reached in meditation in the first stages of practice, until the birth of knowledge. During the stage of *upāsana* (worship through *mantra japa*), the subtle form becomes attainable. Finally, when the seeker's *vāsanās* decline, the causal form becomes attainable.

Instead of the gross-subtle-causal description, an alternative five-fold division into gross, subtle, subtler, subtlest and undivided forms is sometimes given.

Devī's gross form is described in the next fifty names.

7. चतुर् बाहु समन्विता

Catur bāhu samanvitā

She who is four-armed.

Devī has four arms which are adept at giving blessing and which extend in all directions. The number four is very common in Indian imagery: the four directions of the compass, the four faces of Lord Brahmā facing the four directions, the four ages or *yugas* (*kṛta*, *treta*, *dvāpara* and *kali*), the four stages of a human life (childhood, adolescence, youth, old age), the four principal objects of human life (*dharma*, *artha*, *kāma and mokṣa*), the four castes, the four stages of (religious) life (*brahmacārya*, *grahastha*, *vānaprastha* and *sannayāsa*) and the four *Vedas* (*Ṛg*, *Yajus*, *Sāma* and *Atharva*). Similarly, there are the four means of success against an opponent (conciliation, bribery, dissension and punishment), the four forms of sound (*para*, *paśyantī*, *madhyama* and *vaikharī*, as discussed under names 366-371), the four ways in which life originates (life starting in a uterus, life starting as an egg, life that breaks out from the soil and that originated from sweat or dirt) and four kinds of learning (*anvikṣiki*, *trayi*, *vartha* and *daṇḍanīti*).

8. राग स्वरूप पाशाढ्या

Rāga svarūpa pāśāḍhyā

She who is holding the rope of love in Her hand.

Love is the emotion that binds all life together, and it takes the form of a rope. It is this noose of love that binds life to the universe. This love-noose is in Devī's lower left hand.

Love is a basic emotion. It is innate in the wise and the unwise. The tremulousness of love is seen even in normally cruel animals. This fundamental emotion is a weapon in Devī's hand. Love is indeed the rope that binds everything and forces its will on everything. There is wisdom in seeing the divine nature of the poetic concept that describes this emotion as one of Devī's weapons.

9. क्रोधा काराङ्कुशोज्ज्वला

Krodhā kārāṅkuśojjvalā

She who shines, bearing the goad of anger.

Anger is the form taken by love or desire when thwarted. Devī controls everything by the goad of anger.

Anger destroys all relations and crushes all the tender sentiments in life. It is desire that transforms itself into anger. It originates in the *guṇa* of *rajas*. "This is craving, this is wrath, born of the *guṇa* of *rajas*, all-devouring and most sinful," says the *Gītā* (III-37).

Devī carries the goad of anger in Her lower right hand. *Krodha* is sometimes assigned the meaning *jñāna* (knowledge or wisdom). It is pointed out in *Pūrvacatuśśatīśāstra* (a *Tāntric* scripture) that the noose and the goad represent the power of will and the power of knowledge.

10. मनो रूपेक्षु कोदण्डा

Mano rūpekṣu kodaṇḍā

She who holds in Her hand a sugarcane bow that represents the mind.

The mind is the seat of both resolve and doubt (*saṅkalpa* and *vikalpa*). Devī's bow is made of that mind and is pictured as made of sugarcane. The outer skin of the sugarcane is hard and holds no juice, but the inside is sweet. Amma often says, "One who goes after the taste of the tongue does not get to know the taste of the heart." To know the real taste of the mind, it is not enough to tap the outside. One has to remove the outer skin and squeeze the inside. This is the role of *tapas* (penance). Only through *tapas* do we get to enjoy the sweetness. Devī's bow is that sugarcane. It glitters in Her upper right hand. It should be noted that it is a sugarcane in bloom.

11. पञ्च तन्मात्र सायका

Pañca tanmātra sāyakā

She who holds the five subtle elements as arrows.

In *Vedānta*, the five subtle elements correspond to the five senses of sight, taste, smell, touch and sound. The five senses are portrayed here as arrows issued from the bow of the mind. What a sublime image! The more the bow bends the swifter the arrows go. What if the bow does not bend? As it is made of sugarcane, it will bend. Only if the sugarcane is turned into steel will it refuse to bend. *Sādhana* (spiritual practice), then, is for keeping the mind supple and thus subtle.

In names 8 to 11, there are hidden *āyudhamantras*, *mantras* for weapons to be used in warfare. They are not of practical relevance now and are mentioned only to point out to the curious this aspect of the *Sahasranāma*. Perhaps, in ancient days, Rāma and Kṛṣṇa invoked such *mantras* in the application of various weapons.

12. निजारुण प्रभा पूर मज्जद् ब्रह्माण्ड मण्डला

Nijāruṇa prabhā pūra majjad brahmāṇḍa maṇḍalā

She who immerses the entire universe in the red effulgence of Her form.

The sages prescribe that Devī's form should be visualized in red during morning meditation. Creative power is linked to the *rājasic* quality and red is the *rājasic* color. The suggestion here is that Devī is the Power that keeps the entire universe intent on action.

13. चम्पकाशोक पुन्नाग सौगन्धिक लसत् कचा

Campakāśoka punnāga saugandhika lasat kacā

She whose hair has been adorned with flowers like campaka, aśoka, punnāga *and* saugandhika.

A head-to-toe description of Devī's form starts with this name. Her form consists of three parts or *kūṭas*. Her head is spoken of as *Vāgbhavakūṭa*, Her body from the throat down to the waist, as *Madhyamakūṭa* and from the waist down to the feet as *Śaktikūṭa*.

Here, the celebration of Her form starts with Her head. Previously She has been praised as *Cidagnikuṇḍasambhūtā*, one who rose out of the sacrificial fire pit. The first part of Her form to emerge would naturally be Her head. Devī's hair is inherently fragrant. The fragrance of Her hair enriches the flowers in Her hair, not the other way around. Every kind of fragrance is a little portion measured out of Her infinite treasure of fragrance!

14. कुरुविन्द मणि श्रेणी कनत् कोटीर मण्डिता

Kuruvinda maṇi śreṇī kanat koṭīra maṇḍitā

She who is resplendent with a crown adorned with rows of kuruvinda *gems.*

The scriptures say that wearing jewels enhances devotion and gives prosperity. The form of Devī wearing the crown bedecked with many gems thus gives pleasure to the devotees. When we dress up babies in beautiful clothes and precious jewelry, is it for their pleasure or for the pleasure of those who see them? For the babies, a plain black string or a gold chain around their neck would be the same. So it is with Devī's adornments. They do not give Her any pleasure - it is the devotee who revels in that beauty. It is for the devotee's joy that Devī wears the bejewelled crown.

Amma often says, "A policeman does not look the same in civilian clothes as in his uniform. The uniform reveals his official stature. It is for this same reason that Amma puts on Devī's ornaments and decorations." Yet an actor who dresses up as a policeman cannot really assume a policeman's duties - only a real policeman can do that. The devotee who wants to unburden his sorrows in front of Amma knows that She is not just the attire and ornaments, but the Principle behind them.

15. अष्टमी चन्द्र विभ्राजदलिक स्थल शोभिता

Aṣṭamī candra vibhrājadalika sthala śobhitā

She whose forehead shines like the crescent moon of the eighth night of the lunar half-month.

On the eighth night, the moon appears as a half-circle. Devī's forehead thus shines like such a moon under Her crown. *Samudrikaśāstra* (the science that interprets the marks and features on the body) says that a half-moon-shaped forehead indicates high intelligence.

16. मुख चन्द्र कलङ्काभ मृगनाभि विशेषका

Mukha candra kalaṅkābha mṛganābhi viśeṣakā

She who wears a musk mark on Her forehead which shines like the spot in the moon.

The name figuratively suggests that the spot may be a blemish in the case of the moon, but for Devī, the musk mark enhances Her beauty.

17. वदन स्मर माङ्गल्य गृह तोरण चिल्लिका

Vadana smara māṅgalya gṛha toraṇa cillikā

She whose eyebrows shine like the archways leading to the house of Kāma, the god of love, which Her face resembles.

Devī's face is portrayed as Kāma's auspicious abode. Her eyebrows shine like two decorated archways. Curved eyebrows are deemed especially beautiful. If the face is the abode of Cupid, how can anyone gauge the beauty of that face? It is clear that Devī's beauty is beyond imagination.

18. वक्त्र लक्ष्मी परीवाह चलन् मीनाभ लोचना

Vaktra lakṣmī parīvāha calan mīnābha locanā

She whose eyes possess the luster of the fish that move about in the stream of beauty flowing from Her face.

It is suggested that Devī's eyes are capable of readily granting every wish. A fish is a being which does not gasp for breath in water. Devī's glances eagerly come to a devotee's rescue in all situations under all kinds of circumstances.

19. नवचम्पक पुष्पाभ नासा दण्ड विराजिता

Navacampaka pushpābha nāsā daṇḍa virājitā

She who is resplendent with a nose that has the beauty of a newly blossoming campaka *flower.*

A blossoming flower opens up only very gradually, and is especially attractive at that stage. Similarly, Devī's nose is described as being small and attractive like the bud of a flower.

20. तारा कान्ति तिरस्कारि नासाभरण भासुरा

Tārā kānti tiraskāri nāsābharaṇa bhāsurā

She who shines with a nose-ornament that excels the luster of a star.

Tārā means a star or planet, in particular, *maṅgala* (mars) or *śukra* (venus). These two are considered as deities. Devī's diamond-studded nose-ornament excels these celestial deities in its luster. This figure of speech also implies that the radiance of the ornament is eternal.

21. कदम्ब मञ्जरी क्लृप्त कर्णपूर मनोहरा

Kadamba mañjarī kḷpta karṇapūra manoharā

She who is captivating, wearing bunches of kadamba *flowers as ear-ornaments.*

Devī is usually portrayed as sporting a bouquet of *kadamba* blossoms behind each ear. In addition, She is said to dwell in a *kadamba* forest, the *kadamba* being one of Her favorite trees.

22. ताटङ्क युगली भूत तपनोडुप मण्डला

Tāṭaṅka yugalī bhūta tapanoḍupa maṇḍalā

She who wears the sun and the moon as a pair of large earrings.

Devī's ear pendants are the sun and the moon! The implication is that the sun and the moon are so pliant to Her will as to become Her ear ornaments. The sun and the moon are variously portrayed as Her breasts and as Her eyes.

23. पद्म राग शिलादर्श परिभावि कपोल भूः

Padma rāga śilādarśa paribhāvi kapola bhūḥ

She whose cheeks excel mirrors made of rubies in their beauty.

So great is the radiance of Devī's ruddy cheeks that rubies are no match for them even when polished as mirrors.

24. नव विद्रुम बिम्ब श्री न्यक्कारि रदन च्छदा

Nava vidruma bimba śrī nyakkāri radana cchadā

She whose lips excel freshly cut coral and bimba fruit in their reflective splendor.

Devī's red lips shine like freshly cut coral and the bimba fruit.

25. शुद्ध विद्याङ्कुराकार द्विज पङ्क्ति द्वयोज्ज्वला

Śuddha vidyāṅkurākāra dvija paṅkti dvayojjvalā

She who has radiant teeth which resemble the buds of pure knowledge.

Śuddhavidyā (or Śrī Vidyā) is also known as *Ṣoḍaśavidyā.* A sixteen-syllabled *mantra* of great importance; it is the light of knowledge that dispels the darkness of ignorance.

Dvījas are those who have two births; teeth, birds and *brāhmaṇas* are *dvījas.* A *brāhmaṇa* is regarded as a *śūdra* by birth, and becomes a *brāhmaṇa* through the study of the *Vedas.* A bird is born first as an egg and when the egg hatches, the real bird emerges. Teeth also have two births. The baby teeth fall away before the firmer permanent teeth appear. Here, the *dvījas* are Devī's teeth whose radiance is being praised. Like *Śuddhavidyā,* Devī's smile drives away all impurities and spreads light in our hearts.

As pointed out above, *Śuddhavidyā* is the same as *Śrī Vidyā,* the great *mantra* for the worship of Devī. The three hymns, *Tripuramahimāstotra* written by the sage Durvāsas, *Subhagodayastotra* by Gauḍapādācārya and *Saundarya Laharī* by Śrī Śaṅkarācārya, authoritatively deal with *Śrī Vidyā* and *Śrīcakra.* At a practical level, *Lalitāsahasranāma* is the main reference work for *Śrī Vidyā* worship.

Manmatha and Lopāmudrā were the first to worship *Śrī Vidyā.* But Manu, Candra (the Moon), Kubera (the lord of wealth), Lopāmudrā, Manmatha, Agastya, Agni (the god of Fire), Sūrya (the Sun), Subrahmaṇya, Lord Śiva and Durvāsas are all mentioned as seers (*draṣṭas*) of the *Śrī Vidyā mantra.* All of them, however, did not worship using the same *mantra.* Most of those *mantras* have disappeared in the course of time. Scholars say that the *Vidyās* of Manmatha and Lopāmudrā are the ones that have survived.

It is believed that the *mantra* starts from the *mūlādhāra*, the seat of the *Kuṇḍalinī*, and reaches the tongue after passing through the four stages of *parā*, *paśyantī*, *madhyama* and *vaikharī*. These stages represent the stages of the *Śabdabrahman* or *Brahman*-as-sound, the knowledge of the Supreme Spirit consisting of words. *Parā* is the germinal state. It is like the state of a seed that swells when it comes in contact with soil and water. The first sprouting of this seed may be considered as the *paśyantī* stage. The stage in which the sprout is ready to open as two nascent leaves may be compared to *madhyama*. When the two leaves open up as one, that is the *vaikharī* stage - the two leaves of sound and meaning unfold into one undivided entity. Those who lead worldly lives know only about *vaikharī*. The other stages are known only to *yogins* (see *mantras* 366-371).

In infancy, two teeth appear at first. In time, one gets two rows of sixteen teeth each. Sixteen syllables of sound and meaning are likened to two rows of teeth with sixteen in each row. Just as the sixteen-syllabled *mantra* illumines the heart of the worshipper, the gleam of Devī's teeth as She displays Her charming smile dispels all the darkness from the heart and makes it blissful.

Dvījapaṅktidvayā may refer to the thirty-two rituals prescribed for a *brāhmaṇa* doing worship. These rituals (such as *Śuddhavidyā* or *Baladvādaśārdhamatam*) are described in books on *Tantra*. They are to be observed in two parts and are compared here to the thirty-two teeth arranged in two rows.

Śuddhavidyā, which represents Devī's subtle body, is considered to be in three parts, as described by Bhāskararāya in the text *Varivasyārahasya*. The first is the *agnimaṇḍala* (the disc of fire), from *mūlādhāra* (the seat of *Kuṇḍalinī*) to the *anāhatacakra* in the heart and is like the Fire of Dissolution in its brilliance. The second is *Sūryamaṇḍala* (the disc of the sun) from the heart to *ājñācakra* between the eyebrows, bright as ten million suns. The third is the *Candramaṇḍala* (the disc of the moon) from *ājñācakra* to the *brahmarandhra* in the crown, equal to ten million moons in brightness (see *mantras* 85-87).

26. कर्पूर वीटिकामोद समाकर्षद् दिगन्तरा

Karpūra vīṭikāmoda samākarṣad digantarā

She who is enjoying a camphor-laden betel roll, the fragrance of which is attracting people from all directions.

The camphored betel roll (*karpūravīṭika*) is made from several fragrant medicinal substances, such as cardamom, coconut, black pepper, ginger and lime. The fragrance of the betel roll in Devī's mouth reaches far and wide, and people from all around are attracted to come for Her blessings.

27. निज सल्लाप माधुर्य विनिर्भर्त्सित कच्छपी

Nija sallāpa mādhurya vinirbhartsita kacchapī

She who excels even the vīṇā *of Sarasvatī in the sweetness of Her speech.*

The suggestion that the *vīṇā* of Sarasvatī, the Goddess of Speech, is inferior to Devī's speech in its musical sweetness is found also in Śaṅkarācārya's *Saundarya Laharī* (verse 66):

"O Devī, while nodding Your head to applaud Devī Sarasvatī's sweet music on the *vīna*, extolling Lord Śiva's noble deeds, You began to praise Her. She quietly covers Her instrument, the sweet notes of which are far excelled by Your soft melodious voice."

Anyone who has had the good fortune to spend time talking to Amma will come to realize the aptness of this description of Devī's speech.

28. मन्द स्मित प्रभा पूर मज्जत् कामेश मानसा

Manda smita prabhā pūra majjat kāmeśa mānasā

She who submerges even the mind of Kāmeśa (Lord Śiva) in the radiance of Her smile.

Kāmeśa is the one who vanquished Kāma, the Lord of Desire. Devī's smile casts a spell of infatuation even on that Kāmeśa.

Kāma has a special meaning in *Tantraśāstra*. It is the *Bindu* of *Kāmakalā*. The Lord of the *Kāmabindu* is also Śiva.

29. अनाकलित सादृश्य चिबुक श्री विराजिता

Anākalita sādṛśya cibuka śrī virājitā

She whose chin cannot be compared to anything (it is beyond comparison because of its unparalleled beauty).

Śaṅkara makes the same point in *Saundarya Laharī* (verse 67), "There is nothing to which Your chin can be compared."

30. कामेश बद्ध माङ्गल्य सूत्र शोभित कन्धरा

Kāmeśa baddha māṅgalya sūtra śobhita kandharā

She whose neck is adorned with the marriage thread tied by Kāmeśa.

Devī's wedding is described in *Lalitopākhyana*. The *devas* wondered who the appropriate bridegroom would be for Devī, who is "born in the fire-pit of Pure Consciousness." Brahmā, Viṣṇu and Śiva all came before Her and asked Her to choose one of them. Devī threw the wedding garland up in the air. It fell on the neck of Kāmeśa. Accordingly, Kāmeśa tied the *māṅgalyasutra* (marriage thread) around Her neck. Śaṅkara fancies in *Saundarya Laharī* that the three strands of the marriage thread tied by Kāmeśa on that occasion are seen even today as three folds on Devī's neck.

Also, this is the same *māṅgalyasutra* that brought back Kāma, the Lord of Love who was burned by Lord Śiva's wrath.

31. कनकाङ्गद केयूर कमनीय भुजान्विता

Kanakāṅgada keyūra kamanīya bhujānvitā

She whose arms are beautifully adorned with golden armlets.

Aṅgada and *keyūra* are both armlets, ornaments for the upper arms, but *aṅgada* is worn closer to the elbow and *keyūra* still higher, closer to the shoulder. There is a difference in their shapes as well. In the verse for meditating on Lord Śiva, He is portrayed as wearing coils of serpents as *aṅgada* and *keyūra*.

32. रत्न ग्रैवेय चिन्ताक लोल मुक्ताफलान्विता

Ratna graiveya cintāka lola muktāphalānvitā

She whose neck is resplendent with a gem-studded necklace with a locket made of pearl.

Bhāskarāraya separates the word *graiveyacintākalolamuktā* into three words and writes that they (*graiveyacintāka*, *lola* and *muktā*) describe three types of devotees: *Graiveyacintākas* are those who worship Her, but cannot firmly install Devī in their hearts. They are at the medium level spiritually. *Lolacintākas* are those who worship Her prompted by desires for worldly objects and are at the lowest level, and *muktacintākas* are those who worship Her without any desires and occupy the highest level. The main point here is the difference in the innate *vāsanās* of the devotees. Devī grants each devotee the result that matches their devotion. Lord Kṛṣṇa says in the *Gītā* (IV- 11), "Howsoever men approach Me, so do I reward them."

33. कामेश्वर प्रेम रत्न मणि प्रतिपण स्तनी

Kāmeśvara prema ratna maṇi pratipaṇa stanī

She who gives Her breasts to Kāmeśvara in return for the gem of love He bestows on Her.

Seeing Lord Parameśvara's devotion, Devī makes Her breasts the objects of His worship. Here the emphasis is not on play, but on worship. The scholars of old comment that when Lord Śiva offered Her one gem of love, She gave in return the gems that are Her breasts and the gem that is Her fidelity.

34. नाभ्यालवाल रोमालि लता फल कुच द्वयी

Nābhyālavāla romāli latā phala kuca dvayī

She whose breasts are the fruits on the creeper of the fine hairline that starts in the depths of Her navel and spreads upwards.

The Divine Mother's breasts yield the nectar of love for Her children.

35. लक्ष्य रोम लता धारता समुन्नेय मध्यमा

Lakṣya roma latā dhāratā samunneya madhyamā

She who has a waist, the existence of which can only be inferred by the fact that the creeper of Her hairline springs from it.

The suggestion is that Devī's waistline is exceedingly slender, hinting at the eminence of Her beauty.

36. स्तन भार दलन् मध्य पट्ट बन्ध वलि त्रया

Stana bhāra dalan madhya paṭṭa bandha vali trayā

She whose abdomen has three folds which form a belt to support Her waist from breaking under the weight of Her breasts.

According to *lakṣanaśāstra* (the science of body marks and features), three folds in the abdomen enhance the beauty of women. The golden folds in the abdominal region of Devī seem to be three strands of golden cord tied there to strengthen Her waist which might otherwise break, unable to bear the load of Her breasts.

37. अरुणारुण कौसुम्भ वस्त्र भास्वत् कटीतटी

Aruṇāruṇa kausumbha vastra bhāsvat kaṭītaṭī

She whose hips are adorned with a garment as red as the rising sun, which is dyed with an extract from safflower (kusumbha) *blossoms.*

Aruṇa is the charioteer of the Sun. It was common practice to dye garments with the extract of safflower. It is well-known that Devī particularly likes deep red or yellow garments as shown by such descriptions as *pitavastrā* (yellow-robed) and *raktāmśukadhārinī* (one who is clothed in a blood-red garment).

38. रत्न किङ्किणिकारम्य रशना दाम भूषिता

Ratna kiṅkiṇikāramya raśanā dāma bhūṣitā

She who is adorned with a girdle which is decorated with many gem-studded bells.

This girdle is worn over the garment. It is an ornament with bells that tinkle sweetly as Devī moves.

39. कामेश ज्ञात सौभाग्य मार्दवोरु द्वयान्विता

Kāmeśa jñāta saubhāgya mārdavoru dvayānvitā

The beauty and softness of whose thighs are known only to Kāmeśa, Her husband.

Kāmeśa is one who has vanquished Kāma, the Lord of Desire. He is thus desireless. This *mantra* implies that Devī's inner secret is revealed only to one who has conquered desire, and suggests the secret spiritual experience of a learned sage who is like the bee feeding on the nectar in the blossom of unbroken bliss.

40. माणिक्य मुकुटाकार जानु द्वय विराजिता

Māṇikya mukuṭākāra jānu dvaya virājitā

She whose knees are like crowns shaped from the precious red jewel, māṇikya *(a kind of ruby).*

41. इन्द्र गोप परिक्षिप्त स्मर तूणाभ जङ्घिका

Indra gopa parikṣipta smara tūṇābha jaṅghikā

She whose calves gleam like the jewel-covered quiver of the God of Love.

The beauty of Devī's calves covered by Her jewel-studded red garment is portrayed here.

42. गूढ गुल्फा

Gūḍha gulphā

She whose ankles are hidden.

Devī's ankles are hidden from view by the hem of Her garment.

43. कूर्म पृष्ठ जयिष्णु प्रपदान्विता

Kūrma pṛṣṭha jayiṣṇu prapadānvitā

She whose feet have arches that rival the back of a tortoise in smoothness and beauty.

Feet with high arches are a sign of beauty according to the *śāstras*.

44. नख दीधिति सञ्छन्न नमज्जन तमो गुणा

Nakha dīdhiti sañchanna namajjana tamo guṇā

She whose toenails give out such a radiance that all the darkness of ignorance is dispelled completely from those devotees who prostrate at Her feet.

Worship of Devī's feet removes all ignorance. Since Her feet are not visible to humans, some commentators say that the devotees referred to here are Brahmā and Viṣṇu. A touch of the Devī's feet dispels the impurities from the minds of even such exalted divinities. The *Matsya Purāṇa* and the *Padma Purāṇa* actually describe such occasions. Bhāskarāraya says in his commentary that the gem-studded crowns of the *devas*, as they prostrate at Her feet, pale in the radiance from Devī's toenails.

45. पद द्वय प्रभा जाल पराकृत सरोरुहा

Pada dvaya prabhā jāla parākṛta saroruhā

She whose feet defeat lotus flowers in radiance.

Devī's feet excel lotus flowers in radiance, softness, purity and fragrance. While lotus flowers attract mere bees with their indistinct hum, Devī's feet attract gifted poets. There is a limit to the sphere of attraction of the lotus. The attraction of Devī's feet is limitless. The beauty and fragrance of Her feet reach across time and space.

46. शिञ्जान मणि मञ्जीर मण्डित श्रीपदाम्बुजा

Śiñjāna maṇi mañjīra maṇḍita śrīpadāmbujā

She whose auspicious lotus feet are adorned with gem-studded golden anklets that tinkle sweetly.

Devī's worshippers have recorded that during deep meditation they hear the musical tinkle of Her anklets.

47. मराली मन्द गमना

Marālī manda gamanā

She whose gait is as slow and gentle as that of a swan.

This is the gait of someone who has no anxiety. Where is the room for anxiety in someone who is omniscient and all-powerful?

48. महा लावण्य शेवधिः

Mahā lāvaṇya śevadhiḥ

She who is the treasure house of beauty.

Śrī Śaṅkara says that even divine savants such as Lord Brahmā are struggling to describe Her unequalled beauty:

"O Devī, Daughter of the Mountain, even distinguished poets like Brahmā struggle in their attempt to portray Your beauty. Celestial women in their imagination attain union with Lord Śiva, which is difficult to reach even with severe penance, only to see Your unparalleled beauty." (*Saundarya Laharī*, verse 12)

49. सर्वारुणा

Sarvāruṇā

She who is entirely red in complexion.

At the gross level, Devī's ornaments and garments are all portrayed as red in color. At the subtle level, when engaged in the affairs of the universe (such as creation, maintenance, destruction)

She is *rājasic* in Her disposition. Red is the *rājasic* color. It was noted that Śiva is *prakāśa* and Devī is *vimarśa*. The color of *vimarśa* is red.

50. अनवद्याङ्गी

Anavadyāṅgī

She whose body is worthy of worship.

Avadya is despicable; *anavadya* is the opposite, meaning adorable. Every limb of Her body is venerable and glorious. Devī is a treasure house of beauty.

51. सर्वाभरण भूषिता

Sarvābharaṇa bhūṣitā

She who is resplendent with all types of ornaments.

In some texts, this name is given as *Sarvābharaṇa bhāsurā* (although having the same meaning).

Devī shines with many ornaments starting with the crown jewel and gem-studded ornaments on Her body. The *Kālikā Purāṇa* specifies forty ornaments for Devī to wear from head to toe. In *Paraśurāmakalpasūtra* it is made clear that there is no limit to Her ornaments.

Devī's gross body has now been described. Her seat is described next.

52. शिव कामेश्वराङ्कस्था

Śiva kāmeśvarāṅkasthā

She who sits in the lap of Śiva, who is the conqueror of desire.

Śiva stands for the Undivided Self, the principle of Existence-Consciousness-Bliss in which there is no distinction between *jīva* (the individual soul) and *Īśvara* (the Lord).

Kāmeśa is the Lord of Desire, one who can assume any form according to His desire; or, one who has conquered Kāma, one who is desireless. Thus the name means that Devī is one who resides in the Self which is beyond *saṅkalpa* (resolve) and *vikalpa* (doubt).

Kāma also means *prajñāna* (knowledge) which is Śiva Himself. According to the *Vedas*, *Prajñānam Brahma* or Knowledge is *Brahman*, the Universal Self. The *Vedas* also say that Śiva had a *kāma* (desire) to create the universe. Thus, Devī is one who sits in the lap of Śiva who desired creation.

53. शिवा

Śivā

She who bestows all that is auspicious.

According to the *Śaiva* scriptures, Devī is the power which is all-pervading, all-witnessing and all-knowing.

Śivā is the feminine form of Śiva. This difference is only in accentuation. The Supreme Self can be called by the name Śivā.

Śivā is the great Goddess who gives us or takes us to the world of Śiva.

The scriptures declare that Śivā, Devī, is as inseparable from Lord Śiva as heat from fire, radiance from the sun or moonlight from the moon.

Amma's devotees know that the word which is always on Her tongue is "Śiva, Śiva" and that often it becomes "Śivā."

54. स्वाधीन वल्लभा

Svādhīna vallabhā

She who keeps Her husband always under Her control.

Texts on *Tantraśāstra* like *Sūtasamhita*, *Saundarya Laharī* and *Subhagodayam* make it clear that even the trinity of Brahmā, Viṣṇu and Śiva become capable of their tasks only through Devī's blessings.

This *mantra* is also interpreted as "She who blesses wives with dominance over their spouses."

Devī Bhāgavata says that Devī's blessings enabled Śacīdevī to keep her husband, Indra, under her influence.

The story of Sukanyā is also famous. She was the devoted wife of the sage Cyavana, who was old and unattractive. Once the two *Aśvins*, a class of gods, came to her and, after turning her husband into the same handsome form as they themselves, asked her to choose one of the three as husband. Sukanyā, who was thus thrown into a painful dilemma, appealed urgently to Devī for help. With Devī's blessing, she was able to recognize and choose Cyavana from among the three.

55. सुमेरु मध्य शृङ्गस्था

Sumeru madhya śṛṅgasthā

She who sits on the middle peak of Mount Sumeru.

Mount Meru is described as having four peaks. The middle peak is occupied by Devī and the other three by Brahmā, Viṣṇu and Śiva. (*Lalitāstavaratna* verses 2-4)

The meaning of this *mantra* may be found in *Tantraśāstra*. The backbone is referred to as *merudaṇḍa*, the lower end of which is the *trikoṇa*, the triangle; the upper end is the *bindu* in the *sahasrāra cakra* in the head. The *trikoṇa* and the *bindu* form the first *manḍala* of the *Śrīcakra*. The arms of the *cakra* are also known as peaks. Brahmā, Viṣṇu and Śiva occupy these peaks. The central *bindu* is also called a peak. The word peak is to be interpreted as a place that is difficult to reach. Parāśakti dwells on the central peak.

This *mantra* is written as *Sumeruśṛṅgamadhyasthā* in some texts.

56. श्रीमन् नगर नायिका

Śrīman nagara nāyikā

She who is the Mistress of the most auspicious (or prosperous) city.

Devī's city, called Saubhāgyapūra (prosperous city) is on the middle peak of Mount Meru and in the middle of the ocean of nectar. This, too, is a concept with a hidden meaning. The "auspicious city" is the same as *Śrīcakra*, and Parāśakti is its Mistress.

A *cakra* is something that revolves. *Śrīcakra* is a symbol of the revolving Universe.

If we look at a picture of *Śrīcakra*, we see the following: a square at the outset, inside which are drawn three circles. Inside this, there are sixteen petals in a circle and then eight petals inside that; then come, in order going inwards, a *cakra* of fourteen triangles, then one of ten, another one of ten and then one of eight triangles. Finally there is a triangle at the center and a point (*bindu*) at the center. If, instead of a picture on a plain surface, we visualize this as a solid object, at the very top we see the point or *bindu* and below it the triangle. This is the *Tāntric* image of the human body. It may also be viewed as the image of the entire universe. This concept is well-known and contained in the *śāstras*.

Śrīcakra becomes *Merucakra* when turned into an image. Śaṅkarācārya installed *Śrīcakra* in several locations during his victory tour (*digvijaya*).

Śrīcakra has the synonyms *Cakrarāja*, *Navayonicakra*, *Viyatcakra* and *Mātṛkācakra*.

Lalitādevī is Parāśakti, the presiding deity of *Śrīcakra*. Lalitā is one who transcends all the worlds in Her sport, Her *līlā*.

57. चिन्तामणि गृहान्तस्था

Cintāmaṇi gṛhāntasthā

She who resides in a house built of the Cintāmaṇi *(wish-fulfilling) gem.*

Cintāmaṇi is a gem capable of fulfilling every wish. The name suggests an inner meaning instead of a literal one. Isn't the house made of wish-fulfilling gems really one's own mind? Doesn't that gem storehouse (the mind) possess the power to bring even the most unreachable goal within reach? That house is Devī's abode.

Even the *devas* are said to worship Devī in the *Cintāmaṇi* house.

58. पञ्च ब्रह्मासन स्थिता

Pañca brahmāsana sthitā

She who sits on a seat made of five Brahmās.

Devī's mansion has been described as made of *Cintāmaṇi* gems. The bed is Śiva and the pillow the great Īśāna; the mat is Sadāśiva; the four bed supports are Brahmā, Viṣṇu, Rudra and Īśvara according to *Tāntric* texts. Indra is described as Her spittoon! Indra is the highest symbol of comfort and prosperity. If all the worldly and heavenly riches amount only to a spittoon for Devī's use, what is the sense in running after them? The statement that the Trinity and Īśvara are bedposts is also noteworthy. An unsteady object is not fit to be a bedpost. The four divinities standing motionless as pillars to support Devī is a sublime image. Only those who attain such stillness can hold Her within.

The five Brahmās may be interpreted as the five *tanmātras* (subtle elements) in the process of manifestation from the *sakalabrahman* (*Brahman* having parts or *Brahman* with a form).

59. महा पद्माटवी संस्था

Mahā padmāṭavī samsthā

She who resides in the great lotus forest.

The thousand-petaled lotus (*sahasradala padma*) or the thousand-spoked *cakra* (*sahasrāra cakra*) is referred to as the great lotus forest here.

The ultimate fulfillment of *upāsana* (worship) occurs when the *Kuṇḍalinī* rises from the *mūlādhāra* and, reaching the thousand-petaled lotus, merges with Śiva there. In this sense, too, the Devī's playground is the thousand-petaled lotus (see *mantra* 110).

60. कदम्ब वन वासिनी

Kadamba vana vāsinī

She who resides in the kadamba *forest.*

Kadambavana is a picture from *Tāntric* tradition. All around the *cintāmaṇi* mansion there are temples of precious gems and around them *kadamba* trees cast their shade. Śrī Śaṅkara describes Devī's abode as "surrounded by a grove of celestial trees."

61. सुधा सागर मध्यस्था

Sudhā sāgara madhyasthā

She who resides in the center of the ocean of nectar.

The ocean of nectar is said to be the *bindu* at the center of *Śrīcakra*. *Tantraśāstra* says that there are three cities in this ocean. One of these is surrounded by the nectar. Another is the *candramaṇḍala* in the pericarp of the thousand-petaled lotus. The third is the central point (*bindu*) of the *candramaṇḍala* called *aparājita*.

62. कामाक्षी

Kāmākṣī

She whose eyes awaken desire, or She who has beautiful eyes.

Here the desire is not for physical enjoyment, but for the ultimate goal of life: Liberation.

Also, She whose eyes are Sarasvatī (*kā*) and Lakṣmī (*mā*). Knowledge and material wealth are the goals of those who worship Devī. Both are as natural for Her as Her two eyes. Those eyes shower their blessings generously on Her devotees.

63. काम दायिनी

Kāma dāyinī

She who grants all wishes.

Brahmāṇḍa Purāṇa says that the names Kāmākṣi and Kāmadāyini were given to Devī by Brahmā because of Her kindness and generosity.

This *mantra* can also be interpreted as "She who brings good fortune (*ayini*) to Śiva (Kāmada)" or as "She who destroys *kāma*, desire."

Dāya has the meaning of inheritance; in this sense, "She who belongs to Śiva as His inheritance."

The primary meaning of this *mantra* is, however, "She who grants all the wishes of Her devotees."

64. देवर्षि गण संघात स्तूयमानात्म वैभवा

Devarṣi gaṇa saṅghāta stūyamānātma vaibhavā

She whose might is the subject of praise by multitudes of gods and sages.

Saṅghāta is the name of a particular hell. Devī is one who has the power to save *devas* and sages from that hell. The *Purāṇas* have made it clear that *devas* and sages fall from their position in various ways. The *mantra* means that Devī is one who is being praised for saving them from their fall.

If we take *saṅ* as meaning "well" or "properly" and *ghātam* as "killing," then the *mantra* can be interpreted as "She who had the might to kill Bhaṇḍāsura for the sake of the *devas* and the sages" (see next *mantra*). It was Devī who the *devas* and the sages invoked and praised in song for the destruction of Bhaṇḍāsura. After his killing, they again sang in praise of Her. Her majesty is clearly unparalleled. Devī is the embodiment of the Supreme Self.

65. भण्डासुर वधोद्युक्त शक्ति सेना समन्विता

Bhaṇḍāsura vadhodyukta śakti senā samanvitā

She who is endowed with an army of śaktis *intent on slaying Bhaṇḍāsura.*

Recall the fifth *mantra*: Devī is one who manifested for fulfilling the wishes of the *devas*. The killing of Bhaṇḍāsura is the most important deed in this connection.

Lord Śiva incinerated Kāma, the god of love, with the fire from His eye. From the ashes, Citrasena, a member of Śiva's entourage of spirits (*bhūtas*), using his power of penance, created a very powerful being. Seeing the new being, Lord Brahmā uttered the praise, "Well done, Well done (*Bhaṇḍa*, *bhaṇḍa*)!" Thus the new being came to be known as Bhaṇḍa. Since he was created from the ashes of Śiva's fire of wrath by a leader of the *bhūtas*, Bhaṇḍa turned out to be a very powerful demon (*asura*). He did severe penance, made Śiva appear before him and obtained all the boons required for his own protection.

Bhaṇḍa then proceeded to attack the *devas* and the sages. The *devas* panicked and started a sacrifice (*yāga*) for his destruction. But the *yāga* was disrupted by Bhaṇḍa's invasion. The *devas* scattered in all directions.

Indra, the chief of the *devas*, then started an even more powerful *yāga* aimed at pleasing Parāśakti. The *devas* offered their own flesh and limbs in the sacrificial fire. From that fire, Devī manifested in a form known as Tripūrasundarī. The *devas*, the seven great sages and Nārada sang hymns in Her praise. Devī assembled Her army of *śaktis* and prepared to face Bhaṇḍa.

Philosophically, this story has a different meaning. *Bhaṇḍa* means unashamed; *asu* means life and *ra* means one who destroys. Bhaṇḍāsura is one who destroys life with no shame, no conscience. The reason for this lack of inhibition is ignorance. Thus, "Bhaṇḍāsura" is the *jīva* (soul) that is bound to the body due to ignorance. Ignorance makes the *jīva* prone to killing (*himsa*) and incites it to violence of all kinds. The *yāga* or *tapas* is for the removal of ignorance. The seeker burns his attachments, his body-consciousness, his thoughts and emotions in the fire of *tapas*, *sādhana*. It is from this sacrificial fire-pit of the heart that Devī arises. She cuts all the bonds of *karma* and *vāsanās* (habits or tendencies) that bind the *jīva* and gives it Ultimate Liberation. This is the meaning of the allegory of the destruction of Bhaṇḍāsura.

66. सम्पत्करी समारूढ सिंधुर व्रज सेविता

Sampatkarī samārūḍha sindhura vraja sevitā

She who is attended by a herd of elephants ably commanded by Sampatkarī.

The description of the Devī's army of *śaktis* starts here, setting up the background for the killing of Bhaṇḍa. The goddess Sampatkarī assembles an army of elephants under her command to assist Devī. Sampatkarī manifested from the goad one of the weapons carried by Devī.

Sampatkarī is also the name of a *mantra* of unimaginable power for the worship of Devī.

In the *Lalitopākhyāna*, Sampatkarī is described as riding a great elephant named Kolāhala at the very sight of which all other elephants line up behind it. Even though Sampatkarī has chariots, horses and men under her control, the elephant brigade is her chief force.

Sampatkarī is one who generates wealth (*sampat*). Wealth generates pleasure. *Sampatkarīsamāruḍha* means pleasure-giving. The elephant brigade refers to the pleasure-giving senses in this context.

Recall the story of *Gajendramokṣa*, the Liberation of the Elephant King, given in the *Bhāgavata Purāṇa*. A king turns into an elephant as the result of a curse. As the head of a large herd of elephants, he rules the forest. Once, while sporting in a lake with his companions, a big crocodile attacks him and begins to drag him down by grabbing his hind leg with its teeth. The elephant resists and a struggle ensues which lasts for a very long time. The elephant's companions give up all hope of saving him and leave one by one. His thoughts then turn towards Lord Viṣṇu and, plucking the wild lotus flowers in the lake with his trunk, offers them to the Lord, calling for help. His once majestic strength slowly ebbs away, and finally as he is about to be pulled under completely, he makes his last desperate appeal to the Lord for help with the only flower remaining. Lord Nārāyaṇa appears, His *sudarśana cakra* in hand. He kills the attacker and gives *mokṣa* to the elephant.

What does this story mean? Life is the big lake full of lotus flowers. The elephant represents the sense organs and the flowers the sense objects or sensory experiences. The crocodile is the mind. To free the senses from the mind, the *sudarśana* is needed - literally, "good vision."

The elephants represent the senses. Those wild animals must be tamed and brought down to worship at the feet of Devī. Only someone who has tamed the mind and senses in that fashion will be able to enjoy the bliss of *turīya*. *Turīya* is the bliss beyond even the stage of deep sleep.

In the *Gītā* the mind is counted as the sixth sense. In this case, life is the lotus lake, the sense objects are the flowers, the mind is Kolāhala the elephant, the other senses are the elephants in attendance and the intellect is the crocodile. Through a vision of truth (*sudarśana*), the worldly intellect is transformed into divine experience, into knowledge that transcends the senses. *Sampatkarī*, the source of worldly wealth, turns into the source of the wealth of knowledge. When that conversion is firm, the *yogi* can revel in the bliss of the *turīya* state. The inner meaning of this *mantra* then is that Devī is served by such *yogins*.

67. अश्वारूढाधिष्ठिताश्व कोटि कोटिभिर् आवृता

Aśvārūḍhādhiṣṭhitāśva koṭi koṭibhir āvṛtā

She who is surrounded by a cavalry of several million horses which are under the command of the śakti, *Aśvārūḍhā.*

The name Aśvārūḍhā means "seated on a horse." This *śakti* leads many millions of horses and escorts Devī.

Aśvārūḍhā is a goddess described in *Tantraśāstra*. Her *mantra* is thirteen syllables long. She is pictured as the presiding deity of Devī's cavalry.

This goddess is born out of the noose or rope (*pāśa*) which is one of the Devī's weapons. It has been made clear (see *mantra* 8) that this rope stands for love or desire, binding all living things together. Aśvārūḍhā, the deity born of the love-noose, rides a horse named Aparājita, meaning unbeaten.

The horses stand for the senses. The name "unbeaten" is very apt for the senses. A sense-horse is, indeed, very difficult to control. But Aśvārudha controls that wild horse at her will and rides it far and wide at great speeds. Here Aśvarūdha represents the mind and Devī, in turn, is the Self. But Aśvārūḍhā, the mental power which has tamed the unbeatable sense-horse Aparājita, is capable of controlling countless millions of sense-horses in the universe.

The real experience of *yogis* excels such book knowledge. When one is escorted by the Aśvārūḍhā mind, everything becomes a wonder. The land of *yoga* is one of wonders, according to authorities. The mind that reaches that astonishing state of *yogic* experience realizes the essence of Śiva. In this state the will power of the *yogi* is known as "Umā." Other names for it are "Kumāri" and "Parābhaṭṭārikā."

68. चक्र राज रथारूढ सर्वायुध परिष्कृता

Cakra rāja rathārūḍha sarvāyudha pariṣkṛtā

She who shines in Her chariot cakrarāja, *equipped with all kinds of weapons.*

The *Lalitopākhyāna* describes different types of chariots, of which the Devī's *cakrarāja* chariot is the most glorious. It has *ānanda* (bliss) as the flag and has nine levels. It is ten *yojanas* (a *yojana* is a distance of about eight miles) in height and extends for four *yojanas*.

Next comes the *Geyacakra* chariot with large wheels and seven stages. It is occupied by the *śakti* Mantriṇī. Then comes the *Kiricakra* chariot, also with seven stages. The *śakti* named Daṇḍanātha occupies this chariot. These three chariots always travel together (see the next two *mantras*). There is reason to believe that these chariots are *Tāntric* concepts representing the *iḍā*, *piṅgalā* and *suṣumnā nāḍīs* (nerves).

The weapons mentioned in this *mantra* refer to the methods of *sādhana* to attain the knowledge of the Self. According to the *Śaiva* tradition, these weapons are the techniques such as *āṇavopāya*, *śāktopāya* and *śāmbhavopāya*.

We can indeed guess that the *cakrarāja* chariot is the *Śrīcakra*. Then, "*cakrarājarathārūḍha*" means Devī, seated in the Śrīcakra bestowing Her blessings on Her devotees in all their *sādhanas*. One who knows *Śrī Vidyā* knows the secret of *Śrīcakra*. And one who knows that secret transcends the ideas of "I" and "mine" and attains the knowledge of the Self.

69. गेय चक्र रथारूढ मन्त्रिणी परिसेविता

Geya cakra rathārūḍha mantriṇī parisevitā

She who is served by the śakti *named Mantriṇī who rides the chariot known as* Geyacakra.

Geyacakra means a *cakra* whose glories are worthy of being extolled in song. The reference here is to the path of the *Kuṇḍalinī* in its ascent from the *mulādhāra* to the *sahasrāra* at the top. The *geyacakra* is *sūryamaṇḍala* (the disc of the sun) in the middle of that path. This *mantra* implies that the deity seated in the *sūryamaṇḍala* assists Devī, who is Tripūrasundarī or *Kuṇḍalinī Śakti*, to the *sahasrāra* (see *mantras* 99, 110).

In another interpretation, *geyacakra* stands for the main *cakra* or *Śrīcakra*. Devī Herself, seated in the *Śrīcakra*, reveals the power of *mantras* to Her devotees. In this case, the name would mean: "She who is served by the devotees for whom the power of *mantras* has thus been revealed." *Tantraśāstra* says that the Devī's *mantriṇī* (minister) and singer is the deity named Śyāmalāmba. The present *mantra* then means "She who is always served by the deity Śyāmalāmba."

70. किरि चक्र रथारूढ दण्ड नाथा पुरस् कृता

Kiri cakra rathārūḍha daṇḍa nāthā puras kṛtā

She who is escorted by the śakti *known as Daṇḍanāthā, seated in the Kiricakra chariot.*

Kiri is a hog and *kiricakraratha* is a chariot in the shape of a hog or one that is drawn by hogs. *Daṇḍanātha* is the goddess known as Vārāhi. As the commander of Devī's forces, she always travels in front of Her.

In another interpretation, *kiri*, which means "ray," stands for all the beings in creation. *Kiricakra* becomes the wheel of *saṁsāra.*

The deity Daṇḍanātha (the wielder of the stick) is none other than Yama or the Lord of Death. The *mantra* then means "She who is *not escorted (apuraskṛta)* by Yama, who is travelling in his chariot of samsāra." Yama is powerless to go in front of Devī. Even as She is engaged in Her worldly sport, Devī has the inherent power to transcend time.

71. ज्वाला मालिनिकाक्षिप्त वह्नि प्राकार मध्यगा

Jvālā mālinikākṣipta vahni prākāra madhyagā

She who has taken position at the center of the fortress of fire created by the goddess, Jvālāmālinī.

Jvālāmālinī is one who throws flames all around. The fortress of fire stands for the entirety of creation. This fortress is made of sparks or tongues of flame which are only transient. Fire itself is eternal; it is the Truth. The state of a *jñāni* or enlightened one is like the fire. The sparks or tongues of flame are the sense objects and the *jñāni* remains unruffled at the center of these transitory sense objects.

According to *Tantraśāstra*, *jvālāmālinīs* are the five triangles of Śakti. The fortress of fire represent four Śiva triangles covering all four directions. When the five Śakti triangles and the four Śiva triangles merge, *Śrīcakra* is formed. Devī resides in the central *bindu* of the *Śrīcakra*. The work *Uttaracatuṣśati* clearly says, "By the combination of the five Śaktis and the four fires, the *cakra* came into existence."

Recall the name "*Cidagnikuṇḍasambhūtā*" (mantra 4). Devī is at the center of the fortress of fire. Bhaṇḍāsura, the darkness of ignorance, cannot even cast a glance at that center.

Jvālāmālinī is the deity of the fourteenth day of the lunar half-month.

72. भण्ड सैन्य वधोद्युक्त शक्ति विक्रम हर्षिता

Bhaṇḍa sainya vadhodyukta śakti vikrama harṣitā

She who rejoices at the valor of the śaktis *who are intent on destroying the forces of Bhaṇḍāsura.*

Bhaṇḍa is the *jīva* that is bound to the senses and the mind. Bhaṇḍa's army consists of the countless aspects of duality with the myriads of forms and names all around. This *mantra* implies that Devī rejoices at the power of the *sādhana* that has progressed through its many stages, gone beyond the *ājñācakra*, intent on reaching the ultimate experience that eradicates all sense of duality.

The valorous acts of the *śaktis* mentioned in the *mantra* are the forms of *sādhana* that conquer, one by one, the *kośās* or sheaths such as the *annamaya* or food sheath, that shroud the innate bliss of the *jīva*. The *jīva* has two levels of existence: *paśubhūmika* (the "animal" level) and *patibhūmika* (the level of the master). The *jīva* that is steeped in *samsāra* is at the *paśubhūmikā* and one who is free of *samsāra* is at the *patibhūmikā* level. This is why Śiva is called "Paśupati," the master of *paśus* (animals). The realization of the non-dual Self is the process of *paśu* (animal) becoming *paśupati* (the Lord). Whatever the path, reaching this supreme goal is the fulfillment of human life.

73. नित्या पराक्रमाटोप निरीक्षण समुत्सुका

Nityā parākramāṭopa nirīkṣaṇa samutsuka

She who delights in seeing the might and the pride of Her nityā *deities.*

Each day of the lunar half-month has its own presiding deity. They are known as *nityā* (daily) deities. *Nityā* deities provide protection to Devī who is the manifestation of Time. This *mantra* says that Devī is very pleased with the heroism of the *nityā* deities in staying alert and destroying the demonic powers (such as Bhaṇḍa or Damanaka) which impede the seeker's Self-Realization.

Starting with the first day of the lunar half-month, these deities are Kāmeśvari, Bhagamālinī, Nityaklinnā, Bherunḍā, Vahnivāsinī, Mahāvidyeśvarī, Dūtī, Tvaritā, Kulasundarī, Nīlapatākā, Vijayā, Sarvamaṇgalā, Jvālā, Malinī and Citrā. These fifteen goddesses killed fifteen demons such as Citragupta and Damanaka.

Nityā (everlasting) is the eternal power of the Self. The aggressive might referred to in the *mantra* is the mighty will power dedicated to the struggle for gaining knowledge of the Self. Devī's delight is in seeing this. An unshaken will knows no defeat; it only gathers more strength at each step. This happens once the seed of knowledge has sprouted. It will take root and grow stronger steadily.

74. भण्ड पुत्र वधोद्युक्त बाला विक्रम नन्दिता

Bhaṇḍa putra vadhodyukta bālā vikrama nanditā

She who delights in seeing the valor of the goddess Bālā who is intent on killing the sons of Bhaṇḍa.

Bhaṇḍāsura had thirty sons starting with Caturbāhu and Upamāya. They may be thought of as the thirty days of the month. Each day (son) tries to turn the *samsāra*-bound *jīva* (Bhaṇḍa) more and more intoxicated and conceited. The nine-year old Bālā destroys them. Here Bālā refers to the "*Bālāmantra.*" The seeker in the rigor of his *sādhana* becomes unaware of the passage of day and night. This experience is alluded to here. Devī is delighted by this.

75. मन्त्रिण्यम्बा विरचित विषङ्ग वध तोषिता

Mantriṇyambā viracita viṣaṅga vadha toṣitā

She who rejoices at the destruction, in battle, of the demon Viṣaṅga by the mantriṇī śakti.

The *Brahmāṇḍa Purāṇa says*, "Long ago there was the demon chief, Bhaṇḍa, who was capable of creating different types of demons at will. For the preservaftion of the demon world, he created Viśukra from his right shoulder and Viṣaṅga from his left shoulder. These two demons are thus brothers." Of these two brothers, Viṣaṅga was killed by Śyāmalāmba, the mantriṇī *śakti.*

The word *Viṣaṅga* can be interpreted in two ways. As *vi+saṅga*, it means the opposite of "satsanga." This is attachment to or desire for worldly objects. It is the creation of Bhaṇḍa, the *jīva* in bondage. The other meaning is "poisonous in essence" (from *viṣam+ga* that which attains *viṣa*, poison). All worldly enjoyments will seem like nectar at first, but turn into poison for someone seeking Liberation. The mantriṇī *śakti* kills this Viṣaṅga and Devī is pleased with this.

76. विशुक्र प्राण हरण वाराही वीर्य नन्दिता

Viśukra prāṇa haraṇa vārāhī vīrya nanditā

She who is pleased with the prowess of Vārāhī who took the life of Viśukra.

Vārāhī is the *śakti* known as Daṇḍinī. *Tripurāsiddhānta* narrates that Devī appeared before the sage Varāhānandanātha in the form of a boar (*varāhā*) and that since then She is called Vārāhī.

Viśukra can also be interpreted as "one who embraces sorrow" (*vi+śuk+ra*: one who goes to sorrow eagerly). This is also the creation of the *samsāra*-bound *jīva.*

Viṣaṅga and Viśukra are two sides of the *jīva*'s thirst for worldly pleasures. How great indeed is the urge for wealth, wife and children! But the *jīva* shrouded in ignorance does not see that at the core of these lies sorrow. Trapped in the circle of sorrow, the *jīva* stays immersed in countless miseries. Amma sings, "Remember, O mind, this supreme truth always: there is none that is your own!" It is hard for the *jīva* in bondage to understand the meaning of this. The *jīva* immersed in *samsāra* is *jīva* in bondage (*baddhajīva*), and one that has transcended *samsāra* is liberated *jīva* (*muktajīva*).

The last three *mantras* (74-76) deal with the impurities of the mind (they are known technically as *aṇava* impurities), and the power within the seeker to eradicate them. Devī is delighted to see the advances made by the seeker in curbing the affairs of *samsāra* and rising to the path of knowledge.

77. कामेश्वर मुखालोक कल्पित श्री गणेश्वरा

Kāmeśvara mukhāloka kalpita śrī gaṇeśvarā

She who gives rise to Gaṇeśa by a glance at the face of Kāmeśvara.

The demonic powers create many obstacles and prevent the advance of the *samsāra*-bound *jīva* towards Liberation. Seeing this sad state, Devī, in Her compassion, wanted to find a solution. *Brahmāṇḍa Purāṇa* relates one story: "Thus, when the *asuras* threw obstacles in the path of the *devas*, Devī Lalitā looked at Kāmeśvara's face and smiled. From the radiance of that smile was born a deity with the face of an elephant with ichor flowing from the temples. He was Vighneśvara, the remover of obstacles, who shattered all the hindrances from the path of the *devas*." This is why Vighneśvara (Gaṇeśa) is worshipped at the start of all auspicious undertakings.

Kāmeśvara is pure *Brahman*. The "glance at His face" is the knowledge of *Brahman*. *Gaṇa* is the city (meaning the body) formed by eight parts (*puryāṣṭaka*). These eight parts are: the organs of action, the organs of perception, the mind, the five *prāṇas*, the five *bhūtas* (elements), *kāma* (desire), *karma* (action) and *avidyā* (nescience). Gaṇeśvara is the deity presiding over these. The word can also be taken as feminine, "Gaṇeśvarā" which would mean "the Devī who is the controller of the body, the *Ātman*."

Gaṇeśvara also means the presiding deity of the *gaṇeśvaramantra*, a *mantra* of twenty-eight syllables which is used for removing the effects of evil spirits.

78. महा गणेश निर्भिन्न विघ्न यन्त्र प्रहर्षिता

Mahā gaṇeśa nirbhinna vighna yantra praharṣitā

She who rejoices when Gaṇeśa shatters all obstacles.

The journey of the *jīva* from the bonds of *samsāra* towards Liberation is portrayed as a battle.

There are the five birds (the sense organs) that feast on the five kinds of fruits (the sense objects). The birds are enclosed in the stinking cage that is the body, where they fly around artfully dodging obstacles. During countless cycles of birth and death, they play in different cages. These birds have to be done away with; the *vāsanās* born of the senses have to be eliminated. Only then will the embodiment of light, of Self-Knowledge, emerge.

(*Atmopadeśaśataka*, verse 8) Bhaṇḍa's effort is to obscure and topple this embodiment of knowledge.

When Bhaṇḍa saw that the *śaktis* had destroyed his army and that Bālā Devī had killed his sons, he summoned Viśukra and ordered him to use his magical powers and deploy the *jayavighna* (obstacle to victory) *yantra* to overpower Devī's forces. Viśukra struggled for a long time to deploy the *yantra* and finally, artfully hurled it in the direction of Devī's army. With that, the divine forces became dim-witted, sleepy and disinclined to fight. It is easy to identify these effects of the *yantra* with the slothfulness and loss of direction suffered by a seeker at the height of *sādhana*.

It is in this context that Devī looked at Kāmeśvara's face and smiled, creating Gaṇeśa. Gaṇeśa, in turn, shattered the *vighnayantra* which pleased Devī.

Lalitopākhyāna says that the *vighnayantra* had eight corners which were guarded by eight evil spirits.

79. भण्डासुरेन्द्र निर्मुक्त शस्त्रप्रत्यस्त्र वर्षिणी

Bhaṇḍāsurendra nirmukta śastrapratyastra varṣinī

She who showers counter weapons to each weapon fired at Her by Bhaṇḍāsura.

Bhaṇḍa's armaments are the weapons of delusion arising from nescience (ignorance). Devī counters each one of them. If the devotee takes one step towards Her, She will take ten steps towards him. To the devotee thirsting for Self-Knowledge, She gives the power and concentration needed for unbroken self-inquiry.

80. कराङ्गुलि नखोत्पन्न नारायण दशाकृतिः

Karāṅguli nakhotpanna nārāyaṇa daśākṛtiḥ

She who created from Her fingernails all ten incarnations of Nārāyaṇa (Viṣṇu).

Daśākṛti means ten forms. The *Purāṇas* tell the story of Viṣṇu's ten incarnations. *Lalitopākhyāna* explains that each of these incarnations originated from a fingernail of Devī at the appropriate moment. We may consider this reference in *Lalitopākhyāna* to have only an allegorical significance, but we should also remember that the stories of the incarnations of Paraśurāma, Śrī Rāma, Balarāma and Kṛṣṇa have a historical aspect as well. Vālmīki and Vyāsa are not just allegorical figures.

Alternately, *daśākṛti* may be interpreted as the five states (*daśas*) of the *jīva* and the five functions (*kṛtis*) of Īśvara (see *mantras* 256-274). The five states of the *jīva* are waking, dreaming, deep sleep, *turīya* (perception of reality) and abidance in *Brahman* (the state beyond *turīya*). The five functions of Īśvara are creation, maintenance, destruction, the great dissolution and restoration of the universe. Here it is said that all these issue from Devī's fingernails. The *mantra* emphasizes Her sovereignty and might.

81. महा पाशुपतास्त्राग्नि निर्दग्धासुर सैनिका

Mahā pāśupatāstrāgni nirdagdhāsura sainikā

She who burned the armies of the demons in the fire of the missile, mahāpāśupata.

This is the missile of *Paśupati* (Śiva). The fire of *mahāpāśupata* is the fire of *jñāna*, knowledge. That fire burns away all perceptions of duality. Devī is the embodiment of such *jñāna*. The demon army connotes the mental impurities arising from ignorance.

The *mahāpāśupata mantra* is different from the *pāśupata mantra.* Sadāśiva is the deity of the former whereas Īśvara is that of the latter. *Liṅga Purāṇa* says that everything from Rudra to the *piśācas* (evil spirits) is known as *paśu*, and Śiva, the Protector of them all, is *Paśupati* (Lord of *paśus*).

82. कामेश्वरास्त्र निर्दग्ध सभण्डासुर शून्यका

Kāmeśvarāstra nirdagdha sabhaṇḍāsura śūnyakā

She who burned and destroyed Bhaṇḍāsura and his capital Śūnyaka with the mighty Kāmeśvara missile.

In some texts, this *mantra* is given as "*Kameśvarāstra nirdagdha sabhaṇḍāsura* <u>*sainika*</u>." In this case it means that Bhaṇḍa's army was destroyed along with him instead of his capital. Yet another text is "*Kameśvarāgni nirdagdha*," meaning "She who burned and destroyed Bhaṇḍāsura and his capital in the fire of Kāmeśvara."

Brahmāṇḍa Purāṇa describes this episode as follows: "The Supreme Goddess, Mother Lalitā, using the Mahākāmeśvara missile which had the radiance of a thousand suns, killed the fierce and mighty Bhaṇḍāsura, a wicked demon causing much harm to the world, who was boiling with rage, and who was the sole survivor after all his relatives were killed in battle. From the flames issuing from the missile, Śūnyaka, his city, also burned to ashes instantly along with women, children, cattle and wealth. His famous city Śūnyaka truly became '*śūnya*' (empty)."

We may shudder to hear that women and children were all burned to death. But why should we? Is any of our family or wealth with us in our sleep? While asleep do we know where we are lying? And what about someone who is dead? He does not retain ownership of even a pin. If this truth is appreciated while still alive, we can convince the mind of its import and gain the practice needed to lead the mind to its goal with dispassion.

83. ब्रह्मोपेन्द्र महेन्द्रादि देवसंस्तुत वैभवा

Brahmopendra mahendrādi devasamstuta vaibhavā

She whose many powers are extolled by Brahmā, Viṣṇu, Śiva and other gods.

When Devī destroyed Bhaṇḍāsura as described above, the Trinity and the other *devas* were pleased and came to praise Her, according to the *Lalitopākhyāna.*

Alternately, Brahmā, Viṣṇu, Śiva and others became aware of the infiniteness and omnipresence of the Self only when they praised Devī.

84. हर नेत्राग्नि संदग्ध काम संजीवनौषधिः

Hara netrāgni sandagdha kāma sanjīvanauṣadhiḥ

She who became the life-giving medicine for Kāmadeva (the god of love) who had been burned to ashes by the fire from Śiva's eye.

The *devas* who came to praise Devī pointed out Kāma's bereaving widow Rati to Her and requested that Kāma be given back his life. Devī was pleased with their request and glanced at Her consort, Śiva. It is the mother who normally consoles the child who is scolded by the father. The father's anger is also not for lack of love, but from the force of circumstances.

This *mantra* uncovers another secret of life. How many are there in a society who are ready to become Hara (God)? The *Gītā* (VII, 3) says, "Out of thousands of men, only one strives for attaining the Self; out of those who strive and succeed, only one perchance knows Me in essence." One who attains that state truly becomes Hara, Sadāśiva. He has no more worldly attachments. But the existence of the world is based on the process of creation and that process is based on desire *(kāma)*. It is the revival of that Kāma that Devī requested. She thus became the resuscitating medicine for him. She is, after all, responsible for governing the universe.

There is yet another interpretation of this *mantra*. *Hara*, knowledge of the Self; *netra*, that which leads; *agni*, the creations of myriad shapes; *sandagdha*, that which is burned. Devī is the medicine that resuscitates and elevates to Self-knowledge the *jīva* who is burned down by the fire of *samsāra*.

85. श्रीमद् वाग्भव कूटैक स्वरूप मुख पङ्कजा

Śrīmad vāgbhava kūṭaika svarūpa mukha paṅkajā

She whose lotus face is the auspicious vāgbhavakūṭa *(a group of syllables of the* pancadaśi mantra*)*.

A description of Devī's subtle body starts here. The subtle body itself is in three forms: subtle, subtler and subtlest, which are known as *pancadaśākṣari mantra*, *kāmakalā* and *kuṇḍalinī*.

The subtle form is represented by the *pancadaśākṣari* (fifteen-syllabled) *mantra* which itself is divided into three parts: the first part with five syllables is known as the *vāgbhavakūṭa*, the second part containing the next six syllables is the *madhyakūṭa* and the last part with the remaining four syllables is the *śaktikūṭa*. In this *mantra* the *vāgbhavakūṭa* is called Devī's face.

86. कण्ठाधः कटि पर्यन्त मध्यकूट स्वरूपिणी

Kaṇṭhādhaḥ kaṭi paryanta madhyakūṭa svarūpiṇī

She who from Her neck to Her waist is of the form of the madhyakūṭa *(the middle six syllables of the* pancadaśākṣari mantra*).*

The middle syllables are also known as *kāmarājakūṭa*. This part is the trunk of the body, the origin of the manifold actions and conflicts in life that have the aim of fulfillment of desires (*kāma*). Recall also that in *Tāntric* descriptions Devī resides in the heart-space known as *anāhata cakra*.

87. शक्ति कूटैकतापन्न कट्यधो भाग धारिणी

Śakti kūṭaikatāpanna kaṭyadho bhāga dhāriṇī

She whose form below the waist is the śaktikūṭa *(the last four syllables of the* pancadaśākṣari mantra*).*

The *Kuṇḍalinī śakti* in Her dormant state resides in the *mūlādhāra* at the bottom of the spine from where it rises to the top and merges with Śiva. With this merger the *Kuṇḍalinī* is experienced as pure bliss. *Mulādhāra*, *Kuṇḍalinī's* abode in the dormant state, is in the *śaktikūṭa*.

The story of the killing of Bhaṇḍāsura serves as an aid in the portrayal of the gross body of Devī. The images in the story are the means that the ancient sages used for rendering subtle concepts more easily understood. The idea that the *pancadaśākṣari mantra* is Devī's (subtle) body and that it is in three parts is also such a concept.

In verse 32 of Śaṅkara's *Saundarya Laharī*, the *pancadaśākṣari mantra* is encoded:

Śivaḥ śaktiḥ kāmaḥ kṣitiratha raviḥ śītakiranaḥ
Smaraḥ hamsaḥ śakrastadanu ca parā māraharayaḥ
Amī hrillekhabhi stisrubhiravasāneṣu ghatitā
Bhajante varnāste tava jananī nāmāvayavatam.

Kandiyur Mahādeva Śāstry's commentary gives the following code for the interpretation of this verse:

Sivaḥ: the syllable *ka; śaktih:* the syllable *e; kāmaḥ:* the syllable *ī; kṣiti:* the syllable *la; atha:* afterwards; *ravih:* the syllable *ha; śītakirana:* the syllable *sa; smara:* the syllable *ka; hamsaḥ:* the syllable *ha; śakraḥ:* the syllable *la; tadanu:* after that; *parā:* the syllable *sa; maraḥ:* the syllable *ka; hariḥ:* the syllable *la; ami:* these syllables (the first four, then the five and then the three); *avasaneṣu:* at the end of each of these groups of four, five and three syllables; *tisrubhi hrillekhabhi ghatita:* adding a *hrīm* syllable to each of the three; *jananī:* O Mother; *tava namāvayavatam:* as Your name and Your body; *bhajante:* (the devotees) worship.

Using this code, we get the following meaning for the verse: "The syllables *ka, e, ī, la, ha, sa, ka, ha, la sa, ka, la* are taken as three groups of four, five and three syllables. The syllable *hrīm* is added to the end of each making three groups of five, six and four syllables and a total of fifteen syllables. O Mother, Your devotees worship this as Your *mantra* and as Your body." This *mantra* is also known as the *tripurasundarī mantra.*

There is the following additional interpretation for *hrīm*, the *hrillekha. Hrīm* is said to contain the following twelve *tattvas: h, r, ī, bindu, ardhacandra, rodhini, nāda, nādānta, śakti, vyāpika, samana* and *unmanī.*

The three separate *kūṭas* of the *pancadaśākṣarī mantra* and the *mantra* as a whole form four entities. These are associated with many other groupings of four related to *mantras* throughout the *Sahasranāma.*

Creation, preservation, destruction and complete dissolution (see *mantras* 264-271).

Knower, known, knowledge and the combination of all three.

Agnicakra, sūryacakra, somacakra and *brahmacakra.*

States of waking, dreaming, deep sleep and *turīya* (see *mantras* 256-263).

Vāmā, Jyeṣṭhā, Raudrī, Śāntā (see *mantra* 628).

Icchā, Jñāna, Kriya and *Ambikā* (see *mantra* 658).

Kāmeśvarī, Vajreśvarī, Bhagamālinī and *Mahātripurasundarī* (various *mantras*).

Ātmatattva, Vidyātattva, Śivatattva and *Sarvatattva.*

Kāmagiri Pīṭha, Pūrnagiri Pīṭha, Jālandhara Pīṭha and *Oḍyāna Pīṭha* (see *mantra* 379).

Svayambhuliṅga, *Bānaliṅga*, *Itaraliṅga* and *Paraliṅga*.

Parā, *paśyantī*, *madhyama* and *vaikharī* (see *mantras* 366-371).

The conception and development of these associations evoke our wonder.

88. मूल मन्त्रात्मिका

Mūla mantrātmikā

She who is the embodiment of the mūlamantra *(the* pancadaśakṣari mantra*)*.

A *mantra* is something that protects one who repeats it. If a *mantra* by itself has the power to protect, how great will be the power of its presiding deity!

89. मूल कूट त्रय कलेबरा

Mūla kūṭa traya kalebarā

She whose (subtle) body is made of the three parts of the pancadaśākṣari mantra.

Since the word *mūla* also means "subtler" (*sūkṣmatara*), this name may be taken as describing Devī's subtler body known as the *Kāmakalā* form. The parts of the *Kāmakalā* form are the *ūrdhvabindu*, the top, the *hārdakalābindu* at the bottom and the *madhyabindu* in the middle.

90. कुलामृतैक रसिका

Kulāmṛtaika rasikā

She who is especially fond of the nectar known as kula.

After describing *Kāmakalā*, the subtler aspect of Devī's body, we now come to a description of *Kuṇḍalinī*, the subtlest aspect. If *Kāmakalā* or *Tripurasundarī* resides in the universe (*brahmāṇḍa*), *Kuṇḍalinī* resides in the individual body (*piṇḍāṇḍa*).

Dattātreya Samhita says, "*Kula* refers to the six *cakras* starting with *mūlādhāra*."

Kuṇḍalinī śakti is described as a female serpent sleeping in the *mūlādhāra cakra*, coiled in three-and-a-half turns. One awakens the *Kuṇḍalinī* through *yogic* practices. The awakened *Kuṇḍalinī* moves upwards through the *suṣumnā*, passing through the six *ādhāras*, reaches the thousand-petaled *sahasrāra* in the head, and there merges with Sadāśiva, pictured as a male serpent. *Kulāmṛta* is the flow of nectar occurring when the *Kuṇḍalinī śakti* reaches the *sahasrāra*.

Kula (family) refers to the body and to the triad ("*tripūṭi*") of knower, knowing and knowledge. *Yoginihṛdaya* says that in the human body there are thirty-two *Tāntric* "lotuses," and all except the last one (*akula*) are collectively known as *kula*.

Kula is a community of things related by birth. *Kulāmṛta* is interpreted as the sense of unity in diversity. It is the realization of non-duality that occurs as one transcends the sense of the knower, the known and knowledge. It is the sense of identity of the worshipper and the worshipped. Devī revels in that experience.

Kula is defined as the state in which all thoughts of plurality based on the sense of time, place, cause, action and effect dissolve completely. What remains is the nectar of *jñāna*, and Devī is one who revels only in that nectar.

Also, *kula* is *ācāra*, customary observance. Devī is one who enjoys the traditional observances.

91. कुल संकेत पालिनी

Kula saṅketa pālinī

She who protects the code of rituals of the path of yoga *known as* kula.

Kulasaṅketa can be interpreted as the secret of the *cakras*, the *mantras* and the rites. There is a strict injunction that books dealing with *yogic* or *Tāntric* knowledge should be securely guarded by the Guru. The rituals are not something a disciple can put into practice just from book knowledge. It is laid down that such rituals have to be learned from the mouth of the Guru.

92. कुलाङ्गना

Kulāṅganā

She who is well-born (who is from a good family).

Women of high descent do not wander around publicly. Devī, likewise, is one who stays highly secluded. It is implied that while all other knowledge is accessible to anyone, the knowledge of *Śrī Vidyā* is not.

Just like a bride of noble descent, Devī remains veiled. The face of such a bride can be seen only by her husband and her sons. Similarly, Devī's *darśan* is available only to Lord Śiva and to the pure-minded seeker.

The following description from *Kulārṇava* is particularly noteworthy: "All other knowledge is on display like a courtesan; but this knowledge of Devī is hidden like a noble bride." Paraśurāma's view, too, is that "other forms of knowledge are displayed like a harlot." These comparisons are not meant to disparage other forms of knowledge, but to underscore the intimacy and precious qualities of the guru-disciple relationship which is special to the *kula* path.

93. कुलान्तस्था

Kulāntasthā

She who resides in Kulavidyā.

Here *kula* can be taken as special spiritual knowledge, *śāstra*. Recall the lines that Amma sings:

Āgāmāntap porule jaganmayī
Āraríyunnu ninne vidyāmayī...
"O Devī, Essence of all *Vedānta*, Essence of the Universe,
Who knows You, O Essence of Knowledge?"

In some texts, this *mantra* is given as *kulāṅkasthā*, "One who sits in the lap of *kulavidyā*."

Bhāskararāya writes, "She who resides inside the *kula*, between the measurer and the measured in the form of the measure." Or "She who resides between the knower and the known in the form of knowledge."

Kula also means the country or the home. The *mantra* then means, "She who resides as the object of worship in each home, tribe or village." "She is to be worshipped at every place, in every city, village and forest by those who are devoted to Śakti."

94. कौलिनी

Kaulinī

She who belongs to the kula.

Kula has been already explained in various ways. Śakti is referred to as *Kula* and Śiva as *Akula*. Śiva is *svayambhu* - born of Himself and has no *kula* (family). That which pertains to *kula* is *kaula*. *Kaula* is the Supreme Essence that represents the relation between *Kula* and *Akula*. This relation means the unity of Śiva and Śakti; thus, the name *Kaulinī* is synonymous with *Śivaśaktyaikyarūpiṇī* (*mantra* 999).

The thousand-petaled lotus in the *sahasrāra cakra* is known as *kula*. Its petals are occupied by various *śakti* deities and the flower stalk is occupied by Devī, according to the text *Svacchanda Tantra*. Thus Devī is known as *Kaulinī* in the sense that She presides over the deities of the *kula*.

95. कुल योगिनी

Kula yoginī

She who is the deity in the kulas.

Yoga means "relation" and *yoginī* is "one who is joined to." *Kula* here means the six *ādhāracakras* (see *mantra* 99). *Kulayoginī* is one who resides in those *cakras*.

All previously given meanings of the word *kula* are also applicable here when taken together with the word *yoginī*.

96. अकुला

Akulā

She who does not have a family.

Where is the family for Devī who is Ādi Parāśakti, the Primal Supreme Power? The *mantra* means one who has no more *tripūṭi* (distinction of knower-known-knowledge), no body, and one who has no equal.

Svacchandasamgraha explains that Devī who resides in two lotuses below and above the *suṣumnā* is called *Akula.*

97. समयान्तस्था

Samayāntasthā

She who resides inside "samaya."

Samaya is *mānasa pūja,* internal worship, conducted in the *hṛt cakra* (the heart *cakra*). *Yogis* have recorded this as the highest form of worship.

It is worth noting here that Mother has suggested the rules and procedures for *mānasa pūja* (see Introduction).

Samaya is a collection of five *Tāntric* texts composed by Vasiṣṭha, Śuka, Sanaka, Sanātana and Sanatkumāra. *Śrīcakra* worship is their subject. *Samayāntasthā* means "She who is the subject of the *samaya* texts."

Also, *sama*: equal; *ya*: she who has reached or attained; *antah*: end or ultimate aim. The *mantra* means "She who resides within those who have a firm conviction of the equality of Śiva and Śakti."

The *Tāntric* authorities cited above indicate that there is equality between Śiva and Śakti in five different aspects: (1) in abode, in the ocean of nectar in the *bindu* in the *sahasrāra cakra*; (2) in action, Śakti's capabilities are equal to those of Śiva; (3) in dance, Śiva and Śakti engage in *tāṇḍava* and *lāsya* dances; (4) in name, one is Śiva and the other is Śivā and (5) in form, both are of red complexion, for example.

This *mantra* can also be interpreted as "She who, residing within us, awakens an understanding of the principle of the *hṛt cakra* and of the *Tāntric* texts of Vasiṣṭha and other sages."

98. समयाचार तत्परा

Samayācāra tatparā

She who is attached to the Samaya *form of worship.*

Samayācāra is described in the text *Rudrayāmala* in ten chapters. It is a mode of *sādhana* undertaken with the Guru's supervision, for awakening the *Kuṇḍalinī*. The *Kuṇḍalinī* rises from the *mulādhāra* through each of the *cakras*, *svādhiṣṭhāna*, *maṇipūraka*, *anāhata*, *viśuddhi* and *ājñā*. It meets Sadāśiva in the thousand-petaled lotus in the *sahasrāra*, joins Him in the curtained pleasure chamber and emerging from there, returns to the *mūlādhāra*. *Samayācāra* consists of the various steps in this *sādhana* undertaken with the Guru's instructions under his watchful eye. The *mantra* says that Devī is attached to this form of *sādhana*.

99. मूलाधारैक निलया

Mūlādhāraika nilayā

She whose principal abode is the mūlādhāra.

Mūlādhāra is pictured as a lotus with four petals. In the center there is the *bindu* known as *kulakuṇḍa*.The *Kuṇḍalinī* sleeps here with face hidden from view. *Mūla* means the "root" or "base;" *ādhāra* also means "base." The term *mulādhāra* stands for the root of the *suṣumnā* and the base of the *Kuṇḍalinī*.

The *cakras* traversed by the *Kuṇḍalinī* as it rises up are mentioned above. These *cakras* have the following *tattvas* (elements) associated with them:

Mulādhāra	Earth (*Pṛthvi*)
Svādhiṣṭhāna	Fire (*Agni*)
Maṇipūraka	Water (*Jala*)
Anāhata	Air (*Vāyu*)
Viśuddhi	Space (*Ākāśa*)
Ājña	Mind (*Manas*)

The *Kuṇḍalinī* passes through each of these *cakras* by way of the *suṣumnā*. This is the origin of the omniscience of the *yogis*. Nothing remains invisible or unknown to them after this.

Mūlādhāra is described as a four-petaled lotus in the region between the anus and the genitals. *Svādhiṣṭhāna* is a lotus with six petals, at the level of the genitals. Above it, at the navel, is *maṇipūraka*, the ten-petaled lotus. At the heart level is *anāhata*, the twelve-petaled lotus, and above it, at the level of the throat is *viśuddhi*, the sixteen-petaled lotus. Above this is *ājña*, the lotus with two petals, situated in between the eyebrows. These are the six *ādhārās*.

Mūlādhāra and *svādhiṣṭhāna* are known as the *Tāmasic* World. They form the Disc of Fire (*Agnimaṇḍala*). *Maṇipūraka* and *anāhata* are known as the Mixed World (*miśra loka*). They form the Disc of the Sun (*Sauramaṇḍala*). *Viśuddhi* and *ājña* are known as the World of Light (*jyotirmaya loka*) and they form the Disc of the Moon (*Candramaṇḍala*).

According to the *yogaśāstra*, the nerves *iḍā* and *piṅgalā* run inside the backbone, on the left and the right respectively. Between these two runs the *suṣumnā*, from the *mūlādhāra* to the *brahmarandhra*, slender as a lotus fiber and radiant as lightning. The six *ādhāras* described above are connected to the *suṣumnā*. When the *Kuṇḍalinī*, normally sleeping in the *mūlādhāra*, is awakened through *yogic* practice and by the grace of the Guru, it races upward through the *suṣumnā*. As it passes through each *cakra*, various chambers of the mind open by themselves. Wondrous sights, unparalleled sounds and indescribable *siddhis* manifest. And as the *Kuṇḍalinī* reaches the *sahasrāra cakra* in the head, the *yogin* transcends all the limits imposed by body and mind.

The moon moves constantly through *iḍā* and the sun through *piṅgalā*. When exposed to the sun's rays, the nectar in the moon melts and flows constantly through the six *ādhāras*. The *Kuṇḍalinī* falls asleep in the *mūlādhāra* after drinking this nectar. The motion of the sun and the moon can be stopped by *yogic* practices. Then the flow of nectar from the moon stops. The *Kuṇḍalinī* suddenly wakes up hungry and starts on Her path upwards.

100. ब्रह्म ग्रन्थि विभेदिनी

Brahma granthi vibhedinī

She who breaks through the knot of Brahmā.

Granthi means a knot. The *Brahmagranthi* is just above the *agnikhaṇḍa* which consists of the *mūlādhāra* and *svādhiṣṭhāna.* Brahmā is the creator and Devī shines in the *Brahmagranthi* as a symbol of creation. The name *Brahmagranthi* is thus symbolic of the creative instinct. The seeker transcends this *granthi* easily by *sādhana* and by Devī's grace. The *granthi* may be thought of as the hurdles caused by *vāsanās* in the course of a seeker's spiritual pursuit.

The sun is said to have twelve parts or *kalās*. Each *kalā* is said to correspond to a portion of the *Lalitāsahasranāma Stotra.* The first *kalā* is linked to the introductory dialogue between Agastya and Hayagrīva and the last *kalā* to the conclusion of the *stotra*. Each of the remaining *kalās* correspond to a hundred names in the *stotra*. This completes the first hundred names, corresponding to the second *kalā* known as the *Tāpinīkalā*.

101. मणिपूरान्तर् उदिता

Maṇipūrāntar uditā

She who emerges in the Maṇipūra cakra.

As explained above, *maṇipūra* is the ten-petaled lotus at the navel level. In the course of *samayācāra* worship (see *mantra* 98), the *sādhak* decorates Devī's image with *maṇipūras* or jewelry as the *Kuṇḍalinī* reaches this *cakra*. Hence, this *cakra* is known as the *maṇipūra cakra.*

During *mānasa pūja*, the seeker can imagine Devī's navel region adorned with a ten-petaled lotus and diamond jewelry.

102. विष्णु ग्रन्थि विभेदिनी

Viṣṇu granthi vibhedinī

She who breaks through the knot of Viṣṇu.

Viṣṇugranthi is just above the *maṇipūraka* in the Disc of the Sun. This is the abode of Viṣṇu, hence the name *Viṣṇugranthi.*

The two *cakras*, *maṇipūraka* and *anāhata*, together are said to represent the radiant *Viṣṇugranthi* which confers all *siddhis* (psychic powers) on the seeker.

When the *Kuṇḍalinī* breaks through this *granthi* and rises above, the seeker gets indescribable bliss and astonishing powers. But the experienced sages warn that he will fail to reach the ultimate goal if trapped by these *siddhis*.

103. आज्ञा चक्रान्तरालस्था

Ājñā cakrāntarālasthā

She who resides at the center of the Ājñācakra.

Ājñācakra is the region between the eyebrows, where a two-petaled lotus blossoms. *Ājña* means "to know, to understand." To a *sādhak* whose *Kuṇḍalinī* has entered the *ājñācakra*, all knowledge is as accessible as "a berry in the palm of his hand."

104. रुद्र ग्रन्थि विभेदिनी

Rudra granthi vibhedinī

She who breaks through the knot of Śiva.

The *Rudragranthi*, which is most auspicious, is situated in the *viśuddhi* and *ājña cakras*. Its name is derived from the fact that it is the abode of Śiva.

Alternately, the *Śrī vidyā mantra* has four parts (*khaṇḍas*): *Agni*, *Sūrya*, *Soma* and *Candrakalā* (These are also called four *kūṭas*, as described in *mantras* 85 to 90: *Vāgbhava*, *Kāmarāja* or *Madhyama*, *Śakti* and *Turīya*).

Viśuddhi and *ājñā cakras* together are known as *candrakhaṇḍa*. Thus the three *granthis* (knots), *brahmagranthi*, *viṣṇugranthi* and *rudragranthi* correspond to *agni*, *sūrya* and *candra khaṇḍas*. We can infer that these three *granthis* are symbols representing the origin, existence and disappearance of the body made of the five elements.

105. सहस्राराम्बुजारूढा

Sahasrārāmbujārūḍhā

She who ascends to the thousand-petaled lotus.

The thousand-petaled lotus (*sahasrāra*) is above the *ājñācakra* and just below the *Brahmarandhra* (an aperture in the crown of the head).

106. सुधा साराभिवर्षिणी

Sudhā sārābhivarṣiṇī

She who pours out streams of ambrosia.

Those who drink ambrosia are deathless. The shower of ambrosia occurs when the *Kuṇḍalinī* reaches the *sahasrāra*. On drinking this nectar of spiritual bliss, one attains deathlessness. Think of the countless mighty lords and kings who have lived, died, and are now forgotten. Yet none who have experienced Devī's shower of nectar will ever be forgotten. The lineage of *ṛṣis* sets the example. "Let the feet of Devī, which send out torrents of nectar, make us content forever." (*Taittiriya Brāhmaṇa*, III, 12, 3)

107. तडिल् लता सम रुचिः

Taḍil latā sama ruciḥ

She who is as beautiful as a flash of lightning.

"She who is radiant as the lightning," says the *Śruti*. (*Taittiriya Āraṇyaka*, X,13,2)

The radiance of lightning makes the eyes blink. Likewise, Devī's radiance is so great that the eyes cannot look at Her directly without blinking.

108. षट् चक्रोपरि संस्थिता

Ṣaṭ cakropari samsthitā

She who resides above the six cakras.

The six *cakras* are *mūlādhāra*, *svādhiṣṭhāna*, *maṇipūraka*, *anāhata*, *viśuddhi* and *ājña*, as previously explained.

109. महासक्ति

Mahāsakti

She who is greatly attached to the festive union of Śiva and Śakti.

The name can be interpreted also as "She who is fond of light or luster."

Another meaning is, "She who has great love." The love Devī has for everyone - enemy and friend, the righteous and the unrighteous - is implied here. The children who have enjoyed Amma's nectar of love can understand this meaning easily. Amma's love, which overflows the entire world, is nothing but the love that flows from Parāśakti.

110. कुण्डलिनी

Kuṇḍalinī

She who has the form of a coil.

The nature and abode of *Kuṇḍalinī* have already been described. "In the *mūlādhāra*, at the center of the radiant fire, resides the essence of *jīva*, known as *Kuṇḍalinī*, in the form of *prāṇa* and as the embodiment of effulgence. When someone with both ears closed cannot hear the constant hiss of the *Kuṇḍalinī* in the center of the *suṣumnā*, he is close to death." (*Tantrarāja*)

The *Vāmakeśvara Tantra* describes *Kuṇḍalinī* thus: "The *Kuṇḍalinī* lies at the lower end of the *suṣumnā* (which reaches up to the *Brahmarandhra* in the crown), enjoying the pericarp of the lotus in the *mūlādhāra*, coiled like a serpent with its tail in its mouth, fine as a lotus fiber and lustrous as lightning."

"Seated in the lotus position, keeping the anus contracted, keeping the mind focussed on *kumbhaka* (a breath control exercise), the yogi should turn the *prāṇa* upwards. Then the fire in the *svādhiṣṭhāna* blazes up. Through the pressure of air and fire,

Kuṇḍalinī, the serpent queen residing in the *mūlādhāra*, wakes up startled and moves upward breaking through the Brahmā, Viṣṇu and Rudra *granthis* and transcending the six *cakras*, reaches the *sahasrāra* and joins with Śiva there. This is the Supreme State. It is also the cause of Final Liberation."

The *Aruṇopaniṣad* calls on seekers, "O Bhāratas, arise; sleep not! Kindle the fire!" "Bhāratas" are seekers of Bhārati who is Sarasvatī or Vidyā, or *Śrī Vidyā* in the present context. Bhāskararāya says that the *Upaniṣad* is addressing the worshippers of *Śrī Vidyā.*

The *Devī Purāṇa* describes *Kuṇḍalinī* as "having the form of *sṛṅgātaka.*" *Sṛṅgātaka* means a triangle. The corners of this triangle are the powers of desire, wisdom and action (*icchāśakti, jñānaśakti* and *kriyāśakti*). These three powers are to be understood as the attributes of the *Kuṇḍalinī.*

Kuṇḍalinī is also the name of *vāgbhavabīja*, corresponding to the first *kūṭa* of the *pancadaśi mantra.*

The following words of Amma are most relevant and noteworthy here: "Children, *Kuṇḍalinī* is the life-force in living things. This power dwells at the bottom of the spine in the form of a coiled serpent. It is awakened by meditation and by the grace of the Guru. Once awake, it rushes upward through the *suṣumnā* driven by the urge to meet the male serpent residing in the head. Each *ādhāra* appears as a minute passage in the *suṣumnā*. When the *Kuṇḍalinī* passes from one *ādhāra* to the next, there will be many changes in the body. There will be a burning sensation throughout the body, as if the body is covered by a paste of chili peppers. The body will feel very hot. Often one will feel the hairs standing on end. Water will ooze, like sweat, from pores all over the body. Occasionally, even blood may issue from the pores of the body. The body will become emaciated like a skeleton. The seeker may become fearful when experiencing these changes for the first time. That is why it is said that *Kuṇḍalinī sādhana* should be undertaken only in the presence of a *Satguru* (Self-Realized Master)."

"Children, at this stage, the seeker should be very careful. The body should not move at all. He should not try to lie down, not even on a mattress, as even wrinkles on the mattress may be unbearable to him. He should sleep on a straight smooth wooden board. No shock should be given to the backbone as it can create serious repercussions. With the awakening of the *Kuṇḍalinī*, the seeker becomes a center of great attraction. He may be approached by women who are attracted to him. If a *Satguru* is not present to give proper instructions, he may squander all the hard-earned power by indulging in the pleasures of the body."

"The *Kuṇḍalinī* perfects each *ādhāra* that it reaches and then ascends to the next higher one. Passing the six *ādhāras* in this manner, the *Kuṇḍalinī śakti* reaches the thousand-petaled lotus. Once it reaches there, the body cools. There will be the shower of ambrosia throughout the body."

"What remains is not the old body. It is a new body filled with the power of the Self!"

111. बिस तन्तु तनीयसी

Bisa tantu tanīyasī

She who is fine and delicate as the fiber of the lotus.

"The auspicious *śakti*, called *Kuṇḍalinī*, resembling the lotus fiber," states the *Vāmakeśvara Tantra*. The beautiful *Kuṇḍalinī*, fine as the lotus fiber, resides in the *mūlādhāra* in the form of a serpent. The *Taittiriya Āraṇyaka* says, "Fine as the point of an ear of rice, saffron colored, radiant and resembling an atom."

112. भवानी

Bhavānī

She who is the wife of Śiva.

In Kālidāsa's *Śākuntala*, the stage-manager (*sūtradhāra*) says in his invocation: "May Śiva, who manifests in eight forms, protect you!" The eight forms are earth, water, fire, air, ether, the sun, moon and consciousness. Among these, Śiva who is in the form of water is known as Bhava. His wife is Bhavānī.

Devī Purāṇa gives the meanings: "ocean of *samsāra*" and

"Manmatha (the god of desire)" for the word *bhava*. Bhavānī is one who gives life to them.

In the *Saundarya Laharī* (verse 22), Śaṅkarācārya says, "When the devotee wants to pray, 'O Bhavānī, You must cast Your compassionate glance on me,' and starts by saying 'Bhavānī, You..(*Bhavānī tvam..*),' You instantly bless him with Your own Supreme State, which Viṣṇu, Brahmā and Indra worship, performing *nīrājana* (waving of lights) with their crowns." "Bhavānī tvam" also means, "I am You."

In short, Devī bestows the Supreme State even on the devotee who does not expect it. The devotee's request is small; the result is unparalleled, immeasurable. Fire burns even one who touches it unintentionally.

113. भावनागम्या

Bhāvanāgamyā

She who is unattainable through imagination or thought.

"The mind and words withdraw from there," that is, from what is real, from the Supreme Power, according to the *Śruti*.

This *mantra* can also be interpreted as "She who is attainable by purifying the mind through the path of action."

Bhāvana yoga (or *yoga* of meditation) and *Kuṇḍalinī yoga* are two modes of *yoga* described in books on Śakti worship. *Bhāvana yoga* is the *yoga* leading to the goal through meditation, with the aid of *mantra* chanting and breath control. *Kuṇḍalinī yoga* is the *yoga* in which the *Kuṇḍalinī* is awakened and brought into union with the Supreme Self in the *sahasrāra*.

The *yoga* of meditation is in itself of three types: *brāhmi*, *maheśvari*, and *akṣara*. It is also described as of two types, *arthabhāvana* (*bhāvana* of meaning) and *śabda bhāvana* (*bhāvana* of sound). There is yet another division of meditation: *sakala*, *niṣkala* and *sakala-niṣkala*. According to Bhāskararāya, meditation from *mūlādhāra* to *ājñācakra* is *sakala*, that from *indu* to *unmanī* is *sakala-niṣkala* and that in the Supreme Abode (*mahābindu*) is *niṣkala*.

Śrī Śaṅkara describes *bhāvanā* in his commentary on the *Gītā* (II-65) as "the devotion to Self-Knowledge." Whatever method of worship is followed, it will become a desire for Self-Knowledge in the end.

114. भवारण्य कुठारिका

Bhavāraṇya kuṭhārikā

She who is like an axe to clear the jungle of samsāra.

The jungle of existence is not man-made. Its nature is not determined by man. The poet Bhasa says, "Even if cut down from time to time, the forest grows back again and again." *Vāsanās* are also like that.

When dispassion arises, worship, *japa* and meditation may sometimes bear fruit. However, if the root of *vāsanās* still remains dormant, they will sprout again. There is a well-known story of a monk who kept a pet cat. Having renounced his family and home, the spiritually-inclined man retired to the forest to lead the life of a hermit. However, his peace of mind was disturbed by the mice which regularly ate away at his loin-cloth which was spread outside for drying. He decided to keep a pet cat to catch the mice, but the cat, brought in from the village, needed to be fed. Therefore, he went back to the village and got a cow so that the cat could be given milk regularly. The hermit discovered that the cow needed much greater attention. Soon his wife and children were summoned to the forest to take care of both the cow and the cat. A house was put up for everyone's comfort in the forest. Feeding a family is no easy task. A wandering friend of the monk visited him a few months later only to find the would-be *sannyāsi* sinking ever deeper into the mire of *samsāra.*

"Repeated births, repeated deaths, repeated lying in the mother's womb - this *samsāra* is difficult to cross. Save me, O Kṛṣṇa, through Your grace!" says Śaṅkara in the *Bhaja Govindam.*

Devī is the axe that cuts away forever the roots of the forest of samsāra which is thick, dark, and filled with cruel animals.

The word *kuṭhārika* in the *mantra* is suggestive. It is a small hand-held axe used for small cutting jobs. It is suggested that it is relatively quick and easy to win Devī's favor and thus to gain a release from the misery of *samsāra*. Amma once advised a devotee of Kṛṣṇa: "Son, chant Devī's name also; don't you want to eat?" In short, worship of Devī is the easiest means of obtaining all material and spiritual riches.

115. भद्र प्रिया

Bhadra priyā

She who is fond of all auspicious things, who gives all auspicious things.

Also, the beloved of Bhadra; Śiva.

The word *bhadra* also means prosperity, Mount Meru and a family of elephants of superior quality. Devī is fond of all these. Meru may also stand for *merudaṇḍa* or the backbone. The *suṣumnā* nerve, the path of *Kuṇḍalinī*, passes through it and reaches the *candramaṇḍala* in the head. It is therefore dear to Devī. She is said to be fond of the *bhadra* elephants. Devī's army includes a brigade of elephants.

116. भद्र मूर्ति

Bhadra mūrti

She who is the embodiment of auspiciousness or benevolence.

Devī has been celebrated as "the most auspicious among the auspicious." The *Viṣṇu Purāṇa* says, "It is known that auspiciousness is nothing but *Brahman*." Devī is thus the embodiment of *Brahman*.

Also, *Bhadra mūrti* may mean "one who has taken the form of Bhadra." The *Purāṇas* say that Devī took the form of Bhadrakālī and killed the demon Dāruka.

117. भक्त सौभाग्य दायिनी

Bhakta saubhāgya dāyinī

She who confers prosperity on Her devotees.

Subhagā is one of Devī's names (see *mantra* 761). *Saubhāgya* stands for Her qualities in general.

Devī was described as intent on promoting the cause of the *devas* (*mantra* 5). Here it is said that She is very generous in giving prosperity to Her devotees as well. For the sick, prosperity means a cure, for the destitute, wealth, and for the seeker, knowledge. Devī is one who gives all these.

118. भक्ति प्रिया

Bhakti priyā

She who is fond of (and pleased by) devotion.

Nārada Bhakti Sūtra describes *bhakti* (devotion) in many different ways:

"That, verily, is of the nature of Supreme Love."

"And it is the immortal bliss of Freedom (Liberation) itself."

"Devoid of all attributes, and free from all selfishness, it is an unbroken inner experience, ever growing, subtler than the subtlest."

Śāṇḍilya's *Bhaktimīmāmsā sūtra* says, "It is supreme longing for the Lord." Devotion is the love for God. It is a dissolution of the mind in God, forgetting oneself. "An enquiry into one's own true form is devotion," according to Śrī Śaṅkara.

Devotion is of two kinds: *mukhya* (primary) and *gauṇa* (secondary). Unending, unbroken devotion is primary devotion. It is also known as *parābhakti* and is described in the paragraph above. *Gauṇa* devotion is the devotion shown through service to the Lord according to scriptural rituals.

The *Garuḍa Purāṇa* says, "One who has devotion, even if he is a barbarian, is the best of *brāhmaṇas*; he is a *sannyāsin*, he is prosperous, he is an ascetic and a scholar."

The sign of devotion is service. We should learn that service of man is service of God. Mother says, "Children, kindness towards the poor is our duty to God."

The *Bhāgavata Purāṇa* talks about nine forms of devotion: "Hearing the glories of the Lord, singing about them, remembrance of the Lord's name, service at His feet, worship through offering of flowers, prostration, servitude, comradeship of the Lord and surrender of one's self." In addition, the sages have described devotion as love for the beloved (*premabhakti*), as love for God as one's own child (*vātsalyabhakti*), peaceful devotion, sweet devotion and devotion of the servant.

The Divine Mother is fond of all these forms of devotion.

119. भक्ति गम्या

Bhakti gamyā

She who is attained only through devotion.

Devī cannot be reached through high position, nobility, high caste, strength of the family, wealth or knowledge. Only sincere devotion is dear to Her. Only through this devotion can one reach Her. Lord Kṛṣṇa declares in the *Gītā* (XI-54), "O Arjuna, only through undivided devotion can I be known, seen and entered into."

120. भक्ति वश्या

Bhakti vaśyā

She who is to be won over by devotion.

Devī is free from all bonds. If She is to be won over, it is possible only through devotion.

Once a conversation took place between Lord Viṣṇu and Nārada.

"Nārada, what is the greatest thing in the universe?"

"Need You ask, my Lord? Isn't it the earth?"

"The earth? But doesn't it lie in the ocean? Only two-fifths of it is land!"

"That is true. It must be the ocean, then."

"Oh, no! Isn't it well-known that Agastya took the entire ocean up in his hand for his ablutions?"

"Oh, that is true, of course. The greatest one must be none other than Agastya!"

"Can you say that, Nārada? Isn't Agastya a constellation? It stands in just one corner of the sky!"

"Right, Oh Lord! I was wrong. The sky is the greatest thing."

"Really? Didn't I measure the earth, the sky and the netherworld all in just three steps?"

"Why are You playing with me as if I am a little monkey, Lord? Couldn't You just say this earlier? Of course, You are the greatest!"

"Come on, Nārada, don't you know even this? Am I not just a prisoner in My devotees' hearts? Isn't the heart of a devotee the greatest thing?"

This is the greatness of devotion. Nārada composed the *Bhakti Sūtras* because he understood this. The path of devotion is easier and shorter than the paths of knowledge, action and *rāja yoga.*

The sages say that even though Devī is free of all bonds, She is bound by devotion.

121. भयापहा

Bhayāpahā

She who dispels fear.

The cause of fear is the belief that there is something other than oneself. Svami Vivekānanda once said, "If you ask me the essence of the *Upaniṣads* distilled into two letters, I will say, '*Abhih!*' (Fear not!)." The greatest fear is the fear of death. It is to become free from this fear that the sages of India have recommended the *Upaniṣadic* path. "He who knows the bliss of *Brahman* does not fear anything." (*Taittiriya Upaniṣad*, II,9,1)

Devī is the essence of *Brahman*. She removes all fears. Bhāskararāya quotes the *Vāyu Purāṇa*: "In the forest and other places, in water, on earth, in the presence of a tiger, before wild beasts and robbers, and especially in all diseases, the names of Devī should be repeated."

It is said, "As the mind, so the world." When the mind is full of Devī, where is room for fear? Our *ṛṣis* (sages) are the best proof of this fearlessness.

122. शाम्भवी

Śāmbhavī

She who is the wife of Śambhu (Śiva).

Śambhu is the giver of happiness and prosperity. This *mantra* also means, "Mother to those who worship Śambhu."

The *Śāmbhavī mudrā* (*mudrā* is a gesture made during worship using the fingers) is well-known in *hatha yoga* and in *Tantra.* Devī uses this *mudrā* or She abides in it.

The *Kalpasūtra* of Para śurāma mentions three types of initiations (*dīkṣas*) namely, *śāmbhavī*, *mantra* and *śakti*. Devī is to be reached by the *śāmbhavī* initiation.

The word *śāmbhavī* also means a girl of eight years. Devī is to be worshipped in the form of such a girl. This is called *Kumāri pūja.*

123. शारदाराध्या

Śāradārādhyā

She who is worshipped by Śāradā (Sarasvatī, the Goddess of Speech).

Śāradā is one who is able or is an expert. *Śāradārādhya* is one who is worshipped by *sāttvic*-minded scholars.

Also, *śarad* means great and *a* means Brahmā or Viṣṇu. Thus, the *mantra* means "She who is worshipped by the exalted Brahmā and Viṣṇu." In *Saundarya Laharī*, Śaṅkarācārya has included Śiva also among Devī's worshippers: "Therefore, is it possible for those who have not earned merit to either worship or praise You who are worshipped even by Viṣṇu, Śiva, Brahmā and others?"

Śarad is the autumn season (the months of Aświn and Kārtik; mid-September to mid-November). *Śāradārādhya* means "one who is worshipped in the *śarad* season." The *navarātri* (worship of Devī for nine nights) is in this season.

124. शर्वाणी

Śarvāṇī

She who is the wife of Śarva (Śiva).

Śiva in His earth-form is known as Śarva (one of Śiva's eight forms which are listed under *mantra* 112). The *Liṅga Purāṇa* says, "Those who have transcended all the *śāstras* call the *Deva* who is the essence of the earth as Śarva. His wife is known as Sukeśi and His son as Aṅgāraka." Aṅgāraka is Mars, also known as Kuja. Kuja literally means "the son of the earth" (ku: earth). There is also an astronomical theory that Mars is a part that broke off from the earth.

125. शर्मदायिनी

Śarmadāyinī

She who confers happiness.

"She gives happiness to Her devotees; hence She is called the 'Bestower of happiness.'" (*Devī Bhāgavata*)

Happiness (*śarma*) is not only material happiness here, but also happiness beyond this life. It has been made clear in the beginning that Devī's worshippers get both material happiness and Liberation.

126. शाङ्करी

Śāṅkarī

She who gives happiness.

"She is *Śaṅkarī* whose habit it is to give happiness."

Śāṅkarī is also the wife of Śaṅkara (Śiva). The *Kālikā Purāṇa* says that Devī is celebrated by the names *Śaṅkarī* and Rudrāṇī because She accompanies Śiva in a female form during the acts of creation, preservation and destruction.

127. श्रीकरी

Śrīkarī

She who bestows riches in abundance.

That which meets the needs is wealth, and beyond that is *Śrī*, abundance.

Śrīkara is Viṣṇu. Devī is called *Śrīkarī* meaning Viṣṇu's sister.

128. साध्वी

Sādhvī

She who is chaste.

Lord Śiva is the only one who has known Devī. Her essence is so secret.

Sarasvatī, Brahmā's wife, yields to all learned men. Lakṣmī, the goddess of wealth and Viṣṇu's wife, is always on the move and accessible to all. But Devī, Maheśvara's wife, yields to no one. While being a paragon of virtue, She who is Parāśakti is also absolutely free. The implication is that learning and wealth can be achieved by anyone with effort, but Self-Realization is extremely difficult.

129. शरच्चन्द्र निभानना

Śaraccandra nibhānanā

She whose face shines like the full moon in the clear autumn sky.

By singling out the autumnal moon, it is hinted that the moon's radiance is not constant through the seasons. The beauty of Devī's face is superior, as it does not change with time.

130. शातोदरी

Śātodarī

She who is slender-waisted.

Śātodara is also defined as "having hundreds of caves," meaning Himavat, king of the mountains. Śātodarī is his daughter, Pārvatī.

131. शान्तिमती

Śāntimatī

She who is peaceful.

Peacefulness is Devī's nature. She forgives every fault of Her devotees, with no agitation and with abundant kindness. Devī's ultimate aim is the peace and welfare of the universe. She will not tolerate anything which hurts that cause. That is why She appeared to be cruel towards Bhaṇḍāsura.

Śāntimatī is also one who is not overly eager for anything.

132. निराधारा

Nirādhārā

She who is without dependence.

Devī is the support for everything. Therefore She needs no support.

Tantraśāstra describes six *ādhāras* or *cakras*. Devī transcends all of them and is, therefore, without support.

This *mantra* also refers to the form of Parāśakti worship known as *nirādhāra*. This worship is described as follows in *Sūtasamhita* (verses 11-19): "There are two forms of worship, external and internal; the external is divided into *Vedic* and *Tāntric* and the internal is divided into *sādhāra* (*saguṇa*) and *nirādhāra* (*nirguṇa*). *Sādhāra* worship is by means of images, while *nirādhāra* worship is not based on any form. Worship of Devī in images or in sacred syllables is *sādhāra* worship. *Nirādhāra* is the best form of worship. In this method, the dissolution of the mind occurs during meditation on Pure Awareness which is nothing but the Supreme Śakti. Therefore, for freedom from *samsāra*, one should worship the Parāśakti as the very Self, as witness, free from the attributes of the manifold universe. Knowing Devī as the Self from direct experience, She should be worshipped with devotion. This is the worship that leads to Liberation."

133. निरञ्जना

Nirañjanā

She who stays unattached, bound to nothing.

"Attachment is the impure *vāsanā* of the mind which produces joy from the gain of an object and anger at its loss." (*Yogavāsiṣṭha*) Devī is free from all such attachments; She is the Pure Spirit.

Rañjana is desire and *nirañjanā* means one who is desireless.

Also, *añjana* is the eye salve collyrium and *nirañjana* is one whose eyes are not smeared with the black salve of *avidyā* (ignorance) that arises from illusion. Thus, *nirañjana* is "She who has no blemishes arising from ignorance."

Some argue that whatever is seen by the eye is the only truth. Are the stars that appear to be unmoving in the sky really not moving? When a bird soaring up into the sky is no longer visible, can we say it does not exist? When we make a slide from a thin section of a plant and look at it under the microscope, we see a colorful view. Which is the truth, the black smear that we see with the naked eye or the colorful display seen under the microscope? In the same way, the view seen by the eyes smeared with the collyrium of *Māyā* is not the same as that seen by eyes free of *Māyā*.

Several *mantras* now follow which describe Devī's attributes which help in formless worship.

134. निर्लेपा

Nirlepā

She who is free from all impurities arising from action.

The lotus leaf does not get wet even when lying in water. Similarly, even though Devī governs the universe, that bond of action does not really bind Her. Lord Kṛṣṇa says, "Actions do not bind Me; neither do I have any desire for the fruit of any action." (*Gītā*, IV-14) Rising to this level is the true fulfillment of a devotee of Devī.

135. निर्मला

Nirmalā

She who is free from all impurities.

Mala (impurity) is ignorance. Ignorance is the seed of delusion regarding the nature of the world. The Self, which is knowledge, is covered by ignorance; due to this, man becomes subject to *moha* (delusion) and does not attain knowledge. Devī is "forever pure, knowing and free."

Impurities are of three kinds: *āṇava*, *bheda* (*māyika*) and *kārmika*. *Āṇava* impurity is the bondage arising from not fully knowing the real nature of the Self. This is the minutest or subtlest impurity (*anu*: atom). *Bheda* or *māyika* impurity is the perception of duality - difference between self and non-self - arising from *Māyā* (*bheda*: difference). *Kārmika* impurity is the bondage due to action (*karma*) that causes birth and death.

Devī is one who is not tainted by even the subtlest of these, the *āṇava* impurity. Those who have only *āṇava* impurity are known as *vijñānakevalas*; those who have both *āṇava* and *māyika* impurities are *pralayakālas*, and those who are affected by all three types are *sakalas*. According to *Setubandha*, *vijñānakevalas* worship Devī in the *mahābindu* (*niṣkaladhyāna*); *pralayakālas* worship Her from *ājñācakra* to *unmanī* (*sakala-niṣkala dhyāna*), and *sakalas* from *mūlādhāra* to *ājñācakra* (*sakaladhyāna*). These terms were mentioned previously under *mantra* 113.

136. नित्या

Nityā

She who is eternal.

Devī is eternal since She does not undergo dissolution in the three periods of time. "This Self, my dear, is indeed unchangeable and indestructible." (Yājñavalkya to Maitreyi in *Bṛhadāraṇyaka Upaniṣad*, IV,5,14) This name refutes the theory that there is nothing that is eternal.

Other interpretations are: "She who has the form of the daily deities of the fortnight (*nitya devatas*)" and "She who is of the form of the *nitya mantra.*"

137. निराकारा

Nirākārā

She who is without form.

Form is based on the *guṇas* (attributes). Devī is beyond the three *guṇas* and therefore without form.

The notion that God is without form is not foreign to Hindu philosophy. But a mind whose essence is in the *guṇas* cannot imagine such a formless God. One statement in the *Śruti* clarifies this point: "The mind and words withdraw without reaching it."

The formless God was given a form for the mind to grasp Him. The wise know that this is a product of the imagination, and imagination is tied to the sense of beauty and the power of the intellect. This *mantra* refutes the theory that everything has a form.

138. निराकुला

Nirākulā

She who is without agitation.

The reason for agitation and sorrow is ignorance. There is no sorrow for one who is established in wisdom. The mark of such a person is keeping the mind free of agitation in the face of profit or loss, victory or defeat, honor or dishonor. Being one who is thus established in Awareness, Devī is free from agitation while killing Bhaṇḍāsura, while blessing him or while playing with Sadāśiva.

139. निर्गुणा

Nirguṇā

She who is beyond all three guṇas *of nature, namely* sattva, rajas *and* tamas.

She who is not tied to - who is beyond - the objects of the senses of sight, taste, touch, smell and sound.

The *Viṣṇu Bhāgavata Purāṇa* says, "It (*Brahman*) is not *deva*, demon, human, animal, male, female, living being, quality, *karma*, presence or absence. It is the infinitude that remains after all negations."

The qualities of love and affection used to describe Devī are not *guṇas* but Her inherent nature.

140. निष्कला

Niṣkalā

She who is without parts.

Kalā is a fraction or a part. This name discards the theory that *Brahman* has limbs or parts.

Bhāskarācārya makes it clear that the name *niṣkala* refers to meditation on *Brahman* without qualities. He quotes from the work, *Vijñānabhairavabhaṭṭāraka*, "*Niṣkaladhyāna* is meditation (on *Brahman*) without parts, since He is without dependence and without a fixed resting place. It is not meditation on a form with face, hands." This *mantra* means that Devī is to be realized in such formless meditation. Descriptions such as "without parts, without action, tranquil, blameless and stainless" all apply to Devī who is Herself undivided *Brahman*.

141. शान्ता

Śāntā

She who is tranquil.

She who abides in the mood or sentiment of tranquility, "*śānta rasa*," which is one of the nine sentiments in poetry. The basic feature of this sentiment is the absence of the sense of ego. The sages say that, "in the *śānta rasa* there is no sorrow, no happiness, no thoughts, no anger or love or desire; there is perfect equanimity."

The composite word consisting of the previous and the present *mantras* can be split differently, as follows: *niṣkalāśānta*: *niṣkala* + *āśānta*. Then the *mantra āśāntā* means "She who pervades to the end of all directions (*āśā*: directions)."

The last syllable of the *amṛtabīja mantra* is *śā*. Thus, *śāntā* (*śā* + *antā*) is the "embodiment of the *mantra* whose last syllable is *śā*."

142. निष्कामा

Niṣkāmā

She who is without desire.

What desire is there for Devī who can realize anything just by Her *saṅkalpa*? The *Devī Bhāgavata* states: "When the fruits of all wishes are contained within Her, what desire can remain for Her?"

143. निरुपप्लवा

Nirupaplavā

She who is indestructible.

Upaplava means calamity, destruction. It also means "by whom abundant flow of nectar occurs in the body of the *jīva*." The *mantra* thus refers to the *Kuṇḍalinī* which rises to the *sahasrāra* and causes the flow of abundant streams of ambrosia in the body (see *mantra* 110).

144. नित्यमुक्ता

Nityamuktā

She who is ever free from worldly bonds.

It is clear that all the deeds of Devī recounted here, such as the slaying of Bhaṇḍāsura, blessing the *devas*, or sporting with Sadāśiva, are acts attributed to Her and that She is indeed free from all these.

Another meaning is "One who gives eternal Liberation to devotees and in whom the liberated ones merge eternally." She is Liberation personified and is thus eternally free.

145. निर्विकारा

Nirvikārā

She who is unchanging.

Devī is one who does not have *vikāra* (change). She is the Cause of the universe. The cause does not undergo any change, the effect does. The rope does not move, but the serpent superimposed on the rope appears to move. That is why we feel the illusion of the serpent. The causal principle does not itself feel or cause the feeling of illusion, but the effect does; so it undergoes change.

The *Sāṅkhyatattva kaumudī* has made this clear: "The *mūlaprakṛti* (the root of all) does not change. The seven principles, starting with *mahat*, cause and undergo changes; the remaining sixteen principles undergo changes but do not cause them. The soul neither changes nor causes changes." Devī is the unchanging *mūlaprakṛti* referred to here.

146. निष्प्रपञ्चा

Niṣprapañcā

She who is not of this universe.

Prapañca denotes the five elements (*pañca bhūtas*) that make up the universe. Devī is separate from the aggregate of these. Thus She is called *Niṣprapañcā.*

147. निराश्रया

Nirāśrayā

She who does not depend on anything.

Devī is the refuge of everything in the universe. She does not have any refuge. It is said in the *Śruti*, "Where is the foundation of Her on whom the whole universe is founded?"

Dependence is an "*upādhi*," a conditioning. The *jīva*'s *upādhis* extend from the mind - *antaḥkaraṇa* - to the body. When the *jīva* is conditioned by the body attributes, there arise notions such as "I am fat, I am lean;" when conditioned by the sense organs, notions such as "I am blind, I am deaf" arise and when conditioned by the mind, notions such as "I wish, I imagine" arise.

All such conditioning belong to the *samsārins* - those bound by worldly bonds. Devī is pure Existence, without any *upādhi* or conditioning.

148. नित्यशुद्धा

Nityaśuddhā

She who is eternally pure.

Limitations related to purity and impurity are put on embodied beings to help them achieve mental purity. Devī is untouched by blemish and is above and beyond such limitations. It is said that "the body is very impure, but the dweller in it is very pure." Impurity is only for the body, not for the *Ātman* (Self).

149. नित्यबुद्धा

Nityabuddhā

She who is ever wise.

Devī, who is *cit* (awareness) itself, contains all knowledge;

hence, She is eternally wise. The *Śruti* says, "There cannot be absence of knowledge from the knower." (*Bṛhadāraṇyaka Upaniṣad*, IV,3,30) Thus, knowledge of *Brahman* is not separate from the knower.

150. निरवद्या

Niravadyā

She who is blameless or She who is praiseworthy.

Devī is to be worshipped by all as She is the cause of all auspiciousness or prosperity. "Blameless and spotless" says the *Śruti*. (*Śvetāśvatāra Upaniṣad* VI,19)

Avadya also means hell. *Niravadyā*, then, means "One who guards Her devotees from falling into hell." Bhāskararāya quotes from *Kūrma Purāṇa*, "Hence if anyone remembers Devī day and night, he does not go to the hell that is *avadya*, as he is cleansed of all sins." According to the *Liṅga Purāṇa* there are twenty-eight *crores* of hells. Such descriptions of hell dissuade people from sins and turn them towards good deeds. Fear of committing sins and faith in God are the two wheels of the chariot of life.

151. निरन्तरा

Nirantarā

She who is all-pervading.

Devī fills the universe without any gaps (without *antara*: hole or gap). In short, She is the "glory that fills inside and outside."

We may also take the meaning "difference" for *antara*. The *Taittiriya Upaniṣad* (II,7) says, "He who sees even the slightest difference or separateness in this (*Brahman*), in him fear arises." Devī makes no distinction such as Her kind, others or Herself.

152. निष्कारणा

Niṣkāraṇā

She who is without cause.

Since Devī is the cause of everything, She does not have a cause. Here the cause is eternal and the effects are all transient. She is the Universal Mother who is the cause of everything.

153. निष्कलङ्का

Niṣkalaṅkā

She who is faultless.

Taking the meaning, *kalaṅka* (sin): "She who eradicates the sins of Her devotees."

Sin and merit (*pāpa* and *puṇya*) are the results of *karma*. As Devī is actionless and detached, there is no space in Her for sin or merit.

"Pure, untouched by sin," says *Īśāvāsya Upaniṣad* (verse 8).

154. निरुपाधिः

Nirupādhiḥ

She who is not conditioned or has no limitations.

Upādhi refers to the conditioning effect imposed by something that is situated nearby. Just as a clear crystal takes on the color of a flower kept nearby, consciousness (*caitanya*) takes on the sense of plurality that is born of ignorance; this is *upādhi*. Devī is without such conditioning. She is without a trace of ignorance, has no divisions, no limitations of the whole or part. Also, She is the ocean of spontaneous kindness. She showers blessings on Her devotees without any limitations.

On the still surface of a lake we can see inverted images of trees standing on the shore. Here, the motionless water surface is the *upādhi*. Those of us who have discrimination know that the trees are not standing upside down, but a child may be confused by this sight. As far as the universe is concerned, many of us are like the child. A few people know that it is the *upādhi* of the water that creates the contradiction. Even for those who know the truth, the immediate experience that the images are upside down still exists.

It will continue as long as the *upādhi* continues. It is the same reasoning that makes the universe appear real as long as there is the conditioning of body-consciousness. This reality is known as "illusory reality." One should not insist that this is the Ultimate Reality.

155. निरीश्वरा

Nirīśvarā

She who has no superior or protector.

Since Devī is the protector of everything, She has no overlord.

All the philosophies of the world can be divided into two groups, theistic and atheistic. Both these are the same for Devī; in other words, both are indistinct from Her.

156. नीरागा

Nīrāgā

She who has no desire.

As Devī has no desires, She does not have the other emotions such as anger either, by implication.

According to the *Śāṇḍilya Sūtra* (I.6), *rāga* connotes devotion. "Devotion is longing, and it is opposed to hatred; it is expressed by the word *rasa*." Devī is free from it as She longs for nothing.

We can take this *mantra* to be made up of two words, *nīra* (water) and *agā* (mountain). The water here is Gangā and the mountain is Himavat (Himālaya). If we understand that the daughter of the mountain is not distinct from the mountain, then this *mantra* would mean "She who is Gangā and Pārvatī."

157. राग मथनी

Rāga mathanī

She who destroys desires (passions).

Rāga is the ardent attachment to worldly life. Normally, the sense organs are inclined to indulge in worldly enjoyment. As the inclination towards the Divine Power gets stronger, the attachment to physical objects weakens. Devī removes emotions such as longing and anger from the devotee's heart and liberates him from worldly sorrows by awakening pure *sāttvic* emotions in him. She churns the passions and produces dispassion, just like churning the curd to extract butter.

158. निर् मदा

Nir madā

She who is without pride.

Even though She is omnipotent and omniscient, Devī does not have even a trace of pride. Beauty, youth, power, wealth, each of these is a seed for pride and when all of these come together, intense pride is sure to follow. But in Devī, who is a model for the world, there is not even a trace of pride, even though She is unparalleled in each of these attributes.

Amma often says, "I am the servant of servants." As the *Gītā* (III, 21) says, "Whatever a great man does, that the other men also do; whatever he sets up is the standard that the world follows."

159. मद नाशिनी

Mada nāśinī

She who destroys pride.

Not only is Devī free from pride, but She also destroys pride in others. However proud one might be, it is but natural that on getting close to Her, all pride vanishes and one becomes humble.

This name can also be understood as "One who swallows (destroys) *madana* (another name for Kāma, the god of desire)." *Madana* creates agitation in the mind of the devotee. Devī destroys him. Her devotee gets firmness of mind and attains his goal.

160. निश्चिन्ता

Niścintā

She who has no anxiety in anything.

Where is room for anxiety in one who knows everything? *Cintā* (anxiety) is like *cita* (a funeral pyre). The pyre burns the corpse, while anxiety burns one who is alive.

"As a boy, one is attached to sports; as a youth, one is attached to a young woman. An old person is attached to anxiety but to the Supreme *Brahman*, alas, no one is attached!" marvels Śaṅkarācārya. The anxiety in old age is really that of the funeral pyre. The spiritual path must start early in life, and the training to become free of anxiety like Devī must become deep-rooted in the devotees. This *mantra* can be used as a guiding light.

Cintā is also interpreted as deceit or delusion. *Niścintā* is one without delusion or illusion.

161. निर् अहङ्कारा

Nir ahaṅkārā

She who is without egoism. She who is without the concept of "I" and "mine."

Depending on the proportion of the *guṇas sattva*, *rajas* and *tamas*, egoism is said to be of three kinds: *vaikārika*, *taijasa* and *bhūtādi*.

Egoism is the root of all calamities. If we were to extract the essence of our *Purāṇas* and epics into one sentence, it would undoubtedly be: "Cut the roots of egoism." There are many stories in the *Purāṇas* in which even exalted sages like Nārada, Durvāsas and Viśvāmitra had to take the bitter consequences of their egoism.

Not only is Devī Herself free of egoism, but Her devotees also become free of it. Eruttacchan, the saintly Malayalam poet, has said it well: "O Hari, Thou who art Pure Bliss, Lover of the Gopis, let me not have the feeling of I; yet if I do, let me feel that all is 'I', O Nārāyaṇa!"

162. निर् मोहा

Nir mohā

She who is free from delusion.

Moha can be desire, lack of discrimination between good and bad as in the passage from the *Gītā*, "From *krodha* (anger) arises *moha*," or loss of consciousness. None of these affects Devī even remotely.

Moha is the bewilderment that arises from ignorance (*avidyā*). As the *Śruti* says, "What delusion can there be, what sorrow, when all things are seen as one with the Self?" (*Īśāvāsya Upaniṣad*, 7)

163. मोह नाशिनी

Moha nāśinī

She who destroys delusion in Her devotees.

All the meanings of *moha* given in the last *mantra* apply here also.

164. निर् ममा

Nir mamā

She who has no self-interest in anything.

A sense of possession and delusion are the seeds of the sorrows of *samsāra*. In the *Gītā*, Arjuna becomes powerless on the battleground because he came under the sway of such a sense.

When we say that Devī is without a sense of ownership, it does not mean that She lacks love or that She is without interest in others. We have already noted that She is unaffected by the effects of *karma* (see *mantra* 133). It is this unaffectedness that is the root of Her absence of self-interest.

165. ममता हन्त्री

Mamatā hantrī

She who destroys the sense of ownership.

Not only is Devī devoid of self-interest, She also destroys that sense in Her devotees. She causes the same mental transformation that took place in Arjuna after listening to Kṛṣṇa's advice.

The greatest benefit of spiritual training is the victory over selfishness at each step.

166. निष्पापा

Niṣpāpā

She who is without sin.

Devī is ever pure, ever knowing and ever free. In addition, She is not affected by any bonds of *karma* which cause sin.

The *Gītā* (V.10) says, "He who performs actions offering them to *Brahman*, abandoning attachment, is not tainted by sin, as a lotus leaf by water." If this is the state of a *karmayogin*, must we say anything about Devī who is Herself *Brahman?*

She governs the world with the good of the world in mind. There is no attachment in Her. "I have no attachment to the fruit of action," says Lord Kṛṣṇa.

167. पाप नाशिनी

Pāpa nāśinī

She who destroys all the sins of Her devotees.

Whoever has knowledge of the Self, does penance along with *japa* and meditation, and spends time in holy places, will not be tainted by sin. Any sin committed by such people either unknowingly or due to force of circumstances (even if as great as Mount Meru) is instantly reduced to ashes like cotton in a fire. For someone who has taken total refuge at Devī's feet, however, there is no need to even perform spiritual practices as mentioned above.

168. निष्क्रोधा

Niṣkrodhā

She who is without anger.

Desire is the mother of anger. If there is no desire, there is no anger. Since Devī is free from desires, it is clear that She has no anger.

Anger is destructive. One should consciously control it and thus gain freedom. It is said that *ahimsa* is the greatest *dharma* (*Ahimsa* is abstaining from killing or giving pain to others in thought, word or deed). The mental refinement needed for *ahimsa* is freedom from anger.

According to Lord Kṛṣṇa, desire and anger born of *rajoguṇa* (the quality of passion) are the enemies, all-devouring and all-sinful. (*Gītā*, III.37) Conquering these enemies is life's greatest victory. All penance, sacrifice, *japa* and meditation should be directed towards this goal.

169. क्रोध शमनी

Krodha śamanī

She who destroys anger in Her devotees.

We can also say that the anger in one will automatically vanish in front of Devī.

170. निर्लोभा

Nirlobhā

She who is without greed.

Greed is one of the eight emotions (*aṣṭarāgas*) that are impediments to Liberation (The other seven emotions are desire, anger, delusion, pride, envy, conceit and spite). Greed is the evil tendency to hoard what is already in one's possession, and to acquire and enjoy what is someone else's. Greed is the enemy of renunciation. The *Śruti* says, "*Tyāgenaike amṛtattvamānaśuḥ*": "Only through renunciation can one enjoy immortality." Greed blocks the divine path to immortality. Devī is without greed. To Her, who fulfills all the needs of Her devotees, there is no need of anything from anyone. She is the breeding ground of generosity.

171. लोभ नाशिनी

Lobha nāśinī

She who destroys greed in Her devotees.

Man's greed is at the root of all social ills and injustices. Greed is a barrier to compassion, kindness, giving and selfless service.

Devī eliminates greedy thoughts in Her true devotees in order to destroy evil tendencies, and to encourage the blossoming of good qualities.

172. निःसंशया

Niḥsamśayā

She who is without doubts.

In Devī who is the embodiment of Truth, there is no room for doubt. She who is the Guru of all should be free of doubt. A Guru is one who is able to give unequivocal advice on everything.

Devī is one who should not be doubted in any way. She is the Supreme Being in whom anyone can take refuge, without a trace of hesitation.

173. संशयघ्नी

Samśayaghnī

She who kills all doubts.

A devotee or *sādhak* may have many different doubts. Devī removes them as they arise and awakens appropriate responses within the seeker. This awakening of knowledge is the Guru's grace (*Gurukaṭākṣa*: glance from the corner of the Guru's eye). It will be faultless.

Devī removes doubts and showers Her blessings even on someone who approaches Her with a questioning attitude. This shows Her kindness. However, doubts do not totally disappear before achieving knowledge of the Self, and so this *mantra* implies that Devī is one who bestows Self-Realization.

"With Self-Realization, all the knots of the heart break by themselves; all knots are cut away and all bondage of *karma* withers." (*Muṇḍakopaniṣad*, II 2:8)

174. निर् भवा

Nir bhavā

She who is without origin.

Devī is without origin or end; She is the embodiment of eternity.

175. भव नाशिनी

Bhava nāśinī

She who destroys the sorrow of samsāra *(the cycle of birth and death)*.

According to the *Brahajjābāla Upaniṣad*, there is a river named *Bhavanāśinī*. Those who bathe in it are not reborn.

176. निर् विकल्पा

Nir vikalpā

She who is free of false imaginings.

"*Vikalpa*" is something that does not exist, but creates the impression of being real. The *Yoga Sūtra* gives the definition, "*Vikalpa* is a notion conveyed by mere words, but of which there is no object corresponding to reality." See the following example:

"Here comes the son of the barren woman, after a bath in the waters of the mirage, wearing sky-flowers in his hair, and holding a bow made of rabbit-horns." There are barren women, but they do not bear children; the sky exists, but not sky-flowers; rabbits exist, but do not have horns. This is *vikalpa*.

All *vikalpa* ends at the height of meditation (*nirvikalpa dhyāna*). Devī is one who remains in that state always. The *Gautama Sūtra* (IV.50) states, "Anything that is created by the mind is not real." Devī, on the other hand, is unconditioned eternal Knowledge.

Also, *vikalpa* is that which is opposed to *śāstras* (scriptures) and *nirvikalpa* is not opposed. Devī is not separate from various *śāstras*; therefore, no *śāstra* can negate Her.

177. निराबाधा

Nirābādha

She who is not disturbed by anything.

Ābādha is incorrect knowledge or understanding. One may have the illusion of seeing a serpent instead of a rope in dim light. The illusion is removed when there is bright light. Devī is beyond this kind of illusion.

178. निर् भेदा

Nir bhedā

She who is beyond all sense of difference.

To Devī there are no similarities or differences in the qualities of beings or things. The *Kūrma Purāṇa* says, "Thou art the Supreme Ruler, infinite and the Supreme Śakti, devoid of all differences and destroyer of all differences." Those who are ignorant think that Śiva and Śakti are separate, but those *yogins* who meditate on the Truth recognize Their singular identity.

179. भेद नाशिनी

Bheda nāśinī

She who removes from Her devotees all sense of differences born of vāsanās.

The universe consists of myriad names, forms and themes. The fulfillment of the devotee is in experiencing the oneness inherent in all this diversity. Devī is the one who brings about that fulfillment.

The notions of separateness and opposites, such as friend and foe, ours and theirs, victory and defeat, are the cause of all wordly sorrow. Once this sense of difference is removed, there is no more sorrow.

180. निर्नाशा

Nirnāśā

She who is imperishable.

Bhaṭṭathiripāḍ says in the *Nārayaṇīyam*, "(It is) beyond time, space and all such limitations; it is eternally free." Devī has no end. As the *Gītā* (II.17) proclaims, "Know That to be imperishable by which all this is pervaded. None can cause the destruction of That - the Imperishable."

181. मृत्यु मथनी

Mṛtyu mathanī

She who destroys death.

Yama, the Lord of death, makes clear in the *Kaṭhopaniṣad* (I-ii-10): "I know that treasure is transient, for the Eternal is not obtained by things which are not eternal. Therefore, the *Naciketa* fire (a *Vedic* ritual) has been propitiated by me with perishable things, and I have obtained the Eternal."

Yama declares that his own position as the Lord of Death must be obtained through merit. Thus even Yama is not eternal. Devī is powerful enough to seat or unseat him.

This *mantra* means, "She who saves Her devotees from Yama (the cycle of birth and death) and, by merging them in Herself, blesses them with an eternal status."

Through Her Will, Devī removes the sickness and suffering and even the fear of death, arising from *prārabdha karma*, through Her blessing.

182. निष्क्रिया

Niṣkriyā

She who remains without action.

There are no actions for Devī who is the *Ātman*. But what about the cycle of creation, maintenance and destruction? Does that constitute action?

When a flower blossoms, its fragrance spreads everywhere. It is the inherent nature of the flower. There is no special *karma* or action here on the part of the flower. The acts of creation are like this. This is why Devī is called actionless.

Śaṅkara makes it clear from his own experience in *Manīṣāpañcaka* that actions by one who abides in *Brahman* are not actions at all. This idea is also explained in the *Gītā* (V. 8-9): "I do nothing at all, thus would the truth-knower think, steadfast though seeing, hearing, touching, smelling, eating, going, sleeping, breathing, speaking, letting go, seizing, opening, and closing the eyes, remembering that the senses move among the sense-objects."

183. निष्परिग्रहा

Niṣparigrahā

She who does not acquire or accept anything.

She is complete in Herself, with all wishes fulfilled.

Devī is one who does not amass anything. *Parigraha* means spouse, children, grain, wealth, and so on. None of these apply to Her.

Why, then, does the actionless Devī need temples, *pūja*, offerings of food, money and the like? It is the desire of the devotees; it is for their pleasure and peace of mind. We put diamonds and jewelry on children according to our wealth. What need does a child have for jewelry? The child does not know its value. It is all for the happiness of the adults.

Amma says, "It is our mind that we should give to God. Then we will get it back purified. Presently our strongest attachment is to our wealth. Therefore, when we give wealth, it is like giving our mind. The benefit is not to God, but to ourselves."

The dictionary says that *parigraha* also means "root." Since Devī is the root cause of everything, She Herself is without root (*niṣparigrahā*).

184. निस्तुला

Nistulā

She who is incomparable, unequalled.

Devī is so exalted that there is nothing similar, comparable or superior to Her. She is Brahman. "She who is without cause or comparison," says the *Tripuropaniṣad*.

185. नील चिकुरा

Nīla cikurā

She who has shining black hair.

Her luxuriant, long, curly locks of hair give Her great beauty.

186. निर् अपाया

Nir apāyā

She who is imperishable.

Apāya means separation. As Devī is omnipresent and all-pervading, from what is She separate? Recall Lord Kṛṣṇa's words in the *Gītā*: "Everything is arranged in Me, as pearls in a necklace."

187. निरत्यया

Niratyayā

She who cannot be transgressed.

The word *atyayā* has the following meanings: transgression, destruction, decay and punishment. Devī is without these.

Even Brahmā, Viṣṇu and Śiva do not go beyond Devī. Just as She cannot be transgressed, She Herself does not transgress. Although She has created the entire universe, She does not transgress the rules and the rulers She has provided for the protection of the cosmos. In Nature's storehouse, even Īśvara will show great restraint.

This *mantra* is also interpreted as, "She who removes the dangers faced by devotees from time to time."

188. दुर्लभा

Durlabhā

She who is won only with much difficulty.

Devī is not accessible to everyone. She is won only by those who are pure at heart. Amma says, "Children, without purity of heart one cannot attain God." She also sings,

> *"You may give Her endless wealth,*
> *But your heart, to Her, is dearest."*

189. दुर्गमा

Durgamā

She who is approachable only with extreme effort.

Even *yogis* cannot reach Her easily.

The present *mantra* may also be read as *adurgamā* which means, "She who is reached easily." Devī becomes easily attainable through pure devotion. It can also mean that Devī has no place that is unattainable or no obstacle that is impassable.

190. दुर्गा

Durgā

She who is the Goddess Durgā.

Durgā is the name that is dearest to Devī. Durgā is one who rescued the *devas* from fear. Devī is celebrated by the name Durgā because She slew the great demon Durgama. She Herself claims this in *Mārkaṇḍeya Purāṇa*: "There I will kill the great demon Durgama and My name will become famous as Durgā." The name *Durgama* merits examination. It means one who travels on evil paths. What other demon than the mind wanders in search of evil paths? Durgā is the power of the *mantra* that destroys that demon. Durgā is one who turns the mind away from its thirst for evil and establishes it in the pursuit of good. That is the greatness of Durgā worship.

Ācārya Bhāskararāya describes further: "Indra and other *devas* were delivered from mental and physical fear in battle; hence Devī is called Durgā, the Deliverer."

The image of Devī installed in Varanāsi by the king Subāhu is known as Durgā. *Devī Bhāgavata* says that when Devī appeared in front of him and granted him a boon, he prayed to Her to establish Herself in the city under the name Durgā.

Durgā is known also as "One who helps us to cross the ocean of *samsāra*."

191. दुःख हन्त्री

Duḥkha hantrī

She who is the destroyer of sorrow.

Duḥkha (sorrow), literally means corrupted or evil (*duh*) sense organ (*kha*). The opposite is *sukha*, happiness. The implication is that sorrow and happiness do not belong to the soul, but are based on the senses. The mind is to be viewed as a sense organ; the *Gītā* describes the mind as the "sixth sense." Conquer the mind and there is no more sorrow, the sorrow of *samsāra*.

192. सुख प्रदा

Sukha pradā

She who is the giver of happiness.

Devī gives happiness in this world and the next with the bliss of ultimate Liberation.

The *Taittiriya Upaniṣad* (II.7) states, "Only after obtaining this Essence does one become blissful." Devī is the embodiment of that *ānanda* (bliss).

Amma says, "Children, the mother who gave birth to you may look after you in this life. Even that is rare today. But Amma's aim is to lead you to happiness in all of your births!"

193. दुष्ट दूरा

Duṣṭa dūrā

She who is unapproachable by sinners.

It is the result of one's prior evil deeds that one comes to hate and malign Devī. She does not distance Herself from them; they themselves move away from Her. On cold days people gather around the fire for warmth. Those who are close to the fire do not feel cold. Those who sit far from the fire shiver due to the cold, but that is not the fault of the fire; it is because they don't come near the fire. Those who are *sāttvic* in nature come closer and closer to Devī. They enjoy divine bliss.

Another interpretation of this *mantra* is, "She is one who drives away evil people for the protection of Her devotees."

194. दुराचार शमनी

Durācāra śamanī

She who stops evil customs.

Customs that go against the scriptures are evil. She removes sins accruing from such acts.

The good codes of conduct laid down for the security of the society become corrupted due to the passage of time and due to the innate selfishness of man. Devī manifests to correct this, and to reestablish the righteous code of life. Lord Kṛṣṇa declares in the *Gītā* (IV-7), "Whenever there is a decay of righteousness, O Arjuna, and a rise of unrighteousness, I then manifest Myself."

195. दोष वर्जिता

Doṣa varjitā

She who is free from all faults.

Desire and anger are some of the faults implied here. From these faults arise all of the dangers to society. We should cast away all such evils just as we would fling away a serpent that we have picked up by mistake.

How many self-centered thoughts hide within even the most pious of minds! Worshipping Devī, the remover of faults, helps us to discover these and eradicate them.

196. सर्वज्ञा

Sarvajñā

She who is omniscient.

She knows That; knowing which, one knows all.

Even a great scholar's knowledge is partial. His knowledge is measured by the amount of grace he has received from Devī.

Devī who pervades everything knows the course taken by each animate and inanimate object. The devotee's duty is not to hide anything from Her who knows all.

197. सान्द्र करुणा

Sāndra karuṇā

She who shows intense compassion.

Devī showers Her compassion on everyone incessantly. We can see that same Devī in Amma, in Her great kindness, when She ignores not even one devotee among the thousands that throng for Her *darśan*.

198. समानाधिक वर्जिता

Samānādhika varjitā

She who has neither equal nor superior.

According to the *Śruti*, nothing equals or excels That. *Śvetāśvatāra Upaniṣad* (VI-8) declares, "No action (effect) or instrument (organ) of His is found. There is not seen His equal or superior. The great power of the Supreme is declared in the *Vedas* to be of many different kinds. His knowledge, strength and action are described as inherent in Him."

199. सर्व शक्ति मयी

Sarva śakti mayī

She who has all the divine powers.

The description of Devī's *saguṇa* (with qualities) form begins with this *mantra*. She is the Power in which the power of all the deities is concentrated. Bhāskarācarya quotes from the *Lakṣmī Tantra* of *Pāñcarātra* Devī's own words: "O Indra, I am Mahālakṣmi in the age of Svāyambhuva (Manu). I am born as the slayer of the demon Mahiṣa for the well-being of all *devas*. Those portions of My powers which came from the bodies of the *devas* together became My supremely beautiful form."

Any spark of life we see in nature is a trace of Her power. Thus, *Mārkaṇḍeya Purāṇa* says, "Those who are wise know that whatever energy objects possess is all Devī Herself." The *Śruti* also says, "The power of the Supreme is of many different kinds." (refer to the quotation under the previous *mantra*)

The universe is held together by forces of different kinds and of infinite extent. It is this scientific fact that is represented by the image that the universe is supported by the thousand hoods of the great serpent Ananta (infinite).

200. सर्व मङ्गला

Sarva maṅgalā

She who is the source of all that is auspicious.

Bhāskarācārya quotes from the *Devī Purāṇa*, "She gives all the good fortune that we long for in our hearts and all the desired objects; hence She is called *sarvamaṅgalā*. She gives to Hara all the best and choicest things, and removes the pain of the devotees; hence She is *sarvamaṅgalā*."

Thus ends the third *kalā* or "ray of the sun," called Dhūmrikā, with the second hundred mantras.

201. सद् गति प्रदा

Sad gati pradā

She who leads into the right path.

Sadgati is the journey of the *jīva* from the experience of heaven to final Liberation (*mokṣa*).

Sat is *Brahman* and *gati* is knowledge. The *mantra* then means "She who gives knowledge of the Self." *Sat* also means righteous and *gati*, refuge. Devī is one who gives total refuge to those who are righteous.

202. सर्वेश्वरी

Sarveśvarī

She who rules over all the living and nonliving things.

Not even a leaf falls without Her wish. Not even an ant moves. She is the one who controls and protects everything, the one with the power to act one way or the other, or not to act at all, according to Her wishes.

203. सर्वमयी

Sarvamayī

She who pervades every living and nonliving thing.

All the *tattvas* (cosmic elements) from the earth to Śiva are contained in Devī.

According to the *Kāmika Tantra*, there are two hundred and twenty-four worlds. Meditating upon these as if they were hairs on the body of Śiva is the *bhuvana* method of meditation. Meditating on the fifty letters (*varṇas*), visualizing them on the skin of the trident-bearing Lord is the *varṇa* method. Meditating on the seven *crores* (one crore is a measurement of ten million) of *mantras* arising from the *Vedas*, visualizing them as Śiva's blood is the mantra method. Meditation on the words of the *mantras* as Śiva's flesh and blood vessels is the *pada* (word) method. Meditating on the thirty-six *tattvas* beginning with the earth as Śiva's sinews, bones and marrow is the *tattva* method.

Since Śiva and Devī are one, Devī is all-pervading.

204. सर्व मन्त्र स्वरूपिणी

Sarva mantra svarūpiṇī

She who is the essence of all the mantras.

The ancient wisdom acknowledges seven *crores* of *mantras*. Each *mantra* revealed itself to the *ṛṣis* in the form of a deity. Before chanting a *mantra*, the corresponding *ṛṣi* is remembered. *Mantra* means something which, when meditated upon, leads to salvation.

The *Śrividyā mantra* (the fifteen-syllabled *mantra*) is at the center, leading all of the other *mantras*, according to the *Sundarītāpanīya Upaniṣad*.

205. सर्व यन्त्रात्मिका

Sarva yantrātmikā

She who is the soul of all yantras.

A *yantra* is a symbol which represents a deity in the form of a picture, or as a *cakra* (figure) or syllables. Devī is the support behind whichever deity is being invoked.

206. सर्व तन्त्र रूपा

Sarva tantra rūpā

She who is the Soul of all the Tantras.

Devī is the goal of all *Tāntric* paths. All the paths laid down by the *śāstras* merge in Her, just as rivers in the ocean. The easiest and most readily available *Tāntric* method is meditation on Her form from head to toe.

The various *Tantras* have been described as parts of Devī's body. *Kāmika Tantra* is described as Her feet, *Yogaja* as heels, *Kāraṇa* and *Prasṛta* as toes, *Ajita* as knees, *Dīpta* as thighs, *Amśuma* as back, *Suprabheda* as navel, *Vijaya* as stomach, *Niśvāsa* as heart, *Svāyambhuva* as the bosom, *Anala* as the three eyes, *Vīrāgama* as the throat, *Ruru Tantra* as ears, *Makuṭa* as the crown, *Vipula* as the arms, *Candrajñāna* as the chest, *Bimba* as the face, *Prodgīta* as the tongue, *Lalita* as the cheeks, *Siddha* as the forehead, *Samtāna* as the earrings, *Kiraṇa* as the gems, *Vātūla* as the garments and all the other *Tantras* as hair on Her body.

207. मनोन्मनी

Manonmanī

She who is Śiva's śakti.

Manonmanī is the name of Śiva's *śakti* according to the *Śruti*.

Saubhāgyabhāskara quotes from *Bṛhannāradīya*: "When the object of meditation, the act of meditation and the meditator all become one, the state of *manonmanī* arises in which the experience of the nectar of *jñāna* occurs." The experience of Devī which occurs in such a state is also *manonmanī*.

Also, Devī is *manonmanī* as in one who uplifts the mind of the devotee (unma: lifting up).

Manonmanī is the point just below the *brahmarandhra*, the eighth point counting upwards from the middle of the eyebrows. The eight points are, *indu*, *rodhinī*, *nāda*, *nādānta*, *śakti*, *vyāpinī*, *samanā*, and *unmanī* or *manonmanī*. These are extremely subtle locations and must be learned under direct instructions from a Guru.

Manonmanī is also the name of a yogic posture in which the eyes are held slightly open without blinking, the breath is controlled without inhaling or exhaling, and the mind is made blank and free of speculation and doubt. Devī is to be meditated upon in this state.

The *Tripuropaniṣad* says that when the mind is free from all sensory connections and is concentrated in the heart, one reaches the state of *unmanī*. Devī is the one who bestows this state on the *yogi*.

208. माहेश्वरी

Māheśvarī

She who is the wife of Maheśvara.

Maheśvara (Śiva), when predominantly in the *tāmasic* (dormant) state, becomes Rudra, the Destroyer. When predominantly *rājasic* (active), He is Brahmā, the Creator, and when predominantly *sāttvic* (peaceful), He is Viṣṇu, the all-pervading Protector. Thus, Maheśvara is the source or support for the Trinity and is devoid of the three *guṇas*. This is how Maheśvara is described in the *Liṅga Purāṇa*. The *liṅga* is the symbol of Maheśvara. It should be worshipped with a pure heart and while observing celibacy.

Maheśvara is the lord of all creation and the lord of human greatness, according to the *Mahābhārata*. The *Vātulaśuddha Āgama* describes Maheśvara as the sum total of the twenty-five *tattvas*.

209. महा देवी

Mahā devī

She who has the immeasurable body.

The entire cosmos is Her great body. "Her body is immense and cannot be measured by any instruments. The root '*mahā*' means worship; therefore, She is called Mahādevi," according to the *Devī Purāṇa*. Devī cannot be measured by words, mind or intellect and is worthy of worship in all possible ways.

Mahādevī is the wife of Mahādeva (Śiva). Also, She is Mahādevī as She is the greatest (*mahā*) of the goddesses.

210. महा लक्ष्मी

Mahā lakṣmī

She who is the great Goddess Lakṣmī.

Lakṣma means mark or sign; Lakṣmī is one who possesses all divine attributes. Mahālakṣmi is the great Lakṣmī and the wife of Mahāviṣṇu.

In the previous *mantra*, it was explained that Viṣṇu is Maheśvara Himself in a predominantly *sāttvic* role. In a corresponding role, Devī becomes Mahālakṣmī.

The name "Lakṣmī" can also mean Pārvati. According to the *Śiva Purāṇa*, "The all-beautiful, dark-complexioned *śakti*, who sits in Maheśvara's lap, is called Mahālakṣmī."

"Lakṣmī is the origin of everything that manifests in the form of the three guṇas." (*Mārkaṇḍeya Purāṇa*)

Devī became famous as Mahālasā and Mahālakṣmī as She slew the demon Mahāla.

A girl of thirteen years is called Mahālakṣmī according to *Dhaumya Smṛti.*

211. मृड प्रिया

Mṛḍa priyā

She who is the beloved of Mṛḍa (Śiva).

Mṛḍa is the form of Śiva who is predominantly *sāttvic* and bestows happiness on everything in the universe.

212. महा रूपा

Mahā rūpā

She who has a great form.

According to the *Viṣṇu Purāṇa*, the four forms of the Supreme *Brahman* are *Puruṣa*, *Pradhāna* (unmanifested), *Vyakta* (manifested), and *Kāla* (time). These forms are the basis for creation, preservation and destruction. Devī has a form beyond all of these.

213. महा पूज्या

Mahā pūjyā

She who is the greatest object of worship.

Devī is worthy of worship even by Brahmā, Viṣṇu and Śiva.

214. महा पातक नाशिनी

Mahā pātaka nāśinī

She who destroys even the greatest of sins.

A glance from Devī burns to cinders all of our sins. The *Brahmāṇḍa Purāṇa* makes it clear that the remembrance of the holy feet of the Parāśakti is the most effective atonement for all sins committed knowingly or unknowingly.

Pātaka is that which causes fall. Devī removes impurities such as desire and anger which cause our fall from the plane of Self-Knowledge.

215. महा माया

Mahā māyā

She who is the Great Illusion.

Devī is one who can cause illusory agitation even in Brahmā, Viṣṇu and Śiva.

"That divine Mahāmāyā forcibly draws away the minds of even the sages and leads them to delusion," says *Mārkaṇḍeya Purāṇa*.

Also, She is Mahāmāyā because She links the *jīvas* to both happiness and sorrow.

According to the *Kālika Purāṇa*, She is the Supreme Goddess Mahāmāyā, who takes knowledge away from the being who possesses knowledge while in the womb. She gives him birth, leads him to the many desires according to prior *saṃskāra*, makes him subject to the feelings of confusion, egoism and doubt. Day and night he is a victim of anxiety arising from anger, sorrow and greed, the Goddess at times bringing him sorrow and at times joy.

It is the same great *Māyā* that finally lifts the *jīva* up from the darkness of illusion and immerses it in the ocean of bliss. The *jīva's prārabdha karma* is the deciding factor in both cases. However intense the darkness a mere candle light is enough to dispel it. In the same way, even someone who is totally bound in *Māyā* can undergo transformation instantly by the nearness of Realized Souls and association with them. As the poet sings,

> *"It takes but an instant*
> *For knowledge to brighten within*
> *And for pain-giving darkness*
> *To fade away."*

Māyā is the state in which something seems to be what it is not. *Māyā* is not the absence of something. A flower is not a flower, it is *caitanya*, the Essence or Existence. The sun is really not the sun, it is Existence. So is the earth. What hinders us from seeing it as such is *Māyā*. When *Māyā* is lifted, one can experience that all is *Brahman*. This is not a conjecture, but established truth; however, to gain this state one needs the grace of Mahāmāyā!

Mahāmāyā can also be interpreted as the treasury of unparalleled compassion.

216. महा सत्त्वा

Mahā sattvā

She who possesses great sattva.

Sattva means power, existence (*caitanya*), intelligence, *sāttvic* quality, strength, substance and reality. All of these meanings are applicable to Devī with the adjective *mahā* (great).

217. महा शक्तिः

Mahā śaktiḥ

She who has great power.

Just as the brightness of a fire spreads in all directions, Devī's power extends in all directions. Just as the warmth of the fire diminishes as we go away from it, so does our experience of Her power. Even when She is near, one needs the merit from previous good *karma* to get drawn to Her and to gain Her blessings. As it is said in the *Gītā* (VII.3), "Only one in thousands strives for perfection; and even among those successful strivers, only one perchance knows Me in essence." Divine Grace is essential to achieve this perfection.

Bhāsakarācārya interprets Mahāśakti as the broad and many-sided power required to protect and nurture the entire universe.

Śakti means army, ability and weapons. Devī possesses all of these in great measure.

Mahāśakti also represents *Kuṇḍalinī śakti.*

218. महा रतिः

Mahā ratiḥ

She who is boundless delight.

A life of sensory delights, however sweet and wonderful, is lowlier than the life of an insect, conversely, a sage's life is like that of a bee who falls into the blossom of unbroken bliss and feeds on the nectar there. Devī is the source of that bliss. If there were not such an indescribable bliss in spiritual attainment, would anyone forsake worldly delights and set out on the path of *tapas*? Worldly delight is ephemeral while spiritual delight is eternal.

219. महा भोगा

Mahā bhogā

She who has immense wealth.

Bhoga means riches such as money, grain or other goods. Those who take refuge in Devī obtain worldly wealth automatically.

Another definition of *Mahābhoga* is, "She who has great *ābhoga*," meaning completeness or extension. Thus, Devī is *mahābhoga* when we think of the extent of Her form, which fills the whole universe.

220. महैश्वर्या

Mahaiśvaryā

She who has supreme sovereignty.

Devī is the seat of the six *aiśvaryas* (godly qualities): lordliness (*aiśvarya*), valor (vīrya), fame (kirti), auspiciousness (śrī), wisdom (jñāna) and dispassion (vairāgya). There are eight superhuman abilities (*siddhis*) which are also considered as *aiśvaryas* (see *mantra* 224). Devī is incomparably rich in all of these qualities and hence She is known as Mahaiśvaryā.

221. महा वीर्या

Mahā vīryā

She who is supreme in valor.

Devī effortlessly killed several powerful *asuras*. Her valor and strength are beyond measure.

Vīrya means semen, might, glory and strength according to the *Viśvakośa*.

222. महा बला

Mahā balā

She who is supreme in might.

Balā has many meanings: might, smell, taste, form, soul, corpulence or crow.

Yogavāsiṣṭha says that Bhuṣuṇḍa, the crow, with his twenty brothers, worshipped Devī for many years. Devī gave all of them

Liberation even while they were in their physical bodies.

223. महा बुद्धिः

Mahā buddhiḥ

She who is supreme in intelligence.

"Many salutations to Her, who exists in all beings in the form of intelligence." (*Devī Māhātmya*)

Devī is one who bestows great intelligence. When that intelligence is firmly fixed on Her, everything becomes known. "Which when known, all is known," says the *Chāndogya Upaniṣad*.

Intelligence is the basis of all our achievements. When it is dead, all is dead. Not only our own lack of intelligence, but the absence of it in others also brings us peril. That is why in the *Gāyatri mantra* we pray, "Kindly awaken our intelligence!"

"From loss of intelligence comes utter ruin," warns Lord Kṛṣṇa in the *Gītā* (II.63).

224. महा सिद्धिः

Mahā siddhiḥ

She who is endowed with the highest attainments.

The eight *siddhis* (attainments) are: the power to become as minute as an atom at will (*animā*), to grow as large as the universe (*mahimā*), to become as light as a cotton fiber (*laghimā*), to become as heavy as a mountain (*garimā*), to lord over everything (*īśitva*), to win over and control everything (*vaśitva*), to effortlessly reach places that are even beyond imagination (*prāpti*), and to manifest wherever and whenever needed (*prākaśya*).

What *siddhi* is greater than creating this unimaginably complex universe and guarding it? Devī possesses that miraculous *siddhi*.

This *mantra* can also be interpreted as: "She who confers great *siddhis* on Her devotees."

225. महा योगेश्वरेश्वरी

Mahā yogeśvareśvarī

She who is the object of worship even by the greatest of yogis.

Yogis, spiritual adepts, are not like ordinary men. They see themselves as *Īśvara*. The scriptures, after all, say that the knower of *Brahman* becomes *Brahman*. Even to such persons, Devī is the Goddess.

226. महा तन्त्रा

Mahā tantrā

She who is worshipped by the great Tantras *such as* Kulārṇava *and* Jñānārṇava.

Seeing that the sixty-four *Tantras*, originally formulated by Lord Śiva, conferred only insignificant *siddhis* which deluded the human soul without leading it to the ultimate goal, Devī asked the Lord to bring forth *Śrī Vidyā* which confers the supreme goal of life, as Śaṅkara points out in *Saundarya Laharī* (verse 31).

The list of sixty-four *Tantras* is given below. It is clear that the aim of these is only the gain of physical desires and powers.

1. *Mahāmāyāśambara* (The practice of magic); 2. *Yoginī jālaśambara* (To get *darśan* of the host of *yoginis*, through worship in cemeteries); 3. *Tattvaśambara* (*Mahendrajāla*, a higher level of magic); 4-11. *Bhairavāṣtaka Tantras* (Worshipping *Siddha-*, *Vatuka*, *Kankāla-*, *Kāla-*, *Yogini-*, *Maha-*, *Śakti-* and *Kālāgni Bhairavas*. These fall under the rituals of the sect of *Kāpālikas*); 12-19. *Bahurupāṣṭaka Tantras* dealing with the deities *Brāhmi*, *Māheśvari*, *Kaumāri*, *Vaiṣnavi*, *Vārāhi*, *Māhendri*, *Cāmuṇḍa* and *Śivadūti*; 20-27. *Yamalāṣṭaka Tantras* (All 64 *Tantras* are sometimes called "*yamalas*" in the sense that they are outside the *Vedas*); 28. *Candrajñāna*, also a part of the religion of *Kāpālikas*. There is also a different *Candrajñāna* which is more acceptable as it is part of *yogaśāstra*; 29. *Mālinīvidya*, which enables travelling over the ocean and involves the *siddhi* known as *jalastambhana*.

There is a story connected with Chāṭṭampi Svāmi. Once he was bathing in the river at Kodanad with his disciples. He went to the middle of the river and sat there in *padmāsana*. Thinking that he was sitting on a rock, his disciples started approaching him. He told them not to. When asked later why he did not allow them to go near, he pointed out that the water there was very deep and that he was checking to see whether he had forgotten the *siddhi* of *jalastambhana* ("immobilizing the water"); 30. *Mahāsammohana*, the *siddhi* of putting people to sleep. This power is obtained through the means of "cutting a child's tongue" and is thus considered unacceptable; 31. *Vāmajuṣta*; 32. *Mahādeva*; 33. *Vātūla*; 34. *Vātulottama*; 35. *Kāmika*; 36. *Hṛdbheda Tantra*; 37. *Tantrabheda*; 38. *Guhya Tantra* (These last two are to be practiced through the killing of many living things and hence are also contrary to the scriptures.); 39. *Kalāvāda*. This deals with the art of love, and is contrary to the *Vedas* as it includes relationships with extramarital partners; 40. *Kalāsara*; 41. *Kundikāmata*; 42. *Matottara*; 43. *Vīnākhya*, which is aimed at the *yogini* known as Vīnāyogini; 44. *Trotala*; 45. *Trotalottara*, which supposedly allows the direct vision of sixty-four thousand *yakṣinis* or celestial females; 46. *Pañcāmṛta*, through which many *siddhis* connected with the five elements are said to be attained; 47 to 53. Seven *Tantras*, *Rūpabheda* etc., connected with *māranas* or rites for causing death; 54-58. Five *Tantras* starting with *Sarvajñāna* practiced by *Kāpālikas* and the sect of *Digambaras*; 59-64. *Tantras* connected with the *Digambara* sect.

227. महा मन्त्रा

Mahā mantrā

She who is the greatest mantra.

Mantras are meant to invoke various deities. As indicated earlier, *mantras* are said to have appeared in front of the great sages in the form of deities. The greatest of *mantras* is the *Śrī Vidyā*, a form of Devī.

228. महा यन्त्रा

Mahā yantra

She who is in the form of the great yantras.

Devī is worshipped through the great *yantras*. The greatest *yantra* is the *Śrīcakra* which is the *yantra* of *Śrī Vidyā*. In *Tantraśāstra, cakras*, letters, inscriptions are all known as *yantras* which are figures of special power. All of the one hundred verses in *Saundarya Laharī* have *yantras* associated with them as pointed out in the various commentaries. Books such as *Kulārṇava* explain these *yantras* in detail.

229. महासना

Mahāsanā

She who is seated on great seats.

The thirty-six *tattvas* (principles) from the earth to Śiva are considered as Her seats, but it is said that the seat dearest to Her is the heart of a sincere devotee. The *Gītā* (XVIII.61) says, "The Lord dwells in the hearts of all beings, Arjuna."

230. महा याग क्रमाराध्या

Mahā yāga kramārādhyā

She who is worshipped by the ritual of mahāyāga.

Mahāyāga is a worship meant for pleasing Devī, done with elaborate preparations following prescribed rules. It is the worship of sixty-four *yoginis* who are parts of such deities as Brahmī. Bhāskararāya quotes *Bhāvanopaniṣad* here and says that *Mahāyāga* is a sacrifice performed by *Śivayogins*.

In its inner meaning, *mahāyāga* can be considered as the process in which the worshipper-seeker sacrifices his *vāsanās* one by one in the fire of wisdom and the seeker becomes one with what he seeks, thus reaching the ultimate bliss of unity with the Supreme.

231. महा भैरव पूजिता

Mahā bhairava pūjitā

She who is worshipped even by Mahābhairava (Śiva).

In the name Bhairava, "Bha" denotes creation, "ra" preservation, and "va" destruction. Devī is worshipped by Lord Śiva who performs all three of these tasks.

The three syllables are also interpreted as standing for the words *bha*rana (protecting), *ra*mana (pleasing) and *va*mana (discarding). Everything in the world is subject to these. Can we, in the end, avoid discarding anything that we nourish and make happy? That is why everything in this world is called *Māyā*. Amma says, "Anything that is not permanent is *Māyā*."

Lord Śiva, Bhairava, is thus responsible for nourishing, pleasing and discarding everything. Devī is worshipped even by Him. According to *Padma Purāṇa*, "Śiva, the Source of the Universe, holding a rosary in His hand and performing *nyāsa*, worships the beneficent Devī, who is the *Śakti* of the *mantras*." (*Nyāsa* means the assignment of the various parts of the body to different deities, accompanied by prayer and corresponding gestures.)

232. महेश्वर महाकल्प महाताण्डव साक्षिणी

Maheśvara mahākalpa mahātāṇḍava sākṣiṇī

She who is the witness of the great dance of Maheśvara (Śiva) at the end of the great cycle of creation.

The great dissolution (*mahāpralaya*) is the destruction of the universe. Śiva, the Destroyer, in great bliss, performs the *tāṇḍava* dance, according to the *Purāṇas*. Devī, who is beyond everything, is the sole witness of this dance. Ācarya Bhāskararāya quotes from *Pañcadaśīstava*: "Victory to Your form, bearing the noose, goad, sugar-cane bow and the arrow of flowers, who is the only witness of the *tāṇḍava* dance of the axe-bearing Parabhairava, at the time of His drawing the universe into Himself." The *Devī Bhāgavata* describes Devī at the time of the dissolution (of the universe) as sporting, after absorbing all beings into Herself and drawing in the entire universe. In either case, we see the beauty of the *ardhanārīśvara* (half-female, half-male god) concept. Mahādevī is the only witness to Mahādeva's cosmic dance, as They indeed are joined together as word and meaning and are the parents of the universe!

233. महा कामेश महिषी

Mahā kāmeśa mahiṣī

She who is the great queen of Mahākāmeśvara.

234. महा त्रिपुर सुन्दरी

Mahā tripura sundarī

She who is the great Tripurasundarī.

Bhāskararāya interprets "*tripura*" as the "city of three": the measurer, the measuring and the thing measured or, in other words, the knower, knowledge and that which is known.

Tripura can also be the three bodies: gross body, subtle body and causal body. Isn't Devī the *Sundarī*, the beautiful *Śakti* who dwells captivatingly in all three? What is more beautiful than this essence of life? Indeed, that is why the *Śruti* says, "This Self is dearer than a son, dearer than wealth, dearer than all other objects, being nearer than everything, being inside; one should meditate on the Self alone as dear." (*Bṛhadāraṇyaka Upaniṣad* I.4.8) The *Mahābhārata* also says, "Therefore, the Self is the dearest of all things to living beings."

In all of this, the beauty of the *Atman* and our great love for It becomes clear.

The *śakti* of the individual *jīva* is known as *Kuṇḍalinī* and the *Śakti* of Sadāśiva is Tripurasundarī.

235. चतुः षष्ट्युपचाराढ्या

Catuḥ ṣaṣṭyupacārāḍhyā

She who is adored in sixty-four ceremonies.

The sixty-four ceremonies are those described in Paraśurāma's

Kalpasūtra. In other *Tantras*, eight more are described. Bhāskararāya describes these *upacāras* in the *pūja* chapter of the *Varivasyārahasya*.

Of these sixty-four ceremonies, sixteen are the most important. They are known as *ṣodaśopacāras* (*ṣoḍaśa*: sixteen). The sixteen are: invocation (*āvāhana*), offering of a seat (*āsana*), water for washing the feet (*pādya*), offering of water or other materials (*arghya*), water for rinsing the mouth (*ācamana*), bath (*snāna*), clothes (*vastra*), ornaments (*ābharana*), fragrance (*candana*), flowers (*puṣpa*), incense (*dūpa*), a lamp (*dīpa*), food (*naivedya*), betel leaves (*tāmbula*), circumambulation (*pradakṣina*) and prostration (*namaskāra*).

Some *Tantras* refer to seventy-two ceremonies instead of sixty-four.

236. चतुः षष्टि कलामयी

Catuḥ ṣaṣṭi kalāmayī

She who embodies the sixty-four fine arts.

Kala means "a part," a fraction; every *kalā* (art) is a part of the splendor of the Self. Lord Kṛṣṇa tells Arjuna in the *Gītā* (X.41), "Whatever being is glorious, prosperous or strong, know that to be a manifestation of My splendor."

Kalā (art), is a facile ability for display. Wherever there is this ease of performance, there is art. Arjuna earned the epithet "Savyasācin" because of his natural ability to shoot arrows with his left hand. He is the symbol of art. It is well-known from the *Vedas* that Indra is a symbol of the *Atman*. Arjuna is the son of Indra; art is the creation of the *Atman*. Everything that can be called an art is a part of Devī's glory.

In *Vāmakeśvara Tantra*, there are sixty-four books named *kalās*. Devī can be thought of as shining in the form of these books. One list of the sixty-four "arts" is given below. There are variants of this list depending on the source. 1. Music; 2. Playing musical instruments; 3. Dance; 4. Acting; 5. Painting; 6. Making emblems; 7. Flower art, making garlands and other artful creations; 8-9. Art work in mattresses and bedspreads; 10. Techniques for enhancing the beauty of the body; 11. Decorating the house; 12. Musical instruments using water, like *jalataranga;* 13. Making sound effects in water; 14. Art of attire; 15. Making necklaces with pearls; 16. Hair decoration; 17. Dressing; 18. Art of making ear ornaments; 19. Flower decoration; 20. Decorations in food items; 21. Magic; 22. Decoration of surroundings 23. Manicuring; 24. Making savories, cakes etc; 25. making drinks; 26. Sewing; 27. Making nets; 28. Riddles; 29. Poem recital; 30. Commentary talk on epics, poetical works; 31. Reading; 32. Seeing plays; 33. Completing *samasyas* (a *samasya* is a verse left incomplete as a challenge for others to complete); 34. Making furniture articles with cane; 35. Wood working; 36. Debate; 37. Architecture; 38. Assessing gold and gems; 39. Refining of metals; 40. Cutting and polishing diamonds; 41. Searching for ore; 42. Special knowledge about trees and plants; 43. Cock fighting; 44. Interpreting the sounds of birds; 45. Massaging; 46. Hair care; 47. Sign language; 48. Learning foreign languages; 49. Scholarship in local languages; 50. Predicting the future; 51. Making machinery; 52. Strengthening memory power; 53. Learning from hearing; 54. Instantaneous verse-making; 55. Decisiveness in action; 56. Pretending; 57. Prosody (study of metrical structure of verses); 58. Preserving clothes; 59. Gambling; 60. Playing dice; 61. Playing with children; 62. Rules of respectful behavior; 63. The art of a bard or minstrel; 64. Grasping the essence of subjects.

237. महा चतुः षष्टि कोटि योगिनी गण सेविता

Mahā catuḥ ṣaṣṭi koṭi yoginī gaṇa sevitā

She who is attended by sixty-four crores *of bands of* yoginis.

There are eight main *yoginis* attending Devī: Brāhmī, Maheśvari, Kaumāri, Vaiṣṇavi, Vārāhi, Mahendri, Cāmundi and Mahālakṣmi. Each of them has eight *Śaktis*, making a total of sixty-four. Each of these, in turn, has a *crore* (ten million) of *yoginis* as parts of herself. In each of the nine *cakras*, starting from *Trailokyamohana*, resides such a group of sixty-four *crores* of *yoginis*. All of them are collectively referred to in this *mantra*. Devī is worshipped by them all.

The countless thousands of energies of desire (*icchāśakti*) that revolve around the mind are implied here by these groups of *yoginis*.

238. मनु विद्या

Manu vidyā

She who is the embodiment of manuvidya.

Manuvidya is Devī Herself embodied in the *Śrividya mantra. Manuvidya* is the collective name for the method of worship used by the following twelve devotees of Devī: Manu, Candra, Kubera, Lopāmudrā, Agastya, Manmatha, Agni, Sūrya, Indra, Skanda, Śiva and Krodhabhaṭṭāraka (Durvāsas).The method of worship formulated by each of them is given in *Jñānārṇava.*

239. चन्द्र विद्या

Candra vidyā

She who is the embodiment of Candravidya.

Candravidya is a form of *Śrividya* (see previous *mantra*). The meaning of the *mantra* is, "She who is worshipped through *candravidya.*"

240. चन्द्र मण्डल मध्यगा

Candra maṇḍala madhyagā

She who resides in the center of candramaṇḍala, *the moon's disc.*

The *candramaṇḍala* in the *Śrīcakra* is referred to here.

The *śakti* residing in the individual *jīva* (*piṇḍāṇḍa*) is the *Kuṇḍalinī*, and the *śakti* in the cosmos (*brahmaṇḍa*) is Tripurasundarī. Recalled in this *mantra* is the experience in which the *Kuṇḍalinī* breaks through the six *ādhara cakras* and enters the *sahasrāra*, the thousand-petaled lotus, and reaching its pericarp (known as *candramaṇḍala*), causes the flow of nectar.

Bhāskararāya quotes from the *Śiva Purāṇa*: "I reside in the flame of fire, and You in the head of the moon; this world consisting of fire and moon is presided over by Us."

The moon and fire are symbols for cold and heat, happiness and sorrow, and all other pairs of opposites. It is implied that Śiva and Śakti manifest everywhere in the universe in this dual aspect.

241. चारु रूपा

Cāru rūpā

She who has a beauty that does not wax or wane.

Devī's form is eternally beautiful in accordance with the imagination of the devotee. That beauty does not dim or fade. Her form is ever radiant, constantly giving new awakening to the devotees' hearts.

242. चारुहासा

Cāruhāsā

She who has a beautiful smile.

Moonlight is Devī's smile, according to the poets. She is able to captivate the whole world with Her smile which is as pure as moonlight and which awakens ultimate knowledge. It is the pure nectar of wisdom which flows through Her smile.

243. चारु चन्द्र कलाधरा

Cāru candra kalādharā

She who wears a beautiful crescent moon that does not wax or wane.

A crescent moon that does not wax or wane is known as "*sāda*." Bhāskararāya recalls in this context a story from *Devī Bhāgavata* - the story of a beautiful princess of Kāśi called Candrakalā. She was very *sāttvic* and had all the auspicious attributes. Devī gave *darśan* to her in a dream and told her, "O beautiful girl, marry the prince Sudarśana, my devotee, who will be able to fulfill all your wishes. You will have all happiness and prosperity." Thus Devī became the refuge and support (*dhara*) of Candrakalā.

Recall the epithet "Tārānāyakaśekhara" in Devī's meditation verse (*dhyānaśloka*). Tārānāyaka is the king of stars - the moon. Devī wears the moon in Her crown.

244. चराचर जगन्नाथा

Carācara jagannātha

She who is the ruler of the animate and inanimate worlds.

245. चक्र राज निकेतना

Cakra rāja niketanā

She who abides in the Śrīcakra.

Śrīcakra is the most important *cakra* in *Tantra* and is called the King of *cakras* (*cakrarāja*). Devī dwells in the nine *cakras*, beginning with the *Trailokyamohana*, which are within *Śrīcakra*.

The book *Śrīcakra* says, "The nine *cakras* from *Trailokyamohana* to *Sarvānandamaya* are nine coverings. Before perceiving the Truth directly, the nine layers have to be transcended or nine curtains have to be removed." It is clear from this that Devī who dwells in the *Śrīcakra* is not easily attainable and that constant worship is the way to obtain Her *darśan*, that unalloyed devotion alone is sufficient to win Her blessings.

246. पार्वती

Pārvatī

She who is the daughter of the Mountain (Mount Himavat or Himālaya).

The *Purāṇas* tell the story of Sati, daughter of Dakṣa Prajāpati and wife of Śiva. To protest the insult shown to Her and Her husband by Her father, Sati offers Herself to the fire created through Her *yogic* power known as *Agneyi*. She then takes birth as the daughter of Himavat, the king of the mountains. Kālidāsa also refers to this self-sacrifice by Sati in his *Kumārasambhava.*

247. पद्म नयना

Padma nayanā

She who has eyes that are long and beautiful like the petals of the lotus flower.

Padma (lotus) is a synonym for purity. Devī's eyes see only the good in everything.

248. पद्मराग सम प्रभा

Padmarāga sama prabhā

She who has a resplendent red complexion like the ruby.

Padmarāga is red in color and is one of the nine types of jewels. Devī's complexion is described everywhere as red, in phrases like "shining like the pomegranate flower" (*dāḍimīkusumaprabhā*), "with body as red as saffron" (*sindūrāruṇavigrahā*), and "red-hued and eyes full of compassion" (*aruṇām karuṇā taraṅgitākṣīm*).

249. पञ्च प्रेतासनासीना

Pañca pretāsanāsīnā

She who sits on the seat formed by five corpses.

Brahmā, Viṣṇu, Rudra, Īśvara and Sadāśiva are the five corpses here. They are also known as the five Brahmas (see *mantra* 58). Brahmā conducts his task of creation by the power known as *vāmaśakti* obtained from Devī; without it he is as powerless as a corpse. Similarly, Devī's *śakti* is indispensable to Viṣṇu, Rudra, Īsvara and Sadāśiva in performing their tasks. Without it they are all like corpses. One becomes a corpse when the inner Existence leaves.

The five corpses may refer to the five elements (*bhūtas*) in creation: earth, water, fire, air and space (ether). Devī, who is pure Existence, abides in this universe made of these five elements. She is *pañcapretāsanāsīnā* in this sense also.

250. पञ्च ब्रह्म स्वरूपिणी

Pañca brahma svarūpiṇī

She whose form is composed of the five Brahmas.

The five Brahmas are five different forms of Śiva: Īśana, Tatpuruṣa, Aghora, Vāmadeva and Sadyojāta.

According to the *Liṅga Purāṇa*, the five Brahmas are the individual soul, primordial nature, intellect, ego and mind. They also stand for the five organs of perception, the five organs of action or the objects of the five senses. The entire cosmos consisting of the five elements may be suggested by *pañcabrahma*. The *Śruti* concurs by saying, "Everything, indeed, is *Brahman*." Devī is that *Brahman*. Hence, this *mantra* can be interpreted as "The Devī whose form is the cosmos."

In the commentary on the previous *mantra*, the five divinities were called the five Brahmas. According to the present *mantra*, they may be understood as Devī's own forms.

251. चिन्मयी

Cinmayī

She who is consciousness itself.

Devī is described in this *mantra* as formless awareness.

252. परमानन्दा

Paramānandā

She who is supreme bliss.

Once pure awareness is reached, there is no more sorrow. There is only constant bliss. The supreme bliss may be understood also as Liberation (*mokṣa*). Devī is of the form of *mokṣa*.

The scale of bliss is analyzed in *Taittirīya Upaniṣad* (II.8). Consider the sequence of beings: human, human gandharva, celestial gandharva, pitṛdeva, karmadeva, Indra, Bṛhaspati, Prajāpati and Brahmā. The bliss felt by each increases a hundredfold as we go from one being to the next in this order. Thus the bliss of one who abides in *Brahman* is countless times higher than the happiness of man. Devī is the embodiment of that supreme bliss.

253. विज्ञान घन रूपिणी

Vijñāna ghana rūpiṇī

She who is the embodiment of all-pervading solid Intelligence.

Intelligence (*vijñāna*) is interpreted also as *jīva*. (*Bṛhadāraṇyaka Upaniṣad*) *Ghana* is solid mass. Thus *vijñānaghana* denotes the aggregate of *jīvas*. Devī is the aggregate of all *jīvas*.

254. ध्यान ध्यातृ ध्येय रूपा

Dhyāna dhyātṛ dhyeya rūpā

She who shines as meditation, meditator and the object of meditation.

According to the *Yoga Sūtra* (III:2), "Meditation is the unbroken flow of thought toward an object."

Dhyāna is the seventh *yoga* in the eight forms of *yoga* (*aṣṭāṅga yoga*): *yama* (self-control), *niyama* (control of the organs), *āsana* (posture), *prāṇāyāma* (breath control), *pratyāhāra* (withdrawal of the organs), *dhārana* (concentrating the mind), *dhyāna* (meditation) and *samādhi*.

255. धर्माधर्म विवर्जिता

Dharmādharma vivarjitā

She who is devoid of (who transcends) both virtue and vice.

According to Jaimini, *dharma* is action according to the *Vedas* and *adharma* is the opposite. This distinction does not apply to

Devī. *Samvarta Smṛti* also says that *dharma* is that conduct which is in accordance with the scriptures and tradition.

According to the *Nityahṛdaya Tantra*, *dharma* is bondage and *adharma* is Liberation. Often the implication of such statements appear contrary to the *śāstras*. Here *dharma* really means *karma*. According to the *Tantra*, Devī is one who has no bondage or Liberation.

Dharma is that which creates equality or happiness; *adharma* is that which creates inequality or sorrow. Devī is free of happiness and sorrow.

According to *mantraśāstra*, *dharma* stands for the sacred letter (*bīja*) for Śakti, and *adharma* that for Śiva. *Vivarjita* here means "greatly increased." Devī is one who imparts great power to the sacred syllables of Śiva and Śakti in *mantras*.

The word *dharma* comes from the root *dhṛ*, to carry, and *ma* meaning "great." Thus *dharma* is that which is carried by the great (according to *Matsya Purāṇa*).

According to Yājñavalkya, sacrifice, good conduct, self-control, non-injury (*ahimsa*), gift-giving and scriptural study all constitute *dharma*, but the supreme *dharma* is the realization of the Self.

Dharma and *adharma* apply to the unenlightened. Devī is beyond them.

256. विश्व रूपा

Viśva rūpā

She who has the whole universe as Her form.

In the *Devī Bhāgavatā*, Devī says, "I Myself am the universe, there is nothing different from Me." This and several succeeding *mantras* describe the different states of the *jīva* and *Īśvara*.

In the process of creation, the first to be manifested is *tamas* (darkness).

Subsequently, *mahat*, *ahaṅkāra* (ego) and the five great elements (*pañcamahābhūta*) emerged. At the same time there arose the five energies of knowledge (*jñānaśakti*) and the five energies of action (*kriyāśakti*). From the five energies of knowledge collectively the *antaḥkaraṇa* ("inner instruments," which manifests in the four forms of *manas*, *buddhi*, *ahaṅkāra* and *citta*) arose, and from each individually the five sense organs (*jñānendriyas*). Similarly, from the five energies of action collectively the *prāṇa* (vital air) arose and from each of these the five organs of action (*karmendriya*). From the five subtle elements arose the five gross elements.

In the waking state, the *jīva* acts, equipped with the five organs of knowledge, the five organs of action, *antaḥkaraṇa*, the five *prāṇas* (vital airs) and the gross body. This *jīva* who takes pride (*abhimāna*) in the gross body is known as *Viśva*.

257. जागरिणी

Jāgariṇī

She who is in the waking state, or She who assumes the form of the jīva *who is in the waking state.*

The waking state is the normal state of action. The *jīva's* pride in its gross body becomes evident in this state. The *jāgarī* (waking-state) *jīva* is that which manifests externally to all the senses and which is the same essence that inhabits and is dear to all beings. Devī is in the form of that *jīva*.

258. स्वपन्ती

Svapantī

She who is in the dream state or She who assumes the form of the jīva *in the dream state.*

Here, the dream state is the state in which the ideas and knowledge of things, which are latent in the mind, are manifested.

259. तैजसात्मिका

Taijasātmikā

She who is the soul of Taijasā.

Taijasā is the *jīva* in the dream state, proud of its subtle body.

Dreams occur in sleep; sleep is darkness to the external eye. But the inner self is the lustrous and glorious essence (*tejas*); and *taijasā* is that which pertains to *tejas*. This *mantra* (*taijasātmikā*) reinforces the idea that Devī is the embodiment of the inner essence.

260. सुप्ता

Suptā

She who is in the deep-sleep state or assumes the form of the jīva *experiencing deep sleep.*

Deep sleep is the state in which there is no power of discrimination. The experience in deep sleep is indeed "I know nothing." What remains afterwards is only the memory of "I knew nothing." There are three forms of *avidyā* (ignorance) in play here - ignorance, selfishness and love of pleasure or comfort. Ignorance creates the condition of "I knew nothing." Selfishness creates the experience, "I fell asleep." The experience "I slept comfortably" is created by the attachment to pleasure, a creation of *Māyā*.

The body which experiences the deep sleep state is the causal body.

261. प्राज्ञात्मिका

Prājñātmikā

She who is not separate from Prājña.

The *jīva* who is in the state of deep sleep is known as *prājña*. (See the commentary on *mantra* 256, *Viśvarūpā*.)

262. तुर्या

Turyā

She who is in the state of turya.

Devī is one who has assumed the fourth state known as *turya*.

This does not imply the process of going from one state or place to another. There is no state where the all-pervading, and therefore, motionless Devī does not exist. In that sense, She transcends the states of waking, dreaming and deep sleep.

Turya is the state in which the experience known as *śuddhavidya* is attained - the ultimate realization of the *Ātman*.

Śivasūtra talks about five states: waking, dream, deep sleep, *turya* and the state beyond *turya* (*turyātīta*). The *jīva* who is in the *turya* state is not affected by the experiences of the lower states. In *turya* the *jīva* exists just as a witness. But the ultimate union with Śiva occurs only in the fifth state, the state beyond *turya*.

In the deep sleep state the *jīva* acts through the causal body whereas in the *turya* state it acts through the conditioning known as *mahākāraṇa*, "the great causal body." Devī is called *Turyā* because She is not separate from the individual *jīva* or the aggregate of *jīvas* in that state.

Varadarāja says, "The supreme state of *turya* can only be described as a wonder. *Yogins* consider only this state as real." The concept of *turya* is one that astonishes modern psychology. The modern intellect retreats from the effort after talking about the conscious, subconscious and unconscious mind, whereas thousands of years ago, the *ṛṣis* of India declared the existence of the *turya* state which was attained by the *yogins*.

In a verse that reads as if written as a commentary on this *mantra*, Śaṅkara portrays Devī in *Saundarya Laharī* (verse 97) thus: "O Devī, You, who are the Supreme *Brahman*, are praised by the knowers of the *Vedas* as Sarasvatī, the wife of Brahmā, as Lakṣmī, the wife of Viṣṇu and as Pārvatī, the wife of Śiva. But You are Turyā, the state beyond their reach. As Mahāmāyā, the seat of powers that can be grasped only with the greatest effort, You whirl the universe around constantly."

In one interpretation, *Turīyā* is the name of a *śakti* and Devī is said to be indistinct from her.

Also, *Tripurasiddhānta* says that Devī blessed through Her *darśan* a certain *siddha* known as Turīyānandanātha, and thus She became famous as *Turīyā*.

263. सर्वावस्था विवर्जिता

Sarvāvasthā vivarjitā

She who transcends all states.

There is a fifth state beyond the *turya* state. It is enjoyed only by the *yogins* who have transcended *turya*. This state has no special name. One who has reached this state enjoys the condition described in the *Śruti* as "He is not born again."

The *yogin* who has reached the state beyond the *turya* is known as a *mahāyogin*. *Śivasūtra* describes the condition of such a man: "His entire life is worship, all his conversation is *japa*, and whatever he gives is the knowledge of *Brahman*." According to the *Yogasūtra*, "His soul revels in the state of non-differentiation (*nirvikalpa*); all truth is known to him." The *Śruti* says, "All his words become *mantras*, because his mind is pure." *Yogavāsiṣṭha* says, "Such great souls should always be approached because, even when they are not instructing, their conversation itself is instruction." His "every movement is a gesture of worship; even his prattle is *japa*." (*Saundarya Laharī* verse 27) And *Vārttika* explains: "Thus, the *yogin* who constantly abides in his own *Ātman*, always being equal to Śiva, is called a *mahāyogin*. He imparts the knowledge of the Self to his disciples." Since Devī is not distinct from such *yogins*, individually or in their aggregate, She is called, "One who transcends all states." This state is called "Turyātīta" ("beyond *turya*") in *Varivasyārahasya*.

Varadarāja, the great teacher of *Tantra*, says, "The seeker, through frequent abidance in the fourth state, reaches the state beyond, and becomes equal to Śiva who is the Soul of the universe and who is pure bliss."

The doctrine of the state beyond *turya* is an independent and original concept in *Tantra*. An obvious difference between *Advaita* (the doctrine of nonduality) and *Tantra* is that, while everything other than *Brahman* is false in *Advaita*, nothing is false in *Tantra*. The implication in *Tantra* is that the knot of each state does not break and cease to exist, but simply becomes loose and slips away. In *Śrīcakra* it is said, "The *ṛṣis* of the *Vedas* and the great teachers of *Tantra* affirm that partial truth need not be discarded in order to reach the full truth. There is no sense in attaining God by losing the world. The entire truth has to be realized. Partial truths must also be seen in the perspective of that realization. The *Parāśakti* (*Brahman*) in the central *bindu* does not negate the other deities in *Śrīcakra*." The fact that separate rules of worship are prescribed for these deities is proof of this non-negation.

In *mantras* 256-263, the five states of the *jīva* have been described. Now in the following *mantras* up to 274, the five states of *Īśvara* are discussed.

264. सृष्टि कर्त्री

Sṛṣṭi kartrī

She who is the Creator.

The creation of the entire universe is implied here. The creation, preservation and destruction of the universe are performed by Brahmā, Viṣṇu and Śiva representing the three *guṇas*. Śaṅkarācārya explains that the Trinity get the power to do their tasks from the resolve of Devī (*Saundarya Laharī* verse 24): "O Devī, Brahmā creates the world, Viṣṇu protects it, and Rudra destroys it. Īśvara merges these three in His own body and screens it from view. Taking the order that You give by the slightest movement of Your eyebrows, Sadāśiva creates them all again."

Creation is performed by Īśvara when the *guṇa* of *rajas* is ascendant.

265. ब्रह्म रूपा

Brahma rūpā

She who is in the form of Brahmā.

She who has assumed, for the purpose of creation, the form of Brahmā which is predominantly *rājasic* in nature. In the last *mantra* it was said that Devī is the one who gives orders even to Brahmā. In this *mantra*, it is made clear that Brahmā is none other than Devī.

266. गोप्त्री

Goptrī

She who protects.

This *mantra* means that Devī is also Viṣṇu in whom the *sāttvic* quality predominates. Preservation is the task of Īśvara when *sattva* predominates.

Goptrī is also one who hides. The Devī is the *Mahāmāyā* who hides the real essence of the universe and creates the illusion of myriad forms and names.

267. गोविन्द रूपिणी

Govinda rūpiṇī

She who has assumed the form of Govinda (Viṣṇu) for the preservation of the universe.

The word *go* has many meanings: cow (animal), earth, word, intelligence, ray. "Cow" signifies the *samsāra*-bound *jīva*. Such a *jīva* and the earth, words, intellect, rays of light are all Her manifestations. Taking the meaning "earth," She can be described as one who protects it (*vindana*). There is a celebrated story in the *Purāṇas* describing how the *asura* Hiranyākṣa stole the earth and how Viṣṇu recovered it in His incarnation as Varāha (the Boar). Devī is that protector of the earth (Govinda).

"Govinda" is also Bṛhaspati, the Guru of the *devas*. Devī is then attributed the position of the Guru of all the *devas*.

268. संहारिणी

Samhāriṇī

She who is the destroyer of the universe.

Īśvara, in the form in which the *tāmasic* quality predominates, is responsible for the destruction of the universe.

This *mantra* has also been written as "*Samdhāriṇi*" (bearer), but in the present context *Samhāriṇī* is more appropriate.

269. रुद्र रूपा

Rudra rūpā

She who has assumed the form of Rudra (Śiva) for the dissolution of the universe.

Rudra is the form of Īśvara in whom the *tāmasic* quality predominates. Rudra means "one who weeps." "He wept; therefore he is known as Rudra, the weeper." (*Taittiriya Samhita*) The torrential rain that comes at the dissolution of the universe is the flow of tears from Śiva's solar eye (Śiva's three eyes are the sun, the moon and fire).

Also, Rudra is one who drives away (*dra*) pain and sorrow (*ru*). Human life is subject to periodic pain and sorrow. As the flower blossoms when the sun rises, as the ocean becomes agitated when the moon rises, as leaves fall, flowers bloom and fruits ripen with the seasons, planetary revolutions create seasonal changes in human lives also. But Devī has the power to ward off their effects and protect Her devotees. In this way, Devī is *Rudrarūpiṇī*.

The names from *Sṛṣṭikartrī* to *Rudrarūpā* (mantras 264-269) are described in the *Devī Bhāgavata* as follows:

"She creates the universe according to Her will. She protects it. At the time of dissolution at the end of the epoch, She destroys it. Devī who causes illusion in the universe acts in all three ways. Brahmā, Viṣṇu and Śiva perform their tasks of creation, protection and destruction because of Her blessing. She has bound the entire universe with the bonds of "I and mine." The *yogins* who are free of attachments, who desire Liberation, worship Her alone, who is Śivā and the Mistress of the Universe."

270. तिरोधान करी

Tirodhāna karī

She who causes the disappearance of all things.

Tirodhāna is the complete destruction of everything, the dissolution of even the *tanmātras* (the minutest particles) into *prakṛti* (nature) as in the extinction of light causing complete darkness.

Bhāskararāya says that this aspect of Devī in which pure concentrated *sattva* predominates is called Īśvarī.

Also, the *śakti* called *Tiraskāriṇī* ("one who makes things disappear") is a form of Devī. The *Tripurāsiddhānta* says, "O fair-faced One, because You cause the disappearance of all but Your devotees, You are called *Tiraskāriṇī*."

She who has the power known as *tiraskāriṇīvidya*. This allows one to be invisible to others while being able to see everything clearly. No one is hidden from Devī, but no one sees Her true form. Hence the name *tiraskāriṇī* is very apt for Her. In *Mahābhārata* it is said that King Nala was able to enter the chamber of Damayanti without being observed because of this *tiraskāriṇi* power given to him by Indra.

271. ईश्वरी

Īśvarī

She who protects and rules everything.

Supreme individuality (*parāhantā*) is the quality of Īśvara. Lordship, doership, independence, being consciousness itself, all these are based on this quality. Īśvara and Īśvarī are the same, and all these descriptions apply to Devī.

Jīva is consciousness that is conditioned by mind or ego; Īśvara is consciousness conditioned by the universe. This *mantra* implies that Devī is consciousness as conditioned by the universe.

272. सदा शिवा

Sadā śivā

She who is Sadāśiva, one who always bestows auspiciousness.

Sadāśiva is Lord Śiva in whom superlative, pure *sattva* quality dominates. Devī is not separate from Him.

273. अनुग्रहदा

Anugrahadā

She who confers blessing.

Anugraha is the process in which, after complete dissolution, at the start of fresh creation, the primordial atoms manifest.

Also, *tirodhāna* and *anugraha* are interpreted respectively as bondage and Liberation. In this sense, Īśvara, who is fully manifested externally, causes bondage and Sadāśiva, who is manifested internally, causes Liberation. Īśvara generates ego and the sense of possession in *jīvas* causing bondage, but Sadāśiva, in His infinite compassion gives them Liberation. Īśvara is the one who creates awareness of the world and makes the inner self manifest in the external world. Sadāśiva is the one who dissolves this sense of the external world back into the inner awareness and gives Liberation.

274. पञ्च कृत्य परायणा

Pañca kṛtya parāyaṇā

She who is devoted to the five functions (mentioned in the mantras *above).*

The five functions are creation, preservation, destruction, annihilation (*tirodhāna*), and causing the reappearance (*anugraha*) of the universe.

Books such as *Mṛgendrasamhita* and *Pratyabhijñāhṛdaya* discuss these five functions in detail. According to the *Brahmasūtra*, Īśvara has the three functions of creation, preservation and destruction. But in the tradition of *Śaivadvaita*, the five functions mentioned above are described. Parāśakti, who is identical with Supreme Śiva, as Brahmā performs creation, as Viṣṇu preservation and as Rudra destruction, as Īśvara dissolution and as Sadāśiva the blessing of re-creation. In the *Vaiṣṇava* tradition, these functions are performed by the corresponding manifestations, Vāsudeva, Saṅkarṣana, Aniruddha, Pradyumna and Nārāyaṇa.

275. भानु मण्डल मध्यस्था

Bhānu maṇḍala madhyasthā

She who abides at the center of the sun's disc.

At dusk, Devī should be meditated upon as residing at the center of the solar disc. The *Kūrma Purāṇa* says, "I bow down to the Maheśvara who resides in the solar disc, who is the essence of the *Vedas*, the object of all knowledge, who fills the universe with His brilliance, and who is the cause of the three worlds."

Bhānumaṇḍala, the solar disc, is the lotus in the *anāhata cakra* in the heart. Devī resides there.

276. भैरवी

Bhairavī

She who is the wife of Bhairava (Śiva).

Bhairava is the Śiva who is engaged in the dance of bliss in the cremation grounds.

According to Dhaumya, a girl of twelve years is known as *bhīru*; Devī in the form of such a girl is called Bhairavi.

Bhairavi is the name of a *mantra* (which is obtained by removing the middle "ra" syllable from the *tripuracakreśvarī mantra*). Devī is in the form of that *mantra*.

277. भगमालिनी

Bhagamālinī

She who wears a garland made of the six excellences.

Bhaga means the six attributes of excellence: auspiciousness, supremacy, fame, valor, detachment and knowledge. This list differs according to the source. Another list, for example, gives supremacy, righteousness, fame, prosperity, knowledge and wisdom as the six attributes. As the Ācārya says, "The science of logic is inconclusive. The *Vedas* differ from each other; there is not a single sage whose word is authority. The essence of *dharma* is hidden in the cave of the heart. Great souls reach the good path by it."

There are many meanings in the dictionaries for the word *bhaga*: sovereignty, fame, justice, accomplishment of desire, wisdom, greatness, humility, effort, the womb, worldly concerns, peace. All these are contained in Devī like flowers in a garland.

Wherever *liṅgas* (male emblems) are installed, they are Śiva's glories, and wherever there are *yonis* (female emblems) they are Devī's glories. *Liṅgas* installed for Siva's worship are usually in the form of a combination of the two. All masculine words are, in fact, to be regarded as Śiva's glories and all female words are Devī's glories.

Bhaga means "word." *Bhagamāla* thus becomes a garland of words, a garland of hymns. Devī is thus one who is worshipped by a garland of praise.

278. पद्मासना

Padmāsanā

She who is seated in the lotus flower.

Also, one who is in the form of *Brahman*. Here, *padma* (lotus) is to be understood symbolically. The petals of the lotus are *prakṛti* (nature), the filaments are conditions of time and place, the stalk is knowledge and the stamen is *vāsanā*. Devī has made such a lotus Her seat.

Devī is *Padmāsana*, one who is seated in the lotus and also one who is meditated upon by devotees seated in the lotus posture. In the *Tāntric* sense, *padma* is *bindu*, *vyūha* or *nidhi*. Devī is one who is seated in any of these.

Another definition is "She who distributes prosperity or wealth among Her devotees (*Padma*, Lakṣmī, the goddess of wealth and *san*, to distribute)." "O benevolent Mother, whoever receives Your grace enjoys supreme bliss. He gets a beautiful wife, a house decorated with gold, and other luxuries. But when he displeases You, all his prosperity is lost, his wife deserts him and he becomes supremely unhappy." (Bhāskararāya)

Or, *Padmāsana* is the slayer ("*as*", to kill) of the demon Padmāsura, according to Bhāskararāya.

279. भगवती

Bhagavatī

She who protects those who worship Her.

According to the *Devī Bhāgavata*, *Bhagavatī* is one who knows the origin and dissolution of beings, their comings and goings, knowledge and ignorance. The *Śaktirahasya* says, "The word *bhaga* comes from the root *bhaj*, to worship and *avati*, to protect. Devī is called *Bhagavatī*, as She is worshipped by all the *devas* and She blesses them."

280. पद्म नाभ सहोदरी

Padma nābha sahodarī

She who is Viṣṇu's sister.

The story of Māyādevi who took birth in the womb of Yaśoda to protect Kṛṣṇa, born to Devaki, is well-known from the *Purāṇas*. By taking Kṛṣṇa's place, She rescued him from being killed by Kamsa. Slipping away from Kamsa's hands, She rose up in the sky and disappeared.

In *Kūrma Purāṇa* and in *Ratnatraya Parīkṣā* by Appayya Dīkṣitar, we find the following description: The one *Brahman* divided and took two separate forms; one as attributes (*dharma*) and the other as possessor of attributes (*dharmi*). The *dharma* further divided into male and female forms. The male form, Viṣṇu, is the material cause of the universe. The female form became the spouse of Paramaśiva. In short, Śiva, Viṣṇu and Devī together are *Brahman*.

The sounds *ma*, *ha* and *ra* of this *mantra* are the *bījākṣaras* (seed syllables) of the the first part (*vāgbhava kuṭa*) of the fifteen syllabled (*pañcadaśi*) *mantra*. *Bījākṣaras* are like an electric current. The same current, flowing through different instruments, gives rise to sound and light and can also become the protector and the destroyer.

Similarly, following the will of the worshipper, the *bījākṣaras* exhibit different powers. The present *mantra*, as it contains the *bījākṣaras* of the *vāgbhava kuṭa mantra*, suggests that Devī is the embodiment of that *mantra* (see *mantra* 85).

281. उन्मेष निमिषोत्पन्न विपन्न भुवनावलिः

Unmeṣa nimiṣotpanna vipanna bhuvanāvaliḥ

She who causes a series of worlds to arise and disappear with the opening and closing of Her eyes.

When Devī opens Her eyes, the universe is created; when She closes Her eyes, it is destroyed. Just by Her will, She performs creation and destruction with the simple blinking of Her eyes. It is a *līlā*, a sport for Her; no effort is involved.

As *Ājñāvatāra* says, "By Her mere wish, the entire universe appears and disappears." Kālidāsa also praises Her thus: "Before You think of creation, this universe consisting of the seer, the seen and seeing exists in You in its entirety; when You open Your eyes at will, the universe appears and when You close Your eyes, it disappears."

Śrī Śaṅkara introduces the same idea in *Saundarya Laharī* (verse 55): "O Daughter of the King of the Mountains, the sages say that the blinking of Your eyes causes the cosmos to be born and to be dissolved. I believe that You now remain awake without closing Your eyes to protect this world, which was created when You opened Your eyes."

282. सहस्र शीर्ष वदना

Sahasra śīrṣa vadanā

She who has a thousand heads and faces.

The *Puruṣa Sūkta* says, "The cosmic man (*puruṣa*) has a thousand heads, a thousand eyes and a thousand feet." The *Gītā* (XIII - 13) describes the Supreme: "He exists in the world enveloping all, with hands and feet everywhere, with eyes, heads and mouths everywhere, with ears everywhere." The *Devī Bhāgavata* describes the cosmic form of Devī: "The Devī is effulgent with a thousand eyes, a thousand hands, a thousand heads and a thousand feet."

The word "thousand" is employed to indicate "countless." Devī's body is the universe. Everything in the universe is a limb or a part of Her body.

The *ṛṣis* imagined that Ādiśesha (Ananta), the thousand-headed serpent, supported the earth. Ananta is the symbol for the power of countless faces - an attractive power. It is that power which keeps the celestial bodies revolving in their paths without crashing into each other. This fact is symbolized by the picture of Ananta, the serpent, supporting the earth on his hooded head. The force of attraction was known in India even in *Vedic* times. Proof of this is given in later works like *Āryabhaṭīya*. Varāhamihira gives the illustration that the earth is suspended in a cage formed by the stars in the same way a ball of iron would be suspended in the center of a cage made of magnets. Thus they had seen that the stability of the solar system was based on the force of mutual attraction.

283. सहस्राक्षी

Sahasrākṣī

She who has a thousand eyes.

Anything that shines in the universe is one of Devī's eyes. Thus there are countless eyes. In the same way, it is in reference to their luminous nature that the sun, moon and fire are referred to as Devī's eyes and so She is called *Trinayanā* (She who has three eyes).

284. सहस्र पाद्

Sahasra pād

She who has a thousand feet.

Anything that moves is one of Her feet.

The middle and last *kuṭas* of the *Pañcadaśi* are contained in *mantras* 281-284 according to *Tantra*. Thus these *mantras* signify that Devī is in the form of these two *kuṭas*.

285. आब्रह्म कीट जननी

Ābrahma kīṭa jananī

She who is the mother of everything from Brahmā to the lowliest insect.

286. वर्णाश्रम विधायिनी

Varṇāśrama vidhāyinī

She who established the order of the social division in life.

Varṇas are the divisions of society: *brāhmaṇas*, *kṣatriyas*, *vaiśyas* and *śūdras*.

Brāhmaṇas are those in whom only *sāttvic* qualities are present. They have praiseworthy qualities like truthfulness, not stealing, not acquiring or accepting wealth, and they engage in the study of the scriptures. They live by the power of their intellect. They are teachers or priests.

Those in whom *rājasic* qualities predominate over *sāttvic* ones are *kṣatriyas* - warriors. Truth, *dharma*, anger towards injustice - these are their qualities. They lead in battle. Might is important to them, as they are rulers and warriors. That which controls their might is their intellect.

Those in whom *rājasic* qualities predominate over *tāmasic* ones are *vaiśyas*. They are diligent, skillful, and enterprising. They are merchants and industrialists, known to occasionally employ a bit of deceit to aid in their pursuits. They hold the stomach and the heart as important.

Those in whom *tamas* predominates are *śūdras*. Having less intelligence, they encounter many dangers, and are thus used to misery. They do not have any special attachment to truth and *dharma*. They are satisfied with performing menial tasks.

Taking the *Virāṭ Puruṣa* as society, the above four types of individuals were pictured as his head, hands, the trunk of his body including chest, abdomen and waist, and his feet. This division into four groups is based solely on the *guṇas*.

Four stages (*āśramas*) are prescribed in life: those of *brahmacarya*, *grahastha*, *vānaprastha* and *sannyāsa*. A vision of the completeness of life underlies this order.

The *brahmacāri* is the adolescent who should be engaged solely in studies. If he indulges in pleasures of the senses or in agitations, he ruins his own life without knowing it. He forgets the meaning and goal of life. His future will not contain a contented life, lofty in ideals.

An uncontrolled life as a youthful householder will cause premature aging and even an untimely end. On the other hand, one who spends his youthful years wisely can later entrust the burdens of the family with his children and spend his time helping them and others, thus enriching his own life. That is *vānaprastha*. One feels pity seeing old men struggling day and night to acquire more riches and status. The poet must have had such men in mind when he wrote, "Alas, you poor black bee, not only do you fall into the flame, but you put out the lamp, too!"

Amma sings, " Always remember, O mind, this supreme truth: there is none that is your own!" *Sannyāsa* is leading one's life mindful of the truth of this saying.

Such a classification of the stages of life was not impractical. That is why these injunctions are known as *Sanātana Dharma*, the Eternal Code of Life.

287. निजाज्ञा रूप निगमा

Nijājñā rūpa nigamā

She whose commands take the form of the Vedas.

Nigamas are *Vedas* and the *Tantras* which are in accordance with the *Vedas*.

Devī says in the *Kurma Purāṇa*, "At the beginning of creation, the supreme and ancient Śakti, according to My command, manifested in the form of the *Vedas*: *Ṛg*, *Yajus* and *Sāma*."

It is well-known that the twenty-eight *Tantras* which follow the *Vedas* emerged from the mouth of Śiva in accordance with Devī's commands. Five of these *Tantras*, starting with *Kāmika*, came from the face of Śiva known as *Sadyojāta*; five, starting with *Dīpta*, emerged from the *Vāmadeva* face; five starting with *Vijaya* emerged from the *Aghora* face; five starting with *Vairocana* emerged from the *Tatpuruṣa* face; and eight starting with *Prodgītā* emerged from the *Īśāna* face of Śiva, as explained by Bhāskararāya.These twenty-eight *Tantras* form what is known as the upward current.

There are also *Tantras* like *Kāpāla* and *Bhairava* which arose from the lower power of Śiva and are opposed to the *Vedas*.

288. पुण्यापुण्य फल प्रदा

Puṇyāpuṇya phala pradā

She who dispenses the fruits of both good and evil actions.

The fruit of *puṇya* (good deeds) is happiness; the result of *apuṇya* (evil deeds) is sorrow.

A basic factor in the systems of philosophy of India is *karma*. No one is free from the effects of *karma*. The only way to be free is to completely relinquish the desire for the fruits of one's actions. This is the message of the Gītā. In the commentary to the *Brahmasūtras*, Śaṅkara explains repeatedly that rituals, such as *yāgas*, are not a path to Liberation, since there is a desire for heaven or reward behind them.

Those who desire Liberation (*mokṣa*) are very rare in society. Most people eagerly run after material things. There are many who cry out Devī's name in the middle of this pursuit, yet everyone has to bear the fruits of *karma*.

"The Lord makes one who is immersed in worldly *karma* bear its fruits strictly according to the rules. The real devotee gets away lightly. The *brāhmaṇa's* wife takes a child as a companion in her walk to the temple. When she takes someone else's child, she makes him walk all the way. But when she takes her own child for company, she will carry him in her arms and play with him most of the way; she will make him walk only when someone is watching! A *karmi* - one who is immersed in worldly actions - is the slave of those actions. A devotee is a slave of *karma* only in the eyes of the world; in reality, he is the Lord's darling child." (Oṭṭūr Unni Nambūdiripaḍ)

A mother punishes her erring child not out of spite, but for its own good. "Even someone who slips on the ground and falls, has to fall on that same ground. Likewise, O Devī, even for someone who errs against You, the real refuge is only You!" This is the sense in which Devī is called "the dispenser of the fruits of good and evil deeds." We must gain the insight that even our bitter experiences flow from Her compassion.

Amma says, "When someone steps on a thorn, he becomes upset. But there is a ditch just beyond and the thorn saved him from breaking his leg by falling into the ditch. Because of the thorn in his foot, he took his steps carefully, so he did not fall into the ditch. A devotee must see unhappy experiences in this light."

289. श्रुति सीमन्त सिन्दूरी कृत पादाब्ज धूलिका

Śruti sīmanta sindūrī kṛta pādābja dhūlikā

She is the one the dust from whose feet forms the vermillion marks at the parting line of the hair of the Śruti devatās *(Vedas personified as goddesses).*

The sacred dust from the lotus feet of Devī becomes the decoration on the forehead of the *Vedas*. How is that? It has been explained that Devī is the origin of the *Vedas*. The *Vedas* prostrate before Devī who is their mother. At that time, the dust from Her lotus feet smears on the hair of these auspicious goddesses. Thus they become even holier.

Bhāskararāya interprets this *mantra* as follows: The *Vedas* are incapable of describing the true form of Devī properly. *Śivastava* says, "O Parameśvara, the scriptures which are the seat of all knowledge and are very dear to You, are unable to describe You adequately and fall silent like women silent from bashfulness. If even they can describe You only by saying, "Not this, not this," how can a mere mortal like myself do it properly?"

Bhāskararāya quotes from *Rudrayāmala*: "The place reached by the *Vedas* is reached also by the *Tantras*. Hence, *brāhmaṇas*, *kṣatriyas*, *vaiśyas* and *śudras* are all fit to worship it." This makes it clear that all four *varṇas* are fit to worship Her through *Tantra*.

290. सकलागम संदोह शुक्ति सम्पुट मौक्तिका

Sakalāgama sandoha śukti sampuṭa mauktikā

She who is the pearl enclosed in the shell made of all the scriptures.

If the scriptures collectively form a shell, Devī is the pearl inside that shell. From the size of the shell one can perhaps guess the size of the pearl, but cannot gauge its quality and greatness. Similarly, one can only approximate the form of Devī through the *Vedas* but cannot arrive at Her real nature. As the *Kaṭha Upaniṣad* (I-ii-23) says, "This *Ātman* cannot be attained by the study of the *Vedas*, nor by intelligence, nor by much hearing." Then how is it to be reached? "Whoever is chosen by the *Ātman*, to him alone is its real nature revealed." This *Upaniṣadic* statement reveals the true meaning of this *mantra.* As Amma says, "Looking for Truth outside is like drying up the ocean to catch fish. One should look deep within. Only then will Truth be revealed."

The way in which the *Vedas* describe ultimate reality may be likened to "*arundhati nyāya.*" *Arundhati* is a little star and can be pointed out only with the help of the larger stars nearby. Similarly, the *Vedas* can only give some indications as to the form of Ultimate Reality. The *Vedas* are like Devī's jewelry; they are not Her true form.

291. पुरुषार्थ प्रदा

Puruṣārtha pradā

She who grants the (four-fold) objects of human life.

These objects are *dharma* (morality), *artha* (wealth), *kāma* (desire) and *mokṣa* (Liberation).

The *Brahmāṇḍa Purāṇa* says, "Those who worship the Supreme Śakti, whether or not following the rules, are no longer in *samsāra*; they are, no doubt, liberated souls." Worshipping Her feet is the means for liberation from *samsāra*, for prosperity and for peace in this worldly life.

This *mantra* has a different meaning in the *Tantra. Puruṣa* is Śiva and *artha* is Liberation. Devī is one who gives Liberation even to Śiva. *Saundarya Laharī* begins by saying that Śiva is only able to move because of association with Śakti: "When Śiva joins You, O Śakti, He is able to engage in His cosmic tasks; otherwise He cannot even move about!" Thus Devī is the one who liberates Śiva from a virtually lifeless state.

292. पूर्णा

Pūrṇā

She who is always whole, without growth or decay.

As the *Śruti* says, "*Pūrṇamadaḥ pūrṇamidam purṇāt pūrṇamudacyate; pūrṇasya pūrṇamādāya pūrṇamevāvaśiṣyate*" (The whole is all That. The Whole is all This. The Whole was born of the Whole. Taking the Whole away from the Whole, what remains is the Whole).

This wholeness or completeness of the divine power is evident to us in nature. A child born of its mother is whole in itself. The seedling sprouting from the seed grows to the fullness contained in the seed, and gives rise to countless new whole seeds. The calf grows to be as whole as the cow, yet it does not make the other less than whole.

If this is the condition of things in the physical world, what needs to be said about the Parāśakti, governing the universe? The cause is whole and the universe, the effect born of the cause, is also whole. Here, cause and effect are not different from each other, according to the sages.

Pūrṇa is the deity of the fifth, tenth and fifteenth day of the lunar half-month. The deity of the fourteenth night of the bright half of the lunar month is also *Pūrṇa*. All these deities are forms of Devī.

Pūrṇa is the name of a river which is also another form of Devī.

293. भोगिनी

Bhoginī

She who is the enjoyer.

Devī is one who enjoys, through all the life forms, everything there is to be enjoyed.

She is also *bhoginī* in the sense of one who consumes (*bhuj*) everything in the universe.

Bhoga also means the hood of a serpent; in this sense, She is one who has taken the form of a serpent maiden.

294. भुवनेश्वरी

Bhuvaneśvarī

She who is the ruler of the universe.

Devī is the protector of all fourteen worlds (*bhuvana*). *Bhuvana* is also water. Thus, Devī is the protector of the land and the oceans.

In *mantraśāstra*, Bhuvaneśvarī is one who is in the form of the *bīja* (seed), *hrīm*. This *bīja* contains all the worlds. Devī is *Bhuvaneśvarī* also because She is worshipped in all the worlds.

Tripurāsiddhānta recounts that Devī gave Her blessings to a guru known as Bhuvanānandanātha and that She is called *Bhuvaneśvarī* because of this.

295. अम्बिका

Ambikā

She who is the mother of the universe.

Ambikā is Sarasvatī, the earth, and the embodiment of the *śaktis* of *icchā*, *jñāna* and *kriyā*, the powers of will, knowledge and action (see *mantra* 658).

Ambikā also means night or sleep. *Māyā* (illusion) also has the synonyms *rātri* (night) and *nidra* (sleep). The *Gītā* (II-69) says, "What is night to all beings, in that the self-controlled man keeps awake; where all beings are awake, that is night for the sage who sees." Clearly that night is the darkness created by *Māyā*, and the self-controlled man is awake when others are enveloped by the darkness of ignorance. Thus, sleep and night connote the nature of *Māyā*. *Ambikā* is thus the embodiment of *Māyā*. "Night is the great Devī and day is Lord Śiva," according to the *śāstras*.

296. अनादि निधना

Anādi nidhanā

She who has neither beginning nor end.

Nidhana means death. According to the system of *Vararuci* (representing numbers by letters), *ādi* stands for the number eighty. The *mantra* then means that Devī delivers one from eighty causes of death. Man is mortal; he turns to the worship of Devī to become immortal.

Of the eighty causes of death, twenty-eight are called *vadha* (killing) and the rest are called *pāśa* (bondage, rope). Thus, the *Viṣṇu Purāṇa* says, "Egoism and self-conceit are of the nature of *vadha* and are of twenty-eight kinds." According to the *Liṅga Purāṇa*, "The fifty-two *pāśas* arise from the knot of *avidyā*, ignorance." Devī protects Her devotees from both kinds of harm. The sole refuge of fearless worshippers residing in the forests infested with cruel animals is their unshaken faith in the divine will.

297. हरि ब्रह्मेन्द्र सेविता

Hari brahmendra sevitā

She who is attended by Brahmā, Viṣṇu and Indra.

The *Śrīcakra* is pictured as a city. Between the fourteenth and the fifteenth walls of the city, Indra and the other guardians of the worlds reside. Between the fifteenth and the sixteenth walls is the abode of Viṣṇu. Between the sixteenth and the seventeenth walls lives Brahmā. Each of them worships Devī from His place.

In addition to these divinities, Varuṇa, Yama, Vāyu, Agni and Kubera also worship Devī. Rather than worshipping all these who themselves are under Devī's control, it is advisable to worship Her directly.

298. नारायणी

Nārāyaṇī

She who is the female counterpart of Nārāyaṇa.

Nāra is water and *ayana* is abode. *Nārāyaṇī* is one whose abode is water.

Nārāyaṇī also means the sister of Viṣṇu (see *mantra* 280). Devī is also considered to be identical to Lakṣmī, Sarasvatī and Pārvatī depending on the context.

Nāra is also the knowledge of the Self. *Nārāyaṇī* is thus the seat of Self-Knowledge - She who is established in the knowledge of the Self. Here there is no distinction between the support (*ādhāra*) and the supported (*ādheya*) - both are Devī Herself. *Nārāyaṇī* is one who resides in *nāra* and creates both men (*nāra)* and women. She is also Devī who is in the form of Viṣṇu (Nārāyaṇa).

299. नाद रूपा

Nāda rūpā

She who is in the form of sound.

According to *Tantraśāstra*, there are eight notes (*varṇas*) above the *bindu* of the *bīja* syllables such as *hrīm*. They are *ardhacandra, rodhinī, nāda, nādānta, śakti, vyāpikā, samānā* and *unmanī.*

Śrī Nārāyaṇa Guru starts his *Kalikanātaka* thus: "Salutations to You who are the essence of the *nādabindu*, who has no end, whose holy feet are worshipped by Nārada and other sages!"

The first motion in the universe arose as sound, or *praṇava*, the syllable OM. Devī is indeed the embodiment of OM.

"Her worshippers should meditate on Devī seated on *nāda* which is effulgent like a thousand suns, resembles the filament of the lotus, surrounded by innumerable cities and is situated above *rodhinī*," according to *Mahāsvacchanda Tantra.*

300. नाम रूप विवर्जिता

Nāma rūpa vivarjitā

She who has no name or form.

There are five aspects of the universe: existence (*sat*), knowledge (*cit*), bliss (*ānanda*), name (*nāma*) and form (*rūpa*). Of these, the first three (*sat-cit-ānanda*) are *Brahman* and the other two are the physical world.

There is a seeming contradiction in describing Devī as having no form after calling Her *Nādarūpa*, one who is in the form of sound. There is really no contradiction. For anything that is perceived by our senses, name and form are unavoidable. All things seen in the universe have names and forms as they are explicit manifestations of *Brahman*; but the essence of that Supreme Existence is without name or form. When manifested (*vyākṛta*), Devī is of the form of sound (*Nādarupa*) and when unmanifested (*avyākṛta*), She is formless and nameless.

As Bhāskararāya points out, "Whatever remains after name and form is eliminated, that is knowledge, that is *Brahman*."

Whatever name is used or whatever form is described, it will not reveal Devī's name or form totally. Ultimate Reality is referred to as that which is not revealed to words (*vācām agocaram*).

With mantra 300, the fourth *kalā* of the sun called *marīchi* is complete.

301. ह्रींकारी

Hrīmkārī

She who is in the form of the syllable hrīm.

Hrīm is the *bijākṣara* (seed syllable) known as *bhuvaneśvarī*. According to *Tantra*, the sounds "h", "r", "i" when accompanied by "m" denote creation, preservation and dissolution. Thus, *hrīm* is the *mantra* that represents the power of Devī who is the personification of the functions of creation, preservation and dissolution.

In another interpretation, *hrīm* is "shame." Devī is one who creates a sense of shame in sinful acts. The sense of shame urges man to desist from such acts. If this sense is gone, there will not be any hesitation in performing actions however reprehensible. Since Devī saves us from this fate, She is the *hrīmkārī*.

302. ह्रीमती

Hrīmatī

She who is endowed with modesty.

The implication is that Devī does not appear easily in front of Her devotees. Modesty is the sign of nobility; it is an ornament of feminine nature. Modesty is a cover of protection given to women by nature. Devī is endowed with that.

303. हृद्या

Hṛdyā

She who abides in the heart.

Devī is one who settles amiably in the heart of Her devotee. She has no special abode. Her devotee's heart is, indeed, Her abode. There is no doubt that Devī dwells in the heart of both friend and foe. She shines in the hearts of even Her foes, albeit in a sense of enmity. The devotion of a foe is called *virodhabhakti* (devotion through enmity).

Also, She is delightful, one who gives delight to everyone.

304. हेयोपादेय वर्जिता

Heyopādeya varjitā

She who has nothing to reject or accept.

Nothing is prescribed or forbidden for Her: nothing is to be accepted or rejected.

The injunctions and prohibitions indicated in the scriptures do not apply to those who know the Truth. Since everything in the universe is the play of the Ultimate Truth, what is forbidden to a Realized one? What is to be accepted? Devī is always in such a state.

305. राज राजार्चिता

Rāja rājārcitā

She who is worshipped by the King of kings.

The King of kings refers to Manu or Kubera. Manu was the first king of humankind who had the power of discrimination. Devī has been worshipped from the time man became a thinking being.

Kubera is the Master of wealth according to the *Purāṇas*. When wealth increases, there is a tendency to drift away from God. Only those who have accrued merit through good deeds can get closer to the Lord, though worldly wealth increases.

306. राज्ञी

Rājñī

She who is the queen of Śiva, the Lord of all kings.

She is the queen because the sovereignty of the worlds rests in Her. Devī's uniqueness, commanding power, sovereignty and universal venerability are all revealed in this name.

307. रम्या

Ramyā

She who gives delight; She who is lovely.

Devī's presence gives much joy and energy to Her devotees' hearts.

Incomparable is the beauty of Her form from head to toe, resplendent with all Her ornaments.

308. राजीव लोचना

Rājīva locanā

She whose eyes are like rājīva.

Rājīva means lotus, deer and fish. Thus Her eyes are long and open like lotus petals, tremulous like those of a deer, or glowing like those of a fish.

She is capable of giving Liberation to Her devotees through Her glance, just as a fish hatches its eggs by looking at them.

Devī's form, with the most captivating eyes, melts the devotees' hearts in love.

309. रञ्जनी

Rañjanī

She who delights the mind.

She who creates a sense of unity by bringing together Her devotees' hearts. All questions of social status and position vanish in front of devotion. Only devotion is capable of merging hearts in this manner.

Rañjanī also means dyeing or coloring. Bhāskarāraya says that Devī is *Rañjanī* because She colors the pure Paramaśiva by Her presence just as a red (hibiscus) flower colors a clear crystal.

310. रमणी

Ramaṇī

She who gives joy.

She is the one who melted the heart of Śiva who had cut all bonds and had become established in *yoga*. Similarly, She delights the hearts of Her devotees and deserves to be praised as *Ramaṇī* by all.

311. रस्या

Rasyā

She who is to be enjoyed; she who enjoys.

The *Śruti* says, "He alone is the essence." That essence is the bliss of *Brahman*. Devī is one who revels constantly in that bliss. Simultaneously, She creates this enjoyment in Her devotees.

312. रणत् किङ्किणि मेखला

Raṇat kiṅkiṇi mekhalā

She who wears a girdle of tinkling bells.

Devī wears the girdle over Her garment. In the verse of invocation, Devī is described as "decorated with all the ornaments (*sarvālaṅkārayuktā*)."

313. रमा

Ramā

She who has become Lakṣmī and Sarasvatī.

Devī is both Sarasvatī, who loves knowledge, and Lakṣmī who loves to dance.

314. राकेन्दु वदना

Rākendu vadanā

She who has a delightful face like the full moon.

315. रति रूपा

Rati rūpā

She who is in the form of Rati, the wife of Kāma.

She who has taken a form which is pure joy and imparts the height of that bliss to everyone.

The *Gītā* (VII.11) says, "Of the strong, I am the strength devoid of passion and attachment; and in all beings, I am *kāma* (desire), that is unopposed to *dharma*, O Arjuna!"

316. रति प्रिया

Rati priyā

She who is fond of Rati; She who is served by Rati.

Śiva became angry at Kāma for obstructing His *tapas* and burned him in the fire from His third eye. The bereaved Rati, stricken with grief, lamented, crying out Devī's name. Devī felt love for Rati and with Her blessing, Rati won Kāma back. Thus Devī became dear to Rati and Rati to Her.

Rati is conjugal pleasure and is indispensable for the survival of the universe. Devī is favorably disposed to Rati for this reason.

317. रक्षा करी

Rakṣā karī

She who is the protector.

Devī is the protector of Her devotees.

Rakṣa means "holy ashes," hence She is also the destroyer, one who reduces the world to ashes. By reducing all the sins and afflictions of Her devotees through Her blessing, She, indeed, becomes the protector.

Lord Śiva decorates Himself with holy ashes. Thus, *Rakṣākari* also means Śiva's wife.

318. राक्षसघ्नी

Rākṣasaghnī

She who is the slayer of the entire race of demons.

There are two types of tendencies in humans, one leaning towards the divine and the other towards the demonic. The *Gītā* (IX.12) explains these two types. The demonic type is: "Of vain hopes, of vain actions, of vain knowledge, devoid of discrimination, partaking only of the delusive nature of *rākṣasas* and *āsuras*." They take pride in their vain abilities and are heartless. In such individuals the quality of *tamas* predominates and they negate God.

On the contrary, the divine type "partake of the nature of the *devas*, worship Me with their minds turned to none other, knowing Me as the imperishable source of all beings." Persons of the divine type will be constantly engaged in good actions.

Both types are found in nature. The *rākṣasic vāsanās* are destroyed by Devī's power.

319. रामा

Rāmā

She who gives delight.

Devī is one who creates delight in *yogins*.

Rāmā is also an epithet of Lakṣmī.

Rāmā means "woman." "Whatever is feminine in nature is Devī and whatever is masculine is Paramaśiva," says the *Liṅga Purāṇa*. The *Brahmavaivarta Purāṇa* echoes the same: "Whatever in the three worlds appears in female form, all that, O Devī, is Thy form." And the *Parāśarasmṛti* says, "When women are pleased, the gods are pleased. When women are angry, the gods are angry. When women are pleased, the family thrives. When they are dishonored, the family perishes."

320. रमण लम्पटा

Ramaṇa lampaṭā

She who is devoted to the Lord of Her heart, Lord Śiva.

The implication is that Devī instills and maintains unshaken love and devotion in each woman towards her husband.

321. काम्या

Kāmyā

She who is to be desired.

Devī is to be desired more than any form of divinity by those who seek Liberation.

Also Kāmya is the deity of the twelfth night of the dark lunar fortnight. Devī is in that form.

322. काम कला रूपा

Kāma kalā rūpā

She who is in the form of Kāmakalā.

In *Tantra*, there are three *bindus*: they represent *Īśvara*, the world and the *jīva*.

In our physical world, if we take away one from three, two remain. But in spiritual science, if we remove one out of three, only one remains. We have the object, a mirror that reflects the object and the reflection - the object is *Īśvara*, the mirror is the *jīva* and the reflection is the world. If we remove the mirror, the reflection also disappears and only the object remains.

The object is "*kāmabindu*" and the reflection is "*kalābindu*." The mirror is the *jīva*. We know the *jīva* as the *antaḥkaraṇa* - the ego. Thus we think of the *jīva* in the sense of "I."

The *bindus* are known respectively as *vāgbhavakūṭa*, *madhyakūṭa* and *śaktikūṭa* (see *mantras* 85-87). *Vāgbhavakūṭa* is to be taken as *kāmabindu* and *śaktikūṭa* as *kalābindu*.

Kāmabindu is the union of Śiva and Śakti. *Kalābindu* is its manifested form. *Kāma* is invisible and *kalā* is visible. The *mantra* "*Kāmakalārūpā*" includes both of these.

The physical universe survives because of the strength of *Kāma*. The attraction between male and female is contained in *Kāmakalā*. According to this *mantra*, Devī represents this aspect. *Kāmakalā* is the art of love. *Kāma* (desire), is one of the four *puruṣārthas*, objectives of life (see *mantra* 291). Marriage is the fulfillment of desire. Married life has the name "domestic sacrifice" (*gṛhamedha*). Marriage is a *yajña* (sacrifice), not just because it is performed with *agni* (fire) as a witness. The core of a *yajña* is sacrifice. Marriage is for practicing sacrifice, selflessness and not just for satisfying physical desire. This is where the real meaning of the statement, "Devī is the embodiment of *Kāmakalā*" is to be found. Mentally one has to evolve to a level which perceives that *kāma* is not just physical desire. In the poet's words, "Love is not body-bound."

323. कदम्ब कुसुम प्रिया

Kadamba kusuma priyā

She who is especially fond of Kadamba flowers.

324. कल्याणी

Kalyāṇī

She who bestows auspiciousness.

Kalyāṇī also means, "She who utters auspicious words."

325. जगतीकन्दा

Jagatīkandā

She who is the root of the whole world.

Kanda is root, seed and cloud. Devī is the root cause of the birth of the universe. She is a cloud that is beneficial to the world. She is also the one who provides food for the survival of the world through rainfall at regular intervals. "From rain arises food," as the *Śruti* reminds us.

Here, "cloud" may also refer to the cloud that comes at the end of the epoch (*kalpa*). Devī, in other words, is the one who causes the *pralaya*, the flood at the end of the age. She is the root cause of the universe, She is the food for its continued existence and She is the flood that dissolves it.

326. करुणा रस सागरा

Karuṇā rasa sāgarā

She who is the ocean of compassion.

The meditation verse (*dhyāna śloka*) calls Her "*Karuṇātaraṅgitākṣī*," one whose eyes reflect waves of compassion. She is a fountain of compassion that never dries up. There are many stories in the *Purāṇas* in which She speaks and acts with great kindness towards those who are helpless. She always shows sympathy at the time of need to those who worship Her and leads them with great kindness towards Liberation.

Amma often says, "In the old days, gurus used to initiate their disciples with a *mantra* and then advise them to chant the *Lalitā Sahasranāma* daily, because the compassionate Devī will carefully look after the welfare of Her devotee."

Kṛṣṇa will throw His devotees into the deep waters of sorrow and obstacles and will make them gasp for breath, though He will guard them from going under. The ever-compassionate Devī, however, will come running to the rescue of a devotee in trouble. That is why She is called "the ocean of compassion."

327. कलावती

Kalāvatī

She who is the embodiment of all arts.

The sixty-four forms of art are all Devī's limbs.

Kalā also means a part of the moon, a crescent. Devī is one who wears a crescent moon.

328. कलालापा

Kalālāpā

She who speaks musically and sweetly.

Devī is one who turns sweet speech into different art forms.

She is *Kalālāpā* also because Her devotees sing sweet hymns in Her praise.

Ka is *Brahman*, *lala* is saliva and *āpa* is one who is reached. Thus, She is one who enables Her devotees to reach *Brahman* as naturally as saliva flows in the mouth, according to Bhāskararāya.

329. कान्ता

Kāntā

She who is beautiful.

One who is very attractive to Her devotees.

Ka is *Brahman*, *anta* is final; thus this *mantra* means that Devī is decidedly the undivided *Brahman*.

Devī is in the form of *Kāntā*, the "daily deity" presiding over the eleventh night of the dark lunar fortnight.

330. कादम्बरी प्रिया

Kādambarī priyā

She who is fond of mead.

What is described here is not ordinary spirits, but the bliss of *Brahman*. Devī is one who is constantly immersed in bliss. *Kādambari* is also the name of a drink made from the kadamba flowers. Devī is fond of this drink.

Kādambari is a name of Sarasvatī who is dear to Devī.

331. वरदा

Varadā

She who grants boons generously.

She who grants boons to Brahmā, Viṣṇu and all Her devotees.

Vara also means exalted, highest. She gives all that is best to Her devotees. The best is *mokṣa* (Liberation). Devī is one who gives the highest boon, Liberation.

In *Saubhāgyabhāskara*, Bhāskararāya explains (quoting from *Devī Bhāgavata*) that from the root *vṛ* (to choose) comes the word *varada*, (the giver of what is chosen). Since Devī fulfills all the desires of the *devas* who seek Her boons, She is celebrated as *Varadā*, the bestower of what is chosen.

In *Saundarya Laharī* (verse 4), Śaṅkara says, "O Devī, while other divinities use their hands to protect their devotees from fear and to grant their wishes, You alone do not put on this act. After all, just Your feet are capable of protecting from fear, and granting more than we wish for."

It is said that the worship of Devī on *navami* (the ninth day of the lunar half-month) is especially beneficial. Not that Her worship on other days is without value, but *pūja* on *navami* will be especially fruitful. It is said that "This Devī is always to be worshipped with concentration on *navami;* She will, without doubt, become the bestower of boons on all the worlds."

332. वाम नयना

Vāma nayanā

She who has beautiful eyes.

Vāma means "beautiful" and *nayana* means "eye," that which leads and "shows proof." The *mantra* also means "She who shows evident proofs." *Vāma* also means left side. There is a "left path" (*vāmācāra*) for the worship of Devī. She is one who leads Her devotees to this path. She is also the "eye" of the *vāmācārin*, the devotee who follows this method of worship, and the one who leads them on the correct path.

Vāma also has the meaning, "the fruit of negligence" or the "fruit of *karma*." Negligence leads to sinful acts (implying negligence of goodness and truth). The one who leads us to its unavoidable fruit is also Devī Herself. She is at the root of both good and evil.

Vāsanās push men toward good and evil. *Vāsanās* are, in turn, related to one's *karma*. The question, "Which comes first, *vāsanā* or *karma*?" is the same as "Which comes first, the tree or the seed?" This leads to an endless inconclusive series of questions, an unclear state known as "*anāvastha*" (unsettled) in philosophy.

333. वारुणी मद विह्वला

Vāruṇī mada vihvalā

She who is intoxicated by vāruṇī.

Vāruṇī can be intoxicating liquor, the juice of grapes or of *soma* (an ambrosial drink). It is also the bliss of *Brahman*. She who is in that state of intoxication. Devī revels in the intoxicating bliss of the Supreme, forgetting the affairs of the universe.

The juice extracted from dates is called *vāruṇī* as it was dear to Varuṇa.

An alternative interpretation is obtained by splitting this name as *vāruṇīmat* + *avihvalā*. *Vāruṇīmat* is one who belongs to the region of Varuṇa, one who resides in the ocean, which in the present case means Ananta. *Avihvala* is one who is not perturbed. Just as the great serpent Ananta supports the world effortlessly, Devī supports and governs the universe easily and without anxiety. The *Viṣṇu Purāṇa* says, "Ādiśeṣa (Ananta) worships Devī with his great body." Bhāskararāya remarks that Ananta supports the universe without any fatigue, thanks to Devī's grace.

Another interpretation is one who has conquered the *vāruṇīnāḍī* and become unperturbed. According to *yogaśāstra*, *vāruṇīnāḍī* is a *nāḍī* (nerve) which is above, below and everywhere. Vāyu is its deity.

334. विश्वाधिका

Viśvādhikā

She who transcends the universe.

One who is beyond the thirty-six *tattvas* from earth to Śiva. Here, "transcending the universe" does not refer to the extent. It is meant in the sense of the power that supports countless solar systems. What is supported is contained in the support, in this case. Devī transcends the universe in the sense that She existed before the universe came into being.

335. वेदवेद्या

Vedavedyā

She who is known through the Vedas.

In *mantra* 57, Devī is described as residing in the *cintāmaṇi* (wish-fulfilling) mansion. There are four doors to this mansion. These are the four *Vedas*. Devī is said to be seen through these doors.

There are four *Vedas* (*Mahābhārata* is known as the fifth *Veda*). The eastern quarter belongs to the *Ṛgveda*, the south to *Yajurveda*, the north to *Sāmaveda* and the west to *Atharvaveda* according to the *Śruti*. (*Taittiriya Brāhmana*) The presiding deities of the *Vedas* are: *Śuddhavidya* and attendants, *Saundaryavidya* and attendants, *Turiyāmba* and attendants and *Lopāmudrā* and attendants for *Ṛg*, *Yajus*, *Sāma* and *Atharva Vedas* respectively.

336. विन्ध्याचल निवासिनी

Vindhyācala nivāsinī

She who resides in the Vindhya Mountains.

Devī Māhātmya recounts that in the period of Vaivasvata Manu, Devī incarnated as "Nanda" and slew the *asuras* Śumbha and Niśumbha in the Vindhya Mountains. After this, She took up residence on that mountain in accordance with the wish of the devotees.

337. विधात्री

Vidhātrī

She who creates and sustains this universe.

Also, She who is a special mother, because, unlike ordinary mothers, She immerses Her devotees in bliss out of Her overflowing maternal love and compassion.

Amma says, "Children, the mother who gave birth to you may look after you in this birth. Even that is rare these days. But Amma's aim is to lead you to the enjoyment of bliss in all your lives!"

Also, The wife of Vidhāta (Brahmā).

Dhātri is myrobalan (gooseberry); Devī is especially fond of this fruit.

338. वेद जननी

Veda janani

She who is the Mother of the Vedas.

The *Śruti* says that the *Vedas* are Brahmā's breath: "*Ṛgveda* and *Yajurveda* are the breath that came out of this great being."

Devī Purāṇa says, "The vowels and consonants of the *Vedas* arose from the *Kuṇḍalinī*, which is triangular in form; hence, She is remembered as the mother of the *Vedas*."

339. विष्णु माया

Viṣṇu māyā

She who is the illusory power of Viṣṇu.

Viṣṇu means "one who covers up the universe." In the *Gītā* (VII.14), Lord Kṛṣṇa says, "Verily, this Divine Illusion of Mine, made of the *guṇas*, is hard to surmount; those who take refuge in none other than Me cross over this illusion." And the *Kālika Purāṇa* says, "*Viṣṇumāyā* is that which makes everything manifested and unmanifested according to the *guṇas* of *sattva*, *rajas* and *tamas*."

Māyā is that which is not what it appears to be. It should not be thought of as that which does not exist.

Viṣṇumāyā can be interpreted as one who subjects even Viṣṇu to Her *Māyā*.

340. विलासिनी

Vilāsinī

She who is playful.

Vilāsa is the power of projection under *Māyā*. It is this power of Devī that conceals the real Truth and deludes the mind by projecting the visible universe of names and forms. "*Vilāsa* is Her power of projection," says Bhāskararāya.

Vilāsinī is She who resides in *vila*, which is the *Brahmarandhra* in the thousand-petaled lotus. Hiding in the *Brahmarandhra*, Devī merges with Sadāśiva and indulges in play. *Brahmarandhra* is the region in the crown where the *suṣumnā* ends. The soul of the *yogin* leaves the body by breaking through this. Devī dwells here, attended by *crores* of *Rudras*.

341. क्षेत्र स्वरूपा

Kṣetra svarūpā

She whose body is matter.

The thirty-six "categories" (*tattvas*) from earth to Śiva form Her body.

Liṅga Purāṇa regards Śiva as the knower of matter (*kṣetrajña*) and Devī as *kṣetra* (matter).

342. क्षेत्रेशी

Kṣetreśī

She who is the wife of Śiva, the Kṣetreśa (Lord of matter, of the body of all beings).

Or, She who is Herself the ruler of matter, of the body of all beings.

Ācarya Śaṅkara says in his *Daśasloki*, the ten-verse hymn: "I am neither earth nor water, nor fire, nor air, nor ether, nor sense organs, nor the aggregate of all these; for all these are transient, variable by nature, while the Self is that whose existence is proved by the unique experience of deep sleep. I am the one, auspicious and pure, that alone remains."

343. क्षेत्र क्षेत्रज्ञ पालिनी

Kṣetra kṣetrajña pālinī

She who is the protector of matter and the knower of matter, therefore the protector of body and soul.

This name is to be understood in conjunction with the previous two names.

In *Viṣṇustuti* we find the statement, "This body is known in the world as the 'field' (*kṣetra*)."

In the *Gītā* (XIII-1), Lord Kṛṣṇa says, "This body, O son of Kunti, is called the field (*kṣetra*) and he who knows it is called the knower of the field (*kṣetrajña*) by those who know them."

The *Liṅga Purāṇa* says, "The sages call the twenty-four *tattvas* by the name *kṣetra* and the *Puruṣa* (the enjoyer of the *kṣetra*) by the name, *kṣetrajña*." According to the *Sāṅkhya* system, there are twenty-five basic categories (*tattvas*) in all. Twenty-four *tattvas* are known as *kṣetra* and the *Puruṣa* is the twenty-fifth, the *kṣetrajña*. Adherents of the *Sāṅkhya* system are referred to as "knowers of twenty-five categories."

Also in the *Vāyu Purāṇa*, we find, "The unmanifested (*avyakta*) is known as *kṣetra* and the *Brahman* as *kṣetrajña*." And in the *Brahma Purāṇa*, "*Kṣetras* are the bodies; and the soul united with them, the enjoyer according to his pleasure, is the *kṣetrajña*."

Finally, in the *Manu Smṛti* it is said, "He who prompts the embodied souls to act is *kṣetrajña*, the one who performs the actions is *bhūtātman* (the self in the form of the elements) and the one who, through the body, enjoys pleasure and pain is *jīva*."

We know of "I" and "mine" on the basis of the body. But very few know that Truth is not the body, but the soul inhabiting the body. Devī is one who gives protection to both *kṣetra* and *kṣetrajña* (body and soul), even before the *jīva* has realized this principle.

344. क्षय वृद्धि विनिर्मुक्ता

Kṣaya vṛddhi vinirmuktā

She who is free from growth and decay.

All things in the universe are subject to the six forms of change: birth, existence, growth, transformation, decay and death. Devī is not touched by these six. This is explained in detail in the *Gītā* (II:23-24): "Him weapons cut not, Him fire burns not, and

Him water wets not; Him wind dries not. He cannot be cut, nor burned, nor wetted nor dried up. He is everlasting, all-pervading and eternal."

Devī who is the *Paramātman* is eternal and therefore has no growth or decay. As *Bṛhadāraṇyaka Upaniṣad* (IV.4.22) explains, this is the glory of the knower of *Brahman*. He does not grow or weaken due to action; he neither grows from good actions nor weakens from evil ones.

345. क्षेत्र पाल समर्चिता

Kṣetra pāla samarcitā

She who is worshipped by Kṣetrapāla.

The *devas* became anxious when Devī's wrath was not appeased after killing the demon Dāruka. They searched for a way to calm Her. Śiva took the form of an infant and, lying in front of Devī, started to cry aloud. Seeing the infant, Her anger ebbed away and She took the baby in Her arms and began to suckle it. The baby drank Her anger along with the milk. Devī calmed down. Śiva in the form of that infant is known as Kṣetrapāla. The *mantra* means that Devī is worshipped by this Kṣetrapāla.

Kṣetra is the body as explained above and Kṣetrapāla is the protector of the body, the *samsāra*-bound *jīva*. The *jīva* is the worshipper and Devī is worshipped by him.

Kṣetra means "the site of sacrificial ceremonies" such as *yāgas*, and also a temple. Devī is worshipped by the keepers (*pāla*) of these.

346. विजया

Vijayā

She who is ever-victorious.

Also, one with special knowledge.

Devī was named *Vijayā* after killing the *asura*, Padma.

In the science of architecture according to Viśvakarma, *Vijayā* is the name of an auspicious kind of building.

Vijayā is also the name of a deity in Kashmir, which is one of sixty-eight sacred places.

Also, *Vijayā* is the name of an auspicious hour. On the tenth day (*daśami*) of the bright fortnight in the month of *Āśvina* (September-October), the hour when the stars appear is known as the hour of *Vijayā* (*Vijayadaśami*). It falls between seven and nine p.m. This is an auspicious hour for all undertakings. Devī is Vijayā, since She is worshipped at this auspicious hour of *Vijayadaśami*.

347. विमला

Vimalā

She who is without a trace of impurity.

Vimalā is a sacred house. Viśvakarma has built ten kinds of sacred houses according to the *Purāṇas*: *Dhanya, Dhruva, Jaya, Manorama, Nanda, Nidhana, Sumukha, Vijaya, Vimalā* and *Vipula*.

According to the *Padma Purāṇa*, *Vimalā* is the deity at the holy place, Puruṣottama.

348. वन्द्या

Vandyā

She who is adorable, worthy of worship.

Devī is worthy of worship by all. The *Saundarya Laharī* indicates this by the description, "O Devī, Thou art worshipped by Viṣṇu, Śiva, Brahmā and others."

349. वन्दारु जन वत्सला

Vandāru jana vatsalā

She who is full of motherly love for those who worship Her.

350. वाग् वादिनी

Vāg vādinī

She who speaks.

She who gives Her devotees the ability to speak the appropriate words on any occasion.

What interest is shown towards a scholar who has no flair for speech? The gift of speech is a blessing, as is scholarship. It is obtained by the grace of Devī.

It has been mentioned that all vowels and consonants arose from Devī. The present *mantra* says that She is the one who makes the words, consisting of those sounds, arise on our tongues appropriately.

In *Laghustava*, Devī is praised thus: "As Thou alone art the origin of all the words, Thou art known in the world as *Vāgvādinī*."

Also, *Vāgvādinī* is the name of a deity who is none other than Devī.

351. वाम केशी

Vāma keśī

She who has beautiful hair.

Vāmakeśa is the Lord of Men, or Śiva (*Vāmaka*: man, *īśa*: lord).

Vāmakeśī is the wife of Śiva.

Also, Vāmakeśa is one of twenty-eight *Tantras*.

Vāmakeśī is the name of the deity of Jaṭa, one of sixty-eight holy places.

352. वह्नि मण्डल वासिनी

Vahni maṇḍala vāsinī

She who resides in the disc of fire.

Vahni means fire. *Vahnimaṇḍala*, the disc of fire, is said to be in the *mūlādhāra* or in the *paramākāśa*, the Supreme Ether.

There are three kinds of fire mentioned traditionally: the fire that burns in the funeral pyre, the fire in the sacrificial arena, and the fire in the home.

Vahnimaṇḍala is interpreted as three discs (according to Bhāskararāya); hence the *mantra* means "She who resides in the three *maṇḍalas* (discs)," those of sun, moon and fire. It has been mentioned that Devī presides over these three "discs" in the *Śrīcakra*: the *agnimaṇḍala* (disc of fire) in the *svādhiṣṭhāna*, the *sūryamaṇḍala* (disc of the sun) in the *anāhata* and the *candramaṇḍala* (disc of the moon) in the *sahasrāra* (see *mantras* 99, 240). Thus, Devī is present in all fires, both internal and external.

353. भक्तिमत् कल्प लतिका

Bhaktimat kalpa latikā

She who is the kalpa *creeper to Her devotees.*

The *kalpa* tree and *Kāmadhenu*, the sacred cow, are said to have the power to grant all wishes. Like the *kalpa* tree, this creeper yields all the wishes of the devotees.

Bhaktimat kalpa also refers to imperfect devotees; Devī is one who gives Her imperfect devotees the chance to flourish and climb (like a creeper), to become perfect ones.

Śaktirahasya makes it clear that the worship of Devī done imperfectly or even with incomplete devotion leads, in course of time, to perfect devotion.

Kalpa has the meanings of musk and jasmine. Devī is one who showers fragrance on Her devotees.

354. पशुपाश विमोचिनी

Paśupāśa vimocinī

She who releases the ignorant from bondage.

Paśu means "animal." That which sees (*paśyati*) is *paśu*. The *samsāra*-bound *jīva* is no better than an animal. Devī is one who liberates him by cutting off his bond (*pāśa*) of *karma*.

Paśu literally means an animal that is not free. It is implied that living things are inherently bound and are like pet animals kept by Īśvara. The *Liṅga Purāṇa* says that, from Brahmā to a tree, all living things subject to *Māyā* are *paśus* of Lord Śiva because they show the nature of beasts.

According to the *Bṛhadāraṇyaka Upaniṣad* (I.4.10), *paśu* is one who still maintains a sense of separateness (duality): "He who adores God, thinking 'he is different from me, and I am different from him,' does not know; he is like an animal (*paśu*)."

Man, *manuṣya*, is one who thinks; remember that *paśu* has a long way to go to become man.

Pāśa means rope; that which binds. In the words of Eruttacchan in *Bhāgavata Kirtana*:

"Bonds are man's karma;
Break they must, for him to be free,
By eating the fruit of karma;
Make bonds no more!"

Pāśa is the bond of thirst and hunger (*pa* and *āśa*). Devī liberates one from this bond. One who is immersed in Her worship does not know hunger and thirst. "*Paśus* are those who desire to eat and drink. They do not talk of *Brahman*. They are not aware of this world or the next, the present or the future," according to the *Śruti*.

Pāśa is the bond of ignorance and *paśu* is one whose freedom is lost because of this bond. In the language of spirituality, *Māyā*, the three *guṇas* and *karma* are the forms of bondage. The term *pāśa* connotes everything that arises out of these.

There are fivefold afflictions that affect the *jīvas* in bondage. These are also *pāśas*. Devī liberates man from these bonds through the power of *yoga*. These five afflictions, according to *yogaśāstra*, are nescience, egoism, desire, anger and intense attachment. Nescience (*avidyā*) is ignorance, the inability to discriminate between the self and nonself. Egoism (*asmita*) is the misconception that the body is the self. Desire (*rāga*) is the attraction arising from the wish for pleasure. Anger (*dveṣa*) is the aversion to anything that obstructs the enjoyment of pleasure. Intense attachment (*abhiniveśa*) is clinging to sense objects even when it is known that they are harmful to one's welfare.

Corresponding to these afflictions mentioned in the *yogaśāstra*, the *Purāṇas* give the list, darkness (*tamas*), bewilderment (*moha*), great delusion (*mahāmoha*), anger or darkness (*tāmisra*), and deep darkness of the soul (*andhatāmisra*). *Liṅga Purāṇa* asserts clearly that these are the same afflictions as those given above.

The word *pāśa* connotes the number fifty-two; it is said that there are fifty-two forms of *pāśa* or bonds. *Śivarahasya* says that Devī rescues Her devotees from the five afflictions and fifty-two *pāśas*.

According to *Śaiva* scriptures, there are three types of bondages *anupāśa, bhedapāśa and karmapāśa.*

Anupāśa is the misconception that the indivisible and unlimited Self is limited in some respects. This is known also as "*aṇava* impurity" or *aṇava mala* (*mala* is something not innate). *Bhedapāśa* is seeing the Self as having many different forms. The Self is one and unique. According to *Śaiva* philosophy, the root cause of seeing it as many distinct forms is *Māyā*. Therefore, this bondage is also known as "*māyā* impurity" or *māyāmala* (Māyā is considered the sixth *tattva*. The other five are *Parāśiva*, *Sadāśiva*, *Īśvara*, *Rudra* and *Brahmā*). *Karmapāśa*, the third type of bondage, is the result of actions that cause the *jīva* to assume a body. This is also known as "*karma* impurity" or *karmamala*. Actions that are approved by the scriptures lead to higher births and those that are prohibited lead to lower births.

Those who are bound only by *anupāśa* are known as *vijñānakevalas*. Those bound by *anu-* and *karmapāśas* are known as *pralayākalas* and those bound by all three are known as *sakalas*. One who frees himself of all three forms of bondage becomes Śiva Himself - omniscient and omnipotent.

Devī is not different from the Śiva who liberates the *jīva* from all three forms of bondage; hence She is known by the name "Liberator from bondage."

This *mantra* can also be interpreted as "She who liberates from *samsāra* those who desire to reach *Paśupa* or Śiva, the protector of *paśus*." *Paśupa* can also mean Viṣṇu.

Again, bonds (*pāśas*) are said to refer to sixteen forms of ignorance and seven forms of sorrow. Devī is one who gives liberation from all these.

Pāśa also means "dice." Bhāskarācārya gives the following meaning to this *mantra*: "While playing dice with Śiva, She conquers Him, throwing the dice on the board."

We have already said that the *jīva* in *samsāra* is *paśu*. *Jīvas* are of three kinds: worldly ones, *yogis*, and knowers (*tattvajñas*). In worldly ones, the bonds grow stronger and thrive. In *yogis*, they turn to ashes. In the knowers, the bonds lie dormant without awakening. Devī liberates all of them from their bonds as they deserve.

355. संहृताशेष पाषण्डा

Samhṛtāśeṣa pāṣaṇḍā

She who destroys all heretics.

Those who speak and act against *dharma* are heretics. They sometimes unite and form their own religion. Devī is one who destroys them all. Another form of this *mantra* is "Samhṛtāśeṣapākhaṇḍā." *Pākhaṇḍa* is one who disputes the meaning of the *Vedas*.

356. सदाचार प्रवर्तिका

Sadācāra pravartikā

She who is immersed in (and inspires others to follow) right conduct.

Devī acts strictly in accordance with the values of truth, righteousness, love and *ahimsa* (noninjury). Likewise, She ensures such conduct in others. She inspires people to follow the precepts laid down in the *karmakāṇḍa* and the *jñānakāṇḍa* of the *Vedas* (the sections of the *Vedas* dealing with rituals and with true spiritual knowledge, respectively).

In the *Kūrma Purāṇa*, Devī Herself declares: "O King, according to My command, the eighteen *Purāṇas* were created by Vyāsa and the supplementary *Purāṇas* (*upapurāṇas*) by his disciples, to establish *dharma* (righteousness). In each age (*yuga*), Vyāsa, who knows the essence of *dharma*, performs this task. The principles of *dharma* are promulgated in the four *Vedas*, in the four supplementary *Vedas* (*upavedas*), in the six auxiliaries to the *Vedas* (*vedāngas*), in the philosophical system of *mīmāmsa*, in *nyāya* (logic), in *dharmaśāstra* (law) and in the *Purāṇas*, altogether in eighteen sources of knowledge. This *dharma* established by Brahmā, Manu, Vyāsa and others at My command will last until the dissolution of the universe." The four supplementary *Vedas* or *upavedas* are: *āyurveda* or science of medicine, *dhanurveda* or military science, *gandharvaveda* or music, and *sthāpatyaveda*, architectural science. The six auxiliaries to the *Vedas* or *vedāngas* are *śikṣā* (the science of articulation and pronunciation or phonetics), *kalpa* (the science of rituals or ceremonies), *vyākaraṇa* (grammar), *nirukta* (the etymology of *Vedic* words), *chandas* (prosody) and *jyotiṣa* (astronomy).

357. ताप त्रयाग्नि सन्तप्त समाह्लादन चन्द्रिका

Tāpa trayāgni santapta samāhlādana candrikā

She who is the moonlight that gives joy to those burned by the triple fire of misery.

The three forms of misery are *ādhyātmika* (from one's own body), *ādhibhautika* (from the elements) and *ādhidaivika* (from divine forces).

Sorrows arising from the body and mind of the individual fall in the first category. The elements - fire, water, wind, earth - are the cause of miseries in the second category. Unexpected calamities prompted by divine will are in the third category.

Misery is usually compared to fire. *Tāpa* in this *mantra* can also be understood as heat. Devī is the moonlight of joy which cools down the flames of all kinds of miseries.

358. तरुणी

Taruṇī

She who is ever young.

Old age does not touch Her who is beyond time. She is immune to changes. As She is the one who controls time, how can time bring about changes in Her?

359. तापसाराध्या

Tāpasārādhyā

She who is worshipped by ascetics.

She is worshipped not only by the great sages, but also by Śiva Himself, the greatest of all ascetics.

This *mantra* can also be interpreted as "She who is to be meditated on as long as the misery of *samsāra* persists." (*Tāpa* is the misery of *samsāra*; *sāra* is the essence, in this case the *jīva*; *ā*, "till end" and *dhya*, "to be meditated upon".)

360. तनु मध्या

Tanu madhyā

She who is slender-waisted.

A slender waist is considered a sign of feminine beauty. Devī is the embodiment of beauty. When all the beauty seen in the world is just a fraction of Hers, what more can one say about Her immeasurable beauty?

Also, Devī is of the nature of time. Time consists of the past, present and future. The past and the future extend endlessly, but the present is just a fleeting instant. Devī is one who has a very slight middle - the present. The present is so slender or short that one is not sure whether it even exists (see *mantra* 847).

Tanumadhyā is the deity worshipped in the area of Kāñcī. It is also the name of a tree.

361. तमोपहा

Tamopahā

She who removes the ignorance born of tamas.

Devī is the one who dispels ignorance. Ignorance is illusion, *Māyā*. Devī removes the devotees' illusion.

Tamas is the root cause of all misfortune. The *Bhagavad Gītā* addresses, on many occasions, the ignorance, dullness, and stupor arising from *tamas*.

Tamas is darkness. Devī is indeed the primordial sun which rises up, piercing the darkness.

362. चित्

Cit

She who is in the form of pure intelligence.

Bhāskararāya says that *cit* is the embodiment of wisdom opposed to ignorance (*avidyā*). *Cit* stands for *icchā* and *jñāna*, the powers of will and knowledge. It is the independent power of knowledge (*jñānaśakti*) which is the cause of the creation of the universe. The power of action (*kriyāśakti*) arises only when the power of knowledge and the power of will (*icchāśakti*) exist. There must be awareness of something; there must be the will or desire; only then does action follow. The three powers are thus complimentary (see *mantra* 658).

363. तत् पद लक्ष्यार्था

Tat pada lakshyārthā

She who is the embodiment of Truth (which is indicated by the word "Tat").

Tat tvam asi - That thou art. *Tat* is *Brahman*. *Brahman* is described as conditioned or unconditioned (*sakala* and *niṣkala*). The terms *saguṇa* and *nirguṇa* also indicate the same distinction. The desire and knowledge for the creation of the universe occur in the conditioned (*sakala*) *Brahman*: "He desired to become manifold." The unconditioned (*niṣkala*) *Brahman* is beyond the powers of will, knowledge and action.

According to Bhāskararāya, while the literal meaning of *tat* is the conditioned *Brahman*, it indicates indirectly (*lakṣya*) the unconditioned *Brahman*. Thus, *tat* indicates the absolute *Brahman* which has no imaginable form. The formless and unmanifested nature of Devī is again imagined here.

364. चिद् एक रस रूपिणी

Cid eka rasa rūpiṇī

She who is of the nature of pure intelligence. She who is the cause of knowledge.

Cit, pure intelligence, is the attribute of the unconditioned *Brahman*.

Conditioned and unconditioned (*saguṇa* and *nirguṇa*) *Brahman* are not really different. They are spoken of as different due to conditioning. In essence they are the same, and Devī is that single essence, as this *mantra* declares.

365. स्वात्मानन्दलवी भूत ब्रह्माद्यानन्द सन्ततिः

Svātmānandalavī bhūta brahmādyānanda santatiḥ

She who makes the bliss of Brahmā and others insignificant compared to Her own bliss.

The collective bliss of everyone from human beings to Lord Brahmā pales before the bliss of Devī. "What good is gaining even Indra's state; it is so empty," sings Eruttacchan.

If spiritual bliss, the solid immortal bliss of oneness with the Self, were not the highest, would brave *yogins* have persisted in searching for it, forsaking all the pleasures of the physical world? Even one instant of that bliss makes life immortal and invaluable. Devī is the pure manifestation of that *amritānandam* - immortal bliss.

366. परा

Parā

She who is the supreme; She who transcends all.

Parā is the manifestation of *Brahman*-as-sound (*Śabdabrahman*) in the individual body (*piṇḍāṇḍa*). The four forms of *Brahman*-as-sound, *parā*, *paśyantī*, *madhyamā* and *vaikharī* are described in this and the next several *mantras*.

During *pralaya*, the time of dissolution, the universe is merged in *Brahman* and the *jīvas*, unaware and actionless, are contained in it. This state in which *Brahman* is bound by *Māyā* itself in the form of their unripe actions is called *ghanībhūta*, the Congealed State (a state in which it is not clear when or how creation is to start). The state in which the actions begin to ripen and creation is imminent is known as *vicikīrṣā* (longing for action). The state in which actions become ripe, with the unfoldment of *Māyā*, is the start of creation and is known as *avyakta* (not yet manifested). This state is endowed with the three *guṇas*. As it is the sprout of the universe, it is called the *kāraṇabindu* (the Causal Point). *Prapañcasāra Tantra* says that the congealed *Brahman* (*ghanībhūta*) became the causal point due to the desire for action.

From the *kāraṇabindu* (Causal Point) are formed the following, at the start of creation: *kāryabindu* (Effect Point), which is *parā*, or supreme, *nāda* or sound which is subtle and *bīja* which is gross. Among these, *parā* is intelligence (*cit*), the *nāda* ("subtle") is a combination of intelligence and non-intelligence (*cit-acit*) and the *bīja* ("gross") is pure nonintelligence (*acit*).

When parallel changes take place in the individual *jīva* (*piṇḍāṇḍa*) corresponding to the above process in the cosmic being (*brahmāṇḍa*), thoughts and words form.

In the individual, the *śakti* corresponding to the *kāraṇabindu* is the *Kuṇḍalinī* residing in the *mūlādhāra*. When the all-pervading, unmanifested *Brahman*-as-sound first appears motionless in the *mūlādhāra*, it is known as *parā*. When this sound rises up to the *maṇipūraka cakra* in the navel (some sources say, up to the *svādhiṣṭhāna*) and amplifies, it is called *paśyantī*. *Paśyantī* is known as *sāmānyaspanda* or "simple motion." As it grows and rises to the *anāhatacakra* (in the heart region) and merges with *buddhi* (intellect) it is known as *madhyamā*. *Madhyamā* is endowed with *viśeṣaspanda* or "special motion" and corresponds to the subtle, *nāda* stage in the cosmic creation mentioned above. As the sound ascends further through the throat (*viśuddhicakra*) it develops in the mouth and becomes audible. This gross sound is known as *vaikharī*. This is endowed with *spaṣṭaspanda* or "manifested motion" and corresponds to the *bīja* or gross stage of cosmic creation.

We are acquainted with only *vaikharī* in our normal lives, yet it is well established that the other three stages *parā*, *paśyantī* and *madhyamā*, are known to *yogins*. Such conclusions are difficult to prove intellectually. Only a divinely inspired intellect can perceive this. The testimony of those who have experienced this is the real proof. The seers who have experienced these stages of sound have unanimously recorded this process.

Saubhāgyabhāskara furthers this discussion. There, Bhāskararāya quotes from *Nitya Tantra*, "Sound is born in the *mūlādhāra* as *parā*; the same sound rises and manifests in the *svādhiṣṭhāna* as *paśyantī*; rising slowly from there to the *anāhata*, it unites with *buddhi* and becomes more amplified, where it is known as *madhyamā*. Again rising, and awakened by the *prāṇa* (vital air) known as *vikhara*, it becomes the sound known as *vaikharī*, endowed with audible syllables."

The word "*parā*" has the common meaning of supreme. Also, the *Tripurāsiddhānta* interprets *parā* in the following ways: Devī is *parā* because She was pleased with the guru known as Paramānandanātha, because She is celebrated in the work known as *Parānanda* and because She is the supreme source of grace.

367. प्रत्यक् चिती रूपा

Pratyak citī rūpā

She who is of the nature of unmanifested consciousness or of unmanifested Brahman.

A consciousness looking at itself by facing in a direction opposite to the usual is *pratyakciti*. In other words, it is the inward-looking *Ātman*. All the sense organs are inherently outward-looking, preventing them from reaching the inner Self. The seeker starts his quest for the Self by turning the extroverted senses in the opposite direction - inward. Once the five birds, that are the senses clamoring for names and forms, are shot down, then the inner Knowledge manifests Itself. Thus *pratyakciti* is the unmanifested *Brahman* that begins to shine when the senses become directed inward. Devī is of the nature of that *Brahman.*

368. पश्यन्ती

Paśyantī

She who is paśyantī, *the second level of sound after* parā, *in the* svādhiṣṭhāna *(as explained above).*

Devī has already been described as *nādarūpa* (of the nature of sound; see *mantra* 299). Since Devī sees all in Herself, She is *paśyantī* (one who sees). Since She rises above the path of *karma* and shines in the path of knowledge, She has also acquired the name *Uttīrṇā* (one who has risen).

369. पर देवता

Para devatā

She who is the supreme deity; Parāśakti.

370. मध्यमा

Madhyamā

She who stays in the middle.

She is between the two forms of sound, *paśyantī* and *vaikharī.*

371. वैखरी रूपा

Vaikharī rūpā

She who is in the form of vaikharī.

Vaikharī is sound in the manifested, audible form.

Vai is certainly; *kha*, the cavity of the ear; and *ra*, to enter. Thus *vaikharī* is sound that enters the ears. The *tāraka mantra*, uttered in the ear at the time of death to help the upward passage of the *jīva*, is implied here; it is known as *vaikhara*. In *yogaśāstra*, there is a *prāṇa* (vital air) known as *vaikhara*. It is through this *prāṇa* that *yogins* realize Devī.

372. भक्त मानस हंसिका

Bhakta mānasa hamsikā

She who is the swan in the minds of Her devotees.

The lake called Mānasa is celebrated in the *Purāṇas* as the abode of swans. Just as the swans play in Lake Mānasa, Devī sports in the hearts of the devotees spontaneously and undisturbed.

Amma often says, "Mother does not have a place of Her own. Her children's hearts are the abode that is dearest to Her."

373. कामेश्वर प्राण नाडी

Kāmeśvara prāṇa nāḍī

She who is the very life of Kāmeśvara, Her consort.

Śrī Śaṅkara explains in *Saundarya Laharī* (verse 22): "Even the *devas* who have consumed the nectar that removes old age and death perish in the great dissolution (*pralaya*). But Śiva who has consumed virulent poison can defy death even at that time. The reason for this, O Mother, is the power of Your ear ornaments!" In the brilliance of those ornaments, the darkness of the poison fades and the poison ceases to be virulent. This is how Devī becomes the vital nerve (*prāṇa nāḍi*) of Śiva. Widows do not normally wear such ornaments.

374. कृतज्ञा

Kṛtajñā

She who knows all of our actions as they occur.

Also, She who rewards the worship and offerings of Her devotees by imparting knowledge, *jñāna*.

Kṛta may also mean *Kṛta Yuga*, the first of the four ages. It was the age when *dharma* (righteousness) was whole. In *Tretā Yuga*, *dharma* declined to three-fourths while *adharma* (unrighteousness) took the remaining quarter. In *Dvāpara Yuga*, *dharma* and *adharma* are balanced half and half and in *Kali Yuga*, *adharma* occupies three-fourths and *dharma* only a quarter. *Kṛtajña* means Devī has knowledge of the *dharma* of *Kṛta Yuga* and implements it again in time.

Devī is witness to every action. Amma says, "Son, a thorn pricks your foot and it hurts instantly. You feel the pain because a message about the prick of the thorn arrives in the brain. Similarly, the Lord in your heart knows each of your good and bad actions then and there. This is not a blind belief. It is the truth declared by the scriptures."

It is said that "The sun, the moon, time, Yama (the Lord of Death) and the five elements are the nine witnesses for every action." Time and Yama are indeed one and the same although here they are referred to separately. Again, "The sun, moon, air, fire, sky, earth, water, the heart, Yama, day, night, the twilights and *dharma* are witness to every act of man." All these are Devī's *vibhūtis* or glories and through them She bears witness to everything.

In the game of dice, there are four throws called *kṛta*, *treta*, *dvāpara* and *kali*, with values of four, three, two and one respectively. The one who makes a throw of *kṛta*, which has the highest value, wins the game. When Devī plays dice with Sadāśiva, She always throws *kṛta* and wins. She is so certain of the *kṛta* in the game of dice that She is called *kṛtajña* - knower of *kṛta*.

375. काम पूजिता

Kāmā pūjitā

She who is worshipped by Kāma.

Kāma is born of the mind. He is *Ananga* - one without a body, one without a definite form. His bow is full of flowers (made of a sugarcane in blossom); the bowstring is a line of bees; the five arrows are the five flowers: lotus, aśoka, mango, jasmine and blue-lotus; his deputy is *vasanta*, the spring season; his battle-chariot is the wind from the Malaya mountain (unlike other chariots which need roadways, this one can be driven anywhere). With such equipment, Kāma, with no body, conquers and subjugates the whole world because of the grace of Devi's glance! (*Saundarya Laharī*, verse 6)

Also, She who is worshipped at Kāmarūpa (see *mantra* 379).

376. शृङ्गार रस सम्पूर्णा

Śṛṅgāra rasa sampūrṇā

She who is filled with the essence of Love.

Śṛṅgāra, the sentiment of love, the erotic sentiment, is the king of the nine sentiments in poetry and art. It is the foundation of the union of hearts. It turns all human relations sweet and full of sentiment, not just the relation between a pair of lovers. Devī is the embodiment of that love sentiment. She is, in short, the string of love that ties together all beings.

The word *Śṛṅgārarasasampūrṇā* can be split as *śṛṅgā* (horn, usually two) + *āra* (petals) + *rasa* (flavor, usually six) + *sampūrṇā* (full). Thus *Śṛṅgārarasa* means two times six, or twelve petals - the twelve-petaled lotus which is the *anāhatacakra*. Devī, in Her full form, inhabits its center. *Anāhata* is the heart-lotus. "Arjuna, the Lord resides in the heart of all beings," says Kṛṣṇa in the *Gītā*.

Another interpretation is as follows: *Śṛṅgā* means peak, principal (the highest thing); *ārara*, covering; *sa*, with; *sampūrṇā*, complete. Thus, Devī is one who resides in the entire world, along with *avidyā* (ignorance), the covering that hides the highest truth, *Brahman*. She resides everywhere accompanied by *mukhyāvidya*. This *mantra* implies that She is both the conditioned and the unconditioned *Brahman*.

There are four locations on earth known as *Śaktipīṭhas* (centers of Śakti). They represent the four *cakras* in the body: *mūlādhāra*, *anāhata*, *viśuddhi* and *ājña*. Of these *pīṭhas*, the *Pūrṇagiripīṭha*, corresponding to *anāhata*, is represented by this *mantra*. In this interpretation, the previous *mantra* represents *Kāmagiripīṭha* (which corresponds to *mūlādhāra*).

377. जया

Jayā

She who is victorious always and everywhere.

Jayā is the deity worshipped on the Vārāha mountain. Devī is in the form of that deity. Also, Jayā is one of the eight *yoginis*.

378. जालन्धर स्थिता

Jālandhara sthitā

She who resides in the Jālandhara pīṭha.

According to the *yogaśāstra*, *Jālandhara* is the *viśuddhicakra* in the throat region. Devī is one who resides there as the embodiment of *Brahman*-as-sound. According to *Padma Purāṇa*, the Devī who resides in *Jālandhara* is also called Viṣṇumukhī.

379. ओड्याण पीठ निलया

Oḍyāṇa pīṭha nilayā

She whose abode is the center known as Oḍyāṇa.

Devī resides at Kāmarūpa as Śāntādevī, at Pūrṇagiri as Vāmadevī, at Jālandhara as Jyeṣṭhadevī and at Oḍyāṇa as Raudrīdevī.

Oḍyāṇa is another name for *ājñācakra*, which is the highest of the six *cakras*. Devī is one who resides there, between the eyebrows, where the sandalwood paste mark is applied.

380. बिन्दु मण्डल वासिनी

Bindu maṇḍala vāsinī

She who resides in the bindumaṇḍala.

Bindumaṇḍala is the center of *Śrīcakra*, the *bindu* called *sarvānandacakra*.

Bindu also means "white in color." *Bindumaṇḍala* then refers to the white center, the *Brahmarandhra* at the top of the crown. Devī is one who resides there.

The residence of Devī in *bindumaṇḍala* is what Śrī Śaṅkara describes in the *Saundarya Laharī*, (verse 9), "In the thousand-petaled lotus, You sport." *Bindu* also refers to the *kāraṇa-*, *kārya-* and *nāda bījas*. Devī is one who resides in these *bindus*.

381. रहो याग क्रमाराध्या

Raho yāga kramārādhyā

She who is worshipped in secret through sacrificial rites.

Rahoyāga may be interpreted as the secret meeting between Śiva and Śakti in the *sahasrāra*, and *krama* is "stepping into." The *mantra* then means that Devī is to be worshipped by the stages of *sādhana* that allow us to enter into the bliss of the union of Śiva and Śakti in the *sahasrāra*.

Ācārya Śaṅkara describes this in *Saundarya Laharī* (verse 9): "O Devī, after passing the *mūlādhāra* containing the *bhūtattva* (earth), the *maṇipūraka* in the navel containing the *jalatattva* (water), *svādhiṣṭhāna* in the genital region containing *agnitattva* (fire), *anāhata* in the heart containing *vāyutattva* (air), *viśuddhicakra* in the throat containing the *ākāśatattva* (ether), the *ājñācakra* between the eyebrows containing *manastattva* (mind), thus breaking through the *kūla* path containing the six *cakras*, You sport in secret seclusion with Your Husband in the thousand-petaled lotus."

Here one deviation from normal is noted. The Ācārya talks about *svādhiṣṭhāna* only after passing *maṇipūra* which comes higher in the *Kuṇḍalinī's* path. Great sages do not err in these matters. Here Śaṅkara is following the act of creation well-known in the *Upaniṣads*, going from the gross to the subtle in the following order: earth, water, fire, air, ether and mind. This is why starting, from the *mūlādhāra*, the seat of earth, he mentions *maṇipūraka*, the seat of water before going to *svādhiṣṭhāna*, the seat of fire.

The sacrificial fire here is the fire of consciousness - *cidagni* (recall *mantra* 4). This secret sacrifice is done in the fire of consciousness with the support of the *Kuṇḍalinī śakti*. Thus, Devī is one to be worshipped in secret, according to the rites, by sacrificing all good and bad actions in the fire of consciousness.

382. रहस् तर्पण तर्पिता

Rahas tarpaṇa tarpitā

She who is to be gratified by the secret rites of worship.

The sacrifice of everything from earth principle to Śiva principle in the fire of consciousness is meant by *tarpaṇa* here. This sacrifice should be learned only from the Guru. When the words in a *mantra* have many different meanings which often depend on the pronunciation, it is dangerous to practice *Tāntric* rites on the basis of book knowledge alone.

383. सद्यः प्रसादिनी

Sadyaḥ prasādinī

She who bestows Her grace immediately.

A mother does not withhold her love and blessings from her children for long. When she gets angry, even that anger is the lightning before the rain of compassion. The children may be unable to understand. That is why the mother is quick to be pleased.

384. विश्व साक्षिणी

Viśva sākṣiṇī

She who is witness to the whole universe.

Devī, with neither beginning nor end, is the eye of the universe. She thus witnesses everything.

385. साक्षि वर्जिता

Sākṣi varjitā

She who has no other witness.

There must be someone different from Her to be Her witness. *Brahman* is One, non-dual and with nothing distinct from Itself. For one who is that *Brahman*, who can be a witness?

386. षडङ्ग देवता युक्ता

Ṣaḍaṅga devatā yuktā

She who is accompanied by the deities of the six parts.

The six *aṅgas* are heart, head, hair, eyes, armor and weapons. *Ṣaḍaṅgadevata* is Śiva who presides over six *aṇgas* and Devī is one who is united (*yukta*) with Him. Śiva's *aṅgas* are: omniscience, contentment, knowledge of the Self, independence, unfading power, and infinity or eternity according to the *Devī Bhāgavata Purāṇa*.

Ṣaḍaṅga may also refer to the six *vedāngas*, auxiliaries to the *Vedas*, the science of rituals, grammar, prosody, phonetics, etymology and astronomy. Devī is accompanied by the deities presiding over these.

387. षाड्गुण्य परि पूरिता

Ṣāḍguṇya pari pūritā

She who is fully endowed with the six good qualities.

The list of the six qualities differ with context. In the code of statecraft, the six are peacemaking, war, victory march, staying in camp, dividing the enemy's forces and refuge.

In philosophy, the six qualities are commonly given as prosperity, valor, dispassion, fame, wealth and wisdom. Devī possesses all of these in full measure.

388. नित्य क्लिन्ना

Nitya klinnā

She who is ever compassionate.

Klinnā is one who is melting. Devī is the embodiment of compassion.

Nityaklinnā is the deity of the third day of the bright lunar fortnight. According to the *Garuḍa Purāṇa*, She is *Tripurasundarī* and the bestower of good luck and Liberation.

389. निरुपमा

Nirupamā

She who is incomparable.

Since there is nothing in the world that is different from Her, Devī is unique and unequalled. The scriptural statements such as "There exists nothing similar to it," and "Only one, without a second," reveal Her incomparable status.

390. निर्वाण सुख दायिनी

Nirvāṇa sukha dāyinī

She who confers the bliss of Liberation.

Ni means without and *vāṇa* (*bāna*) signifies arrow or body. The body is indeed the arrow shot by the fruits of *karma*. It is the cause of all unhappiness. The senses run after objects of enjoyment. The mind awakens *saṅkalpa* and *vikalpa* and strengthens desires, and in the haste to fulfill them, one falls into numerous miseries. In deep sleep, in which there is no body sense, the *jīva* enjoys its innate bliss. Thus, *nirvāṇa* is the bliss unblemished by body sense. Devī confers that bliss.

This bliss is enjoyed by *jīvanmuktas* (those who gain Liberation from the sorrows of *samsāra* while still alive). It is not given only after death. It is an experience which is attainable in this life. This is how King Janaka came to be called *Videha* (one without body).

In the *Kūrma Purāṇa*, Devī tells Himavat, the King of Mountains, "Neglecting Me, the pure and peaceful state of *nirvāṇa* cannot be attained. Therefore, worship Me seeing Me as one or as many or in both ways, and reach that highest state."

391. नित्या षोडशिका रूपा

Nityā ṣoḍaśikā rūpā

She who is in the form of the sixteen daily deities.

The fifteen daily deities are the following: Kāmeśvari,

Bhagamālinī, Nityaklinnā, Bherunḍā, Vahnivāsinī, Mahāvajreśvarī, Śivadūtī, Tvaritā, Kulasundarī, Nityā, Nīlapatākinī, Vijayā, Sarvamaṇgalā, Jvālāmālinī, and Citrā. Presiding over all of them is Tripurasundarī who is, indeed, the governing force in the universe as a whole.

Ṣoḍaśikā is the presiding deity of the sixteen-syllabled (*ṣoḍaśī*) *mantra*. *Śaktirahasya* says that a single utterance of that *mantra* pleases Devī more than the performance of *crores* of *ṣoḍaśayāgas* ("sixteen sacrifices") or horse sacrifices. The meaning of *Nityāṣoḍaśikā* can be understood as "one who is worshipped daily (*nitya*) using the *ṣoḍaśī mantra*."

Another interpretation is: "She who is pleased by daily worship done in the home (*ṣoḍaśikā*)."

392. श्रीकण्ठार्ध शरीरिणी

Śrīkaṇṭhārdha śarīriṇī

She who possesses half of the body of Śrīkaṇṭha (Śiva). She who is in the form of ardhanārīśvara *(half-female, half-male god).*

Here, *śri* means poison. Śiva is one with poison frozen in place in His throat.

Śiva and Śakti are one, but in connection with different tasks, they are thought of as different. When the tasks are completed, they become one again. This is the concept of *ardhanārīśvara*.

Devī is one who has half of Her body darkened like Śrikaṇṭha (poison). *Vāyu Purāṇa* says that Devī is pictured as Gauri (white) in Her right half and as Kālī (black, dark) in Her left half.

According to the *Śaiva* school, while doing *nyāsa* (meditating on certain deities in different parts of the body), half of the body is imagined as filled with Śakti and the other half with Śiva.

According to the *Mantrakośa*, *Śrīkaṇṭha* is a synonym for the syllable *a*. Bhāskararāya gives the quotation, "*A* is all the speech; it takes on different forms in combination with different consonants." The sound A is the "first utterance" (original syllable) and is said to be *parā*. All the vowels and consonants that emerge in the form of audible sound (or *vaikharī*, see *mantra* 366-371) are transformations of A.

The *Sūta Samhita* says, "The *Parāśakti*, Devī, the embodiment of consciousness, arises as the speech, known as *par^ā*. I constantly worship with devotion She who is half the body of Śiva."

Kālidāsa's words from *Raghuvamsa* are worth recalling here: "To understand speech and meaning well, I bow to Pārvatī and Parameśvara, the parents of the universe, who are joined together like speech and meaning."

393. प्रभावती

Prabhāvatī

She who is effulgent.

She who is endowed with eight *aiśvaryas* or *siddhis* which are termed luminous. In one of the meditation verses invoking Devī ("....*Animādibhirāvṛtām maheśīm*...") this is made clear. "I imagine the Great Goddess who is surrounded by the golden rays of *animā* and other *siddhis*."

Śrī Śaṅkara says in the *Saundarya Laharī* (verse 30), "You are served by the golden luminaries, the eight *siddhi* deities, that emerge from Your own body. Any devotee who worships this form of Yours with the conviction that 'Thou art my own Self,' attains such endowments as to make those of Lord Śiva worthless. And the great fire of *pralaya* (dissolution) becomes a flame of worship for him (*nīrājana*)."

394. प्रभा रूपा

Prabhā rūpā

She who is effulgence.

The previous *mantra* says that Devī is accompanied by the eight *aiśvaryas*, stating that they are indeed Devī Herself. There is no distinction between the attributes and the one who possesses them.

395. प्रसिद्धा

Prasiddhā

She who is celebrated.

She is one who is celebrated by Her devotees as "Thou alone am I." There is no one who is not aware of "I."

Eruttacchan points out that the sense of "I" may be of two kinds.

"O Lord, Nārāyaṇa, Who art Consciousness-Bliss Itself, Beloved of the Gopis, let there not be the sense of 'I' in me; and if there is, let it be that everything is 'I.'"

As the initial "I" sense (egoism) disappears, one sees everything as oneself. The subject of this sense of "I" in everyone is Devī Herself. Since this sense is universal, She is *prasiddha*, famous or celebrated.

396. परमेश्वरी

Parameśvarī

She who is the supreme sovereign.

Parama is most exalted; the highest protector. Devī is the most exalted protector of all.

One who protects is called *īśvara* or *īśvarī*. One who feels "there is no one to protect me" is *nirīśvara*, one without God. One who feels solace in the belief that "there is a protector for me" is one who has God.

The *Devī Bhāgavata* says, "I worship Her that is the Self in all, She who is the First, She who is Knowledge!"

397. मूल प्रकृतिः

Mūla prakṛtih

She who is the first cause of the entire universe.

She is the original principle behind the entire creation. *Brahman* is beyond the rules of cause and effect.

Mūla is root and *prakṛti* is the essential cause of creation. In *prakṛti*, the *pra* denotes the three *guṇas* of *sattva*, *rajas* and *tamas*. Thus creation, nature, is endowed with the three qualities. *Pra* also means "pre- or before." Thus *prakṛti* is that which existed before creation.

Pāñcarātra Āgama says, "Devī Sarasvatī is the Mother of the universe, the Mother of the *Vedas* and has no other cause; hence She is called the Primal Cause." According to *Devī Bhāgavata*, Durgā, Lakṣmī, Sarasvatī, Sāvitrī and Rādhā are forms of this original cause.

The *Śrīvidyā mantra* is called *Mūlaprakṛti*. *Mūlaprakṛti*, the original cause, is also said to be in the form of *prakāśa* which stands for the syllable A and *vimarśa* which stands for the syllable *Ha*. The Sanskrit alphabet starts with A and ends with *Ha*. Thus, these two syllables represent the entire universe. Therefore, Devī, the Original Cause, is the creator of this entire universe which the letters of the alphabet represent.

Creation is said to be of six forms: *Tāmasa* (ignorance), *mahat* (universal mind), *ahaṅkāra* (egoism), the five subtle elements, eleven senses and the deities starting with *Dik* (deities presiding over the quarters). Since Devī is the cause of all these, She is called the Original Cause.

According to Bhāskararāya, the first two letters of *mūlaprakṛti*, *ma* and *la* stand for the numbers five and three respectively. They represent the five elements and the *avyakta*, *mahat* and *ahaṅkāra*. Devī is the origin of all eight of these and hence She is the Original Cause.

Prakṛti is cause and *vikṛti* is effect or product. Cotton is *prakṛti* and thread is *vikṛti*, or thread is *prakṛti* and garment is *vikṛti*. The effect of one thing becomes the cause of something else in turn.

Taittiriya Upaniṣad (II.1) states that of the five great elements, water is the *prakṛti* (cause) for earth, fire for water, air for fire, and ether for air. *Brahman* is the *prakṛti* for ether.

In *Sāṅkhya* philosophy, *mūlaprakṛti* is one of the two basic principles which themselves have no cause: *Puruṣa* and *Prakṛti*. Everything else we see is the result of transformations (*vikṛti*) of that original cause (*prakṛti*). The following twenty-three entities are the *vikṛtis* arising from the original cause: universal mind, egoism, individual mind, the five *tanmātras* (sound, touch, form, taste and smell), the five elements (earth, water, fire, air and ether), the five sense organs and the five organs of action.

The *Sāṅkhya* system accepts *Prakṛti* and Īśvara (*Puruṣa*) as truth. For one who follows *Advaita*, the non-dual philosophy, the two are the same.

Svāmi Vivekānanda has said that the tower of *Advaita* is built on *Sāṅkhya* but that the crowning piece is purely *Advaitic* or nondual. He has also said that all the philosophies of the world are related in one way or other to Kapila, the founder of *Sāṅkhya* philosophy.

Mūlaprakṛti is said to be *Kuṇḍalinī*, enveloped by the *suṣumnā* in the form of eight *vikṛtis*. (*Mṛgendrasamhita*)

"In the beginning, there was only the Supreme Self, the *Paramātman*, which is knowledge-bliss. Dormant in it was the essence of time, later manifesting as visible objects. When the desire for creation arose in the supreme *Ātman*, this power developed. From this, *prakṛti* or *Māyā* arose which is endowed with the three *guṇas*. When the *Paramātman* entered the undifferentiated *prakṛti* in the form of *Kṣetrajña* (knower of the field), the principle of *mahat* arose. From *mahat* there arose three types of egoism: *sāttvic*, *rājasic* and *tāmasic* (also known respectively as *vaikārika*, *taijasa* and *bhūtādi*). From the *sāttvic* egoism arose the mind, from *rājasic* egoism arose the senses and from *tāmasic* egoism arose the five great elements." (*Bhāgavata Purāṇa*)

The process of creation is described differently in different sources.

398. अव्यक्ता

Avyaktā

She who is unmanifested.

In Sāṅkhya philosophy, *prakṛti* is known as *pradhāna*; it is the state in which the three qualities of *sattva*, *rajas* and *tamas* are not distinctly different. *Pradhāna* is the unmanifested (*avyakta*) state.

In *Vedāntic* terms undivided (*niṣkala*) *Brahman*, when intent on creation, becomes covered by *Māyā* and turns into *Sakala Brahman* - the one with parts. *Avyakta* is the first movement of that *Māyā* (See also the commentary on *parā, mantra* 366). Devī is that unmanifested state, for there is nothing in the universe that is not a form of Hers.

Avyakta refers to the unmanifested *Brahman*. "He is not grasped by the eye, nor by speech, nor by other senses nor by penance, nor by good actions." (*Muṇḍaka Upaniṣad*, III.1.8)

In the *Liṅga Purāṇa*, *avyakta* is included among the names of Viṣṇu who is always capable of creation: *pradhāna*, *avyaya*, *yoni*, *avyakta* and *prakṛti*.

399. व्यक्ताव्यक्त स्वरूपिणी

Vyaktāvyakta svarūpiṇī

She who is in the manifested and unmanifested forms.

The universe with forms is Devī's manifested state while the indwelling vital essence is Her unmanifested state. The tree is the manifested state (*vyakta*) and the procreative power in its seed is the unmanifested state (*avyakta*).

Whatever is perceived by the senses is Her manifested form, yet *Māyā* does not permit us to see this correctly. When someone touches his body and says "I," he does not touch the real "I." The real entity is the unmanifested state.

Śrī Śaṅkara remembers his Guru at the start of *Vivekacūḍāmaṇi*: "Salutations to Śrī Satguru Govinda who is of the nature of absolute bliss, who can be perceived only through the essence of *Vedānta* and who is beyond the normal means of perception." The Guru who is both manifested and unmanifested (*vyaktāvyakta*) is remembered here.

Vyakta is perishable and *avyakta* is imperishable. (*Matsya Purāṇa*) The former is the effect and the latter, the cause. Devī is thus both cause and effect. Or, *vyakta* is individual and *avyakta* is collective, aggregate. (*Narasimha Purāṇa*) Devī is in both individual and aggregate forms. Again, *vyakta* consists of seventy-three categories of things (*tattvas*) and *avyakta* is the Supreme *Prakṛti* or Nature. (*Brahma Purāṇa*) Then, Devī is both in the form of *tattva* and *Prakṛti*.

There are three kinds of Śiva *liṅgas*: *vyakta*, *avyakta* and *vyaktāvyakta*. Worship of *vyaktaliṅga* (*svayambhu* or self-existing *liṅga*) is aimed at salvation; worship of *avyakta liṅga* (*bāṇaliṅga*) is aimed at worldly prosperity and *vyaktāvyakta liṅga* (*śailaliṅga* - made of stone) at both worldly happiness and salvation. Devī is present in all three in the corresponding states.

By *vyakta* we may understand that She is manifest to Her worshippers and by *avyakta* that She is one who never reveals Herself to those bound in *samsāra*.

Vyakta also means *parāhanta*, who is none other than Tripurasundarī.

In another interpretation, She is said to be manifested (*vyakta*) in those whose actions (*karma*) have ripened and unmanifested (*avyakta*) in those whose actions are not ripe, those still bound in *Māyā*. Both are Devī's alternate forms. She is manifested in those whose sins are washed away and who are pure, and unmanifested in those who are still bound by their actions and impurities.

400. व्यापिनी

Vyāpinī

She who is all-pervading.

Amma sings:

"*Thou art the Creation, thou art the Creator,*
Thou art the Essence, thou art the Truth entire,
Thou art the Director of the Cosmos,
Thou indeed art the beginning and the end,
Thou art the truth in the minutest atom,
Thou art the Five Elements."

The Devī who thus fills the entire cosmos, who is the cause and effect of all, is *vyāpinī*.

This name ends the fifth *kalā* of the sun known as *jvālinī*.

401. विविधाकारा

Vividhākārā

She who has a multitude of forms.

Creation is of two kinds: *vaikṛta* and *kaumāra*. *Vaikṛta* creations are plants, animals, ghosts and spirits (The life force (*prāṇa*) of plants moves upwards, that of animals works sideways and that of ghosts goes downwards). *Kaumāra* creations are humans, *gandharvas* and *devas*. Devī is the one responsible for the creation of all these forms, hence She is *vividhākārā*, one with multiple forms.

402. विद्याविद्या स्वरूपिणी

Vidyāvidyā svarūpiṇī

She who is in the form of both knowledge and ignorance.

The understanding that "I am the Self" is knowledge (*vidyā*). The understanding that "I am the body" is ignorance (*avidyā*). Perception of oneness is *vidyā* and perception of plurality is *avidyā*. The attitude that "The Lord makes me do everything," is *vidyā*; the attitude that "I do all," is *avidyā*. The attitude that "I am neither the doer nor the experiencer, but pure consciousness," is *vidyā*; the attitude that "I am the doer and experiencer," is *avidyā*.

According to the *Liṅga Purāṇa*, Śiva has three forms: *bhrānti* (confusion), *vidyā* and *parā*. The knowledge of many forms, plurality, is *bhrānti*; the knowledge of the *Ātman* is *vidyā*; and the knowledge of *Brahman* without any ambiguity is *parā* (supreme).

One who discriminates between knowledge and ignorance partakes of the nectar of immortality - and Devī, of course, is the one who initiates this. One who immerses himself in the river of ignorance goes through thousands of cycles of "repeated births, repeated deaths and repeated lying in the mother's womb." That, too, is due to the power of Devī's *Māyā*.

Devī, in the form of *vidyā*, liberates Her devotees; She Herself, in the form of *avidyā*, binds the worldly beings in *samsāra*.

403. महा कामेश नयन कुमुदाह्लाद कौमुदी

Mahā kāmeśa nayana kumudāhlāda kaumudī

She who is the moonlight that gladdens the water-lilies that are Mahākāmeśa's eyes.

Kumuda is the water-lily and *kaumudi* is moonlight. *Kaumudi* is the full moon of the month of *Kārtika* (October-November). Lotuses are said to blossom at sunrise and water-lilies at moonrise. Similarly, the *darśan* of Devī gladdens and opens the eyes of Śiva, the Self.

Also, *kumuda* is meaningless and inferior (*ku*) worldly pleasure (*muda*); *nayana* is one who leads; *āhlāda* is the supreme bliss or salvation; and *kaumudi* is light. Thus, the *mantra* means "She is the light that leads to Śiva, the ultimate bliss, by taking us away from insignificant worldly pleasures."

404. भक्त हार्द तमो भेद भानुमद् भानु सन्ततिः

Bhakta hārda tamo bheda bhānumad bhānu santatiḥ

She who is the sunbeam which dispels the darkness from the heart of Her devotees.

The darkness in the heart is nothing but evil thoughts, evil feelings and ignorance. Devī is one who shines with the brightness of a million suns, wiping out this darkness whenever it rises in the hearts of Her devotees.

405. शिव दूती

Śiva dūtī

She for whom Śiva is the messenger.

It can also mean "She who is Śiva's messenger."

A story in the *Devī Māhātmya* is the basis for this name. There were two demons, Śumbha and Niśumbha. Before slaying them, Devī sent Śiva to them with Her message: "Either give back the celestial world to Indra and the other *devas* and return to the netherworld or prepare for battle, ready to die." Śiva thus became Her messenger.

406. शिवाराध्या

Śivārādhyā

She who is worshipped by Śiva.

Śiva is said to have performed austerities using the *mantra* known as "*Śivadūtī*." This is mentioned in the *Brahmāṇḍa Purāṇa*: "By worshipping whom even Śiva, through the power of meditation (using the *Śivadūti mantra*), became the half-female, half-male god (*ardhanārīśvara*)." That Devī is *Śivārādhyā*.

407. शिव मूर्तिः

Śiva mūrtiḥ

She whose form is Śiva Himself.

The forms of Śiva and Śakti are indeed inseparable and not distinct from each other. Bhāskararāya gives the following quotation from the *Śruti*: "One Rudra is hidden in all beings; He is endowed with *Māyā*; He is with parts and without parts; He is Devī and not distinct from Her; by knowing this, one attains immortality."

"Śiva" means *mokṣa* (Liberation). In that sense, Devī is of the nature of Liberation. She is also known as the embodiment of auspiciousness.

408. शिवङ्करी

Śivaṅkarī

She who confers prosperity (auspiciousness, happiness). She who turns Her devotee into Śiva.

How numerous are the souls like Vyāsa, Jābāli, Śabari, Kanakadāsa and Kannappa, who, through the paths of *karma*, *bhakti* and *jñāna*, became great souls, worshipped by the wise!

"At birth one is born a *śūdra*, but by deeds is one born a *brāhmaṇa*."

How numerous are the small lives that have became full of Śiva, full of auspiciousness, through Devī's grace! Devī is *Śivaṅkarī* in this sense also.

409. शिव प्रिया

Śiva priyā

She who is beloved of Śiva.

She to whom Śiva is dear. Also, She who has made everything that is *śivam* or auspicious dear to Herself.

410. शिवपरा

Śivaparā

She who is solely devoted to Śiva.

One who is beyond even Śiva. Śiva depends on Śakti. This is what Śaṅkarācārya means in the opening verse of *Saundarya Laharī*: "When Śiva joins You, O Śakti, He is able to engage in His cosmic tasks; otherwise He cannot even move about!" It is in this sense that Devī transcends Śiva.

411. शिष्टेष्टा

Śiṣṭeṣṭā

She who is loved by the righteous. She who is the chosen deity of devotees. Also, She who loves righteous people.

Śiṣṭam can mean "prescribed ceremonies and rituals of worship;" *śiṣṭas* are those who perform such worship without the desire for the fruits. Devī is dear to them.

According to the *Vāsiṣṭha Sūtra*, "*Śiṣṭas* are those who control the organs of action and knowledge, who have learned the *Vedas* according to tradition and draw inspiration from them and who are worshippers of *Brahman*."

412. शिष्ट पूजिता

Śiṣṭa pūjitā

She who is always worshipped by the righteous.

Righteous thoughts and *sāttvic* attitudes derive from the *vāsanās* one has at birth. There are also some individuals who turn righteous due to a sudden transformation in life. In such cases, the *samskāra* from previous births must be at work. As the *Gītā* (VII.3) says, "Out of thousands of men, only one strives for attaining the Self; out of those strivers, only one perchance knows Me in essence." *Śiṣṭas* are those who proceed on the spiritual path in this manner. Devī is one who is constantly worshipped by them.

413. अप्रमेया

Aprameyā

She who is immeasurable by the senses.

The syllable *a* stands for Brahmā, Viṣṇu and the other gods and *prameyā* is "to be known." Therefore, She is to be known only by Them.

Ap + *rameya* is one who abides in water; She who abides in sacred rivers like the Gangā. The sacred rivers are invoked to sanctify water before bathing or using in *pūjas*: "O Gangā, Yamunā, Godāvarī, Sarasvatī, Narmadā, Sindhu, Kāverī, kindly grace this water by your presence!"

414. स्वप्रकाशा

Svaprakāśā

She who is self-luminous.

"He shines and everything shines after Him; by His light, all these shine." (*Kaṭha Upaniṣad* II.2.15) Devī is that *Brahman* Itself.

By splitting this name as *su* (well) + *ap* (water) + *ra* (fire) + *kāśa* (one who shines), one understands the meaning as "She who shines well in water and fire." Note that water and fire are the primary powers of life.

415. मनो वाचाम् अगोचरा

Mano vācām agocarā

She who is beyond the range of mind and speech.

Mind and speech are two of the means of knowledge. Reliable knowledge beyond the reach of eyes and ears is obtained from the words of the trustworthy. The other path to knowledge is through the mind. New knowledge arises when the mind analyzes what is heard or read. Yet Devī is beyond these means of obtaining knowledge. As *Taittiriya Upaniṣad* (II.9.1) says, "From where speech and mind turn away without reaching," That is *Brahman*, the Reality behind all. That is Devī's unmanifested form.

Mind and speech are illumined by Devī; they cannot illumine Her. The electricity makes the lamp shine; the lamp cannot make the electricity shine.

Mind and speech are the motions of the *cit*, the consciousness. They have to subside before Devī can be known.

Another interpretation of this *mantra* is: "She who is unknowable by minds and words that are impure." The *Śruti* itself says, "It is to be perceived by mind alone." (*Kaṭha Upaniṣad* II.4.11) According to Śaṅkarācārya's commentary on the *Brahma Sūtra*, it is known by pure minds, but unknowable by impure minds.

416. चित् शक्तिः

Cit śaktiḥ

She who is the power of consciousness.

Cit is knowledge, consciousness. It is the power that is in all beings. Its nature is to know, to enjoy bliss. It is the power that wipes out *avidyā*, ignorance.

"Both knowledge and ignorance are hidden in the imperishable *Brahman*. Knowledge is imperishable and ignorance is perishable; but entirely different from these two is *Brahman* who rules them both." (*Śvetāśvatāra Upaniṣad* V.1)

417. चेतना रूपा

Cetanā rūpā

She who is pure Consciousness.

She who is Self-Knowledge. The power of Consciousness of the Lord is called *caitanya.* (*Śārīrakācārya*)

Devī Bhāgavata praises Devī in the form of the *Kūtatraya Gāyatri.* This *mantra* is also known as Tripartite *Gāyatri* (*Tripāda Gayatri*). "We salute the Consciousness in all, which is the original Knowledge; may it inspire our intelligence!" Devī is the power that confers consciousness to all and gives Her devotees the power to overcome the senses, according to the *Devī Bhāgavata.*

Śrī Śankarāraṇya explains in his *Vidyāratna* that the *vimarśa* form of Devī is *cetana.* In the language of Śakti doctrine, this refers to the Self-manifest Reality surveying or experiencing Itself (see *mantra* 548).

418. जड शक्तिः

Jaḍa śaktiḥ

She who is the Māyā *that has transformed itself as the power of creation.*

"All is *Brahman,*" according to the *Śruti.* Modern science is in accordance with this ancient idea of the *ṛṣis.* Energy cannot be created or destroyed. It can only be transformed from one form to another.

"The energies in living beings are not easily grasped by our intellects. The energies of *Brahman* are a hundred times more difficult to grasp. They are contained in *Brahman* as heat is contained in fire. *Brahman* is the instrumental cause of the creation of the universe. The creative powers are, on the other hand, the material causes. They depend on *Brahman* who is the instrumental cause." (*Viṣṇu Purāṇa*)

419. जडात्मिका

Jadātmikā

She who is in the form of the inanimate world.

Devī is the *Māyā* that manifests in the form of the inanimate world.

420. गायत्री

Gāyatrī

She who is the Gāyatrī mantra.

Gāyatrī is a meter consisting of twenty-four syllables. "I am *Gāyatrī* among the meters," says Lord Kṛṣṇa in the *Gītā* (X.35). That *Gāyatrī* is Devī.

Gāyatrī is that which protects (*tra*) one who sings (*ga*). Devī's holy names are equal to the *Gāyatrī mantra*. In the *Padma Purāṇa*, Gāyatrī Devī Herself says, "After bathing in the morning, one should repeat Me, the Mother of the *Vedas*. I abide in parts of eight syllables, yet I fill the entire universe."

The *Gāyatrī mantra* is considered to be the most exalted *mantra*. Being the source of all *Vedas*, having become the seed for all four *Vedas* - *Gāyatrī* is celebrated as the Mother of the *Vedas* and as the wife of Lord Brahmā.

Om bhur bhūva svāḥ
Tat savitur vareṇyam
Bhargo devasya dhīmahi
Dhiyo yo naḥ pracodayāt

Gāyatrī is Brahmā's wife. There is a story in the *Padma Purāṇa*. Once Brahmā was conducting a sacrifice in Puṣkara. He called his wife Sāvitrī, who was talking at the time with Lakṣmī Devī, to join him at the sacrificial altar. Sāvitrī, who was immersed in her conversation, agreed to join him but did not, in fact, do so. Brahmā became annoyed at this and he wedded, according to the *gāndharva* rites, a cowherd girl named *Gāyatrī* who was presented to him by Indra, and made her sit with him at the altar.

In the *Vāsiṣṭha Rāmāyana*, Devī is referred to as Gāyatrī because "She is in the form of song."

421. व्याहृतिः

Vyāhṛtiḥ

She who is of the nature of utterance. She who presides over the power of speech.

The *vyāhṛtis* ("utterances") are: *bhuh*, *bhuvah*, *svah*, *mahah*, *janah*, *tapah and satyam*. Since these are used for invoking Devī, She is called *Vyāhṛtiḥ*. *Vyāhṛti* is the name of a *mantra*. As Devī is invoked by uttering this *mantra*, She is known as *Vyāhṛtiḥ*, according to *Vāyu Purāṇa*.

These *vyāhṛtis* represent the gross and subtle levels of the sphere of consciousness. *Bhuh* is the grossest and *satyam* is the subtlest (These syllables are used for invoking the *Gāyatrī mantra*).

422. सन्ध्या

Sandhyā

She who is in the form of twilight.

Sandhyā is that which joins day and night together. Here, Devī is said to be that. She is also *Yugasandhya*, one who joins two *yugas* (ages) together.

According to the *Mahābhārata*, *sandhyā* is the *cit* (consciousness) that abides in the sun. Brahmā, Viṣṇu, Indra and all other beings are the rays of that *sandhyā*.

Mādhavācārya says that Devī is known as *Sandhyā* as She is worshipped at the three *sandhyas* (twilights).

Kālika Purāṇa tells the story that Sandhyā (which also means "meditation") is the celestial beauty that arose in the mind of Brahmā as he sat in meditation.

According to *Renuka Purāṇa*, the *śakti* known as *Iḍā* is Kālī, *Piṅgalā* is Lakṣmī and *Suṣumnā* is Ekavirā. *Sandhyā* is the combination of all three.

Sandhyā is the symbol of beauty, sacredness and auspiciousness which is, indeed, a form of Devī.

Sandhyā (san+dhya) is "She who is to be meditated upon with one-pointedness."

During meditation, the moment in which the meditator realizes that he is none other than the Supreme is called *Sandhyā*.

The *Smṛti* says that the knowers call *Brahman*, witness to everything, by the name *Sandhyā*. During *sandhyas* (twilights), worshippers meditate on Devī, who is *Brahman*, as manifested in the sun.

One interpretation says that *sandhyā* is the "mental sheath" (*manomayakośa*) among the five sheaths or *kośas* that cover the *Ātman*.

According to Dhaumya, a one year old girl is called *Sandhyā*.

423. द्विज वृन्द निषेविता

Dvija vṛnda niṣevitā

She who is worshipped by the twice-born.

By birth all men are *śūdras*. *Karma* makes a *śūdra* into a *dvija*, a twice-born, commonly interpreted as a *brāhmaṇa*. The great sage Vyāsa is proof that in India, actions decided a person's caste (*varṇa*). Devī is one who is worshipped by those who become twice-born through their actions.

Dvija means teeth. Devī's teeth were compared in *mantra* 25 to thirty-two forms of worship starting with *Śuddhavidyā* or *Śrīvidyā*. The present *mantra* can be interpreted as She who is to be worshipped by these means.

Devī is Sandhyā, and according to the *Renuka Purāṇa*, "This Sandhyā is to be worshipped by the twice-born, *devas* (gods) and *mahātmas* (great souls) always, while sitting, walking, eating and sleeping."

The three names, *vyāhṛtiḥ*, *sandhyā* and *dvijavṛndaniṣevitā*, connote the three states of waking, dreaming and deep sleep. *Vyāhṛtiḥ* connotes the operation of speech and symbolizes the waking state. *Sandhyā*, being in between the other two, connotes the dream state. *Dvija* (twice-born) also means birds, here referring to *jīvas*. Just as the birds, who are fatigued from flight finally come to their nests, the *jīvas* after waking and dreaming, merge with *Brahman* in the state of deep sleep. The *Bṛhadāraṇyaka Upaniṣad* (IV.3.19) says, "Just as a hawk or falcon flying about for a long time is exhausted and comes to its nest, so does this person hasten to this state where, falling asleep, he desires nothing nor sees any dream." In the *Chāndogya Upaniṣad* (VI.8.1), it is written, "When a man is said to be sleeping, then dear boy, he has become united with *Brahman*."

424. तत्त्वासना

Tattvāsanā

She who has tattvas *as Her seat (*āsana*). She who abides in* tattva.

Tattvam is the truth in everything (*tat+tvam*: That is you). Devī resides in everything as the inner Truth. The *Sāṇkhyas* are called "Knowers of the twenty-five *tattvas*." Devī is the inner power in all these *tattvas*.

Tattva also means "a cosmic element." She abides in all the elements from the earth to Śiva. (There are considered to be thirty-six *tattvas*, the last one being Śiva who is not distinct from Devī)

Āsana means "one who discards." In this sense, Devī is one who discards all the twenty-four *tattvas* of *Sāṇkhya* or the thirty-five cosmic elements. There is only one Truth left and that is Devī Herself. Recall the statement "*Neti, neti*," (Not this, not this) used in describing the Supreme Truth.

Gāyatrī, the Mother of the *Vedas*, has three levels of manifestations - *vyāhṛtiḥ* at the gross level, *sandhyā* at the subtle level and *tattvāsana* at the causal level. All these are creations of Devī. She abides in all. They are steps leading to Her.

425. तत्

Tat

She who is meant by "That," the Supreme Truth, Brahman.

When knowledge of *Brahman* arises in the intellect, *Tat* (that) is the word used to signify that *Brahman* (See *mantra* 363).

Tat is a pronoun - a word which is employed to refer to something that is already indicated. All known things are included in *tat* because behind everything is Devī, the Supreme Consciousness.

In the *nāmāvali* form of the *Sahasranāma* in which Devī is invoked name by name, this *mantra* becomes *Om Tasmai Namah. Tasmai* is the dative form of the pronoun *Tat.*

426. त्वं

Tvam

She who is referred to, by "Thou."

One *jīva* is distinguished from another by means of the difference in conditioning. The ant's body is very different from that of the anteater. But the soul is one and the same. Here the conditioning is the body. In the present *mantra, Tvam* (Thou) refers to the unconditioned *Ātman.* That *Ātman* is Devī.

This and the previous *mantra* reveal the identity of the individual soul (*jīvātman*) with the Supreme *Brahman* (*Paramātman*) given by the *mahāvākya* (great declaration from the *Upaniṣads*): "*Tat tvam asi,*" meaning "That thou art."

There are four such *mahāvākyas* in *Vedānta*:

Prajñānam brahma:	Consciousness is *Brahman*
Tat tvam asi:	That thou art.
Ayam ātma brahma:	This Self (*ātman*) is *Brahman.*
Aham brahmāsmi:	I am *Brahman.*

Each of these declarations comes from a different *Upaniṣad,* each connected to one of the four *Vedas.* Thus each *Veda* has given rise to a *mahāvākya.*

"*Prajñānam Brahma*" is contained in the *Aitareya Upaniṣad* of *Ṛgveda*. "*Tat tvam asi*" is from the *Chāndogya Upaniṣad* of *Sāmaveda*. "*Ayam ātma brahma*" is from the *Māṇḍukya Upaniṣad* of *Atharvaveda* and "*Aham brahmāsmi*" occurs in the *Bṛhadāraṇyaka Upaniṣad* of *Yajurveda*.

Of the four, "*Prajñānam brahma*" is known as the "*Vākya* (statement or declaration) of Definition." "*Tat tvam asi*" is the "*Vākya* of Instruction." "*Ayam ātma brahma*" is the "*Vākya* of Contemplation" and finally, "*Aham brahmāsmi*" is the "*Vākya* of Experience." Hearing, contemplation and conviction through experience - those aspects define the greatness of *Vedāntic* philosophy.

The body is what gives the illusion of diversity. The soul is nothing but the one and only *Brahman*.

Once a devotee asked Mother, "Amma, if the soul of all of us is the same, then when one person realizes the Truth, shouldn't everyone get that realization at the same time?" Mother said, "Son, when you turn on the main power switch, the electricity reaches all the rooms - the living room, the kitchen, the bedrooms. But if you want light in your room, you have to turn the switch on in that room. The mind is the switch. Only if each person switches on his mind, will the light inside him be revealed." The names *Tat* and *Tvam* indicate that light. Devī is that light.

Tat (That) may be regarded as *Nirguṇa Brahman* (attributeless *Brahman*) and *Tvam* (Thou) as *Saguṇa Brahman* (*Brahman* with attributes).

In the *nāmāvali*, this *mantra* becomes *Om Tubhyam Namah. Tubhyam* is the dative form of the pronoun *Tvam*.

427. अयी

Ayī

Oh, Mother!

"Ayī!" addresses the Mother as the "dear one." This *mantra* brings out the oneness of the heart of the worshipper and that of Devī, the object of his worship. This address is not only respectful, but is also filled with the utmost feeling of love.

Tattvanārāyanīya makes it clear that the three words *Tat*, *Tvam* and *Ayī* indeed make up the *mahāvākya*, "*Tat tvam asi*" (see previous *mantra*). Perception of this meaning will not arise merely from the study of the scriptures. It arises directly in one's experience, inspired by a worshipful attitude.

428. पञ्च कोशान्तर स्थिता

Pañca kośāntara sthitā

She who resides within the five sheaths.

In *Tantraśāstra*, the five sheaths are *paramjyoti*, *parā*, *niṣkalaśāmbhavi*, *ajapā* and *matṛka*, according to *Jñānārṇava*. Inside these sheaths, at the center, is the *cakra* of bliss (*sarvānandamayī cakra*) in the form of the *bindu*. Devī *Srīvidyā* resides there. In each of these sheaths, a Devī with the same name as the sheath is worshipped.

In another interpretation, the five sheaths represent five levels of *samādhi*: *sāmya*, *laya*, *vināśa*, *atyantabhāva* and *aikya*. In *sāmya*, the difference between the *jīva* and the *Paramātman* persists. In *laya*, this difference begins to disappear, but the sense of identity is not complete. In *vināśa*, the differentiation disappears. In the next stage, the sense of identity becomes stronger and in *aikya*, complete oneness of *jīva* and *Paramātman* is attained.

In *Vedānta*, the five sheaths (*kośas*) are as follows: *annamaya*, *prāṇamaya*, *manomaya*, *vijñānamaya* and *ānandamaya kośas* (the food sheath, the vital air sheath, the mental sheath, the intellectual sheath and the bliss sheath, respectively). Inside the innermost sheath (bliss sheath), Devī shines as Pure Consciousness.

The system of these *kośas* is one of the loftiest analytical concepts reached by our sages. Seekers of knowledge marvel at this achievement.

In the *Brahma Gītā*, it is said that *Brahman*, which is the essence of existence, wisdom and oneness, fills the *ānandamaya kośa* (bliss sheath) as the support and witness of all. It is the eternal essence of everything.

Krodhabhaṭṭāraka says, "O Mother, he alone is the knower of *Brahman* who knows You, blazing with radiant light inside the five sheaths of *anna*, *prāṇa*, *manas*, *buddhi* and *ānanda*, as described in *Mahopaniṣad*."

In Śrī Śaṅkara's commentary on the *Brahma Sūtras*, both the ancient views and Śaṅkara's own theory on these *kośas* are discussed. *Taittiriya Upaniṣad* (*Brahmānanda Valli*) discusses the five *kośas* in detail as well.

429. निःसीम महिमा

Niḥsīma mahimā

She whose glory is limitless.

Everything in the universe, other than *Brahman*, possesses only limited attributes. Only the glories of *Brahman* are limitless. Devī, with unlimited glory, is none other than *Brahman*.

430. नित्य यौवना

Nitya yauvanā

She who is ever youthful.

Devī is not subject to any change of state, because She Herself is the creator of time; time does not create Her. All beings go through stages of growth and decay brought about by time. Devī is not affected by these and remains ever youthful.

431. मद शालिनी

Mada śālinī

She who is shining in a state of inebriation or intoxication.

Here, the reason for the inebriation is the enjoyment of the bliss of *Brahman*. Devī is in that state of intoxication. The face and eyes redden under intoxication. It is implied that the beauty of Her face is highly enhanced by this bliss.

Bhāskararāya describes *mada* as that state of bliss which is untainted by worldly things. That is the nature of the bliss of *Brahman*, and Devī is resplendent in that state.

432. मद घूर्णित रक्ताक्षी

Mada ghūrṇita raktākṣī

She whose eyes are reddened, rolling with rapture and in-ward-looking.

The state of great bliss is indicated by Her half-closed eyes. It is implied that She is enjoying secret internal bliss. The message of those eyes is one of great joy felt by Devī as She sees Her devotee progressing on the spiritual path, forsaking worldly attachments.

433. मद पाटल गण्ड भूः

Mada pāṭala gaṇḍa bhūḥ

She whose cheeks are rosy with rapture.

The Divine Mother's cheeks become rosy in the rush of love She feels seeing the spiritual progress made by Her devotees. This rosy hue may become even more beautiful because of the constant nearby presence of Her beloved, Kāmeśvara.

Mada also means musk. *Pāṭala* is the name of a certain flower. In his work, *Śākuntala*, Kālidāsa describes the forest breeze carrying the fragrance of *pāṭala* flowers. The *mantra*, then, means that Devī's cheeks are rendered fragrant by musk and by the *pāṭala* flowers She wears in Her ears.

434. चन्दन द्रव दिग्धाङ्गी

Candana drava digdhāṅgī

She whose body is smeared with sandalwood paste.

Sandalwood paste is used to give beauty and coolness to the body. During *pūja*, it is customary to bathe Devī's idol in milk, ghee, sandalwood paste and rose water. Mother includes this *abhiṣeka* (bathing ceremony) as part of the *mānasapūja* (mental worship) She has prescribed.

435. चाम्पेय कुसुम प्रिया

Cāmpeya kusuma priyā

She who is especially fond of Campaka *flowers.*

Campaka flowers have a special property. It is said that a bee drinking honey from such a flower dies immediately. *Campaka* flowers are therefore not blemished by contact with bees. Devī is especially attached to them.

Worldly pleasures are like poison. Even the relation to one's wife and children, though sweet at first, feels like poison as detachment grows.

The view of *yogins* is described in the *Gītā* (XVIII.37): "That which is like poison at first, but like nectar in the end, that pleasure is declared to be *sāttvic*, born of the purity of one's own mind."

The bliss felt by the mind which has pulled itself away from the sensory objects is described as nectar here. The pleasure that the mind and body derive through the senses is perishable, mortal and ephemeral. *Campaka* flowers symbolize those who, revelling in the Self, do not touch worldly pleasures.

436. कुशला

Kuśalā

She who is skillful.

The word *kuśala* refers to a disciple who cuts the *kuśa* grass he has discovered and brings it, before sunrise, for his guru's *pūja*. Thus it is an adjective that is used to describe one who has foresight and plans ahead. *Kuśalā* is the feminine form. Similarly, Devī is one who is very skillful in saving Her devotees from danger.

Also, *kuśa* means water, and *lā* is she who accepts. Devī is one who keenly accepts the water offered in prayer by Her devotees. Also, She is one who accepts anything offered by Her devotees even if it is only water.

Bhāskararāya interprets this *mantra* as "She who makes the

moon pale in front of the radiant beauty of Her own face (*ku:* inferior, *śala:* moon)."

437. कोमलाकारा

Komalākārā

She who is graceful in form.

Her gracefulness is an expression of qualities like humility and good conduct, which She possesses in abundance. She who has attractive gestures and expressions.

438. कुरुकुल्ला

Kurukullā

She who is the Śakti, Kurukullā.

This Śakti resides in the "*Vimarśa*" stream in the *Śrīcakra*, which is described as existing between the walls of *cit* and *ahaṅkāra*. The water here is the same as the nectar flowing through the *suṣumnā* (see *mantra* 99). *Kurukullā* is said to be in charge of the boats in this stream of nectar. *Tantrarāja* (chapter 22) describes this deity.

The *Lalitāstavaratna* praises *Kurukullā* as follows: "I meditate always on the Devī, *Kurukullā*, who resides in the *kuruvinda* ruby, whose waist is bent by the burden of Her breasts which put mountains to shame, and whose body is smeared with red paste."

439. कुलेश्वरी

Kuleśvarī

She who is the ruler of Kula.

Here, *Kula* refers to the triad (*tripūti*) of the knower, the known and knowledge.

Remember the truth that the *Upaniṣads* declare: "The light, which is the consciousness that shines when the *tripūti* filling the three worlds to their limits finally breaks, is not visible to a false *yogin*." Devī is the controller of that triad.

Kuleśvarī can mean the *Kuṇḍalinī Śakti.*

Also, Kuleśvara is Śiva and Kuleśvarī is His wife.

Another interpretation states that *Kuleśvarī* is the ruler or presiding deity of the *mūlādhāra cakra. Kula* refers to the *mūlādhāra* because the earth element (*ku*) is contained or dissolved (*la*) in that *cakra.*

440. कुल कुण्डालया

Kula kuṇḍālayā

She who abides in Kulakuṇḍa.

Kulakuṇḍa is the *bindu* at the center of the pericarp in the *mūlādhāra* (lotus). Devī resides there.

The *Kuṇḍalinī* sleeps in this *bindu* (see *mantra* 99). Śrī Śaṅkara describes Her in *Saundarya Laharī* (verse 10): "O Mother, after bathing the universe and the *nāḍīs* (nerves) of the worshipper in the ambrosia flowing from the middle of Your feet, You return from the *sahasrāra* which is in the form of the radiant moon's disc, back to Your abode in the *mūlādhāra* and there sleep, in the pericarp with its minute hole, in the form of the serpent coiled into three and a half turns."

441. कौल मार्ग तत्पर सेविता

Kaula mārga tatpara sevitā

She who is worshipped by those devoted to the Kaula *tradition.*

Kaula is that which pertains to *Kula*, which has already been defined in various ways.

Taking *Kula* to mean family, the *mantra* shows that Devī is one who is worshipped by those following their family tradition.

There are three traditional modes of Devī worship: *samaya*, *miśra* and *kaula*. The *samaya* path is laid down in the *Vedas* and in the *āgamas* of Vasiṣṭha and others. The *miśra* path is described in eight *Tantras* and in works like *Candrakalā*. This path combines the rules from the *samaya* path with the rules from some other paths. The *kaula* path is different from the above two and is described in a set of sixty-four books on *Tantra.*

442. कुमार गणनाथाम्बा

Kumāra gaṇanāthāmbā

She who is the Mother of Kumāra (Subrahmania) and Gananātha (Ganapati).

Ahaṅkāra (egoism) arises from the union of *Ādipuruṣa* (Original man) and Śakti. Kumāra is the deity of this. *Kumāragaṇa* stands for all the qualities arising from egoism. Devī is one who binds and governs all these qualities. Hence She is called *Kumāragaṇanāthāmbā.* The word *Kumāra* is a synonym for egoism and *ambā* stands for one who blocks its forces. Thus, the implied meaning of the *mantra* is that Devī is the one who blocks the path of egoism in the seeker, and opens the path towards Liberation.

Also, *ku* is bad, *maragaṇa* is the aggregate of passions and *amba*, one who restricts. Devī restricts the powers that inspire inferior passions for sensory pleasures.

The next seven names describe Devi's character.

443. तुष्टिः

Tuṣṭiḥ

She who is ever content.

Every being has three states - to exist, to shine and to be happy in that state (*asti, bhāti* and *priya*). Devī abides in the state of happiness.

Mārkaṇḍeya Purāṇa praises Her thus: "Many adorations to the Devī who resides as contentment in all beings."

The *Devī Bhāgavata* says, "That Mother is present in all beings in the form of understanding, fame, firmness, prosperity, power, faith, knowledge and memory."

Tuṣṭiḥ is one of Sixteen Mothers (*Ṣoḍaśamātās*). Here Devī is praised in that form. According to *Padma Purāṇa*, *Tuṣṭiḥ* is the deity at Vastreśvara Tirtha.

444. पुष्टिः

Puṣṭiḥ

She who is the power of nourishment.

The power of nourishment coming from Devī is responsible for the growth of every being which is born. Can any doctor guarantee the survival of a fetus in the womb? If he could, there would be no still births. It is Devī's will that acts as the source of nourishment for all beings.

Puṣṭiḥ is the name of the deity in Devadāruvana, which can be seen as another form of Devī.

445. मतिः

Matiḥ

She who manifests as intelligence.

How does intelligence manifest itself? Through actions. That is worldly intelligence. Spiritual intelligence is the instrument for Self-Realization. Both types of intelligence are manifestations of Devī.

Matiḥ also means "measurement." In this sense, Devī is the measuring rod for the *Vedas*. "We adore the Devī who knows (measures) the *Vedas*, who bestows auspiciousness, who gives bliss, who is supreme, who is worshipped by Viṣṇu and others, who is known as *mati* (intelligence) derived from experience," says the *Sūta Samhita*.

446. धृतिः

Dhṛtiḥ

She who is fortitude.

The fortitude seen in all beings arises from Devī's power.

Also, *Dhṛtiḥ* is one of the Sixteen Mothers. Devī is in that form.

Dhṛtiḥ is also the deity worshipped in the temple at Piṇḍāraka.

447. शान्तिः

Śāntiḥ

She who is tranquility itself.

Śānti is evenness of mind in happiness and in sorrow, in profit and in loss, in victory and in defeat.

According to *Śaivāgama*, *Śānti* is a *kalā* (part) of *Vāyu*. "That *kalā* which dispels the three types of impurities, *aṇava*, *māyā* and *karma*, is called *śānti*." It shows the way for those who are struggling in the illusion of *Māyā* and in actions contrary to one's *karma*, forsaking one's own *dharma* and embracing that of someone else (see *mantra* 354). Slipping away from one's own *dharma* will not bring prosperity; it causes loss of *śānti* (peace). The declaration in the *Gītā* (III.35) that "Better is death following one's own *dharma* (duty); following another's *dharma* leads to fear," is indeed a cornerstone for building a righteous life.

According to *Brahmaparāśarasmṛti*, the area fifteen fingers breadth from the tip of the nose downward is the most auspicious seat of the life force; it is called *śānti*. It is the seat of Devī.

448. स्वस्ति मती

Svasti matī

She who is the Ultimate Truth.

The syllables *su+asti* mean glorious truth. The glorious truth is *Brahman*. Devī is nothing but that Ultimate Truth. "That *Brahman* is the Truth in truth," says the *Bṛhadāraṇyaka Upaniṣad*.

"*Svasti* means immortality itself." (Yāska) *Svasti* means "auspiciousness, benediction, *puṇya* (merit) and abidance in *dharma*." Devī is one who possesses all these. Hence, She is *Svastimatī*, one who possesses *svasti*.

449. कान्तिः

Kāntiḥ

She who is effulgence.

With Her own effulgence, Devī makes everything else shine. *Kāntiḥ*, once seen, awakens the desire to see more and more. Can one have enough of the *darśan* of Devī? The desire for it is ever-rising.

Kāntiḥ also means *icchāśakti* (will power). Devī is one who has indomitable will power.

Kāntiḥ is a mark of excellence in literature. This meaning also applies to Devī, who is the seat of all excellence. The names from 443-449 indicate that all great qualities in human beings are Devi's blessings.

450. नन्दिनी

Nandinī

She who gives delight.

Nandinī is the sacred cow in sage Vasiṣṭha's āśram, providing the sage with the materials for sacrifices, and the residents with everything they need for themselves and for the service of guests. *Nandinī* is a form of Devī.

Nandinī is also a name for Gangā, the sacred river. Gangā is also a giver of delight, one who washes away all sins and provides new energy for body and soul. Devī is in the form of Gangā.

Nandinī is also Nanda's daughter, Viṣṇumāya.

451. विघ्न नाशिनी

Vighna nāśinī

She who destroys all obstacles.

Devī is the one who removes all obstacles arising on both the spiritual and the material paths in life.

452. तेजोवती

Tejovatī

She who is effulgent.

Devī Herself is effulgent and is the support of all that is effulgent.

This is made clear in the *Kaṭha Upaniṣad* (II.ii.15): "The sun does not shine there, nor does the moon, nor does the lightning shine and much less this fire. When He shines everything shines after Him; by His light all these shine." The name *Tejovatī* means that Devī is none other than that *Brahman.*

Tejas also means prowess. Devī has the prowess arising from the eight attributes of excellences (*aiśvaryas*).

453. त्रि नयना

Tri nayanā

She who has the sun, moon and fire as Her three eyes.

Nayana is one who leads. She is one who leads to real knowledge through the three (*tri*) pathways. The three paths, according to the *Manusmṛti*, are perception, inference and word (scriptures).

Alternately, She is one who leads us to the Truth through the three paths of hearing, contemplation and deep meditation.

The three paths may also be those of the south, north and the path of *Brahman*. She leads the *jīvas* through these paths according to what each deserves; hence She is *Trinayanā*.

454. लोलाक्षी काम रूपिणी

Lolākṣī kāma rūpiṇī

She who is in the form of love in women.

Devī is both beautiful (*lolākṣī*) and the embodiment of love or desire (*kāmarūpiṇī*). Her beauty is so great that She engenders desire in beautiful women. She shines as love in women or She has the loveliest form among all the beautiful women.

Kāmarūpiṇī stands for *Yogeśvarī*, the deity of desire (*icchāśakti*), according to *Saubhāgyabhāskara*. In *Varāha Purāṇa*, eight powers and their deities are described. These are: desire (*Yogeśvarī*), anger (*Maheśvarī*), greed (*Vaiṣnavī*), passion (*Brahmāṇī*), bewilderment or delusion (*Kalyāṇī*), envy (*Indrajā*), calumny (*Yamadaṇḍadharā*) and scorn (*Vārāhī*).

455. मालिनी

Mālinī

She who is wearing garlands.

One who is fond of wearing a garland made of the fifty-one letters of the alphabet.

Devī is "resplendent in a garland of red flowers," as described in the verse of invocation (*dhyānaśloka*).

Devī is accompanied by *Mālinī*, a companion of Pārvatī at the time of Her wedding, according to *Vāmana Purāṇa*. *Mālinī* is Gangā, one who wears a garland of waves. Devī is also *Mālinī* when accompanied by that Gangā.

Mālinī is the name of a meter in *Sanskṛt* poetry. Also, *mālinī* is a girl of seven years according to Dhaumya. Worship of young girls during Devī *pūja* is based on this tradition.

456. हंसिनी

Hamsinī

She who is not separate from Hamsas (*the* yogins *who have reached great spiritual heights*).

She who has the special quality of a swan. A swan is said to be able to separate the milk from a mixture of milk and water. Devī is likened to a swan and called *Hamsinī*, because She can clearly separate good from evil.

The *ajapa mantra* is called *Hamsinī*. Devī is in the form of that *mantra*.

457. माता

Mātā

She who is the Mother of the universe.

Also, She who is *Matṛka*. *Matṛkas* are letters of the alphabet. "The Supreme Goddess is called *Matṛka*, as She is the mother of all *mantras*." (*Skanda Purāṇa*)

She is *(pra)māta* or one who knows, the first member of the triad of knower, known and knowledge (*pramāta*, *prameya*, and *pramāna*). Thus the name *Mātā* can be understood as She who knows everything.

Mātā is the deity of the tenth day of the lunar fortnight. She is another form of Devī. Also, *Mātā* is the deity of the Kāyāvarohana temple.

The *Lakṣmibīja mantra* is also called *Mātā*. Devī is considered to be in the form of that *mantra*. *Śrī*, *Mī*, *Ramā*, *Kamalā* and *Mātā* all mean Lakṣmī.

458. मलयाचल वासिनी

Malayācala vāsinī

She who resides in the Malaya mountain.

She is also known as *Malayālayā*, which has the same meaning. This mountain is famous for sandalwood, well-known for its coolness and sacredness.

459. सुमुखी

Sumukhī

She who has a beautiful face.

Devī shines with a face that never loses its luster. The beauty of Her face is heightened by true wisdom. The *Śruti* says, "One who knows It, His face shines." *Chāndogya Upaniṣad* (IV.14.2) also refers to this beauty of wisdom: "Dear child, your face shines like that of a knower of *Brahman*."

Sumukhī is the name of a *nitya* deity who is to be worshipped as part of *ṣodaśī mantra* worship. That deity is none other than Devī.

Sumukhī is a musical *rāga* which is also considered to be a manifestation of Devī.

460. नलिनी

Nalinī

She whose body is soft and beautiful like lotus petals.

Devī's hands, feet, eyes and face are comparable to the beauty of the lotus.

Nalinī is another name of *Gangā.*

King Nala, a devotee of Devī, became one with Her; hence She is called *Nalinī*, according to *Saubhāgyabhāskara.*

461. सुभ्रुः

Subhruḥ

She who has beautiful eyebrows.

The *Ājñā cakra* has a lotus with two petals. Here, the eyebrows symbolize that *cakra.*

462. शोभना

Śobhanā

She who is always radiant.

One who, with Her own radiance, makes everything else shine.

463. सुरनायिका

Suranāyikā

She who is the leader of the gods.

As She is the leader of even the gods, who is there that is not in Her dominion?

Devas are those who shine with special knowledge. Devī is the leader of those who are thus endowed.

464. कालकण्ठी

Kālakaṇṭhī

She who is the wife of Śiva.

When the Ocean of Milk was churned for nectar, the first thing to emerge was poison. No one dared to receive it, as it would burn the whole world down if it fell on the ground. Both the *devas* and *asuras* were equally terrified by it. Lord Śiva received the poison without any hesitation and swallowed it. Devī Pārvatī panicked at the sight and held His throat to stop the poison from descending. The poison became fixed in Śiva's throat and He thus became *Kālakaṇṭha* (dark-throated), *Nīlakaṇṭha* (blue-throated) or *Śrikaṇṭha* (poison-throated).

Kālakaṇṭhī also means She who has a sweet throat (voice). Devī's voice is divinely sweet (see *mantra* 27).

According to *Devī Purāṇa*, Kālanjara is one of the sixty-eight holy places of India. The deity installed there is *Kālakaṇṭhī*.

Liṅga Purāṇa says that Devī took the forms of *Kālī*, *Kapardinī* and *Kālakaṇṭhī* to kill the demon Dāruka.

465. कान्ति मती

Kānti matī

She who is radiant.

The name *Kānti* has already been described (see *mantra* 449). The meanings given there apply here as well.

466. क्षोभिणी

Kṣobhiṇī

She who creates upheaval in the mind.

The upheaval She creates is a creative urge. The *Sāṅkhya* view is that *Puruṣa* (the Cosmic Man) is inherently inactive. Devī (*Prakṛti* or Nature) incites Him to act, to create the universe.

There is a story in the *Varāha Purāṇa*. Vaiṣnavī, the wife of Viṣṇu, went to the Mandāra mountain to do penance. After She was immersed in penance for a long time, Her mind became agitated by desire and from this sprang countless young women of great beauty. The name *Kṣobhiṇī* became synonymous with Devī since that time.

467. सूक्ष्म रूपिणी

Sūkṣma rūpiṇī

She who has a form that is too subtle to be perceived by the sense organs.

There are three kinds of forms - gross, subtle and subtlest (*parā*). In this *mantra*, Devī is described as having a subtle form. "Subtler than the subtle, greater than the great," (*Kaṭha Upaniṣad*, I.ii.20) and "Subtler than the subtle," (*Kaivalya Upaniṣad* 16) is how the Supreme is described.

The word *sūkṣma* also means a *homa* (oblation). There are twelve kinds of oblations. Of these, the greatest is the daily oblation done at the fire in the *mūlādhāra cakra*. This worship is a *mānasa pūja* performed silently in the mind.

This *mantra* reminds us that Devī's real form is not gross, but one that is the subtlest, which is the undivided *Brahman*.

468. वज्रेश्वरी

Vajreśvarī

She who is Vajreśvarī, *the sixth daily deity.*

The *Śrīcakra* has twelve walls built out of diamonds. In the center of the eleventh, there is a river called Vajramayi and *Vajreśvarī* is the deity of this river. She is a part of Devī. Hence Devī is called *Vajreśvarī*.

Devī gave Indra the *vajra* (lightning bolt) weapon, as described in the *Brahmāṇḍa Purāṇa*. Thus She is known as the Goddess of

Vajra (*Vajreśvarī*). Indra performed penance in water; Devī, arising from the water gave him the Vajra weapon and disappeared. Greatly satisfied, Indra returned to heaven.

The *Lalitāstavaratna* describes Her thus: "In that ever-flowing Vajra river which has beautiful banks and in which the graceful swans play on the waves, *Vajreśvarī* shines, decked with diamond ornaments and served by Indra, the wielder of the *vajra* weapon."

Vajreśvarī is also the name of the deity of *Jālandhara Pīṭha.*

469. वाम देवी

Vāma devī

She who is the wife of Vāmadeva (Śiva).

Vāma is "left side" and Vāmadeva is Śiva, the half-female, half-male divinity, whose left side is Devī. *Śiva Purāṇa* says, "The beautiful face of Śiva that faces north, red as vermillion, is called *Vāma.*" This is *Vāmavyūha*, one of the five forms (*vyūhas*) of Śiva.

Vāma also means "good," and "the fruit of *karma.*" Devī is the presiding deity of everything that is good and of all the fruits of action.

Vāma is also beautiful. Devī is the abode of beauty. Truth, auspiciousness and beauty, (*Satyam, śivam, sundaram*) are the attributes of Devī.

Vāmācāra is the left-hand path of Devī worship and *Vāmadevī* is the presiding goddess. According to the *Devī Purāṇa*, "*Vāma* is the opposite or inverted path; Devī gives bliss through that path, hence She is remembered as *Vāmadevī.*" (See *mantra* 332)

470. वयोवस्था विवर्जिता

Vayovasthā vivarjitā

She who is exempt from changes due to age (time).

Devī is beyond the changes such as birth, aging and death.

471. सिद्धेश्वरी

Siddheśvarī

She who is the goddess worshipped by spiritual adepts.

Devī is the one who bestows all *siddhis*; hence this name is apt for Her.

Siddheśvarī is the name of a famous deity of Kāśi (Varanāsi).

472. सिद्ध विद्या

Siddha vidyā

She who is in the form of Siddhavidyā, *the fifteen-syllabled* mantra.

Since the *pañcadaśi mantra* is eternal and universal, the rules regarding preparations, time and place prescribed for other *mantras* need not be followed in its case. Worship using this *mantra* can be done anywhere, at any time.

473. सिद्ध माता

Siddha mātā

She who is the mother of Siddhas.

Siddhas are those who have renounced all worldly attachments. Devī is mother to them all. She undertakes their care and protection like a mother. It is to Her that they turn for everything. She hears their call and gives whatever they need.

Devī is the mother of all those who desire Liberation. She wants them to succeed in their efforts.

474. यशस्विनी

Yaśasvinī

She who is of unequalled renown.

Devī's fame is unparalleled because of Her innumerable and

glorious *līlās* (sports). Her love, compassion and power of protection bring Her great fame.

475. विशुद्धि चक्र निलया

Viśuddhi cakra nilayā

She who resides in the Viśuddhicakra.

Viśuddhi, located in the throat, is the fifth of the six *ādhāra cakras* (see commentary on *mantra* 99). *Ḍākinī* Devī resides there.

In sixty-two names starting with this, the presiding deities of the six *ādhāra cakras* and the *sahasrāra* are described as different forms of Devī. These deities are *Ḍākinī*, *Rākiṇī*, *Lākinī*, *Kākinī*, *Sākinī*, *Hākinī* and *Yākinī*.

She is meditated upon as follows: "In the cavity of the throat, in the center of the *Viśuddhi*, in the sixteen-petaled lotus, I adore *Ḍākinī*, rosy, three-eyed, bearing the club, the sword, the trident and a large skin in Her hands, having one face, striking living beings with fear, always fond of *pāyasa* (sweet milk-pudding), presiding over the organ of touch, surrounded by *Amrita* and other deities and worshipped by warriors."

These attributes are described in detail in the following nine *mantras*.

476. आरक्त वर्णा

Ārakta varṇā

She who is of slightly red (rosy) complexion.

Ḍākinī Devī's complexion is slightly red like the color of the *pāṭala* flower (trumpet flower).

477. त्रि लोचना

Tri locanā

She who has three eyes.

The sun, moon and fire are Her eyes, as are also the past, present and future.

478. खट्वाङ्गादि प्रहरणा

Khaṭvāṅgādi praharaṇā

She who is armed with a club and other weapons.

Khaṭvāṅga is a club with a skull at its end. It is Śiva's weapon. The other weapons refer to a sword, a trident and a rod. From the description in the meditation verse, *Ḍākinī* is to be understood as four-armed, holding the club and other weapons.

479. वदनैक समन्विता

Vadanaika samanvitā

She who possesses only one face.

Ḍākinī Devī, residing in the throat, has only one face. The scriptures prescribe silence while eating. The reason is that the Devī in the *Viśuddhicakra* in the throat has only one face.

480. पायसान्न प्रिया

Pāyasānna priyā

She who is especially fond of sweet rice.

481. त्वक्स्था

Tvaksthā

She who is the deity of the organ of touch (skin).

482. पशु लोक भयङ्करी

Paśu loka bhayaṅkarī

She who fills with fear the mortal beings bound by worldly existence.

"In enjoyment, there is fear of disease; in the family there is fear of decline; in wealth, there is fear from the king; in honor, there is fear of misery; in fine physique, there is fear from young women; in knowledge, there is fear of dispute; in goodness there is fear of evil men; in the body, there is fear of death; all things on earth cause fear without doubt; dispassion is the only freedom from fear, the only refuge."

Everything is a cause of fear for one bound in *samsāra*. The only refuge from fear is dispassion.

Paśu is one who has not realized the oneness of the *jīva* with the Supreme. One who sees (differences) - *paśyati* - is a *paśu*.

483. अमृतादि महाशक्ति संवृता

Amṛtādi mahāśakti samvṛtā

She who is surrounded by Amṛta *and other* śakti *deities.*

The lotus in the *viśuddhicakra* has sixteen petals, each occupied by a *śakti*. The sixteen are *Amṛta*, *Ākarṣini*, *Indrānī*, *Īśānī*, *Umā*, *Ūrdhvakeśi*, *Rudrā*, *Rikarā*, *Likarā*, *Lukarā*, *Ekapādā*, *Aiśvaryātmikā*, *Omkārā*, *Auṣadhī*, *Ambikā*, and *Akṣarā*.

The sixteen *śaktis* represent the internal powers such as intelligence, ego, and the powers of attraction based in the external organs. *Ḍākinī* is surrounded by all these.

484. डाकिनीश्वरी

Ḍākinīsvarī

She who is the Ḍākinī *deity (described by the nine preceding names).*

485. अनाहताब्ज निलया

Anāhatābja nilayā

She who resides in the anāhata *lotus in the heart.*

Mantras 485-494 describe *Rākiṇi* Devī. *Anāhata* is a lotus with twelve petals. *Rākiṇī* resides in its center. She is meditated on as follows: "We meditate upon *Rākiṇī*, the bestower of wishes, residing in the twelve-petaled lotus of the heart, having two faces, with protruding tusks, black in color, holding a disc, a trident, a skull and a drum in Her hands, three-eyed, presiding over blood, served by *Kālarātri* and other attendants, fond of oily food and worshipped by the brave."

486. श्यामाभा

Śyāmābhā

She who is black in complexion.

A sixteen year old girl is known as Śyāma. Devī is an eternal maiden of sixteen.

487. वदन द्वया

Vadana dvayā

She who has two faces.

Everything exists as a pair of opposites - happiness and sorrow, heat and cold, profit and loss.

488. दंष्ट्रोज्ज्वला

Damṣṭrojjvalā

She who has shining tusks.

489. अक्ष मालादि धरा

Akṣa mālādi dharā

She who is wearing garlands of rudrākṣa *beads and other things.*

Saubhāgyabhāskara interprets this in a different way: Akṣa means "the wheel of a chariot." *Akṣamāla* is something that bears (*la*) resemblance (*ma*) to a wheel, a disc. Thus Devī wears a disc and other weapons (trident, etc.) as described in *mantra* 485.

490. रुधिर संस्थिता

Rudhira samsthitā

She who presides over the blood in the bodies of living beings.

491. काल रात्र्यादि शक्त्यौघवृता

Kāla rātryādi śaktyaughavṛtā

She who is surrounded by Kālarātri *and other* śaktis.

The heart *cakra* has twelve petals and there is a *śakti* in each of them. In the pericarp in the center is *Rākiṇi* Devī.

492. स्निग्धौदन प्रिया

Snigdhaudana priyā

She who is fond of food offerings containing ghee, *oil and other substances containing fats.*

493. महा वीरेन्द्र वरदा

Mahā vīrendra varadā

She who bestows boons on great warriors.

Indra is one who knows *Brahman* directly. "He perceived; hence he is known as Indra," according to the *Śruti*. *Mahāvīrendras* are those who are continuously enjoying the nectar of *Brahman*.

Mahāvīra is the vessel in which offerings to gods are placed in the course of a sacrificial ceremony. Indra and other gods partake of these offerings.

She who grants boons to Mahāvīra (Prahlāda), Indra and others. There is mention in the *Devī Bhāgavata* that Indra did penance and pleased Devī.

The great *yogis* who have reached the fourth state of *turīya* are called *mahāvīras*. They are the great warriors who have fought and vanquished the mighty foes of desire, anger and greed. Devī is one who grants boons to these warriors.

Why do such *yogins*, who have reached *turīya*, need boons? They, too, have a state known as *vyuddhānadaśa* in which they provide leadership in worldly affairs.They acquire this strength from the boons given by *Rākiṇi* Devī.

494. राकिण्यम्बा स्वरूपिणी

Rākiṇyambā svarūpiṇī

She who is in the form of the Rākiṇi *deity (described in the nine previous* mantras*).*

495. मणिपूराब्ज निलया

Maṇipūrābja nilayā

She who resides in the ten-petaled lotus in the maṇipūraka cakra.

This is the abode of *Lākinī Yogini*. She is meditated upon as follows: "Let us meditate on *Lākinī* in the lotus in the navel, three-faced, with tusks, blood red in color, bearing in Her hands the dart (or spear, *śakti*), the thunderbolt, the rod and *abhaya* (a weapon), most terrible, attended by *Ḍāmarī* and other *śaktis*, inspiring fear in the ignorant, presiding over the flesh in the bodies of beings, fond of sweet foods, and doing good to all." In each of the ten petals of the lotus in *maṇipūraka* resides *Ḍāmarī* and other *śaktis*. *Lākinī* dwells in the center, in the pericarp.

496. वदन त्रय संयुता

Vadana traya samyutā

She who has three faces.

497. वज्रादिकायुधोपेता

Vajrādikāyudhopetā

She who holds the vajra *(lightning bolt) and other weapons.*

The weapons are *vajra*, the dart, the rod and *abhaya* (a *mudra* bestowing fearlessness).

498. डामर्यादिभिर् आवृता

Ḍāmaryādibhir āvṛtā

She who is surrounded by Ḍāmarī *and other attending deities.*

As mentioned above, *Lākinī* has ten attending deities - ten petals in the lotus and ten attendants. These attendants are discussed in *Pūjāpaddhati.*

499. रक्त वर्णा

Rakta varṇā

She who is red in complexion.

500. मांस निष्ठा

Māmsa niṣṭhā

She who presides over the flesh in living beings.

Thus ends the hundred names in *rucikalā*, the sixth *kalā* of the sun.

501. गुडान्न प्रीत मानसा

Guḍānna prīta mānasā

She who is fond of sweet rice made with raw sugar.

502. समस्त भक्त सुखदा

Samasta bhakta sukhadā

She who confers happiness on all Her devotees.

Happiness in this life and beyond is meant here. There is no doubt that those who worship the Divine Mother get quick results. She is more compassionate and bountiful than any other deity.

503. लाकिन्यम्बास्वरूपिणी

Lākinyambāsvarūpiṇī

She who is in the form of the Lākinī Yoginī *described in the previous eight* mantras.

504. स्वाधिष्ठानाम्बुज गता

Svādhiṣṭhānāmbuja gatā

She who resides in the six-petaled lotus in the svādhiṣṭhāna, Kākinī Yoginī.

Kākinī is now described. Her meditation is: "We meditate upon *Kākinī* who resides in the six-petaled *svādhiṣṭhāna* lotus, four-faced, three-eyed, bearing in Her hands the trident, the noose, the skull and the *abhaya* weapon, ever proud, presiding over the lymph (fat) in the bodies of living beings, attended by Bandinī and others, yellow in complexion, fond of honey and of food mixed with curd, and giver of desires."

The meditation verse literally says "*Veda*-faced," implying that Her four faces are the *Vedas*.

505. चतुर् वक्त्र मनोहरा

Catur vaktra manoharā

She who has four beautiful faces.

There are the four *Vedas*. They are *Kākinī*'s faces as said in the meditation verse.

506. शुलाद्यायुध सम्पन्ना

Śulādyāyudha sampannā

She who possesses the trident and other weapons. Her weapons are the trident, noose (rope), skull and abhaya.

507. पीत वर्णा

Pīta varṇā

She who is yellow in color.

508. अति गर्विता

Ati garvitā

She who is very proud (of Her weapons and Her captivating beauty).

509. मेदो निष्ठा

Medo niṣṭhā

She who resides in the fat in living beings.

510. मधु प्रीता

Madhu prītā

She who is fond of honey and other offerings made with honey.

511. बन्दिन्यादि समन्विता

Bandhinyādi samanvitā

She who is accompanied by Bandinī and other śaktis. Kākinī *resides in the central stalk of the six-petaled lotus surrounded by the six* śaktis *(from Bandinī to Lamboṣṭhī), one in each of the six petals.*

512. दध्यन्नासक्त हृदया

Dadhyannāsakta hṛdayā

She who is particularly fond of offerings made with curd.

513. काकिनी रूप धारिणी

Kākinī rūpa dhāriṇī

She who is in the form of Kākinī Yoginī, *described in the ten previous names.*

514. मूलाधाराम्बुजारूढा

Mūlādhārāmbujārūḍhā

She who is resident in the lotus in the mūlādhāra.

Sākinī Yoginī is described now. The lotus in the *mūlādhāra* has four petals which are occupied by four *amṛta śaktis*. Surrounded by them, *Sākinī* resides in the pericarp. She is meditated on as follows: "We meditate on *Sākinī*, who resides in the four-petaled *mūlādhāra* lotus, five-faced, three-eyed, smoke-colored, presiding over the bones in living beings, bearing in Her hands the goad, lotus, book and *jñānamudrā* (the sign of knowledge), attended by the gentle Varadā and other deities, fond of eating *mudga* beans and intoxicated with mead."

515. पञ्च वक्त्रा

Pañca vaktrā

She who has five faces.

Four of the five faces are turned to the four directions and the fifth is turned upwards.

516. अस्थि संस्थिता

Asthi samsthitā

She who resides in the bones.

She is the presiding deity of the skeleton in living beings.

517. अङ्कुशादि प्रहरणा

Aṅkuśādi praharaṇā

She who holds the goad and other weapons.

She has a goad, a lotus, the *mudrā* (a posture of the hand) of knowledge and a book in Her hands, as indicated in the meditation verse.

518. वरदादि निषेविता

Varadādi niṣevitā

She who is attended by Varadā and other śaktis.

Sākinī resides in the pericarp (*karnika*) of the four-petaled lotus surrounded by Varadā, Sarasvatī and other deities.

519. मुद्गौदनासक्त चित्ता

Mudgaudanāsakta cittā

She who is particularly fond of food offerings made of mudga, *a lentil.*

520. साकिन्यम्बा स्वरूपिणी

Sākinyambā svarūpiṇī

She who is in the form of Sākinī Yoginī *(described in the six names given above).*

521. आज्ञा चक्राब्ज निलया

Ājñā cakrābja nilayā

She who resides in the two-petaled lotus in the ājñācakra.

Now we are describing the *Hākinī Yoginī*, who is meditated on as follows: "We meditate on *Hākinī*, residing between the eyebrows, in the two-petaled *bindu*-lotus, white in color, holding the *jñānamudrā*, drum, lotus, *mālā* (necklace) of *rudrākṣa* beads and skull, six-faced, three-eyed, attended by Hamsavatī and other *śaktis*, fond of food seasoned with turmeric and bestowing good on all others."

522. शुक्ल वर्णा

Śukla varṇā

She who is white.

The *Ājñācakra* is the seat of *candramaṇḍala*, the disc of the moon, hence the whiteness.

523. षडानना

Ṣaḍānanā

She who has six faces.

Ājñācakra is the sphere of the intellect. Recall that there are six *śāstras* (branches of knowledge).

524. मज्जा संस्था

Majjā samsthā

She who is the presiding deity of the bone marrow.

525. हंसवती मुख्य शक्ति समन्विता

Hamsavatī mukhya śakti samanvitā

She who is accompanied by the śaktis Hamsavatī *and* Kṣamāvatī *(in the two petals of the lotus).*

526. हरिद्रान्नैक रसिका

Haridrānnaika rasikā

She who is fond of food seasoned with turmeric.

In many famous temples, rice mixed with turmeric is usually distributed as *prasādam.*

527. हाकिनी रूप धारिणी

Hākinī rūpa dhāriṇī

She who is in the form of Hākinī *Devī (described in the preceding six* mantras*).*

528. सहस्र दल पद्मस्था

Sahasra dala padmasthā

She who resides in the thousand-petaled lotus.

Yākinī Yoginī, who is described next, resides in the pericarp of the thousand-petaled lotus in the *Brahmarandhra* above the *ājñācakra.* Her meditation is as follows: "We meditate on *Yākinī*

Devī, residing in the moon of the pericarp of the thousand-petaled lotus in the *Brahmarandhra*, presiding over the semen, armed with all kinds of weapons, facing all sides, attended by the host of *śaktis* of the letters from *A* to *Kṣa*, shining in all colors, fond of all varieties of food, and devoted to the Supreme Śiva."

529. सर्व वर्णोपशोभिता

Sarva varṇopaśobhitā

She who is radiant in many colors.

Light red, dark red, black and yellow are the main colors (*varṇas*) here.

Varṇa also means "letters of the alphabet." The letters *A* to *Kṣa* (of the Sanskṛt alphabet) are sometimes referred to as the deities from *Amṛtaśakti* to *Kṣamāśakti*. Alternately, one speaks of the *śaktis* from *Amṛtaśakti* to *Hamsavati*; here the reference is to the letters from *A* to *Ha*. In either case, each letter is said to represent a separate *śakti* deity.

If one adds the numbers of petals in the lotuses from *mūlādhāra* to *ājñācakra*, one gets fifty, each bearing a *śakti*. Including both ascending and descending directions through the *cakras*, one has a total of one hundred *śaktis*. In the present *mantra*, the word *upa* stands for ten. When each of the hundred *śaktis* of letters repeat in ten petals, one gets a thousand. This is the significance of the thousand petals. *Yākinī* Devī shines in all one thousand petals in many resplendent colors.

530. सर्वायुध धरा

Sarvāyudha dharā

She who holds all the known weapons.

Yākinī Devī is described as holding countless weapons in Her countless hands.

531. शुक्ल संस्थिता

Śukla samsthitā

She who resides in the semen.

Of the seven *dhātus* (essential ingredients of the body), semen is considered most important. It is believed to be related to the brain. That is why conserving it is very important. Squandering it is harmful even for a householder, the bad effects from which will affect the brain.

Śukla is also the name of the meditation known as *tārakabrahma dhyāna.* Devī is understood to be in the form of *Tārakabrahma.*

532. सर्वतोमुखी

Sarvatomukhī

She who has faces turned in all directions.

533. सर्वौदन प्रीत चित्ता

Sarvaudana prīta cittā

She who is pleased by all offerings of food.

534. याकिन्यम्बा स्वरूपिणी

Yākinyambā svarūpiṇī

She who is in the form of the Yākinī Yoginī *(described in the six preceding* mantras*).*

After describing the various *Yoginīs*, we resume the description of Devī's attributes.

535. स्वाहा

Svāhā

She who is the object of the invocation "svāhā" *at the end of* mantras *chanted while offering oblations to the fire in* yāga *ceremonies.*

Svāhā means "that which is useful in invoking the chosen

deity." *Svāhā* is the wife of Śiva in His manifestation as Agni (fire). The *Linga Purāṇa* says, "*Svāhā* is the essence of fire and one who invokes that name is dear to Śiva." Traditionally, "Om" is chanted at the beginning and "*svāhā*" at the end of *mantras* when making offerings.

Also, *svāha* (*sva+aha*) means one's own speech. The feminine form of this, *svāhā*, is the present *mantra*. The word of the worshipper and the word of Devī become one.

Or, *svāhā* (*su+aha*) is good uttering, good words, words of wisdom.

Bhāskararāya interprets this name also as "She who knows Herself well." That is the knowledge of *Brahman*. Devī is one who possesses the knowledge of *Brahman* and one who confers that knowledge.

536. स्वधा

Svadhā

She who is the object of the "svadhā" *invocation at the end of* mantras.

At the end of *mantras* chanted while making offerings to the ancestors, the word "*svadhā*" is used, just as '*svāhā*" is used at the end of *mantras* for offerings to *devas*.

Svadhā can also be interpreted as "She who carries (nurtures, protects) all beings including Viṣṇu" (*su*, well + *a*, Viṣṇu + *dha*, nourishes).

Devī Māhātmya says, "O Devī, by repeating Your name all the gods are pleased, since You are both *svāhā* and *svadhā*."

Svāhā, *svadhā*, *ṣrauṣaṭ*, *vauṣat* and *vaṣaṭ* are all parts of *mantras* used to invoke various gods while making offerings to them.

537. अमतिः

Amatiḥ

She who is in the form of ignorance or nescience.

Amati, or *Avidyā*, is the deity presiding over actions done according to emotions without applying discrimination.

As the *Kaṭha Upaniṣad* (I.ii.2) explains, the unintelligent man wants to amass objects of pleasure. Therefore he discards the path of the good and chooses the path of pleasure. The same *Upaniṣad* (II.iv.2) also says, "The ignorant (the child-like) pursue external pleasures and fall into the widespread snares of death."

It is *amati* (ignorance) that pushes the *samsāri* into the path of physical pleasures and into the snare of death.

Amati is also interpreted as the first creation, which was without intelligence.

Durgācārya takes this *mantra* as *matiḥ*, interpreting it as knowledge of the Self.

538. मेधा

Medhā

She who is in the form of wisdom (knowledge).

She is the second creation, which is accompanied by intelligence.

Since Sarasvatī is the deity of intelligence, this *mantra* means "She who is in the form of Sarasvatī." *Devī Māhātmya* praises Her as "the Devī who resides in all beings in the form of *medhā* (intelligence)."

According to *Padma Purāṇa*, She is Medhā, a deity of Kaśmīr.

539. श्रुतिः

Śrutiḥ

She who is in the form of the Vedas.

Śruti is what is heard and what should be learned through hearing; *Śruti* is the *Vedas*. *Śruti* is what the sages received through the sense of hearing during their meditation.

The four *Vedas* are: *Ṛg*, *Yajus*, *Sāma* and *Atharva*. They are said to be the outgoing breath of *Brahman*. *Vedas* are the embodiment of knowledge. They are eternal, and therefore the same as *Brahman*. Devī who Herself is *Brahman*-as-knowledge (*jñānabrahman*), is called *Śruti*.

"*Śruti* is Mātā (Mother)," is a well-known saying. It is said that in music, *śruti* (pitch, tone) is the mother and *laya* (time) is the father.

540. स्मृतिः

Smṛtiḥ

She who is in the form of Smṛti.

Smṛtis are works based on the meaning of *Śruti* (*Vedas*).

There are many works which are known as *Smṛtis - Manusmṛti, Bārhaspatyasmṛti, Yājñavalkyasmṛti*. When *Smṛti* and *Śruti* (*Vedas*) give conflicting statements on anything, the statement in *Śruti* should be adopted as ultimate authority. *Smṛti* may change with time.

Smṛti also means memory. Since Devī is the one who awakens and illumines memory, She is called *Smṛti* in this *mantra*.

Devī Purāṇa says that Devī is *Smṛti*, since She is the one who remembers the past, present and future.

541. अनुत्तमा

Anuttamā

She who is the best, She who is not excelled by anyone.

When we praise someone as being unequalled in intellectual or physical strength, we do not compare him to Brahmā, Viṣṇu or Śiva. It is his *śakti* (strength) that we praise as unequalled. That *śakti* is Devī.

542. पुण्य कीर्तिः

Puṇya kīrtiḥ

She whose fame is sacred or righteous.

Devi's glory is such that it sanctifies anyone who remembers and spreads it. It is sanctifying even to hear of Her glory. As Śaṅkarācārya says, "How can one who has not accrued merit even hear of, recall or meditate on Her glory?" (*Saundarya Laharī*, verse 1)

The *mantra* also means "She who is glorified by meritorious or righteous individuals."

543. पुण्य लभ्या

Puṇya labhyā

She who is attained only by righteous souls.

Whoever worships Devī for fulfilling some desire will get what they desire, but not the gift of Her vision (*darśan*). Her *darśan* is obtained only by those who practice *karmayoga* selflessly and by those who are *jñānis* - knowers of the Truth. "Devī, the auspicious Goddess, is seen only by those with merit, those who know the truth of the *Vedas*, those who do *tapas*. Those who are driven by desires do not see Her."

But how few in number are such selfless *karmayogins*! They are the valiant ones, the heroes. They are the anchor for this world.

544. पुण्य श्रवण कीर्तना

Puṇya śravaṇa kīrtanā

She who bestows merit on anyone who hears of Her and praises Her.

Let us praise Her - at least during that time when evil thoughts enter the mind. Freeing the mind from unclean thoughts is meritorious. These unclean thoughts and actions are known as sin. "Through eighteen *Purāṇas*, Vyāsa said just one thing: serving others is *puṇya*, hurting others is *pāpa* (sin)."

Those who hear of and praise the glories of Devī attain merit. In them, there exists no thought of hurting others.

545. पुलोमजार्चिता

Pulomajārcitā

She who is worshipped by Pulomaja.

Pulomaja is Indrānī, Indra's wife.

On the advice of Bṛhaspati, the Guru of the *devas*, Pulomaja worshipped Devī to regain for her husband the kingdom of heaven from Nahuṣa, who had seized it.

Nahuṣa, a king of the lineage of the sun, attained the status of Indra by performing a hundred *yāgas* (sacrifices). But he felt that his status would be complete only if Indrānī became his wife as well. Indrānī became very unhappy at this. She worshipped Tripurasundarī Devī to be able to keep Indra as her husband. Through this worship, a way to avert the misfortune became clear to her.

She demanded that in order to accept Nahuṣa as her husband, he should arrive in a palanquin carried by the *ṛṣis*. The love-sick Nahuṣa agreed to this. He started on his journey to Indrānī's chambers in great splendor, in a dolly carried by the great sages. The sage Agastya, being short, happened to tilt the carriage to one side. Nahuṣa urged him on by tapping on his head saying "*Sarpa, sarpa* (Move, move!)!" Angered by this, Agastya cursed him, "*Sarpo bhava*!" meaning, "Turn into a serpent!" Nahuṣa then turned into a great serpent and slithered to the ground. Thus, through worship of Devī, Indrānī overcame her danger and regained her husband.

546. बन्ध मोचनी

Bandha mocanī

She who is free from bonds; also, She who gives release from bondage.

Devī gives freedom from all kinds of bondage. Queen Ekāvalī was put in prison by the demon Kālaketu. Her attendant worshipped and pleased Devī who released the queen from bondage. Similarly Aniruddha, who was imprisoned by the Emperor Bāna, regained freedom through worship of Devī and was able to marry Bāna's daughter, Uṣā. Nothing is impossible when Devī's grace is present.

547. बर्बरालका

Barbarālakā

She who has wavy locks of hair.

Rich hair is a mark of Devī's beauty. This name is also given as "*Bandhurālakā*" - One with beautiful hair.

548. विमर्श रूपिणी

Vimarśa rūpiṇī

She who is in the form of Vimarśa.

Prakāśa and *Vimarśa* are terms used in Śiva-Śakti doctrine which can be translated as luminosity and reflection. Śiva, *prakāśa*, is pure Consciousness; creative power is latent in It. Śakti, *vimarśa*, is a flash or a throb (*sphurana*) in that consciousness which leads to the cycle of creation, sustenance and dissolution. The process of creation is thus under the control of Devī in the *Vimarśa* form.

Vimarśa and *prakāśa* can be interpreted as word and meaning respectively, as indicated before. Vimarśa may also be understood as shape or form. Thus, Devī manifests as the names and forms which make up the whole universe.

549. विद्या

Vidyā

She who is in the form of knowledge.

Devī is of the nature of knowledge (*vidyā*). She has already been described as the deity of sixty-four forms of art and as having the form of the *Śrutis* and the *Smṛtis*. The present *mantra* refers to the knowledge of the Self; Devī is in the form of that knowledge. *Vidyā* is the knowledge that leads to Liberation.

550. वियदादि जगत् प्रसूः

Viyadādi jagat prasūḥ

She who is the Mother of the universe, which is the aggregate of all the elements starting with the ether.

The *Śruti* says, "The ether arose from the *Ātman.*" (*Taittiriya Upaniṣad* II.2)

551. सर्वव्याधि प्रशमनी

Sarvavyādhi praśamanī

She who removes all diseases and sorrows.

Vyādhi means "old age and disease." Devī is one who dispels all physical and mental diseases. Her grace is capable of removing not only diseases, but even death.

552. सर्व मृत्यु निवारिणी

Sarva mṛtyu nivāriṇī

She who guards Her devotees from all kinds of death.

Death can come from old age or it can be untimely death. Devī's will can postpone both kinds of death.

"Lead me from death to immortality," is a well-known prayer. The statement in the *Śruti*, "Knowing It only, does one transcend death; there is no other path known for this," is proof of the fact that Devī's grace enables one to transcend death. "He who knows Him thus, cuts asunder the fetters of death." (*Śvetāśvatāra Upaniṣad* IV.15)

553. अग्र गण्या

Agra gaṇyā

She who is to be considered the foremost.

Since Devī is the source of the universe, She is indeed the foremost. She is *sat-cit-ānanda*, existence-consciousness-bliss.

"This *Sat* alone, dear child, sits at the forefront," says the *Śruti.*

554. अचिन्त्य रूपा

Acintya rūpā

She who is of a form beyond the reach of thought.

The mind is made up of the three *guṇas* (qualities). Anything that yields to the mind also has to be of the nature of the *guṇas.* Devī, on the other hand, transcends the *guṇas.* For this reason, She is described as "beyond the reach of the mind and speech" (see *mantra* 415).

God-Realization is not a creation of the mind. It is beyond all senses. Thoughts arise in a mind fed by the senses. Devī is beyond such thoughts.

555. कलि कल्मष नाशिनी

Kali kalmaṣa nāśinī

She who is the destroyer of the sins of the age of Kali.

"Just as sunrise dispels darkness and water quenches fire, the chanting of Devī's names washes away the multitudes of sins of the Kali age," says the *Kūrma Purāṇa.* The *Brahmāṇḍa Purāṇa* declares, "The remembrance of the feet of Parāśakti is the highest form of expiation for all sins committed, knowingly or unknowingly."

556. कात्यायनी

Kātyāyanī

She who is the daughter of a sage named Kata.

It is well-known that Kātyāyanī, whose incomparably effulgent body was derived from the radiance (*tejas*) of all the *devas,* is none other than Devī. *Vāmana Purāṇa* says, "That brightness which is the best and the greatest became known in the world as Kātyāyanī. Under that name, She shines and is celebrated all over the world."

Bhāskararāya also points out that Kātyāyanī is the presiding deity in the temple at Oḍyāṇa.

557. कालहन्त्री

Kālahantrī

She who is the destroyer of time (death).

Devī is, of course, beyond time. She is also the one who removes the effects of evil periods in our lives. In Her presence, time is forgotten.

558. कमलाक्ष निषेविता

Kamalākṣa niṣevitā

She in whom Viṣṇu takes refuge.

According to the *Padma Purāṇa*, Viṣṇu attained His own status by always worshipping the sapphire-colored Devī.

559. ताम्बूल पूरित मुखी

Tāmbūla pūrita mukhī

She whose mouth is full from chewing betel.

Devī likes chewing betel leaves with lime, nuts and fragrances. On such enjoyable occasions, She is particularly generous and dextrous in giving Her grace.

Chewing betel enhances the natural beauty of Her face. Picture a mother who, after the household chores, relaxes chewing betel and lovingly watches her children.

560. दाडिमी कुसुम प्रभा

Dāḍimī kusuma prabhā

She who shines like a pomegranate flower.

The color of the pomegranate flower is a particular shade of red which is especially beautiful. In short, Devī's complexion is extraordinarily attractive.

561. मृगाक्षी

Mṛgākṣī

She whose eyes are long and beautiful like those of a doe.

562. मोहिनी

Mohinī

She who is enchanting.

Devī enchants everyone with Her beauty and makes everyone do Her bidding. *Laghu Nāradīya Purāṇa* says, "O beautiful one, as the whole world is enchanted with Thee, Thy name shall be the Enchanting One."

According to the *Brahmāṇḍa Purāṇa*, as Brahmā sat in meditation, Śakti appeared in front of him as Prakṛti, capable of fulfilling the wishes of the gods. This is the first appearance of Mohinī.

The second time was during the churning of the Ocean of Milk. Viṣṇu meditated on the form of Mohinī and assumed Her form. She appeared before the gods and demons who were fighting for the ambrosia generated by the churning of the ocean. Seeing Her, the demons thought it best to entrust Her with the jar of ambrosia for serving everyone fairly. She laid down the condition that all of them should remain with eyes closed while She served, and that She would marry the last one to open his eyes. Any order from the Enchanting One was acceptable to them all, so everyone sat with eyes closed.

Mohinī started serving the ambrosia to the gods. The demons waited, afraid to open their eyes. After a while Rāhu opened his eyes and saw that She had already served the *devas*. Viṣṇu killed him by severing his head with His *cakra*, thus cutting him into two parts.

The deity installed on the bank of the Pratarā River is Mohinī.

563. मुख्या

Mukhyā

She who is the first.

Devī is the first, the first *Prāṇa* (Hiraṇyagarbha, a name for Brahmā meaning "the golden womb" or creative life force).

Devī has already been praised as Agragaṇyā, the first to be counted. She is not only that, but also "the pre-eminent One." "I am the first born of the True." (*Taittiriya Upaniṣad* III.10.5)

564. मृडानी

Mṛḍānī

She who is the wife of Mṛḍa (Śiva).

Mṛḍa is the giver of happiness, Śiva. Devī is not only the wife of Mṛḍa, but is Herself the giver of happiness to everyone. Mṛḍa is Śiva's predominantly *sāttvic* aspect.

565. मित्र रूपिणी

Mitra rūpiṇī

She who is the friend of everyone, the friend of the universe.

Mitra is the sun. This name implies that Devī possesses the splendor of a million suns. She shines as twelve different suns (*dvādaśāditya*) during the twelve months.

566. नित्य तृप्ता

Nitya tṛptā

She who is eternally contented.

Devī is contentment itself. Eternal contentment is present only in *mokṣa*, Liberation. Contentment is the state in which there is no desire. Thus, Devī is Liberation itself. Vyāsa says, "Absence of desire is the ultimate happiness." That is Liberation. *Nityatṛpta* is one who constantly resides in that state.

567. भक्तनिधिः

Bhaktanidhiḥ

She who is the treasure of the devotees.

A treasure is something that fulfills our desires, something that is obtained unexpectedly and gives great pleasure. To the devotee, Devī's *darśan* is a treasure.

A treasure is that which one guards from being lost. Devī is such a treasure, guarded with great care in the hearts of Her devotees.

568. नियन्त्री

Niyantrī

She who controls and guides all beings on the right path.

An episode in *Kena Upaniṣad* states that the all-devouring Agni (Fire) was unable to consume even a blade of grass. Vāyu (Air), which uproots everything could not move the blade of grass even the slightest bit. The burning power of fire and the moving power of air are nothing but the *Māyā* of *Brahman*. Everything in the universe is under the control of that *Māyā*.

569. निखिलेश्वरी

Nikhileśvarī

She who is the ruler of all.

The ruler of everything, living and nonliving.

570. मैत्र्यादि वासना लभ्या

Maitryādi vāsanā labhyā

She who is to be attained by love and other good dispositions.

It is said that there are four types of *vāsanās* (dispositions): *maitri* (friendship), *karuṇā* (compassion), *mudita* (rejoicing) *and upekṣa* (indifference). These are explained in the *Bhāgavata Purāṇa*. One should cultivate friendship of the happy, show compassion towards the miserable, rejoice with the virtuous (take pleasure in association with the virtuous) and show indifference to the sinful. Those devotees in whom these *vāsanās* take root, easily attain Devī or Her grace. *Patānjalī Yoga Sūtra* (I.33) also indicates that undisturbed calmness of mind is attained by cultivating these very same four *vāsanās*.

571. महा प्रलय साक्षिणी

Mahā pralaya sākṣiṇī

She who is witness to the Great Dissolution.

Brahmā, Viṣṇu and Indra all perish at the time of the Great Dissolution. Only Devī remains as a witness. It is said that Śiva's *tāṇḍava* dance creates the Great Dissolution. Brahmā, Viṣṇu and others come to an end and only Devī, who is Rudra's Śakti, remains to witness the dance (see *mantra* 232). Such stories signify that only the Essence of *Brahman* is imperishable and Devī is that Essence.

It is said that Śiva is able to outlive the Dissolution only because Devī is His wife. *Saubhāgyabhāskara* says, "O Devī, You alone remain victorious, bearing the goad, the arrow of flowers and the sugar cane bow, witnessing the *tāṇḍava* dance of the Parabhairava."

572. पराशक्तिः

Parāśaktiḥ

She who is the Original, Supreme Power.

Devī is the Supreme Power that transcends and controls everything.

Kāmikāgama says that the tenth elementary substance (*dhātu*) in the body is Parāśakti. Among the *dhātus*, skin, blood, flesh, fat and bone are derived from Devī, while marrow, semen, breath and vitality are derived from Śiva. The tenth *dhātu* enhances and maintains the above nine and that is Parāśakti.

Wherever there is energy, there is the presence of Devī. The wise see Her as the energy in all substances. (*Liṅga Purāṇa*)

There is a *mantra* known as *parā*, which is also called *parāśakti*. Devī is in the form of that *mantra*.

573. परानिष्ठा

Parā niṣṭhā

She who is the Supreme End, the supreme abidance.

All living and nonliving things gain their final rest in Devī.

All movements need a motionless substratum or foundation. Everything from a blade of grass to the planets move because they have an essence as their support. That support is Devī.

Parāniṣṭha is the knowledge that is the ultimate end of all desires and actions. The *Sūta Gītā* (V 50-54) describes this knowledge. One who has attained it is firmly, unmovably, established in nondual experience. That ultimate end is *Parāniṣṭha*.

574. प्रज्ञान घन रूपिणी

Prajñāna ghana rūpiṇī

She who is pure, condensed knowledge.

A crystal of salt tastes the same inside and outside. Similarly, Devī is pure, uniform Consciousness, with no difference between inside and outside, with no trace of *avidyā* (ignorance). Thus, *prajñānaghana* is solid Consciousness. As discussed under mantra 426, one of the *Mahāvākyas* (Great Sayings) states, "Consciousness is *Brahman*."

575. माध्वी पानालसा

Mādhvī pānālasā

She who is languid from drinking wine; She who is not eager for anything.

The *madhu* (wine) mentioned here is the ambrosia that overflows from the *candramaṇḍala* (disc of the moon) in the *ājñācakra*. Devī is described here as one who is languid from consuming it.

576. मत्ता

Mattā

She who is intoxicated.

Also, *mattā* means "egoism" (the sense of mineness *mat+ta*). Devī is the ego consciousness (*parāhanta*) of Śiva and is therefore called Mattā.

577. मातृका वर्ण रूपिणी

Mātṛkā varṇa rūpiṇī

She who is in the form of the letters of the alphabet.

Mātṛkāvarṇas mean the (fifty-one) letters of the Sanskrit alphabet. *Varṇa* means both letter and color.

Sanatkumāra Samhita assigns colors to the letters. The sixteen vowels are smoke colored, the consonants from *ka* to *da* are red, *dha* to *pha* are yellow, *ba* to *ra* are crimson, *la* to *sa* are golden, and *ha* and *kṣa* are the color of lightning. The letters are said to appear to the inner eye in *yogins*. It is meant here that they are all Devī's own colors. Some say all the letters are white in color.

In *Mātṛkāviveka* it is said, "A is divine, a form of *Brahman*, red in color and protector of all the letters."

The consonants become audible when combined with vowels. Vowels are related to Śakti and consonants to Śiva. Thus, the syllables represent the union between Śiva and Śakti. "Śiva is capable of His cosmic tasks only when joined with Śakti," says the *Saundarya Laharī*.

The *mantra* may also be interpreted as, "She who wears a garland of letters," a garland of *akṣa*; *a* being the first and *kṣa* the last letter of the Sanskrit alphabet. One other interpretation is, "She who created the letters of the alphabet."

In *Tantra*, *mātṛkāvarṇas* are the letters belonging to the *Śrīcakra*. Meditation on the letters and on *Śrīcakra* are the same, according to the sages. The technical term for this form of meditation is *Kailāsaprastāra*. It is the meditation on Devī in the form of letters. In *Tantra*, there are three types of meditation known as *prastāras*: *Kailāsaprastāra* as mentioned; *Meruprastāra* is meditation on the sixteen daily deities and Devī as one and the same; *Bhūprastāra* is meditation on the eight *vāsini* deities and Devī as one.

Some commentators consider this *mantra* as consisting of two names: *mātṛkā* and *varṇarūpini*. Mātṛkā means "one who cuts physical desire and shines as the light of knowledge (*mā:* that which cuts, *tṛ:* tṛṣna, strong desire and *kā:* she who shines)." *Varṇarūpiṇi* is "one who is in the form of letters," as described above.

578. महा कैलास निलया

Mahā kailāsa nilayā

She who resides in the great Kailāsa.

Mahākailāsa means "the abode of Śiva beyond the Kailāsa mountain."

Kailāsa also refers to the *sahasrāra*, in the *Brahmarandhra*. Devī resides there. *Tripurasāra* describes *sahasrāra* thus: "This is known as Kailāsa, the seat of Akula where the Lord of lords, Śiva, resides in the *bindu*." The six *cakras* from *mūlādhāra* to *ājña* are called *kula* and the *sahasrāra* above them is *akula*.

Also, *Mahākailāsa* is the *Kailāsaprastāra* meditation referred to above. The speciality of *Mahākailāsa* is that Vāśini and the daily deities have no place there. They are confined to *Bhu-* and *Meruprastāras*. This last statement takes on greater meaning when recalling that the *mūlādhāra* is the *bhu tattva* (*bhu*: earth) and the backbone is known as *merudaṇḍa*.

579. मृणाल मृदु दोर् लता

Mṛṇāla mṛdu dor latā

She whose arms are as soft and cool as the lotus stem.

The softness indicates Devī's generosity and the coolness Her consoling nature.

580. महनीया

Mahanīyā

She who is adorable.

Mahilā is another word that means adorable. Women are traditionally referred to by this name in India and it shows the stature women enjoyed in olden days. It is the result of that tradition that the "most adorable" status is accorded to Devī.

581. दया मूर्तिः

Dayā mūrtiḥ

She who is the personification of compassion.

To anyone who has enjoyed Amma's loving compassion, the aptness of this name will be evident. Compassion is the basis of all good qualities and lack of it is the cause of all evils.

582. महा साम्राज्य शालिनी

Mahā sāmrājya śālinī

She who controls the great empire of the three worlds.

The "great empire" may mean Mahākailāsa. Then the name means "She who sports in Mahākailāsa in complete freedom."

583. आत्म विद्या

Ātma vidyā

She who is the knowledge of the Self.

One who blesses devotees with the knowledge of the Self.

There is a *mantra* known as "*Ātmāṣṭākṣara mantra*" which is also called *Ātmavidyā*. Devī is also in the form of that *mantra.*

584. महा विद्या

Mahā vidyā

She who is the seat of exalted knowledge, the knowledge of the Self.

The *Vanadurgā mantra* is known as *Mahāvidyā*. Devī is in the form of that *mantra.*

585. श्री विद्या

Śrī vidyā

She who is sacred knowledge.

The *pañcadaśi mantra* is known as *Śrīvidya*. The *Viṣṇu Purāṇa* says that all *vidyā* (knowledge) is a form of Devī. "O Devī, Thou art the science of sacrifices, the secret knowledge of the Self which gives Liberation; in addition, Thou art the science of meditation, the philosophies, the three *Vedas*, the science of trade and justice." All these forms of knowledge lead to *Śrīvidyā*.

586. काम सेविता

Kāma sevitā

She who is worshipped by Kāmadeva.

She who is worshipped for the fulfillment of desires or worshipped according to desire. The *Purāṇas* say that Kāma, the god of love, worshipped Devī with the *Śrīvidyā mantra.*

Kāma is the son of Lakṣmī and is celebrated as *ananga*, one without a body. Even though he has no arms, he worships Devī with joined palms; even though he has no neck, he wears the diamond necklace that is *Śrīvidyā*; even without any sense organs, he enjoys all the senses. Devī is attended by that Kāma.

Kāma, desire, is the son of the goddess of wealth. The more wealth there is, the greater is the desire. Freedom from desire is the real Liberation, the real mental peace.

Kāma is also Mahākāmeśa, Lord Śiva. Devī is worshipped by Him.

587. श्री षोडशाक्षरी विद्या

Śrī ṣoḍaśākṣarī vidyā

She who is in the form of the sixteen-syllabled mantra.

One gets this *mantra* by adding *Śrī* to the *pañcadaśākṣari* (fifteen-syllabled) *mantra.*

A *mantra* does not become potent merely from the syllables arranged in it. The *sāttvic* purity and the sincerity of the persons giving it and using it are very important. That is why it is prescribed that one should be initiated into a *mantra* only by a master who has attained *mantrasiddhi*, one who has realized the efficacy of *mantras* by long practice. This is a fact beyond mere rules of logic.

588. त्रिकूटा

Trikūṭā

She who is in three parts.

The *pañcadaśākṣari mantra* is divided into three *kūṭas* or parts (see *mantras* 85-87).

Trikūṭa is interpreted as representing many different triads, such as the three parts of the fifteen-syllabled *mantra*; the trinity of Brahmā, Viṣṇu and Maheśvara; waking, dreaming and deep sleep; heaven (*svarga*), earth and the netherworld (*pātāla*); *sattva, rajas* and *tamas*; *Ṛg, Yajur* and *Sāma Vedas*. It is implied that Devī is in all these and each of these is Devī Herself.

589. काम कोटिका

Kāma koṭikā

She, of whom Kāma (Śiva) is a part or an approximate form.

Koṭi here means "approximate." Śiva's nature encompasses only a part of Devī. As said before, Śiva is *ardhanārīśvara* (half-female, half-male god). This *mantra* is meant to indicate Devī's immeasurable greatness. Any *kāma*, anything desired, is only a small part of Devī.

590. कटाक्ष किङ्करी भूत कमला कोटि सेविता

Kaṭākṣa kiṅkarī bhūta kamalā koṭi sevitā

She who is attended by millions of Lakṣmīs who are subdued by Her mere glances.

Anyone who has received Devī's glance of grace will be served by countless goddesses of wealth.

591. शिरःस्थिता

Śiraḥ sthitā

She who resides in the head.

Bhāskararāya says that She resides in the *Brahmarandhra* (in the head) in the form of the Guru.

592. चन्द्र निभा

Candra nibhā

She who is resplendent like the moon.

The *candramaṇḍala* (disc of the moon) is just below the *Brahmarandhra*. This region represents one of three *kūṭas* of the *pañcadaśi mantra*. The moon there is said to possess the splendor of many millions of lightning flashes. Devī is as resplendent as that moon.

593. फालस्था

Phālasthā

She who resides in the forehead (between the eyebrows).

The region between the eyebrows is the *ājñācakra.* That is the abode of Devī.

Another interpretation is "She who resides in the forehead in the form of the *bindu* of the *bīja* syllable *Hrīm.*"

594. इन्द्र धनुष् प्रभा

Indra dhanuṣ prabhā

She who is resplendent like the rainbow.

The *bindu* of the syllables Om and *Hrīm* is known as *ardhamātra*; it shines in the forehead in the form of radiance Above it is the half moon which shines with the dazzling beauty of *indradhanuṣ* (Indra's bow), a rainbow; that is the seat of Devī.

595. हृदयस्था

Hṛdayasthā

She who resides in the heart.

The heart is the location of *anāhatacakra.* Devī resides in the *sūryamaṇḍala* (the sun's disc).

In the *Kalpasūtra*, Devī's *parābīja* is called *Hṛdaya* (heart). The worshipper who knows the *parābījaśakti* (the heart of the Supreme), gets all happiness and prosperity.

There is an *Upaniṣad* named *Parameśvarahṛdaya*, which is also called *hṛdaya.* Since Devī is the essence of that *Upaniṣad,* She is called *Hṛdayasthā.*

The seed of everything is in the heart. The heart is called the *viśvabīja*, the seed of the universe. Devī is of the form of that universal seed, and She resides in the hearts of all beings. The Gītā (XVIII.61) says, "The Lord dwells in the heart of all beings, O Arjuna!"

596. रवि प्रख्या

Ravi prakhyā

She who shines with the special brilliance of the sun.

Prakhyā means special brilliance. It also means "resemblance;" hence Devī resembles the sun in radiance. She also has the name, "One who equals a *crore* of suns in radiance."

597. त्रि कोणान्तर दीपिका

Tri koṇāntara dīpikā

She who shines as a light within the triangle.

In the *mūlādhāra*, there is a triangle and within it is the *agnimaṇḍala* (the disc of fire). This is the location of one of the three *kūṭas* of the *pañcadaśi mantra*. According to the *Tantrarāja*, "In all beings, in the *mūlādhāra* there is fire, in the heart there is the sun, and in the head below the *Brahmarandhra*, there is the moon. Thus, the original, eternal *pañcadaśi mantra* is in three parts, representing these three positions."

Viṣṇu Purāṇa says that there are three worlds and three cities that form triangles. The three worlds are heaven, earth and the netherworld. The three cities are the cities of Indra, Candra and Yama. The sun is said to rise in the city of Candra (moon) and set in the city of Yama. Devī shines in all three worlds and three cities at the same time. Hence the present name.

Dīpikā also refers to the *agnimaṇḍala* (the disc of fire).

598. दाक्षायणी

Dākṣāyaṇī

She who is Satīdevī, the daughter of Dakṣa Prajāpati.

The *Purāṇas* celebrate the story of Satī. Angered by Her father's insult of Śiva, Satī burns Her body in the fire of *yoga*, during the sacrifice (*yāga*) conducted by Dakṣa and is reborn as Umā, the daughter of Himavat and is married to Śiva again.

Also, Devī is the enjoyer of the oblations made during the sacrifice known as *Dākṣāyaṇa Yajña*. This sacrifice consists of the repeated performance of the *darśa* and *pūrṇamāsa yajña*.

The deities (of the stars), Aśvini and others, are called Dakṣāyaṇis. They are daughters of Dakṣa. Devī is "one who shines in the form of Aśvini and other stars."

599. दैत्य हन्त्री

Daitya hantrī

She who is the killer of demons.

Devī is the killer of Bhaṇḍa and many other demons (*daityas*).

600. दक्ष यज्ञ विनाशिनी

Dakṣa yajña vināśinī

She who is the destroyer of the sacrifice conducted by Dakṣa.

There are two Dakṣas. Dakṣa Prajāpati, who was Satī's father, is the first (see *mantra* 598). There was also a king named Dakṣa, said to be another incarnation of Dakṣa Prajāpati during the Cākṣuṣa age. Both of them conducted famous sacrifices. Both sacrifices were stopped by Śiva, and Devī, in both cases was the cause.

It was Śiva's curse that caused the rebirth of Dakṣa Prajāpati as Dakṣa, the grandson of Prācīna Barhis, and son of Pracetas, during the age of Cākṣuṣa Manu. Both *Brahmāṇḍa* and *Vāyu Purāṇas* describe this.

With this mantra, the hundred names in the seventh *kalā* known as *suṣumna* are complete.

601. दरान्दोलित दीर्घाक्षी

Darāndolita dīrghākṣī

She who has long, tremulous eyes.

Darāndolita means "moving a little," *dara*, a little and *andolita*, oscillating.

Devī is one who has tremulous eyes. Tremulous eyes are considered a sign of beauty. It is only natural that Devī, who is the very abode of beauty, has eyes which are most captivating.

Another interpretation is "She who drives fear away" (*dara* means fear and *andolita* here means driving away). The meaning, "One whose long eyes move so as to cause fear," is also apt. It is natural that Her eyes move about fiercely when She is engaged in killing Dāruka or Bhaṇḍāsura.

Thus, Her eyes are both fierce and captivating at the same time.

602. दर हासोज्ज्वलन् मुखी

Dara hāsojjvalan mukhī

She whose face is radiant with a smile.

Here also, *dara* can be taken to mean "producing fear." As She stands roaring like a lioness, ready to kill Dāruka, Her laughter is terrifying. The same *mantra* thus describes both of Devī's aspects, one, adept in giving blessing and the other, intent on the destruction of the wicked.

603. गुरुमूर्तिः

Gurumūrtiḥ

She who has assumed a severe form or one who has assumed the form of the Guru.

Just as a pot, a jar or a cup are all different forms of clay, *mantra*, deity and guru should all be understood as different forms of one and the same Truth.

Gu: darkness, *ru:* that which removes; *gurumūrti* is the embodiment of light that dispels darkness. Taking *gu* to mean *Brahman*, and *ru* to mean knowledge, the *mantra* then means, "She who is in the form of the Knower of *Brahman*."

Gurumūrtī is interpreted in *Nityahṛdaya* as the Devī who can assume any form at will.

604. गुण निधिः

Guṇa nidhiḥ

She who is the treasure house of all good qualities.

One who has assumed various forms resulting from combinations of the *guṇas*: *sattva*, *rajas* and *tamas*.

Guṇa means *vyūha* (an aggregate, an arrangement of body or senses) and *nidhi* numerologically corresponds to the number nine. Lord Śiva is said to be in the form of nine *vyūhas*. The nine *vyūhas* are: time, family, name, knowledge, mind, *nāda*, *bindu*, *kalpa* and *jīva*. Thus, the *mantra* means, "She who is the treasure house of the nine *vyūhas*."

Guṇa also means "rope." The *Purāṇas* describe the following incident which occurred at the time of the incarnation of Lord Viṣṇu as a fish. Before the whole world was to be destroyed in the Great Dissolution, all the good seeds in the world and the seven great *ṛṣis* were put in a large boat. The boat was tied to the horn of the Great Fish with a rope called *Vaṭīrikā* (or *rikāvaṭi* in *Matsya Purāṇa*). In order to keep the rope from breaking, Devī infused it with Her strength. As She made the rope (*guṇa*) the repository (*nidhi*) of Her strength, She is called *Guṇanidhi*.

605. गो माता

Go mātā

She who became Surabhī, the cow that grants all wishes.

The word *go* has many meanings. Some of the meanings are: word, intelligence, heaven, rays from stars, lightning, moon, eye, hair, earth, direction, arrow, water, fire, face, truth and path. Devī is the mother of all these, and so She is *Gomātā*.

606. गुह जन्म भूः

Guha janma bhūḥ

She who is the Mother of Guha (Subrahmanya).

Guha also means "covered or veiled" and *janmabhū* is "birthplace."

There is the statement, "The essence of *dharma* is hidden in the *guha*," which may be interpreted as "The essence of *dharma* is veiled." It is also said, "Truth remains behind darkness."

The *jīvas* who are bound by ignorance are indicated by the word "*guha*" in the sense given above. Devī is their mother. All creation, after all, comes from that Mother, just as sparks scatter from fire. Therefore, She is called *Guhajanmabhūḥ*.

607. देवेशी

Deveśī

She who is the protector of the gods.

608. दण्डनीतिस्था

Daṇḍanītisthā

She who maintains the rules of justice without the slightest error.

Devī abides in the system of justice, laws and codes for the maintenance of a *dhārmic* life.

Some seeds sprout quickly. Others may take days or even months. There are seeds that lie dormant under the soil for years. The results of man's *karma* are also like that. Some acts bear fruit immediately. Others take time, possibly many lifetimes. Nature does not allow any action to go to waste. She sees to it that every action is a seed that sprouts, sooner or later.

The ancients knew this truth and divided the actions of man clearly into two groups, those that bring merit and those that are sinful (*puṇya* and *pāpa*). Those who follow the wrong path driven by selfish desires blame the Lord when they suffer the consequences of their evil acts. God has no special role in this except to administer the code of punishment. That is how Devī is the purveyor of the code of justice, or *Daṇḍanītisthā*.

609. दहराकाश रूपिणी

Daharākāśa rūpiṇī

She who is the subtle Self in the heart.

Dahara means small, and *ākāśa* means subtle space, connoting *Brahman*.

Daharākāśa means the small space of the heart - the subtle space in the lotus of the heart. Devī is in the form of that subtle space, which is *Brahman*.

Chāndogya Upaniṣad (VIII.1.1) says, "Now, in this city of *Brahman*, there is a mansion in the shape of a small lotus, with a small inner *ākāśa*. What is within that should be sought; that, indeed, one should desire to understand."

610. प्रतिपन् मुख्य राकान्त तिथि मण्डल पूजिता

Pratipan mukhya rākānta tithi maṇḍala pūjitā

She who is worshipped daily starting with pratipad *(first day of the lunar half-month) and ending with the full moon.*

She who is worshipped by the entire group of *nitya devatas* (daily deities) starting with Kāmeśvari for *pratipad* and Citra for *paurnami* (full moon).

According to *Varāha Purāṇa*, the following is the list of the *nitya* deities (which is different from that given under *mantra* 73): Agni, Aśvinikumāras, Gaurī, Gaṇapati, the Nāgas, Ṣanmukha, Sūrya, the Mātṛs, Durgā, the Quarters, Kubera, Viṣṇu, Yama, Śiva and Candra. Devī is worshipped by all of these.

611. कलात्मिका

Kalātmikā

She who is in the form of the kalās.

Kalā is interpreted in different ways. There are ten *kalās* (parts) of Agni (Fire), twelve of the Sun, and sixteen of the Moon. There are also sixty-four *kalās* or forms of art. Devī is the essence of all these.

In addition, there are four *kalās* in each of the four states: waking, dreaming, deep sleep and *turīya*. These are known as *kāmakalā*. The four *kalās* in the waking state are: rising, staying awake, consciousness (*bodha*) and continuous mental action. The four *kalās* of the dreaming state are: desire, confusion, anxiety and dwelling on sense objects. Those of the deep sleep state are: death, oblivion, insensitivity, and sleep enveloped in darkness. Finally, the four *kalās* of the *turīya* state are: dispassion, desire for Liberation, discrimination of the real and unreal and *samādhi*. Since these are all contained in Devī's Śakti, She is called *Kalātmikā*.

612. कलानाथा

Kalānāthā

She who is the mistress of all the kalās.

Kalās have been previously described.

Kalānāthā is also the moon. Recall the disc of the moon in the *Śrīcakra*. Devī reigns there as queen.

613. काव्यालाप विनोदिनी

Kāvyālāpa vinodinī

She who delights in hearing poetry.

Devī takes delight in listening to the reading of the glorious *Purāṇas*, epics such as *Rāmāyana*, *Mahābhārata* and *Devī Māhātmya*.

614. सचामर रमा वाणी सव्य दक्षिण सेविता

Sacāmara ramā vāṇī savya dakṣiṇa sevitā

She who is attended by Lakṣmī on the left side and Sarasvatī on the right side, bearing ceremonial fans.

615. आदिशक्तिः

Ādiśaktiḥ

She who is the Primordial Power, the Parāśakti who is the Cause of the universe.

The whole universe arises from Devī, exists in Her and dissolves in Her. She is the cause and the universe is the effect; the effect finally dissolves into the cause.

616. अमेया

Ameyā

She who is not measurable by any means.

Science has not yet determined the extent of the universe. How can we then measure the One who is the cause of all the cosmic bodies? She is therefore considered immeasurable. *Liṅga Purāṇa* says, "In all the eight worlds of the *brahmāṇḍa* (cosmos) starting with heaven or *pātāla* (the nether regions), whatever can be measured is Umā Herself, and the one who can measure is Maheśvara."

617. आत्मा

Ātmā

She who is the Self in all.

The self (Ātman) in each *jīva* (*jivātma*) is the same as the Supreme Self (*Paramātman*). As Śaṅkarācārya makes clear, "*Jīva* is not distinct from *Brahman*."

Liṅga Purāṇa says, "Just as sparks in fire, all the *jīvas* exist in Śiva, who is the Supreme Self." According to *Śiva Purāṇa*, "The supreme eighth body of Śiva is called *Ātman*; it pervades all the other seven; hence Śiva is the Universe." And Vasiṣṭha says, "The bodies of all embodied souls are forms of Devī, and all the embodied souls are parts of Śiva."

The word *ātma* also means body, mind, intellect, nature and firmness. Devī is referred to in all these ways according to the context.

618. परमा

Paramā

She who is the Supreme.

Paramā means one who measures (*ma*) the Supreme (*para*). The Supreme *Brahman* is beginningless and undivided. Devī is the power that makes that *Brahman* appear to be divided and take birth in myriad forms. That which is divided becomes measurable. Thus, Devī is one who measures the Supreme.

Para is known as Śiva and *mā* as Lakṣmī. Devī is Śiva's Lakṣmī or Śiva's glory.

Also, Devī is one who transcends the four forms of *Parabrahman*: *Puruṣa* (the Cosmic Man), *avyakta* (unmanifested), *vyakta* (manifested) and *kāla* (time).

619. पावनाकृतिः

Pāvanākṛtiḥ

She who is of sacred form.

Ākṛti means "form" and also "wisdom or knowledge." Seeing Devī's form and praising Her actions creates purity of mind and awakens *jñāna*, wisdom.

Yājñavalkya Smṛti points out, "Penance and knowledge are the means of purifying the embodied soul. The knowledge cleanses the intellect and the soul (*kṣetrajña*) is purified by the knowledge of the Lord." For the *bhūtātma* (embodied soul), penance and knowledge help purify the mind and control the organs of perception, the mind and the intellect.

620. अनेक कोटि ब्रह्माण्ड जननी

Aneka koṭi brahmāṇḍa jananī

She who is the creator of many crores *of worlds.*

Brahmāṇḍa literally means *Brahman*-as-egg. Everything in the universe is egg-shaped - the sun, moon and atoms all have nearly spherical forms. Collections of atoms may take different shapes, but at the microcosmic level, all are egg-shaped. The ancient sages say there are many millions of worlds. Modern science also agrees and talks of millions of galaxies. The sages have spoken of the "orbs" of the moon and the sun and of *brahmāṇḍas* thousands of years ago. These words are examples of the foresight that the *ṛṣis* brought to the analytical study of the universe. Devī is the mother of countless *crores* of such worlds.

She is also the mother of *Virāṭ*, *Svarāṭ* and *Samrāṭ*. *Virāṭ* is the cosmic individual with the sixteen modifications or *ṣoḍaśa vikāras* (five gross elements, five sense organs, five organs of action and the mind). *Svarāṭ* is the power that takes pride in itself as the collective subtle body (*liṅga śarira*) of the cosmos. *Samrāṭ* is the cause of these two. The *Śruti* declares that *Virāṭ Purūṣa* is commonly thought of as *Brahmāṇḍa*, *Svarāṭ* as its nature and *Samrāṭ* as both.

Virāṭ and *Svarāṭ Purūṣas* preside over countless *brahmāṇḍas*. *Samrāṭ Purūṣa* is a combination of those two, and Devī is the mother of them all.

621. दिव्य विग्रहा

Divya vigrahā

She who has a divine body.

This name may be interpreted in the following way: taking *vigraha* to mean "fight" and *divya* as pertaining to the sky, *divyavigrahā* means "one who fought in the sky, without touching the ground." In *Mārkaṇḍeya Purāṇa*, Devī is described as fighting and destroying the *asuras* in the sky. The demons, who had magical powers, were experts in fighting in the sky. In order to destroy them, Devī also took to the sky and fought without any support. Thus, She became *Divyavigrahā* in this way as well.

622. क्लीङ्कारी

Klīṅkārī

She who is creator of the syllable klīm.

Also, Devī is one who has the name *Klīm*. *Klīm* is called Kāmabīja. It is a *mantra* syllable, with Devī as its creator.

Also, *Klīṅkāra* is Kāmeśvara. Devī is *Klīṅkārī*, Kāmeśvara's wife.

623. केवला

Kevalā

She who is the absolute, as She is complete, independent and without any attributes.

Kevalā is one who is not touched by changes arising from Her own kind, from others or from Herself.

She who is in the form of Absolute Knowledge, the knowledge of *Brahman*.

The word *klīm* of the previous *mantra* can be split as ka + la + im. *Klīm* is known as Kāmabīja and *īm* as Kāmakalā. Kāmabīja and Kāmakalā refer to worldly life and Liberation (*mokṣa*) respectively. The first three goals of life - morality (*dharma*), wealth (*artha*) and desire (*kāma*) - are obtained from Kāmabīja and Liberation (*mokṣa*) is obtained from Kāmakalā. Kāmakalā is the state of *turīya*. That state is known as *Kevala*.

624. गुह्या

Guhyā

She who is to be known in secret.

Guhyā is "one who is hidden in a cave." Devī is one to be reached by secret modes of worship in the cave of the heart. "Secret mode" implies worship done in solitude with total surrender.

625. कैवल्य पद दायिनी

Kaivalya pada dāyinī

She who bestows Liberation.

Kaivalyapada is the fifth state - the state beyond *turīya*. Devī is one who bestows that.

Kaivalya is beyond the states described as *sālokya*, *sārūpya*, *sāmīpya and sāyūjya*. *Sālokya* (sameness of world) is reaching the same world as the deity being worshipped. *Sārūpya* (sameness of form) is meditating on the deity as not separate from oneself, becoming equal to the deity with similar qualities. *Sāmīpya* (nearness) is the state in which the worshipper is able to be constantly near the deity; this state is obtained through worship done in strict celibacy, according to the rules. In *sāyūjya* (becoming one), the worshipper becomes one with the deity - all sense of separateness is lost; this is the realization of *Īśvara* with attributes. Finally, *kaivalya* is the eternal state obtained through knowledge in which the Self is realized as Pure Awareness.

626. त्रिपुरा

Tripurā

She who is older than the Three.

According to Bhāskararāya, Devī is called *Tripurā* because She is older than the Trinity (Brahmā, Viṣṇu and Śiva). According to Gauḍapāda, She is *Tripurā* as She is the one *tattva* (Essential Principle, *Brahman*) divided into three. Eruttacchan also talks about the "Essence of Omkāra that splits into three."

Tripurā also refers to three nerves, *iḍā*, *piṅgala* and *suṣumnā* and to the three forms of the *antaḥkaraṇa* (mind): *manas*, *citta* and *buddhi*. Devī is *Tripurā* as She resides in these. (*Tripurārṇava*) The three bodies, gross, subtle and causal are also called *Tripurā*, as Devī dwells in them as well. In fact, Devī resides in everything that is threefold: the three divinities (trinity), three *Vedas*, three *agnis* (fires), three energies (of *mantra*, *prabhu* and *utsāha*), three worlds, three cities (of Indra, Yama and Candra) and three bodies. She is *Tripurā* in all these senses.The Trinity of Father, Son and Holy Ghost can also come under this description.

"*Tripurā* is the Supreme Power," says the *Laghustava*.

627. त्रिजगद् वन्द्या

Trijagad vandyā

She who is adored by the inhabitants of all three worlds.

Devī is worshipped even by the *asuras*.

628. त्रिमूर्तिः

Trimūrtiḥ

She who is the aggregate of the Trinity (of Brahmā, Viṣṇu and Śiva).

Devī takes the form of Brahmā, Viṣṇu and Śiva as required for creation, preservation and destruction.

This mantra also means "She who manifests in the three colors of red, white and black." *Devī Bhāgavata* says, "Śāmbhavi is white, Śrī Vidyā is red, and Śyāma is black in color; the three Śaktis represent the three *guṇas*." It is clear that the three Devīs have assumed the colors of the three *guṇas*, *sattva*, *rajas* and *tamas* and that they represent these *guṇas*.

A girl of three colors, white, red and black, came in front of Brahmā, Viṣṇu and Śiva. They asked Her, "O, smiling one, who are You?" "Don't You know me?" She said. "I am Your own Śakti. I was born in this beautiful form from Your own gaze." They granted Her boons and said, "Please divide Your body into three." Accordingly, the girl took three forms of three colors - white, red and black. (*Varāha Purāṇa*)

In another instance it is said that Parāśakti took a form in white, predominantly *sāttvic*, consisting of the Śakti of Brahmā, a form in red, predominantly *rājasic*, consisting of the Śakti of Viṣṇu and a form in black, predominantly *tāmasic*, consisting of the Śakti of Śiva.

Trimūrtis are thus variously described as Brahmā, Viṣṇu and Śiva; Vāma, Jyeṣṭha and Raudri; Śāmbhavi, Śrī Vidyā and Śyāma, the Śaktis of Icchā, Kriyā and Jñāna.

A girl of three years is known as *trimūrtī*, according to Dhaumyācārya.

629. त्रिदशेश्वरी

Tridaśeśvarī

She who is the ruler of the gods.

Tridaśas are *devas*. There are four stages in life - childhood, adolescence, youth and old age. *Devas* constantly remain in the third (*tri*) stage (*daśa*). They are distinguished by wealth and knowledge. Devī is their ruler (*īśvarī*). The *Purāṇas* say that there are thirty-three *crores* of *devas*. *Tridaśa* also denotes thirty-three *crores*.

Tridaśas are also the three states of waking, dreaming and sleeping. Devī is the ruler of those who remain in these states, the *īśvarī* who is the witness of the three states.

630. त्र्यक्षरी

Tryakṣarī

She whose form consists of three letters or syllables.

Om consists of the three letters *a*, *u* and *m* and is thus a *tryakṣarī mantra* (*mantra* with three letters). Devī is of the nature of *Om*.

She is *Tryakṣarī* as She (and Her *mantra*, the *pañcadaśi*) has three *kūṭas*, each with a seed letter (*bījākṣara*). The three *kūṭas* are *Vāgbhavakūṭa*, *Kāmarājakūṭa* (or Madhya) and *Śaktikūṭa*. "In *Vāgbhavakūṭa* resides Vagīśvarī who is Jñānaśakti, who confers Liberation; in *Kāmarājakūṭa* resides Kāmeśi, who is Kriyāśakti, who fulfills desires; in *Śaktikūṭa* resides Parāśakti, who is *icchāśakti*, who is in the form of Śiva. Devī Mahātripurasundarī is thus three-syllabled." (*Vāmakeśvara Tantra)* Devī is indeed the conjunction of *jñāna-*, *kriyā-* and *icchāśaktis* (see *mantra* 658).

Gauḍapādācārya says that *Śuddhavidyā* and *Kumāri mantras* are three-lettered. *Śuddhavidyā* means the *pañcadaśi* which is three-lettered because of its three *bijākṣaras*, as indicated above.

The *Bṛhadāraṇyaka Upaniṣad* (V.3.1 and V.5.1) says, "The word *hṛdayam* (heart) is three-syllabled" and "the word *satyam* (truth) is three-syllabled." Thus, Devī is of the form of the heart and of truth. Instead of *satyam*, the word *sukṛtam* (good deed) is also given (*su+kṛ+tam*, another three syllabled word, in place of *sa+t+yam*).

Letters are divided into three groups, *yugākṣara*, *māsākṣara* and *nityākṣara* (letters of age, month and day). Devī presides over these and is therefore *Tryakṣarī*.

631. दिव्य गन्धाढ्या

Divya gandhāḍhyā

She who is richly endowed with divine fragrance.

Devī is always surrounded by divine beings and divine things and is, indeed, endowed with divine fragrance. Devī is the most exalted (*ādhya*) of those who carry divine fragrance. Fragrance is verily an attribute of Hers. The earth is fragrant and as the Earth Element (*bhū tattva*) is Devī Herself, who can have more divine fragrance than Her?

It is said in the *yogaśāstra*, the breath of those who reach the height of Devī worship becomes fragrant, according to those who have attained that experience. If even Her worshippers experience this, what need be said about Devī?

Gandha also means *bandha* or relation. Devī is one who is related to the entire living and non-living universe.

632. सिन्दूर तिलकाञ्चिता

Sindūra tilakāñcitā

She who shines with a vermillion mark on Her forehead; She who is decorated with a special paste made of vermilion.

Sindūratilakā also connotes a she-elephant and a woman (whose husband is living) and *añcita* is "one who is worshipped." Thus, this name can mean "One who is worthy of worship among elephants, women and women with a slow and graceful gait resembling that of an elephant."

The *Purāṇas* celebrate the stories of many beautiful women such as Rukminī who worshipped Devī and, through Her grace, gained their desired husbands.

633. उमा

Umā

She who is Pārvatī Devī.

U is Śiva and *Mā* is Lakṣmī. *Umā* is thus the combination of Śiva and Lakṣmī. Happiness and prosperity complement each other and Devī is one who grants both.

Also, *U* is Śiva and *mā* is one who measures. Anything that can be measured has limits. Thus, Devī is one who assigns limits even to Śiva. Brahmā, Viṣṇu and Śiva disappear at the time of the Great Dissolution. That is the limitation of Śiva. Whatever is limited, perishes.

Umā means red, vermillion, fame and radiance.

Kālīdāsa says in *Kumārasambhava* that Mena, the wife of Himavat, dissuaded her daughter Pārvatī from embarking on penance saying, "U mā (Oh, do not attempt to do penance)!" and that Pārvatī got the name *Umā* because of this.

Also, *Umā* means Indukalā, which, according to *Tantra*, creates the waking and sleeping states. Its position is in the pericarp of the lotus of the heart.

Umā also stands for a girl of six years. This is the meaning of *Kumāri Pūja*.

According to *Śaiva* doctrine, *Umā* is *icchāśakti* (will power).

634. शैलेन्द्र तनया

Śailendra tanayā

She who is the daughter of Himavat, the King of the Mountains.

She who leads to the most exalted state of Indra (splitting the name as *śaila* + *indrata* + *naya*).

635. गौरी

Gaurī

She who has a fair complexion.

One who has a golden color is called *Gaurī*. *Devī Purāṇa* says, "Since the Devī who burned Herself in the fire of *yoga* was reborn as the daughter of Himālaya, with the color of the conch, jasmine and the moon, She is known as *Gaurī*."

Gaurī is the deity in the temple at Kanyākubja. Other references say that Varuṇa's wife is known as *Gaurī*, and also a ten year old girl.

636. गन्धर्व सेविता

Gandharva sevitā

She who is served by Gandharvas *(like Viśvāvasu)*.

The science of music is known as *gandharvavidyā*. Devī is one who is worshipped by great musicians, especially during the Navarātri festival.

Gandharva also means horse (*aśva*). Thus, Devī is *Aśvārūḍha* (mounted on a horse) and attended by the *śakti* called Aśvārūḍha (see *mantra* 67). The *aśvārūḍha mantra* is well-known in *Tantra*.

Gandharva also connotes the sun. Devī is worshipped by the sun.

637. विश्व गर्भा

Viśva garbhā

She who contains the whole universe in Her womb.

It is implied that the entire universe emerged from Her womb; She is the mother of the universe.

She is also one who is concealed in the womb of the universe. One who sees the universe does not see Devī, and one who gets Her *darśan* no longer sees the universe. That is the difference between the experience of oneness with the Supreme and all worldly experiences.

638. स्वर्णगर्भा

Svarṇagarbhā

She who is the the cause of the universe.

She who contains sacred *mantra* syllables within Her (*su*: good, *arṇa*: letter, *garbhā*: pregnant with). The word *garbha* also means "shining"; hence, the interpretation "She who gives rise to *mantras*."

639. अवरदा

Avaradā

She who destroys the unholy.

Dā can signify both giving and cutting. *Avara* means "an unholy being, one of demonic nature." The name refers to Devī as the destroyer of *asuras* (demons).

Ava means "shining" and *rada* means "tooth:" thus this name also means "one who has shining teeth."

She who bestows suitable boons on Her devotees (*a*: similar to, as befits the qualifications; *varadā*: bestower of boons).

640. वाग् अधीश्वरी

Vāg adhīśvarī

She who presides over speech.

Devī is Sarasvatī, the Goddess of Speech.

641. ध्यान गम्या

Dhyāna gamyā

She who is to be attained through meditation.

As Devī is beyond the senses, She cannot be seen by the external eyes. She can be realized only by long and regular meditation.

"Engaged in meditation, they (*ṛṣis*) saw the Divine Self hidden in its own *guṇas*." (*Śvetāśvatāra Upaniṣad* I.3)

642. अपरि च्छेद्या

Apari cchedyā

She whose limits cannot be ascertained; unlimited. Only created things can be measured. Devī, who is beyond time and space, and is the cause of all creation, is unlimited and immeasurable.

643. ज्ञानदा

Jñānadā

She who gives knowledge of the Self.

Only through the grace of the Devī who is Śakti can living beings attain Supreme Knowledge which destroys the sorrow of *samsāra*. (*Skanda Purāṇa*)

The *Sūta Gītā* also says that only through the grace of Devī, who is pleased by devotion, can one attain final Liberation which is unlimited and in the form of knowledge, truth and bliss.

644. ज्ञान विग्रहा

Jñāna vigrahā

She who is the embodiment of Knowledge Itself.

Taking *vigraha* to mean "Known through special means," we arrive at the meaning "She who is the knowledge that is obtained through special means," that is, Her worship.

"The Supreme Self is only knowledge. Knowledge is the cause of Liberation and of bondage. Everything in the universe is knowledge. There is nothing beyond knowledge. O Maitreya, know that *vidyā* and *avidyā* are both knowledge." (*Viṣṇu Purāṇa*) Devī is also one "who expands knowledge."

645. सर्व वेदान्त संवेद्या

Sarva vedānta samvedyā

She who is known by all of Vedānta.

Samvedyā means: "She who is known well." The inner essence of all *Vedas* is Devī. She is also the one who makes this known to us. Devī is the object of logic and of *Vedānta*, according to *Varāha Purāṇa*.

646. सत्यानन्द स्वरूपिणी

Satyānanda svarūpiṇī

She whose form is Existence and Bliss.

Satya (existence, reality) is that which does not change with time.

Devī is the sun *(yā)* who is the life force *(sat: prāṇa)* of all beings.

Bliss is the nature of *Brahman*. "*Brahman* is knowledge and bliss," according to the *Śruti*. Thus, Devī is that *Brahman*. Recall the declaration in the *Śruti* that "*Brahman* is Existence, Knowledge and Infinity."

647. लोपामुद्रार्चिता

Lopāmudrārcitā

She who is worshipped by Lopāmudrā, the wife of the sage Agastya.

The *pañcadaśi mantra* is also called *Lopāmudrā*. Thus, "She who is worshipped using the *pañcadaśi mantra*."

The word *Lopāmudrā* can be interpreted as "one who stops trivial pleasures" (*lopa:* less, *mud:* pleasure, *rā:* one who blocks). Worldly pleasures are indeed trivial. "Even Indra's status may be obtained, but for what? It is so worthless," says Eruttacchan. *Lopāmudrārcitā* means the Devī who is worshipped by the *yogins* who, wishing to reach the infinite unequalled bliss, discard all trivial worldly pleasures.

648. लीला क्लृप्त ब्रह्माण्ड मण्डला

Līlā kḷpta brahmāṇḍa maṇḍalā

She who has created and maintained the universe purely as a sport.

How well-defined and firm is the organization of Her universe! A machine created by even the greatest expert becomes outdated with time. How precisely and with what great diversity has She put together this cosmic machine consisting of the sun, the moon, the millions of stars, the towering mountains and vast oceans which keep on working! And all as a sport!

What is said about creation also equally applies to the maintenance and dissolution of this machine. She who puts the cosmos together can guard it and take it apart as well.

Devī Stava says, "O Mother, even Śiva is powerless to create, protect and destroy Brahmā, Viṣṇu and the other *devas*. But to You, governing this universe is just a *līlā*."

649. अदृश्या

Adṛśyā

She who is not perceived by the sense organs.

Only that which is of the nature of the three *guṇas* is subject to the senses. Devī is beyond the *guṇas*. Therefore, She cannot be perceived in any way through the senses. Authoritative sources often refer to Her in this way: "Your form without qualities is not seen by the eyes," and "The Śakti that is beyond the *guṇas* is not easily reached."

650. दृश्य रहिता

Dṛśya rahitā

She who has nothing to see.

One needs to see only the things that are distinct from oneself. There is nothing of any kind that is different from Devī, thus She has nothing to see.

Dṛśya means: "the visible," things in the universe which are impermanent. Devī is not those things. The *mantra* implies that Devī is Eternal, Imperishable.

651. विज्ञात्री

Vijñātrī

She who knows the truth of the physical universe.

Jñāna and *vijñāna* are often used synonymously for knowledge.

For instance, "*Brahman* is *satyam*, *jñānam* and *anantam* (existence, knowledge and infinity)," and "*Brahman* is *vijñānam* and *ānandam* (knowledge and bliss)." However, when a distinction is made, all material knowledge is *vijñāna* and spiritual knowledge is *jñāna*. That which is known through study is *vijñāna* and that which arises from (spiritual) experience is *jñāna*. *Vijñāna* is commonly translated as knowledge and *jñāna* as wisdom.

Thus, the meaning of this *mantra* is: "She who knows everything that is material or physical." Another meaning is: "She who is to be known through special experience." Vijñātrī also means: "She who protects all knowledge."

652. वेद्य वर्जिता

Vedya varjitā

She who has nothing left to know.

She who is omniscient. There is nothing material or spiritual that is unknown to Her. She who is beyond all that is known.

653. योगिनी

Yoginī

She who is constantly united with Parāśiva; She who possesses the power of yoga.

"*Yoga* means the restraint of mental activity," according to Patānjali's *Yoga Sūtra* (I.2). *Yoga* is stopping the activities of the mind and making it abide in Pure Consciousness. *Yoga* is the oneness of *jīva* and *Brahman*. Devī is constantly in union with Śiva.

The Gītā says, "Equanimity is *yoga*," (II.48) and also, "Know that *yoga* is freedom from attachment to pain." (VI.23) Another verse in the *Gītā* (II.50) teaches, "*Yoga* is skill in action." Skill exists in performing actions, but not taking pride in the act, performing fruitful actions, but not having concern for the fruit. Devī is one who has that *yogaśakti*.

Yoga is of four types: *mantra yoga*, *laya yoga*, *hatha yoga* and *rāja yoga*. *Rāja yoga* itself is of three kinds: *Śaṅkhya*, *tāraka* and *amanaska*.

Also, *mantraśāstra* describes seven *yoginīs* starting with Ḍākinī (see *mantras* 475-534). There are countless *yoginīs* as indicated by the *mantra*, *Mahācatuḥṣaṣṭikoṭiyoginīgaṇasevitā* (237). Devī is the greatest *yoginī* of them all, their *Īśvarī*. The eight planetary deities Maṅgala to Sankaṭa are also called *yoginīs*.

654. योगदा

Yogadā

She who bestows the power of yoga.

Devī is one who confers the *yoga* that is the union of *jīvātman* with *Brahman*. She is one who bestows material enjoyment as a form of Her blessing. The *Śākta* doctrine, referred to here, states that divine grace is essential for Self-Realization.

655. योग्या

Yogyā

She who deserves yoga *of all kinds*.

This and the two preceding *mantras* reveal the attributes of observance or practice (*cārya*), giving (*dāna*) and wealth (*sampatti*).

These three *mantras* relate Devī to the observance, gift, and possession of *yoga.*

Under the influence of *Māyā* (which is made up of the three *guṇas*), the Supreme *Brahman* manifests in three forms: the knower, known and knowledge. When *sattva* has ascendancy over *rajas* and *tamas*, it is known as *śuddhasattva.* The corresponding manifestation of Supreme Truth is Īśvara, and is called *Yogadā* (Bestower of *yoga*). When *rajas* is predominant and *sattva* and *tamas* weaker, the same Supreme Truth manifests as *jīva* and is called *Yoginī.* Similarly, when *tamas* is predominant and *sattva* and *rajas* are weaker, the Supreme Truth manifests as the inert universe, and then is called *Yogyā.*

The observance of *yoga* (*yogācārya*) represents the predominantly *rājasic* nature of *Yoginī* - activity is the sign of *rajas.* Giving or bestowing *yoga* (*yogadāna*) is predominantly *sāttvic*; it is related to the generosity of *Yogadā.* The possession of *yoga* (*yogasampatti*) by *Yogyā* represents the *tāmasic* aspect of Devī. Wealth of any kind is related to *tamas.*

656. योगानन्दा

Yogānandā

She who is the bliss attained through yoga *or, She who enjoys the bliss of* yoga.

Also She who is in the state of *Yoganidra,* the sleep of *yoga.* Deep sleep is a state of bliss.

Yoga is the union of Śiva and Śakti. Some commentators take this name as *ayogānanda* and interpret it as *ayoga + nanda. Ayoga* is one who has no attachments ("without *yoga*") and *nanda* is one who enjoys bliss. Thus, She is one who attains bliss through non-attachment. *Ayoga* (*ay+u+ga*) can also mean "One who attains Śiva through auspicious steps (*aya:* auspiciously, *U:* Śiva, and *ga:* one who goes). In this interpretation, *Nanda* is Alakānanda, another name for Gangā, who attains Śiva.

According to *Padma Purāṇa, Nanda* is the name of a sacred

river flowing near lake Puṣkara and the very remembrance of its name is enough to wipe out all sins.

Devī incarnated as Nanda to kill Mahiṣāsura. He took birth again in the Vindhya Mountains under the name of Caitrāsura. Devī incarnated once again as Nanda and destroyed him. *(Devī Purāṇa)*

Mahiṣa represents *ajñāna* (ignorance) and Mahiṣāsuramardini, the Devī as slayer of Mahiṣa, is the power of *jñāna.*

Nanda is the deity of the first, sixth, and eleventh day of the lunar fortnight.

657. युगन्धरा

Yugandharā

She who is the Bearer of the yugas.

Yuga means "age or epoch" (the four *yugas*, Kṛta, Treta, Dvāpara and Kali being four vast ages of time).

Devī bears the responsibility of directing the four *yugas*; hence She is called "Bearer of the *Yugas*."

Yuga also means "yoke or a pair." Just as the bull bears the yoke for the preparation of the field for cultivation, Devī, as *Māyā*, bears the burden of creation, and so is called *Yugandharā.*

Devī Herself is the pair (*yuga*) of Śiva and Śakti. Everything in the universe is of dual nature - heat and cold, happiness and sorrow, victory and loss. As Devī bears the pairs of opposites, She is *Yugandharā.* She is at once the universe which is dual in nature and the Parāśakti which is beyond all duality.

658. इच्छा शक्ति ज्ञान शक्ति क्रिया शक्ति स्वरूपिणी

Icchā śakti jñāna śakti kriyā śakti svarūpiṇī

She who is in the form of the powers of will, knowledge and action.

The original cause of the universe is *Brahman*. At the start of creation, the energy latent in *Brahman* manifests as *icchāśakti*, the power of will or desire (to create). Then arises the *jñānaśakti*, the power of knowledge, deciding that creation should be done in a certain manner. The urge for action then arises and manifests as *kriyāśakti*, the power of creation.

According to *Saṅketapaddhati*, the power of will is Devī's head, the power of knowledge the trunk of Her divine body and the power of action Her lower body from the waist to the feet.

When will or desire for action arises, proper knowledge must follow before action can begin. "He desired to give rise to many." *Brahman* desired, "Why not become several?" The wisdom arose to fulfill this and the universe began to emerge. For every action, the will and proper knowledge are necessary; then only, proper action will take place.

The trinity of Brahmā, Viṣṇu and Maheśvara is another example of this same concept. Bhāskararāya quotes appropriately from *Vāmakeśvara Tantra*: "Devī Tripura is in three forms - Brahmā, Viṣṇu and Śiva; She is the powers of will, wisdom and action."

Kriyāśakti, the power of action, is said to be of five kinds (*Sūta Samhita*): movement (*spanda*), countermovement (*pratispanda*), beginning (*ārambha*), repetition (*āvartana*) and spreading (*pracāra*). A similar division is also seen in *Tarkaśāstra*, the science of logic. There, *karma* is divided as rising, falling, bending, spreading and going forth to the goal.

We should strive to keep our desires, knowledge and actions from being tainted since they are inherently divine. They are Devī Herself.

659. सर्वाधारा

Sarvādhārā

She who is the support of all.

What is meant here is not the usual concept of support and the supported. When we say, "money in the box" or "book on the shelf," the box and the shelf are the supports. That type of support is not implied here. It is like saying, "snake in the rope" or "blueness in the sky." We cannot separate the snake from the rope or the blueness from the sky. In the same way, we cannot separate Devī from the universe. Such is the concept of support meant here. Everything resides in Devī; and nothing is separate from Her.

660. सुप्रतिष्ठा

Supratiṣṭhā

She who is firmly established.

Devī is beyond time and so is firmly established. If we are to call a truth or a philosophy eternal (*sanātana*), it should be unshakably firm through the past, the present and the future. When we label the *Advaita* (nondual) philosophy and all the spiritual doctrines revolving around its axis as eternal, we mean that it has this firmness that transcends the ages.

Supratiṣṭha is the name of a meter (*chandas*) in poetry. Devī is considered to be in the form of that meter.

661. सद् असद् रूप धारिणी

Sad asad rūpa dhāriṇī

*She who assumes the forms of both being and non-being (*sat *and* asat*).*

Both the inert body and the life force are Devī. As the *Śruti* says, "All here is *Brahman*."

One who sees a snake in the rope does not see the rope. He just sees the snake. One who sees the rope does not see the snake. One who was deluded seeing the rope in the dark actually saw the snake. When light came, he realized that it was only a rope and not a snake. Which is the truth, the snake in the delusion or the rope that emerged as the illusion was dispelled? No one is alarmed seeing a totally non-existent snake. To one who is under the illusion, the snake exists; to one whose illusion is removed, the rope is what exists. There is only one thing, but two appearances. Likewise, for one who sees the Truth, this universe is pure

Essence, *Brahman*; for one who has not seen the Truth, it is still the universe. Universe is *asat* (non-being) and *Brahman* is *sat*. Both are Devī. She is therefore called *Sadasadrūpadhāriṇī*.

Sat and *asat* may mean good and bad actions. Actions in accordance with the *Vedas* are good deeds (*satkarma*) and actions that are against the *Vedas* are bad deeds (*asatkarma*). Devī is the support for both and in this way also She is *Sadasadrūpadhāriṇī*.

Devī is in the form of two types of knowledge, *sat* and *asat* - also called *savikalpa* and *nirvikalpa*. *Vikalpa* is "fancy;" it is a notion conveyed by words, but to which there is no corresponding reality. The "horns of a rabbit" are a classic example. Whatever is based on *vikalpa* (*savikalpa*) is *asat* (non-being or unreal) and whatever is not based on *vikalpa* (*nirvikalpa*) is *sat* (being). "Whatever is perceived by the intellect is *asat*," is the ancient wisdom.

662. अष्ट मूर्तिः

Aṣṭa mūrtiḥ

She who has eight forms.

The names of the eight forms are different in different sources. *Matsya Purāṇa* says, "O Sarasvatī with the eight forms, Lakṣmī, Intelligence, Earth, Nourishment, Gauri, Contentment, Radiance and Courage, protect me!"

In *yogaśāstra*, the self is described as having eight different forms depending on the *guṇas*: the embodied soul (*jīvātman*), the Inner Self (*antarātman*), Supreme Self (*paramātman*), Unstained Self (*nirmalātman*), Pure Self (*śuddhātman*), Wisdom Self (*jñānātman*), the Great Self (*mahātman*) and Elemental Self (*bhutātman*). Devī is Self in these eight forms.

In *Śaktirahasya*, the five gross elements plus the sun, the moon and the *jīvātman* are the eight forms of Devī. Heaven or sacrificer appears in some lists in place of *jīva*.

In the Gītā (VII.4) it is said, "Earth, water, fire, air, ether (*ākāśa*), mind, intellect and ego-sense (*ahaṅkāra*) are My eightfold nature." If we take mind to be moon, intellect to be sun and ego sense as *jīvātman* or sacrificer, then there is no contradiction.

663. अजा जैत्री

Ajā jaitrī

She who conquers ignorance.

Avidyā has no beginning, so it is called *ajā* (that which is not born). "There is an unborn being, a female of red, white and black colors who produces many offspring," according to the *Śruti*. *(Śvetāśvatāra Upaniṣad IV.5)* The three colors red, white and black represent the three *guṇas* of *rajas*, *sattva* and *tamas*, respectively. *Avidyā* is a mixture of these *guṇas* and is *ajā*.

It is very difficult to conquer *Māyā*, yet it is effortless for the devotee who has gained Devī's grace. This is the essence of this *mantra*. When we say that Devī conquers *Māyā*, it also means that Her devotees conquer *Māyā*, as we recognize that Her devotees are not distinct from Her.

664. लोक यात्रा विधायिनी

Loka yātrā vidhāyinī

She who directs the course of the worlds.

She is one who directs the lives of all the beings in the world or who directs the motions of the worlds, the cosmic bodies.

665. एकाकिनी

Ekākinī

She who is the lone one.

She is the One. There is no second. She is Non-duality. There is nothing of Her kind or of a different kind that is a second to Devī.

In the *Devī Purāṇa*, She is praised thus: "Alone She consumes the worlds, alone She establishes them, alone She creates the universe; hence She is *Ekākinī*."

666. भूम रूपा

Bhūma rūpā

She who is the aggregate of all existing things.

Bhūma means "many" and also *Brahman*, which is One. Coming just after the name *Ekākinī* (the lone one), this name can be taken to mean "many." *Devī Purāṇa* describes Her thus: "Even though She is only one, through conditioning She is celebrated everywhere as *Bhūma*, "many." As a crystal takes on the colors of the objects nearby, so does She shine as *Bhūma* due to the *guṇas*."

When we take *bhūma* as *Brahman*, the *mantra* means that Devī is none other than *Brahman*. Everything in the universe is only an illusory *(vivarta)* form of *Brahman*. Just as water is one but appears as wave, foam and whirlpool, *Brahman* is one without a second, but appears in many names and forms in the universe.

667. निर्द्वैता

Nirdvaitā

She who is without the sense of duality.

Those who follow a dual point of view do not accept this. Even a non-dualist (*advaitin*) accepts the view that everything is dual until one reaches the Supreme. When he reaches there, he does not see anything perishable or finite. As *Chāndogya Upaniṣad* (VII.24.1) says, "That is the Infinite in which one sees nothing else, hears nothing else, understands nothing else. But that is the finite in which one sees or hears or understands something else. That which is infinite is alone immortal, that which is finite, is mortal."

668. द्वैत वर्जिता

Dvaita varjitā

She who is beyond duality.

It is not appropriate to interpret this *mantra* using the literal meaning of *varjita*, as "one who has discarded or relinquished duality," because that would seem to imply that there was duality in Her to begin with and that She abandoned it. There was only pure Existence to begin with. That is one without a second, according to the *Śruti*.

The notion of two (duality) arises from delusion. Every atom in the universe is the essence of *Brahman*, Devī Herself. The meaning of *Dvaitavarjitā* is that Devī is not tainted by even a trace of the sense of duality.

669. अन्नदा

Annadā

She who is the giver of food to all living things.

Anna primarily means that which helps to sustain and nourish life in all living beings. It also means "all living and non-living things."

The *Gītā* says that food arises from the clouds and the body grows from food. Devī is one who gives not only food, but blesses all living beings with everything needed for the sustenance of life.

Śrī Śaṅkara, in a famous hymn, praises Devī as "Annapūrṇa" (fully endowed with food). Yet, in the hymn, he asks for more than just food. "O Devī, Annapūrṇa, Sweetheart of Śiva, You who are always full, grant me the alms of wisdom and dispassion, O Pārvatī !" (*Annapūrṇā Stotram*)

670. वसुदा

Vasudā

She who is the giver of wealth.

Devī is the giver of all forms of wealth (*vasu*) - grains, money and precious jewels.

One who receives Her blessing will never lack anything - food, clothes or other essentials. "That infinite, birthless Self is the giver of food and the giver of wealth." (*Brihadāraṇyaka Upaniṣad* IV.4.24)

671. वृद्धा

Vṛddhā

She who is ancient.

Devī was the First Cause and was present even before creation.

Vṛddha literally means "advanced or augmented." This may be in four different aspects: One may be advanced in wisdom (*jñānavṛddha*), advanced in righteousness (*dharmavṛddha*), advanced in age (*vayovṛddha*) and advanced in wealth (*dhanavṛddha*). All four descriptions befit Devī as shown by the commentary on the *mantras*.

672. ब्रह्मात्मैक्य स्वरूपिणी

Brahmātmaikya svarūpiṇī

She whose nature is the union of Brahman *and* Ātman.

Brahman is Śiva and *ātman* is *jīva*. *Svarūpa* means "having the form of *sva*," which is a name for the *hamsamantra*. Devī is in the form of the *hamsamantra* which causes the union of the *jīva* with Śiva, the Supreme.

673. बृहती

Bṛhatī

She who is immense.

Bṛhat is *Brahman*. Devī is none other than *Brahman*.

Bṛhatī is a meter (*chandas*) in Sanskrit poetry, with thirty-six syllables. Thus, Devī is in the form of a *chandas*. Recall that *tattvas* are also thirty-six in number.

674. ब्राह्मणी

Brāhmaṇī

She who is predominantly sāttvic.

Brāhmaṇa (feminine, *Brāhmaṇī*) is one in whom the *sāttvic* quality predominates. Devī is the embodiment of wisdom in whom *sattva* is dominant.

Brāhmaṇī is a medicinal plant (also called *Brāhmi*). Devī is in the form of this medicine, which according to the *Smṛti*, "is divine and is consciousness itself."

Parāśara Smṛti describes Śiva as Brāhmaṇa. *Brāhmaṇī* is His wife.

675. ब्राह्मी

Brāhmī

She who presides over speech.

Brāhmī and *Bhāratī* mean "language."
Also, one who pertains to Brahma.

676. ब्रह्मानन्दा

Brahmānandā

She who is ever immersed in the bliss of Brahman.

The nature of bliss according to the *Taittiriya Upaniṣad* has been described (see *mantra* 252). There the scale of bliss from an ordinary human to one who is established in *Brahman* was given.

Brahmānandam is the bliss that arises when the *jīva* returns to the Supreme Awareness from which it originally separated. According to the present *mantra*, Devī is that bliss.

Another division of bliss is: *viṣayānandam*, *vāsanānandam*, *nijānandam*, *mukhyānandam*, *ātmānandam*, *advaitānandam*, *jñānandam* and *brahmānandam*.

677. बलि प्रिया

Bali priyā

She who is especially fond of sacrificial offerings.

Man must show gratitude to Nature in the same measure that She gives Her bounty. To worship the various powers of nature (the *śaktis*) with *mantras* and *pūjas*, the ancient seers prescribed the various *yajñas* (sacrificial ceremonies). Since all *śaktis* are parts of Devī, sacrifices conducted in their honor are dear to Her as well - just as the praise given to children brings joy to their parents.

Bali also means Mahābali. Then, *Balipriyā* means: "She who is pleased by the devotion of King Mahābali."

Bali is also one who has the strength (*balam*) to overcome nescience. Such persons are especially dear to Devī.

678. भाषा रूपा

Bhāṣā rūpā

She who is in the form of language.

Devī takes the form of the language spoken in every region. Since She is the Goddess of Speech, all languages are indeed Her forms. As the Almighty hears our call, whatever language we use, so all languages are Devī's languages. She is therefore *Bhāṣārūpā*.

679. बृहत् सेना

Bṛhat senā

She who has a vast army.

She has sixty-four *crores* of *yoginīs* (*śaktis*) in attendance; in addition, there are regiments of elephants, horses and chariots. Her forces make up a powerful and vast army.

680. भावाभाव विवर्जिता

Bhāvābhāva vivarjitā

She who is beyond being and non-being.

Bhāva is being or existence and *abhāva* is non-being or non-existence. Even before a thing comes into existence, its support, substratum, exists. When it ceases to exist, the substratum continues to exist. Devī is that substratum of all things and is, therefore, beyond existence and non-existence.

The six changes which occur in the course of life are called *bhāvavikāras*, or modifications of existence. They are birth, existence. growth, change, decay and death.

Abhāva, non-existence, is of four kinds: 1) Prior non-existence (*prāgbhāva*), which denotes something not existing before. Before the pot was made, it did not exist; 2) Non-existence due to destruction (*Pradhvamsābhāva*). When the pot is broken, its non-existence falls into this category; 3) Mutual nonexistence (*Anyonyābhāva*). The pot does not exist as the cloth, the cloth does not exist as the pot; 4) Ultimate non-existence (*Atyantābhāva*). The state of something that will never exist.

None of these forms of existence or non-existence touch Devī, who is the substratum of all.

681. सुखाराध्या

Sukhārādhyā

She who is easily worshipped.

This implies that there are no rules to be followed or preparations to be done for Devī's worship.

There are forms of worship that involve inflicting pain or hardship on the body. There is no rule which says that Devī worship should involve hardship to body or mind. She is pleased by the simple chanting of Her names, as long as it is done with devotion. Thus, She bestows Her blessings as a result of worship that is done easily.

The Lord reassures us in the *Gītā* (II.40): "There is no loss of effort here, there is no harm. Even a little of this devotion delivers us from great fear." There is no need to fear an error in procedure or harmful consequences. Even a first step in this direction will protect us from the fear of *samsāra*. Devī's worship gives an optimism that we can completely trust. There is no need to worry that complicated procedures have been neglected. As the Lord says in the *Gītā*, Devī will be pleased with simple offerings of "leaf, flower, fruit and water." The Divine Mother is one who forgives errors that Her darling children make unknowingly.

682. शुभ करी

Śubha karī

She who does good.

She brings good even to those who worship Her imperfectly, since She is the Mother of the Universe. A mother would want only to do what is good even for an erring child.

683. शोभना सुलभा गतिः

Śobhanā sulabhā gatiḥ

She who is attained through a bright and easy path.

Devī shows a bright and easy path to salvation for those who worship Her (*Śobhana*: shining, salvation; *sulabha*: easily attained; *gati:* path or fruit). It is worth recalling here that even a simple hunter like Kannappadāsa could attain immortality through sincere devotion. Total surrender and love for the chosen deity are the most important factors.

"Devī alone is the ultimate goal of all living beings," says the *Kūrma Purāṇa.*

Bhāskararāya points out that this name is sometimes considered as three separate names: *śobhana*, *sulabha* and *gati.*

An alternative interpretation (taking the *mantra* as *śobhana asulabhāgati*) says that Devī is *not* easily attained The reason is that one who attains Her state does not return - is not reborn in this *samsāra. Brahma Purāṇa* says that a "*jīva* attains the fruit of the fifteen-syllabled *mantra* only in his last breath."

The *mantra* can also be interpreted as indicating that those who worship Her become righteous in life. Devī is one who renders glorious that which is difficult to obtain (*asulabhāgati*) such as a human birth. "The lives of those are in vain who do not hear the *Devī Bhāgavata* or do not worship the Original Prakṛti," says the *Devī Bhāgavata.*

684. राज राजेश्वरी

Rāja rājeśvarī

She who is the ruler of kings and emperors.

Devī is Īśvari - Ruler, Controlling Power - not only of human beings but also of Brahmā, Viṣṇu, Śiva, Indra, the Seven Sages and all other beings.

Also, Rājeśvara is Kubera, the God of Wealth. When we say Devī rules even Kubera, it means that the entire wealth in the world results from Her blessing and is controlled by Her.

685. राज्य दायिनी

Rājya dāyinī

She who gives dominion.

Dominion is not only in this world, but also in other worlds such as Vaikuṇṭha, Kailāsa and Brahmāloka. Devī's will decides who has dominion over all these worlds.

Those with faith will not question the statement that all material and spiritual realms are attained only as a result of Her will and pleasure.

686. राज्य वल्लभा

Rājya vallabhā

She who protects all the dominions.

Devī guards not only all of the rulers, but all of their dominions as well.

687. राजत्कृपा

Rājatkripā

She who has a compassion that captivates everyone.

Generally there is a limit to compassion, but Hers is limitless. It flows towards everyone, friend and foe alike. It reaches those who are near and those who are far. That is *rājatkripā*. That is the glory of Her compassion.

688. राज पीठ निवेशित निजाश्रिता

Rāja pīṭha niveśita nijāśritā

She who establishes on royal thrones those who take refuge in Her.

All high positions result as much from divine grace as from our own efforts. Effort alone is not enough. We are stuck in various stages in life without any progress, not because we lack the desire, effort or the ability to go beyond. Over and above all these is the unavoidable controlling factor of divine grace. It has to be in our favor as well.

689. राज्य लक्ष्मी

Rājya lakṣmī

She who is the embodiment of the prosperity of the world.

There is a *mantra* called *rājyalakṣmī*, which is described in *Tantrarāja*. Devī is in the form of that *mantra*.

690. कोश नाथा

Kośa nāthā

She who is the Mistress of the Treasury.

The fact that this name follows the name *Rājyalakṣmī* is food for thought. A rich treasury is essential for the security of a nation. Two elements that control the destiny of a nation are a rich treasury and a strong army.

If we take the word *kośa* to mean "dictionary," then Devī is to be understood as ruling over the entire world of words.

The five *kośas* of the body are also relevant here. Devī is the mistress of these *kośas* (see *mantra* 428).

691. चतुर् अङ्ग बलेश्वरी

Catur aṅga baleśvarī

She who commands armies of four types.

Caturaṅga armies are the four forces consisting of elephants, chariots, horses and men. Devī is the commander of all these forces. There are many well-known stories in which She goes to battle commanding such forces for the protection of the *devas* and the destruction of the *asuras*.

Caturaṅgabala also means four *vyūhas* or aggregates. According to the *Purāṇas*, the Vaiṣṇavas, Śaivas and Śaktas all have their own separate *vyūhas* and Devī presides over them all.

Caturaṅgabala also connotes the four kinds of *Puruṣa*: *Puruṣa* (person) in the body, *Puruṣa* in the Chandas (meter), *Puruṣa* in the *Vedas* and the Great *Puruṣa* (*Mahāpuruṣa*).

692. साम्राज्य दायिनी

Sāmrājya dāyinī

She who is the bestower of Imperial Dominion.

Sāmrājya is the dominion of a *samrāṭ*, a King of kings or an emperor. The title of *samrāṭ* was traditionally obtained by conducting the Rājasūya Sacrifice. Devī is the one who generously gives the grace that is needed for this.

693. सत्य सन्धा

Satya sandhā

She who is devoted to (or maintains) truth.

She who keeps Her promise. She gave Her word that whenever needed for the destruction of the wicked and the preservation of the righteous, She will incarnate. As She keeps this promise strictly, She is called *Satyasandhā*. "Whenever the world is afflicted in this manner, I will incarnate and cause their destruction." (*Devī Māhātmya*, chapter XI)

694. सागर मेखला

Sāgara mekhalā

She who is girdled by the oceans.

She is the Mother Earth, who is girdled by the oceans. The Earth is worshipped as Mother, "rich in water, rich in fruits, cooled by the mountain winds and lush green with vegetation," because She is an image of the Divine Mother. The respect given to the country as Motherland also arises from this.

695. दीक्षिता

Dīkṣitā

She who is under a vow.

Dīkṣa is the observance of a vow with a goal in mind. There are many kinds of *Dīkṣas*, like the observance of celibacy or *sannyāsa*. The vow taken by Pāñchāli (the wife of the Pāṇḍavas), that she would not tie her hair again until it was smeared with Duśśāsana's blood, was an example of a *dīkṣa*.

Dīkṣitā is one who has taken a *dīkṣa*. Devī is under a vow to destroy the wicked and protect Her devotees.

Dīkṣitā is one who gives and also weakens or destroys. The implication here is that Devī is one who gives Her devotees their desires including Liberation, by weakening or destroying their sins. *Parānanda Tantra* says that Devī accomplishes this by initiating them into Her *mantra* (*mantradīkṣa*).

A sense of one's goal - *lakṣyabodha* - is the cornerstone of success in life. *Dīkṣa*, the adherence to a vow, is the means for achieving that goal.

696. दैत्य शमनी

Daitya śamanī

She who destroys the demons, wicked forces.

The stories of Devī's destruction of demons (*daityas*) such as Bhaṇḍa and Dāruka are famous.

697. सर्व लोक वशंकरी

Sarva loka vaśankarī

She who keeps all the worlds under Her control.

Bhāgavata Purāṇa (II V. 42) gives two sets of definitions of worlds (*lokas*). From the feet to the waist is *bhūloka* (earth, the first three worlds), from the waist to the neck is *bhūvarloka*, and from the neck to the crown is *svarloka* (heaven, the highest of the three worlds). All these three are contained within ourselves.

Another more detailed picture contains fourteen worlds. The waist is *bhūloka*; the navel, *bhūvarloka*; the heart, *svarloka*; the chest, *maharloka*; the neck, *janaloka*; the lips form *tapoloka* and the crown is *satyaloka*. The areas below the waist are: the hips form *atala*; the thighs, *vitala*; the knees, *sutala*; the forelegs, *talātala*; the heels, *mahātala*; the tops of the feet, *rasātala*; and the soles of the feet, *patāla*. (*Bhāgavata Purāṇa* II V. 38-41)

Devī is the one who keeps all these worlds under Her sway.

698. सर्वार्थ दात्री

Sarvārtha dātrī

She who grants all desires.

Devī has the ability to bestow all things desired for a good life. She gives, according to the merit and at the proper time, the four ends in life - *dharma* (virtue, moral way of life), *artha* (wealth), *kāma* (sensory desires) and *mokṣa* (Liberation).

699. सावित्री

Sāvitrī

She who is the creative power in the universe.

Devī is Sāvitrī, as She is the mother even of *savitā* (the sun). "The sun is called *savitā* since he creates all beings" says the *Viṣṇu Dharmottara*. Devī is hailed as Sāvitrī as She gives light to the sun and creates the universe, according to the *Bhāradvāja Smṛti*.

Savitā is also a synonym for Śiva. Devī is His wife and is therefore Sāvitrī.

The *Devī Purāṇa* says that She is known as Sāvitrī because She is naturally pure.

According to the *Padma Purāṇa*, the deity in the temple at Puṣkara tīrtha is Sāvitrīdevī.

700. सत् चिद् आनन्द रूपिणी

Sat cid ānanda rūpiṇī

She who is of the nature of Existence, Consciousness and Bliss.

The group of one hundred names forming the eighth kalā of the sun called *bhogadā* (giver of all prosperity) ends here.

701. देश कालापरिच्छिन्ना

Deśa kālāparicchinnā

She who is not limited by time and space; She who is not measured by time and space.

Everything from Lord Brahmā to the lowly insect is limited, because it has a beginning, an end and a form. That which does not exist before the beginning and after the end, does not exist in between (in the present) either. Devī has no beginning or end, since She is none other than *Brahman* - She is unlimited by space and time and is eternal. "Since He is not limited by time and space, He is the Original Guru." (*Yoga Sūtra*)

"He who is all-pervading like the ether, and separate from whom there exists nothing, is not limited by space, time or things." (*Saura Samhita*)

702. सर्वगा

Sarvagā

She who pervades all the worlds and all the living and non-living things; She who is omnipresent.

The *Śruti* says, "Present everywhere like the ether (*ākāśa*) and eternal."

The *Varāha Purāṇa* mentions an incident. Once Devī, in the form of Kriyāśakti (Power of Action) did penance on the Śveta Mountains. Lord Brahmā appeared and enquired what boon She desired. She replied, "O Holy One, I do not wish to be limited to any corner of the world; therefore, I beg you to grant me the boon of omnipresence." A doubt may arise here. How can the *Brahman* which is said to be "eternal, omnipresent, constant and unmoving" do penance? It is all Her *līlā* (sport). Indeed, the credo of the believer is that the formless *Brahman* assumes human form and guides the world on the right path.

From the *Devī Purāṇa*: "O wise One, this is the real truth of Devī. She pervades the *Vedas*, sacrifices, heaven and all the animate and inanimate objects. She is the one who is worshipped and who is sacrificed. She is food and drink. Devī is present everywhere, in different forms and under different names, in trees, in the air, ether, water and fire. She is, therefore, to be worshipped according to the rules. The one who knows Devī's essence will be absorbed in Her."

703. सर्व मोहिनी

Sarva mohinī

She who deludes all.

There are many famous stories in the *Purāṇas* showing that even sages such as Nārada, well-established in the Self, have found the pull of *Māyā* irresistible. Not only common men, but even the wisest ones, after long and hard practice, lead a life rooted in plurality and not in unity with the Self. That sense of plurality is created by *Māyā*'s power of illusion. *Kaṭha Upaniṣad* (II.iv.1) offers an explanation: "The self-existing Supreme has created all the senses with outgoing tendencies; therefore, man beholds the external universe, and not the inner Self." Everyone looks outwards, no one sees the internal Self.

Looking outward leads to plurality, looking inward leads to unity. The natural tendency is to look outward. This urge is also a necessary ingredient in the makeup of the universe. That is why the *Gītā* (VII.3) says, "Among thousands of men, one perchance strives for perfection; even among the most successful strivers, only one perchance knows Me in essence."

One may ask how opposites like eternal and ephemeral, inert and alive, can arise from Devī. The answer is that She deludes everyone and creates the sense of duality, hiding the unity.

In truth, the difference between *Brahman* and the universe is merely an illusion. Śiva says in the *Kūrma Purāṇa:* "This Parāśakti, who is none other than *Brahman*, exists in Me. She, who, as *Māyā*, deludes the whole world, is dear to Me." In another place, Devī says to Himavat, "The *śāstras* such as Kapāla, Bhairava, Sakala and Gautama, which affirm duality in opposition to the *Śruti* and the *Smṛti*, were all created by Me to bewilder the world." *Sūta Samhita* says, "Deluded by *Māyā*, the sinful ones suffer births and deaths, without knowing the Lord." Devī thus deludes all three worlds. There is a *mantra* and a *yantra* by the name "Trailokyamohana," (bewildering all three worlds). The name *Sarvamohinī* may be interpreted as the Devī who is in the form of that *mantra* and that *yantra.*

704. सरस्वती

Sarasvatī

She who is in the form of knowledge.

The *Bhāradvāja Smṛti* says, "She who resides in the tongue of all beings and guides their speech is called Sarasvatī by the great *ṛṣis*." Also, "She is Sarasvatī as She is the one who shows the way for all eyes." (*Vāsiṣṭha Rāmāyaṇa*)

Saras is lake and *vati* is one who possesses. The lake here is the *Brahmarandhra* from which there is a flow of nectar. Thus, the secret meaning of the *mantra* is that Devī is the one with the *Brahmarandhra* from which there is a nectar flow. *Vāsiṣṭha Rāmāyaṇa* also says that *Sarasvatī* is the flow of knowledge or impressions obtained from the senses.

A girl of two is *Sarasvatī* according to Dhaumya.

705. शास्त्रमयी

Śāstramayī

She who is in the form of the scriptures; She whose limbs are the scriptures.

The four *Vedas* were formed from Her outgoing breath and the great *mantras* from Her ego-sense. From Her sweet words were born poetry, drama and rhetoric. From Her tongue, Sarasvatī was born. The six *vedāngas* (supplementaries to the *Vedas*) were created from Her cheeks, and *mīmāmsa* philosophy, *nyāya* (logic), *Purāṇas* and *dharmaśāstra* (the code of justice) from the top of Her throat; medicine and the science of archery, from the middle of Her throat; and the sixty-four arts from the bottom of Her throat; the science of love from Her shoulders and the *Tantras* from Her limbs. (*Brahmāṇḍa Purāṇa*)

What the *śāstras* say is the ultimate truth, not what our sense experience or reason says. Even *Vedānta* agrees with this view. We should accept what the *śāstras* say even when the senses and reason appear to contradict it. We see many examples of the misleading nature of the senses in the physical world. The sun appears to rise in the east and set in the west, yet the science of astronomy says something different.

706. गुहाम्बा

Guhāmbā

She who is the Mother of Guha (Subrahmanya); She who dwells in the cave of the heart.

The *Purāṇas* celebrate the story of the birth of Subrahmanya as the son of Śiva and Śakti to lead the armies of the *devas* to kill the demon Tāraka and liberate the *devas* from the scourge of the *asuras*.

The use of the term *guha* (cave, cavity) for heart is well-known in philosophy. Statements from the *Śruti* like "that which enters the cave and resides there," (*Kaṭha Upaniṣad*) referring to the *jīva* in the cave of the heart, are examples of this.

707. गुह्य रूपिणी

Guhya rūpiṇī

She who has a secret form.

When describing Devī as the Mother of Guha, it may seem as though we are accepting concepts rooted in duality. The present name helps to establish that even though such descriptions follow common sense and a worldly approach, duality is not the result of an analysis of truth. Ultimately, only non-duality survives. And that is, in turn, most secret or not easily perceived. That is why Devī is described as having a secret or hidden form.

The *Sūta Samhita* makes it clear: "We worship the Devī who has assumed the form of the Guru, who has the form of secret knowledge, who is beloved of Her secret devotees and who resides in the secret place."

The Devī who is perceived by the external senses has the form of the material universe; She who is known only by the inner eye is in the form of wisdom, *jñāna*. Devī is *Guhyarūpiṇī* because She is of the nature of wisdom. "Among all the *Upaniṣads*, Devī is the *Guhyopaniṣad*," according to the *Kūrma Purāṇa*.

708. सर्वोपाधि विनिर्मुक्ता

Sarvopādhi vinirmuktā

She who is free from all limitations.

Upādhi is limitation or conditioning and also support. Everything we see has some *upādhi.* In the system of the five Great Elements and their *upādhis* as discussed in *Vedānta, ākāśa* (ether) can be perceived through sound; *ākāśa* is where sound is. The hands that beat to the rhythm of music can produce sound because they enclose a part of *ākāśa. Ākāśa* manifests only through the *upādhi* (conditioning) of sound. The sun's rays falling on the desert causes the illusion of a mirage. Sunlight is the *upādhi* that creates the mirage. On the still water surface of a lake, trees appear upside down. The water surface is the *upādhi* here. All knowledge is associated with such a limitation (*upādhi*). Only Devī is beyond all *upādhis*.

It is clear that limitations or qualifications such as Mother of Skanda, Wife of Śiva or Daughter of Himavat are not the truth; Her true identity is the most secret, non-dual aspect beyond all these. One may ask how we can insist that non-duality is the only reality, when there are scriptures which admit duality and those which admit only non-duality. Duality is the truth of day to day existence, while non-duality is the ultimate truth. All the distinctions seen in the dual world arise from illusion. All the scriptural sayings directly or indirectly explain the non-dual nature of the Supreme *Brahman.* All other sciences deal with the practical day to day world. Therefore, it is enough if we ascribe a significance in the plane of common experience to those *mantras* exhibiting a dual aspect.

This *mantra* also means that the limitations imposed by logicians do not affect Devī; She is beyond them.

709. सदाशिव पतिव्रता

Sadāśiva pativratā

She who is Sadāśiva's devoted wife.

Devī's faithfulness to Lord Śiva has been indicated earlier by the *mantra "Kāmeśajñātasaubhāgyamārdavorudvayānvitā."* (*mantra* 39) Here, She is brought from Her non-dual aspect to the dual aspect.

710. सम्प्रदायेश्वरी

Sampradāyeśvarī

She who is the guardian of sacred traditions.

Sampradāya is that which is given to the disciples in the proper manner, that is, the traditional wisdom imparted to the disciples by the guru's words. Devī is the presiding goddess of that wisdom. Devī is also one who is worshipped using the *pañcadaśi mantra* according to the prescribed rules.

Although Devī is without attributes and without dependence, traditions view Her as having attributes and dependence. Devotees invoke Her in images, *sālagrāma* (sacred stones) and worship Her through traditional *arcana*, and gestures, and obtaining both worldly and spiritual gains. Devī is thus called the *Īśvarī* of sacred traditional rites.

711. साधु

Sādhu

She who possesses equanimity.

The combination of this and the next names is *sādhvi*. Bhāskarācārya takes this name to be *sadhu* - a word in neuter gender - and the next name to be *ī*. This *mantra* is chanted as Om *sādhune namaḥ*.

Sādhu is that which possesses *samatva* (equanimity). As the *Gītā* says, equanimity is abidance in *yoga*. Just as heat is inherent to fire and coolness to water, so is equanimity to Devī.

Bhāskarācārya assigns the meaning "appropriate" to the word *sādhu*. What is appropriate is *dharma*. What is inappropriate is *adharma*. The appropriate aspect is Devī and the inappropriate is Her *Māyā*.

712. ई

Ī

She who is the symbol Ī.

This represents Devī as *Kāmakalā* (see *mantra* 322).

The syllable A is Viṣṇu and *Ī* is Devī, who is Viṣṇu's sister.

The *Brahman*, which is one, becomes twofold for the purpose of creation, dividing into quality (*dharma*) and the thing qualified (*dharmi*). *Dharmi* is Śiva. What is *dharma*? The universe consists of the aggregate (*samaṣṭi*) and the individual (*vyaṣṭi*) forms. *Dharma* is *parāhanta*, the egoism of the Supreme in the form of the individual. It further divides into a masculine and a feminine form. The feminine form becomes the Sister of Viṣṇu and wife of Śiva. She is Kāmakalā. The masculine form, as Viṣṇu, governs the universe.

It is from *Ī*, the Kāmakalā, that creation and the bondage of *Māyā* arise.

The *Vāmakeśvara Tantra* says, "Beyond vowels and the *visarga*, beyond the wave-like knowledge that arises from the *bindu*, when *Ī*, the real nature of light, joins with the flow of vibrations, *Māyā* arises."

According to *Vāmakeśvara Tantra*, Kāmakalā is the state of *turīya*. Kāmakalā is described as red, which is the color of the *guṇa* of *rajas*. Creation is the nature of this *guṇa*.

This name is chanted as "*Om yai namaḥ.*"

713. गुरु मण्डल रूपिणी

Guru maṇḍala rūpiṇi

She who embodies in Herself the lineage of Gurus.

The line of Gurus starting with Paramaśiva and ending with one's own Guru is *Gurumaṇḍala*. That line is not separate from Devī, the Supreme *Brahman*.

"Guru is Brahmā, Guru is Viṣṇu, Guru is Śiva; Guru is the supreme *Brahman*. Salutations to that holy Guru!"

India has a celebrated lineage of Gurus. "I constantly bow to Nārāyaṇa, Brahmā the lotus-born, Vasiṣṭha, Śakti, his son Parāśara, Vyāsa, Śuka, Gauḍapāda, Govinda, his disciple Śaṅkara, Padmapāda, Hastāmalaka, Toṭaka and all my other Gurus." This line of Gurus continues to grow.

The present *mantra* may be interpreted as: "She who is the secret of the *Tantra* of Kāmakalā," as this secret is traditionally preserved by the line of Gurus. Since Guru is not distinct from Devī, the Guru lineage, as a whole, is a form of Devī.

714. कुलोत्तीर्णा

Kulottīrṇā

She who transcends the senses.

Devī is one who transcends (*uttīrṇā*) the inner and outer senses (*kulas*). She is not the object of the senses, and can be reached only through meditation. Likewise, as She is beyond the senses, She is not involved in worldly joys and sorrows.

This is the line of separation between us and God. We experience happiness and sorrow through the senses; the Lord is beyond the entire family of senses.

715. भगाराध्या

Bhagārādhyā

She who is worshipped in the sun's disc.

Here, *bhaga*, the sun's disc, refers to the *anāhata cakra* in the heart. *Bhaga* can be the sun, the moon and Lord Śiva. The *mantra* means: "Devī is one who is worshipped by all of these."

Bhaga also means Kāmakalā. See the *mantras Bhagamālini* (277) and *Bhagavatī* (279) for other references to the word *bhaga*. Thus, Devī is one who is worshipped by the six *aiśvaryas* (attributes of excellences): auspiciousness, supremacy, fame, valor, discrimination and knowledge, as per those references.

716. माया

Māyā

She who is illusion.

Māyā is something that seems to be what it is not. *Māyā* is not the absence of something, but the apparent presence of something that is not real. What *Māyā* gave rise to was not a non-existent snake in the rope; it was a snake that was not the rope, as one is not scared by an absent snake; one is scared by a snake that was not the rope. These two forms of negation are very different in meaning. The world is not something that is non-existent; it is just not what it appears to be. There is only *Brahman*. It appears either as *Brahman* or as the universe. We should not conclude that one is not in the other; we should conclude that one is not something different from the other.

The *Devī Purāṇa* says, "It is called *Māyā* because it is the instrument of marvelous actions producing unimagined results like those in dreams or in magic."

The *jīva* dwells in the world with the mind (*antaḥkaraṇa*) as its instrument (*upādhi*), whereas God dwells here with *Māyā* as His instrument.

Māyā is the strange power that makes the pure appear as impure and knowledge appear as ignorance. It hides the real nature of an object and superimposes on it something that it is not.

It is the power of *Māyā* that creates the seasons, makes the moon wax and wane and the tides rise and fall. That power of *Māyā* is Devī's will power. For the creation of the world, matter and energy are not enough, will is also needed. The three sounds *a*, *u*, and *m*, contained in the sacred syllable *Aum* (Om), stand for matter, energy and will respectively. These are also referred to as *sattva*, *rajas* and *tamas* and as Brahmā, Viṣṇu and Śiva. Devī is that will power that prompts creation and the union of Śiva and Śakti.

717. मधुमती

Madhumatī

She whose nature is as sweet as honey.

Madhu means honey and intoxicating liquor. Since both are dear to Devī, devotees offer Her both during worship. Thus, this *mantra* also means: "She who is offered *madhu* in worship."

According to *yogaśāstra*, there are four kinds of *yogins*. Those of the fourth kind are known as *atikrāntabhāvanas*, those who have transcended the state of *samādhi*. They also have to go past seven stages, the last of which is known as *madhumatī*. In this state, one's knowledge is complete. That knowledge provides freedom from *samsāra*. It is also known as *tārakajñāna* or *samsāratārika* (*tāraka*: that which helps to cross).

There is a sacred river known as Madhumatī. Devī is considered to be in the form of the holy waters of that river. Also, Devī is in the form of the *madhuvidyā mantra*.

718. मही

Mahī

She who is the Goddess Earth.

Devī is the embodiment of patience, like Mother Earth. Also like the Earth, Devī is the support for everything, and so is called the Goddess Earth.

Mahī is the name of a sacred river and Devī is in the form of its waters. She was the given the name *Mahī* since devotees worship Her on the banks of that river.

719. गणाम्बा

Gaṇāmbā

She who is the Mother of Śiva's attendants.

She is the mother of hosts of Śiva's *gaṇas* (attendants) such as Pramatha and others.

Gaṇa also refers to Gaṇeśa (the leader of the *gaṇas*), and Devī is his mother.

Gaṇa is used in the sense of groups of stars or army formations. This *mantra* means that Devī is to be considered the mother of all these.

720. गुह्यकाराध्या

Guhyakārādhyā

She who is worshipped by guhyakas.

Guhyakas are kinds of *devas* such as *yakṣas*, *kinnaras*, *gandharvas* and *kimpuruṣas*.

Guhyaka refers to that which is most secret. It may be assumed, then, that Devī is worshipped in great secrecy, beyond the reach of external disturbances and temptations, and thus the name was applied to Her.

721. कोमलाङ्गी

Komalāṅgī

She who has beautiful limbs.

Devī's entire form is very beautiful.

722. गुरुप्रिया

Gurupriyā

She who is beloved of the Gurus.

Here, Guru is Śiva, the Guru of the World. Devī is His wife and is dear to Him.

The *mantra* also means: "She who is fond of the Guru." The Guru in this case is Bṛhaspati, the Guru of the gods. Devī is one who is fond of that Guru.

As the sacred precept says, "Guru is the Supreme *Brahman* itself." Devī is the *Māyā* who became dear to the *Brahman* with form (or *Brahman*-with-parts, *Sakalabrahman*) who was intent on creation.

723. स्वतन्त्रा

Svatantrā

She who is free from all limitations.

Devī is independent since She does not need the help of anyone during the process of creation. *Sva* means, "Self" and *Tantra* means, "She who depends;" hence, She is one who depends on the Self. Devī abides in union with Śiva who is the Self.

The *mantra* also means, "She who has Her own *Tantras* (*sva*: own)." All the *Tantras* such as *Śaiva*, *Vaiṣṇava*, *Gāṇapatya* and *Śākteya* celebrate Devī. Hence, all *Tantras* belong to Her.

724. सर्व तन्त्रेशी

Sarva tantreśī

She who is the goddess of all Tantras.

There are sixty-four main *Tantras*. Devī is the object of worship in all of them.

725. दक्षिणा मूर्ति रूपिणी

Dakṣiṇā mūrti rūpiṇī

She who is in the form of Dakṣiṇāmūrti (Śiva).

Śiva sat facing south while imparting the supreme knowledge to Brahmā, Viṣṇu and others, and so received the name Dakṣiṇāmūrti (*dakṣiṇa*: south). He became the original Guru as He taught even the gods. This *mantra* means that Devī Herself had assumed the form of Dakṣiṇāmūrti.

Śiva, who did penance in the Himālayas at the loss of Satī, is also known as Dakṣiṇāmūrti.

726. सनकादि समाराध्या

Sanakādi samārādhyā

She who is worshipped by Sanaka and other sages.

Sanaka and the other sages are considered as gurus who prescribed the rites for Devī worship.

The *Brahmāṇḍa Purāṇa* says, "Thou art beginningless, whole and in the form of all cause and effect. The *yogins* such as Sanaka are searching for none other than You." Here searching means worshipping according to all of the prescribed rites.

727. शिव ज्ञान प्रदायिनी

Śiva jñāna pradāyinī

She who bestows the knowledge of Śiva.

Knowledge of Śiva can also be taken as the supreme knowledge of the Self. Devī is one who confers that. *Vāsiṣṭha Rāmāyana* says, "Wind is known by touch and fire by heat; Śiva, who is pure Consciousness, is known only through Śakti, who is the energy that makes Him move."

Conversely, Devī is one whose truth (*svarūpa*) is imparted by Śiva who knows Her essence. In this case, *svarūpa* translates as "the truth of the knowledge of Devī," rather than as the literal meaning of "form."

728. चित् कला

Cit kalā

She who is the Consciousness in Brahman.

Kalā means part. Devī is the Consciousness inherent in *Brahman*, who is *Satcidānanda* or Existence - Consciousness - Bliss. It is not implied that existence, consciousness and bliss are three separate fractions of *Brahman*; only that the *cit* (consciousness) aspect is emphasized in the present *mantra*.

Lord Kṛṣṇa says in the *Gītā* (X.41): "Whatever being is glorious, prosperous or strong, know that to be a manifestation of part of My splendor." He also refers to the soul in everything as "a ray of Myself, the eternal *jīva*, in the world of all living beings." (*Gītā*, XV.7)

This name means that Devī Herself is the Consciousness present in all beings.

729. आनन्द कलिका

Ānanda kalikā

She who is the bud of Bliss.

Her presence is that which is experienced as bliss by all beings. She Herself gives the blessing that makes this bud of bliss blossom, leading the *jīva* into a full bliss that is beyond all the senses. The Self is bliss; that is why it reflects in the senses and we come to experience a little of that. It is like milk turning blue when we immerse a sapphire in it. In truth, the milk is not blue; but the presence of the sapphire gives it a blue color. Likewise, bliss is not inherent in the senses or in the mind, yet when the Self, which is Bliss itself, reflects through them, we come to experience it.

The word *kalika* (bud) is very meaningful. Buds wither and die, but many others blossom and spread fragrance. Buds do not attract our hearts; flowers that have fully blossomed are the attraction. Bees and humans are automatically attracted to them. The *jīva* who is bound in *samsāra* is like the bud that withers and dies. The one who knows the Self attracts thousands of others to him, like the blossom brimming with honey and sending out fragrance.

730. प्रेम रूपा

Prema rūpā

She who is pure love.

The devotion of the worshipper for Devī, and Her compassion for him, are both forms of the *prema* (love) that is Her essence.

"She who has taken the form entirely of love, affection and devotion," says Bhāskararāya. Devī exists as love in all beings. Mutual attraction is the nature of love. Devī is the power that directs that attraction. "Many Salutations to that Devī who dwells in all beings in the form of Love." (*Devī Māhātmya*)

731. प्रियङ्करी

Priyaṅkarī

She who grants what is dear to Her devotees.

Here *priyam* (dear) means "fulfillment of desires." The Divine Mother fulfills the desires that are righteous and beneficial.

732. नाम पारायण प्रीता

Nāma pārāyaṇa prītā

She who is pleased by the repetition of Her names.

"Names" can be those of any deity. She likes them all. Amma once said, "God will respond to any divine name that we utter. Calling Devī, Kṛṣṇa or Śiva all have the same result. Some children address their mother as sister. But the mother knows the child is calling her." "Just as all the water that falls from the sky goes to the ocean, so does prostration to any deity go to Keśava." Keśava is also Devī.

All the letters of the alphabet, from A to *Kṣa* are considered to be Devī's names. According to *Laghustuti* (verse 12), there are 96,874 names in all. Verse 18 mentions an even larger number (195,840) for the total. All of these *mantras* are obtained through different combinations of the fifty-one letters of the *Sanskṛt* alphabet. The letters are known as *mātṛka* letters in this context (see *mantra* 577). Since it is difficult to repeat such a large number of *mantras*, one thousand names have been prescribed in their place - that is the *Lalitā Sahasranāma Stotra*. Thus, the present *mantra* means "One who is fond of hearing the chanting of the *Sahasranāma*." Other similar hymns such as the *Viṣṇu Sahasranāma* also belong here.

Bhāskararāya adopts the number 20,736 as the total number of names. The exact number is not a topic to be debated. It is the result of the direct vision obtained by different seers. It is enough to recognize that there are countless holy names of Devī, starting with the monosyllabic *Om*. In the prologue to the *Sahasranāma*, Devī Herself says, "Whether a devotee worships me in the *Śrīcakra* or not, whether he repeats the *pañcadaśi mantra* or not, if he only recites these thousand names regularly, I will be pleased with him."

Rāmakṛṣṇa Paramahamsa says, "Just as clapping your hands drives the crows away, so does *japa* of holy names drive sins away." There is no greater *yajña* (sacrifice) than *japa*. Chanting holy names is the most powerful means of uniting the hearts of all and raising them to the goal. There is no inappropriate time for *japa*. Eruttacchan, the poet-saint of Kerala, declares firmly, "Chanting Lord Hari's names is not forbidden anytime or to anyone - to a woman having her periods, to a beggar, to one who burns the corpses, to the fallen, or to the *brāhmaṇa* who has performed the fire sacrifice." Such is the universal accessibility of *nāma japa*. It is easy, simple, it yields joy, and finally, leads to Liberation. Hymns like the *Sahasranāmas* have survived as priceless gems for thousands of years, attracting and giving refuge to millions of devotees.

The *Purāṇa* says that when Ajāmila, in the throes of death, called out in pain to his son Nārāyaṇa, the single utterance of that divine name brought him forthwith to Vaikuṇṭha, Lord Viṣṇu's abode. One thing is to be particularly noted: for the divine name to appear on the tongue at the final moment, it has to be deep-rooted in the mind. That recollection will not otherwise be possible. Only the prayer that comes from the depth of the heart will be effective. Mary Magdalene was purified because her prayer was sincere and moving.

733. नन्दि विद्या

Nandi vidyā

She who is the Deity worshipped by the mantra (vidyā) *of Nandi.*

Nandividyā is the *mantra* acquired by Nandikeśvara (one of Śiva's chief attendants) through *upāsana* (worship). Devī is in the form of, or the essence of, that *mantra*.

Nandi also means "Viṣṇu" and "Śiva." Thus we understand that the *Vaiṣṇava* and *Śaiva vidyās* are also Devī Herself.

734. नटेश्वरी

Natesvarī

She who is the wife of Nateśa (Śiva).

Nateśa is the Lord of Dance. Śiva's dance is known as *tāṇḍava* and Devī's dance as *lāsya.*

735. मिथ्या जगद् अधिष्ठाना

Mithyā jagad adhiṣṭhānā

She who is the basis of the illusory universe.

The basis or support for the illusory universe is *Brahman.* This *mantra* means that Devī is the essence of that *Brahman.*

Mithya is that which is illusory, not constant. Everything that changes is illusion. Truth is what is constant. There is only one such truth. That is *Brahman.*

The *ṛṣis* of India recognized thousands of years ago that everything is *Brahman.* The universe manifests in the essence of that *Brahman.* This manifestation persists until one realizes *Brahman.* Until then, this world is indeed the reality. It is called the relative reality. As long as the sense of *samsāra* exists, the world is real. Only for one who has reached the ultimate truth of realization of the Self does the world become an illusion. Those who, without recognizing this, fight the world, merely thinking it to be an illusion, are fighting in vain. One has to recognize that it is a pointless fight doomed to failure.

736. मुक्तिदा

Muktidā

She who gives Liberation.

According to the *Kūrma Purāṇa,* "Anyone desiring salvation should take refuge in Pārvatī Parameśvarī who is the soul of all beings and the essence of Śiva." Also, *Brahmāṇḍa Purāṇa* says, "Those who worship the Parāśakti, whether according to the rules or not, do not get entangled in *samsāra.* They are liberated; there is no doubt."

Mukti is not just Liberation after death. It can be experienced while alive. One who welcomes life as it comes and goes forward, having overcome desire and anxiety with a mind attached to nothing and not dwelling on the fruit while doing any action, is a liberated soul. There are many such liberated ones in India even today. They are known as *jīvanmuktas* - liberated while alive.

737. मुक्ति रूपिणी

Mukti rūpiṇī

She who is in the form of Liberation.

Mukti is bliss. Hence, "She who is in the form of bliss." The wording here may appear to assign a form to that which is formless. In *Saurasamhita* (chapter 14), this state of salvation is described. "This state is not obtained by the removal of ignorance or by reaching *turīya*." It is a blissful experience beyond that.

738. लास्यप्रिया

Lāsyapriyā

She who is fond of the lāsya *dance.*

Śiva's *tāṇḍava* and Devī's *lāsya* are not confined to poetic concepts. Modern science is studying in detail the incessant dance of energy in the molecules of matter. Science is eyeing with wonder the visions of the ancient sages. The visions of the *ṛṣis* are scientific and eternal.

739. लय करी

Laya karī

She who causes absorption.

Laya is a special state of the mind. It is the absorption or dissolution of the mind in the object of meditation, forgetting all surrounding objects. A *laya* is equal to five meditations.

The melting of the heart experienced with the mutual dissolution of pitch and rhythm in music is known as *laya*. "*Śruti* (pitch) is the mother and *laya* the father," is a well-known saying in musical parlance. The *laya* state in music arises from Devī's grace, it is believed. It is noteworthy that many of the celebrated musicians are Devī's devotees. Worship of *Brahman*-as-sound is an important form of *upāsana*, which is still practiced in India.

740. लज्जा

Lajjā

She who exists as modesty in living beings.

"Salutations to the Devī who dwells within all beings in the form of modesty," says *Devī Māhātmya.*

Bashfulness is the external sign of noble birth and modesty. It should not be considered as a weakness, as it is, in fact, an ornament to one's character.

This *mantra* says that the feminine form, which is a part of Devī's gross body, is the embodiment of modesty.

In *mantraśāstra*, the *bījākṣara* (seed syllable) "*hrīm*" is known as *lajjā*. Therefore, it is implied that Devī is in the form of "*hrīm*."

741. रम्भादि वन्दिता

Rambhādi vanditā

She who is adored by the celestial damsels such as Rambhā.

Devī is adored by the celestial damsels (*apsaras*) such as Rambhā, Urvaśī, Menakā and Tilottamā.

Beauty is a gift obtained by divine grace. Rambhā and others have a place in Indra's court as they are leading examples of feminine beauty.

742. भव दाव सुधा वृष्टिः

Bhava dāva sudhā vṛṣṭiḥ

She who is the rain of nectar falling on the forest fire of worldly existence.

Devī is indeed one who showers nectar on the devotees who are scorched by the intense fire of worldly existence.

The above meaning is obtained by splitting the name as *bhava* (worldly existence) + *dāva* (forest fire) + *sudhā* (nectar) + *vṛṣṭi* (rain). A different meaning is derived by splitting it as: *Bhava* (Śiva) + *da* (*dāna*, giving) + *vasu* (wealth) + *dhā* (maintenance) + *vṛṣṭi* (rain). Then it becomes "She who gives us Śiva, the bliss of Self, and also showers on us immense riches without reservation."

One who yearns for the bliss of the Self does not wish for worldly riches; yet when Devī's grace is present, one gets both in plenty. As *Rudrayāmala* says, "Wherever there is worldly enjoyment there is no salvation; where there is salvation, there is no worldly enjoyment. But the highest devotees of Śrī Sundarī receive both salvation and enjoyment into their hands."

743. पापारण्य दवानला

Pāpāraṇya davānalā

She who is like wild fire to the forest of sins.

A forest fire reduces even large trees to cinders. Likewise, Devī's grace burns even heavy sins to ashes. Man hesitates to commit only the first sin. Once begun, sins continue one after the other. Thus, a wild forest of sins grows up around us. Uttering the Divine Mother's name even once with faith and devotion is enough to wipe out all sins.

"Remembrance of the feet of Parāśakti is the best expiation of all sins committed knowingly or unknowingly," declares the *Brahma Purāṇa*. In another context, the same *Purāṇa* says, "O Devendra, hear this great secret which destroys all sins. With devotion and faith, standing in the water after bath, repeat the *pañcadaśi mantra* a hundred and eight times. Worshipping the Supreme Śakti in this way, one is released from all sins."

744. दौर्भाग्य तूल वातूला

Daurbhāgya tūla vātūlā

She who is the gale that drives away the cotton wisps of misfortune.

Vātūla is gale and *tūla* is cotton. A gale can uproot even large trees, so wisps of cotton are not a problem at all. Likewise, Devī's compassion makes misfortunes as light as wisps of cotton and blows them away.

Also, *vātūlā* means certain expiatory actions that remove sins, implying that such actions originate from Devī.

Amma's words are worth recalling here: "Heart-felt prayers and acts of atonement, done with devotion, remove ninety percent of the sorrows from one's *prārabdha*."

745. जरा ध्वान्त रवि प्रभा

Jarā dhvānta ravi prabhā

She who is the sunlight that dispels the darkness of old age.

The darkness that engulfs everything disappears completely, and a new burst of energy awakens in its place, with the emergence of sunlight. Similarly, when exposed to the rays of Devī's compassion, all mental fatigue and bodily ailments of old age disappear.

746. भाग्याब्धि चन्द्रिका

Bhāgyābdhi candrikā

She who is the full moon to the ocean of good fortune.

Just as the full moon causes tides to rise in the ocean, Devī's blessing brings waves of good fortune.

Good and bad fortunes are normal in life. All of us will have to withstand the waves of misfortune at some stage. In the case of Devī's devotees, even ill luck turns into waves of good fortune, because Her grace has the power to challenge even fate.

747. भक्त चित्त केकि घनाघना

Bhakta citta keki ghanāghanā

She who is the cloud that gladdens the peacocks who are the hearts of Her devotees.

Clouds are said to bring such a surge of joy to the hearts of peacocks, that they start dancing. Similarly the hearts of the devotees ascend to the heights of joy at the very thought of the Divine Mother. They start to sing and dance. Singing Her praise is like thunder for them; the flashes of ecstasy from remembering Her are like flashes of lightning, and the joyful tears of devotion are like a cool downpour.

The word *ghanāghanā* means cloud as in the above, or *ghana* is cloud and *aghana* is continual, which emphasizes the meaning, adding that Devī gives continuous nourishment to the devotees' hearts. What sweeter emotion is there than devotion?

748. रोग पर्वत दम्भोलिः

Roga parvata dambholiḥ

She who is the thunderbolt that shatters the mountain of disease.

Dambholi is Indra's thunderbolt (*vajra* weapon). Lord Kṛṣṇa says in the *Gītā*, "I am *vajra* among weapons." For the mountain range of diseases, Devī is the *vajra* weapon. Her *darśan*, touch and embrace are indeed weapons that overpower disease. This truth is revealed only through experience.

There is a reference here to an ancient story. It is said that long ago, mountains were able to fly and that Indra cut off their wings with his *vajra* weapon, thus forcing them to be stationary. Thus, it was Indra's thunderbolt that protected the earth from attacks by the marauding mountains. Likewise, a glance from Devī instantly routs all attacks from diseases, like the thunderbolt.

749. मृत्यु दारु कुठारिका

Mṛtyu dāru kuṭhārikā

She who is the axe that cuts down the tree of death.

Dāru means tree. According to the numerological system, *dāru* signifies the number 28. In one interpretation, this number is said to represent the variety of bonds (*pāśas*) that bind the *jīva* as explained under the *mantra paśupāśavimocinī* (354). Devī is the axe that cuts all those bonds causing the fear of death. The bonds are also understood as sorrows.

As explained before, this is not just a poetic image. Guru's grace has the power to postpone even a death that comes in old age, as proven by experience.

750. महेश्वरी

Maheśvarī

She who is the Supreme Goddess.

Other interpretations are as follows: *Maha* means festival, and Devī presides over festivals; She who is Goddess (Īśvari) to great souls; the wife of Śiva (Maheṣvara).

751. महा काली

Mahā kālī

She who is the great Kālī.

Kālī is one who has transcended time (*kāla*), or one who controls time. Devī is Mahākālī, Kālī of great prowess. One who destroys time and lifts us to the knowledge of the Self which is beyond the past, present and future.

Mahākāla is Śiva and His wife is Mahākālī. There is another belief that Kālī was born from Śiva's third eye.

Kālī is one who is black in color.

The deity installed in Ujjain is Mahākālī. Also, today's Calcutta was originally Kālīghāṭṭa, famous because of Kālī.

752. महा ग्रासा

Mahā grāsā

She who devours everything great or She who is the great devourer.

Devī is one who devours everything, even Brahmā, Viṣṇu and Śiva at the end of the epoch. *Kaṭha Upaniṣad* (I.ii.25) says that for *Brahman*, even all-devouring death is just a side-dish.

753. महाशना

Mahāśanā

She who eats everything that is great.

Since everything in the universe finally merges in Her, She is the great eater. She dissolves into Herself this world and the next.

In *Devī Māhātmya*, Devī is portrayed, during the battle with Chaṇḍa and Muṇḍa, as eating the *asura* army in its entirety, along with the elephants, chariots and horses.

754. अपर्णा

Aparṇā

She who owes no debt.

Aparṇa: apa+ṛṇa; ṛṇa is a debt. Devī is without debt. Just as the lotus leaf does not become wet even when immersed in water, Devī is not beholden to anyone. She fills the universe, yet the universe does not touch Her. She who has no attachments owes nothing to anyone. It is implied that as She fulfills the desires of devotees immediately; She carries no debts.

Aparṇā also means "no leaf" (*a* + *parṇa*). Devī took birth as the daughter of Himavat, and did severe penance to win Lord Śiva as Her husband. The intensity of the penance was such that She did not eat even the leaves falling from trees. Kālidāsa describes Her *tapas* in *Kumārasambhava* (V. 28): "Eating only the leaves falling from trees is indeed the severest form of penance; She gave up even that. Therefore those savants of sweet words who know the ancient stories call Her *Aparṇā*."

Kālikā Purāṇa also gives the same explanation: "She renounced even leaves as food. Hence, the daughter of Himavat is called *Aparṇā* by the *devas*." *Brahmāṇḍa Purāṇa* also recalls this.

Taking *parṇa* to mean "fall," Bhāskarācārya interprets *aparṇā* as "one who has no fall."

755. चण्डिका

Caṇḍikā

She who is angry (at the wicked).

Caṇḍī means anger. Devī shows anger towards evil forces. She became famous as *Caṇḍikā* because of Her wrath towards the demons, Caṇḍa and Muṇḍa.

One who just pretends to be angry is also *Caṇḍikā*. The anger is an act in Her case. How can She be really angry? Can Devī be under the sway of emotions? However, there are times when, as a means of persuasion, show of anger is needed. Then She becomes *Caṇḍikā*.

A girl of seven is also known as *Caṇḍikā*.

756. चण्ड मुण्डासुर निषूदिनी

Caṇḍa muṇḍāsura niṣūdinī

She who killed Caṇḍa, Muṇḍa and other asuras.

Mārkaṇḍeya Purāṇa says, "O Devī, because You captured Caṇḍa and Muṇḍa, You will be known in the world as *Cāmuṇḍā*."

Varāha Purāṇa tells another story in which Devī killed the demon Ruru and because She separated his body-skin (*carman*) and his head (*muṇḍa*) with Her trident, She is called *Cāmuṇḍā*.

757. क्षराक्षरात्मिका

Kṣarākṣarātmikā

She who is in the form of both the perishable and imperishable Ātman.

The perishable (*kṣara*) *ātman* is the *samsāra*-bound *ātman* which mistakes the body to be the Self. The imperishable (*akṣara*) *Ātman* is the Eternal Self. The imperishable and beginningless nature of the Self has been made clear in many places as in the *Bhagavad Gītā* (II. 23), for instance: "Him weapons cut not; Him fire burns not."

Kṣara also means "diverse." A mind that runs in diverse directions is, indeed, perishable.

Akṣara connotes letters of the alphabet or syllables. Devī is thus One who is in the form of letters or syllables. She is known as one-syllabled or many-syllabled. The Devī who is the creator is one-syllabled and the Devī who awakens the sense of diversity is many-syllabled.

Kṣara is *sat* (being) and *akṣara* is *asat* (non-being). Devī is in both forms. Just as gold manifests as pure gold or as various ornaments, Devī is at the same time the *kūṭasṭha* (the Supreme) and the *jīvas* of many names and forms, as indicated by the celebrated passage from the *Gītā* (XV.16): "The perishable includes all creatures; the Supreme is imperishable."

758. सर्व लोकेशी

Sarva lokeśī

She who is the Ruler of all worlds.

759. विश्व धारिणी

Viśva dhāriṇī

She who supports the universe.

The implication is that the universe exists within Devī.

760. त्रि वर्ग दात्री

Tri varga dātrī

She who bestows the three goals of life.

These are righteousness (*dharma*), wealth (*artha*) and objects of desire (*kāma*).

The triad here (*trivarga*) may also be the powers of will, knowledge and action (see *mantra* 658). Devī is one who bestows these on Her devotees. It is from Her that one derives all material riches, a firmly grounded abidance in righteousness and an untiring devotion to action.

761. सुभगा

Subhagā

She who is the seat of all prosperity.

She is one in which all *bhagas* are contained.

There are numerous meanings for the word *bhaga* (see *mantras* 277, 279, 715). Devī is the treasurehouse of all these. Some of the other meanings are wealth, desire, strength, greatness, merit, sun, the womb and Liberation.

If we take the meaning of the womb, it is implied that children are a gift from Her grace.

Subhagā is also the beautiful wife who awakens desire in her husband. In the concept of the universe as consisting of *Puruṣa* and *Prakṛti*, the female (*Prakṛti*) arouses the indifferent male (*Puruṣa*) by her presence and turns him towards creation. Wherever there is a captivating feminine aspect in the universe, there Devī is present as *Subhagā*.

If we take *bhaga* to mean "the sun," the *Śruti* says that the sun is illuminated by a part of Devī's radiance. The sun is also referred to as a manifestation of Viṣṇu. *Viṣṇu Purāṇa* says that *Ṛg*, *Yajus* and *Sāma Vedas* are the dawn, midday and dusk for that sun. In this interpretation, the sun is Brahmā, Viṣṇu and Śiva, the trinity. And the seven rays of the sun are the *devas* (gods), *ṛṣis* (sages), *gandharvas* (celestial musicians), *apsaras* (celestial nymphs), *yakṣas* (demons), *sādhyas* (celestial beings) and *rākṣasas* (other demons). Devī is *Subhagā*, who is the basis and support of all these.

Subhagā may refer to *aṣṭamāṅgalya*, a collection of eight things used on auspicious occasions (or to Devī Herself as the seat of all auspiciousness). The list of these eight things varies according to the source. One list, given by *Padma Purāṇa*, is sugarcane, the *tāla* (palm) tree, *niṣpāva* (a kind of bean), *jīra* (cumin), cow's milk in all its forms, *kusumbha*, flowers and salt. *Kusumbha* may mean the *kausumbha* flower, gold, *kamaṇḍalu* (the water pot of an ascetic) and saffron. Another list gives the following collection: the auspicious *kurava* sound made by women on special occasions, a mirror, a lamp, a *pūrṇakumbha* (a decorated jar full of water presented on auspicious occasions), a cloth, a full jar of grain, a married woman and gold.

A five year old girl is also called *subhagā*.

762. त्र्यम्बका

Tryambakā

She who has three eyes.

"The sun, moon and fire are the eyes of Devī who is therefore called *Tryambakā*."

Tryambakā also means "the mother of three." Parāśakti is the mother of Brahmā, Viṣṇu and Śiva.

763. त्रिगुणात्मिका

Triguṇātmikā

She who is the essence of the three guṇas.

On the basis of the three *guṇas* of *sattva*, *rajas* and *tamas*, Devī is portrayed in three forms - *sattva* as Pārvatī, *rajas* as Durgā and *tamas* as Kālī. This unity in diversity is particularly noteworthy.

The combination or aggregate of the three *guṇas* is called *prakṛti* in *Sāṅkhya* philosophy. At the sight of the *Puruṣa*, the inert *Prakṛti* is enlivened and mates with him, thus becoming the cause of enjoyment and Liberation. Just as a lamp makes nearby objects also shine, the *Puruṣa*, imbued with consciousness, awakens the inert *Prakṛti*. Devī is both *Prakṛti* and *Puruṣa*.

764. स्वर्गापवर्गदा

Svargāpavargadā

She who bestows heaven and Liberation.

Svarga (heaven) is a place of happiness, a pleasant resort, gained through merit. *Apavarga* is Liberation which is eternal. Devī gives both the temporary heaven and eternal Liberation.

The highest state that can be reached by sacrifice (*yāga*) and other rites is the transitory heaven. Some religions consider heaven as the ultimate state to be reached. The *Sanātana Dharma* (the system of eternal tenets that is Hinduism) treats heaven only as a pleasant interlude. Even heaven can be attained only through the accumulation of much merit. As Kālidāsa makes King Duṣyanta observe in *Śākuntala*, "Hope, verily, springs upwards." Thus, the mind will not be satisfied even after reaching heaven. That mind itself has to be dissolved. That is called *amanībhāva* (the absence of mind) - that is Liberation. The *Gītā* (IX.21) says, "Having enjoyed the spacious world of heaven, they return to the world of mortals when their merit is exhausted; thus following the three *Vedas*, desiring objects of enjoyment, they attain the state of *samsāra* (the cycle of birth and death)." For them, the cycle of birth and death does not end.The ultimate aim of the *jīva* is Liberation, and Devī is the one who confers that.

765. शुद्धा

Śuddhā

She who is the purest.

Her purity is the absence of even a trace of *avidyā* (ignorance).

766. जपा पुष्प निभाकृतिः

Japā puṣpa nibhākṛtiḥ

She whose body is like the hibiscus flower.

Japa flower is hibiscus or China rose. Devī's body has the red color of this flower. In the meditation verses, She is described as "*sindūrāruṇa vigraha*" (with body red as saffron)

According to Bhāskarācārya, this name may be taken as *Ajapāpuṣpanibhākṛtiḥ* and then split into two names, *ajapā* and *puṣpanibhākṛtiḥ*. *Ajapā* is a famous *mantra*. This name means that Devī is in the form of that *mantra*. *Puṣpanibhākṛtiḥ* indicates that She is one whose body is as soft as a flower.

Puṣpa may also be interpreted as *puṣpaka*, the vehicle of Kubera, which can go anywhere at will. It has no barriers whatsoever. Devī has no barriers either and can enter anywhere. Thus Devī has a form that can go anywhere like *puṣpaka*. Her form is indeed one that is subtler than the subtlest and grosser than the grossest.

767. ओजोवती

Ojovatī

She who is full of vitality.

Devī is that which shines as vitality (*ojas*) in all beings.

Ojas means light, vitality of life, strength, greatness and radiance. All these are aspects of Devī's essence.

768. द्युति धरा

Dyuti dharā

She who is full of light and splendor. She who has an aura of light.

The light that shines in all beings is Devī's light.

769. यज्ञरूपा

Yajñarūpā

She who is in the form of sacrifice.

The *Śruti* says, "*Yajña* is Viṣṇu." Thus, Devī is in the form of Viṣṇu.

In *Harivamśa* and *Padma Purāṇa*, Viṣṇu's sacrificial form is described. His feet are the *Vedas*; His hands, the materials of oblation; His face, the sacrificial firewood; His tongue, the fire; and His teeth, the posts to tie the sacrificial animals to. His eyes are day and night; His ear ornaments are *Vedānta* and His mouth, the ladle for offering the oblations to the fire. His nose is the *ghee* (melted butter); His voice, the sound of *Sāmaveda*; His head, the *brāhmaṇa* conducting the sacrifice and His hair, the sacrificial rules (which are countless). His nails are the austerities; His motions, the good deeds; His knees, the sacrificial animals; His organ of generation, the *homa* and the *dhātus* (elements) of His body are the fruits. His heart is the gift; and His blood, the *soma* (ambrosial drink). His mental speed is the oblation to the gods and to the ancestors, the *mantras* the rites, His gait, the different poetical meters; His seat, the *Guhyopaniṣad* and His shadow, the wife (to participate in the sacrificial ceremony). This is the form of Viṣṇu as sacrifice. The present *mantra* says that this is truly Devī's form.

770. प्रिय व्रता

Priya vratā

She who is fond of vows.

Bhāskarācārya quotes *Bhaviṣyottara Purāṇa* as authority here. All vows made to any god or goddess please Śiva and Śakti, the creators of the world. There should be no distinction here, because the whole world is made up of Śiva and Śakti.

Also, One who is worshipped by the king named Priyavrata.

771. दुराराध्या

Durārādhyā

She who is difficult to worship.

Devotion should be constant and solid. It is such worship that bears fruit. Only unconditional and selfless devotion will become steadfast. Devī is hard for those who are fickle-minded to worship. Devotion arising from temptations will be wavering and fruitless.

772. दुराधर्षा

Durādharṣā

She who is difficult to control.

The *Śruti* says, "The Self is not attained by the feeble." Only an *upāsak* with extraordinary mental strength can win Devī over. This takes constant worship over a long period of time.

773. पाटली कुसुम प्रिया

Pāṭalī kusuma priyā

She who is fond of the pāṭali *flower (the pale red trumpet flower).*

The *Padma Purāṇa* says, "Śaṅkara is fond of the *bilva* tree and Pārvatī, of *pāṭali*."

774. महती

Mahatī

She who is great.

Devī is one who excels everything else in size, value and greatness, one who possesses great wealth and multifaceted prowess and occupies the highest position.

Maha also means "*pūja*." "Devī is one who is worthy of worship." (Yāska)

Mahatī is one who can measure everything. "The standard to measure anything by," says Śakapūni.

Mahatī is the name of Nārada's *vīna*. The *mantra* then means, "One who is in the form of the *vīna*." Also, Devī is fond of playing the *vīna*.

775. मेरु निलया

Meru nilayā

She who resides in the Meru mountain.

Meru is given different meanings in *Tantraśāstra*. The backbone is called *merudaṇḍa*. *Meruprastāra* is one of the three modes of *Śrīcakra* worship. The other two are *Bhūprastāra* and *Kailāsaprastāra* (as discussed under *mantra* 577).

In *Jñānārṇava*, *meru* is the name of a nine-syllabled *mantra*. Devī is the deity of the *mantra*; hence She is called *Merunilayā*. The nine *bīja* letters of this *mantra* indicate the earth, moon, Śiva, Māyā, Śakti, Kṛṣṇadhvan, *madana*, half-moon and *bindu*.

We can find another explanation in *Tantrarāja* (chapter 18). It is said that there are sixteen daily deities and oceans surrounding them, with *meru* at the center and Devī residing in it. Surrounding the *meru* are fourteen worlds, their presiding *devatas* and, above all these, *Brahman* as *ākāśa* (*ākāśabrahman*). This is a description of the *Śrīcakra* and the human body.

The *Bhūprastāra* with *Vaśini* and eight other *yoginis*, the *Kailāsaprastāra* with the *Matṛkākṣari* deities and the *Meruprastāra* with the daily (*nitya*) deities are all modes of *Śrīcakra* worship. As Devī has made the *Meruprastāra* Her abode, She is called *Merunilayā*.

776. मन्दार कुसुम प्रिया

Mandāra kusuma priyā

She who is fond of the mandāra *flowers.*

Mandāra is a celestial wish-fulfilling tree. Devī is fond of its flower.

There are five kinds of celestial trees: *mandāra*, *pārijāta*, *santāna*, *kalpavṛkṣa* and *haricandana*.

Mandāra is also the white *arka* flower.

777. वीराराध्या

Vīrārādhyā

She who is worshipped by heroic persons.

Vīras are not only heroic warriors, but also knowers of the Self, those who have subdued desire, anger and other negative qualities.

Vīra is one who removes pain. Devī is worshipped by the *Mahātmas* who are intent on helping others.

One who is opposed to duality is also a *vīra*. Devī is the object of worship by *yogins* who have no sense of duality.

Vīra may also be Vīrabhadra. Devī is worshipped by him also.

778. विराड्रूपा

Virāḍrūpā

She who is in the form of the Cosmic Whole.

Chapter 11 of the *Bhagavad Gītā* (XI.10) describes the Cosmic Form of *Brahman*. "With countless mouths, countless eyes, with countless marvelous appearances, countless divine ornaments, countless uplifted divine weapons, (such a form He showed)." The *virāṭ* form consists of the whole universe.

779. विरजाः

Virajāḥ

She who is without rajas.

Rajas means desire and anger. To Arjuna's question, "What draws man to sinful deeds?" the Lord gives the answer, "It is desire, it is anger, born of *rajas*." (*Gītā*, III.37) Devī is beyond these.

This name also refers to the Devī installed in the temple at Viraja. Her *darśan* is said to purify seven generations.

Rajas also means light, water and worlds. All three share the quality of mobility. With the prefix *vi* (meaning distinguished or special), we get *Virajā*, meaning, "one who possesses special radiance, holy waters and exalted worlds."

780. विश्वतो मुखी

Viśvato mukhī

She who faces all directions.

This also implies that Devī is one who guides every living being on life's path. Since She fills the whole universe in the cosmic *virāṭ* form, all life is under Her guidance.

781. प्रत्यग् रूपा

Pratyag rūpā

She who is the indwelling Self.

Pratyagātma is the *jīvātman.*

We should not search for Devī on the outside, but within. Amma says, "Searching for God outside is like thinking that you can catch fish by drying up the sea. We should look for Him within us. We should be frantic to see Him just as a man under water would be frantic for air. God is a thing that exists - He will be found; but not without effort."

Devī's form is to be sought and found by looking inward. The *Śruti* says, "The Self-existent (*Brahman*) created the senses with outgoing tendencies; therefore man beholds the external universe and not the internal Self. A wise man, with eyes averted from sensual objects, desirous of immortality, sees the *Ātman* within." (*Kaṭha Upaniṣad*, IV.1)

782. पराकाशा

Parākāśā

She who is the transcendental ether (which is the material cause of the cosmic and individual bodies).

Ākāśa, (ether or space), indicates *Brahman.* Devī is the Supreme *Brahman.*

The *Chāndogya Upaniṣad* (I.9.1) says, "He said *ākāśa* (is the Essence). All these beings arise only from *ākāśa.*"

"*Ākāśa* is *Brahman* because of the characteristic marks," says the *Brahma Sūtra* (I.1.22).

"She who is called *Ākāśa* is the origin of the universe. The all-controlling beginningless power is also that Maheśvari," according to the *Kūrma Purāṇa.*

Even though we speak of the sky (*ākāśa* in common parlance) as dark, clear or red, those colors do not, in fact, touch the sky. Similarly, attributes of the things of the world, like form or smell do not touch Devī, even though they are suffused with Her essence. The gist of this *mantra* is Her attributelessness, untaintedness and all-pervasiveness.

"He is established in *Parākāśa*," says *Taittiriya Upaniṣad* (III.6.1). *Parākāśa* is the place of manifestation of *Brahman*. This may be understood as the *ākāśa* (space) in the heart, also called *daharākāśa* (see *mantra* 609). Thus, *parākāśa* is sometimes referred to as *daharākāśa*.

The *Cidgaganacandrika* says, "There is no moving sun or moon in the *ākāśa*. What exists is what resides in the heart, which is the energy that produces motion. That is the supreme *ākāśa* - the *parākāśa*."

In *Svacchandasamgraha*, it is said, "Above the forehead, there is a place called *dvādaśānta*. Next to it, next to the top front portion of the skull, inside within two fingers of the front, is *parākāśa*."

Some say *parākāśa* is the space beyond the seven seas. Devī is one who resides there. This only serves to indicate the difficulty of reaching Her.

This name can also be split as *parāka* (hard, laborious) + *āśa* (direction, region). Devī is one to be reached through a difficult path. Or, splitting the name as *para* (great) + *aka* (sin) + *āśa* (one who eats), one gets, "She who eats (removes) even the most severe sins."

Ākāśa (space) can take definite forms, but Devī cannot be attributed to any form. As the Gītā (IV.11) says, "Howsoever men approach Me, so do I reward them."

783. प्राणदा

Prāṇadā

She who is the giver of life.

She who controls the five *prāṇas* and the eleven organs (taking the meaning *da*: to control).

Prāṇa ("vital air") is *Brahman.* Devī is the giver of the knowledge of *Brahman. Kausītakī Upaniṣad* says, "I am *prāṇa,* I am consciousness. Worship Me as life and immortality."

784. प्राण रूपिणी

Prāṇa rūpiṇī

She who is of the nature of life.

As in the previous *mantra, prāṇa* stands for *Brahman.* Also, *rūpa* (literally, form) does not signify a definite form; it implies that Devī is of the nature of *Brahman.*

Chāndogya Upaniṣad (IV.10.4) says, "*Prāṇa* is *Brahman*; bliss is *Brahman*; *ākāśa* is *Brahman.*" In *Manu Smṛti* (XII.123), it is said, "The same *Brahman* some call fire, others call Manu, Prajāpati, Indra, Prāṇa and Maheśvari."

In the *Nitya Tantra,* the sixteen *Nitya* (daily) deities are called *Prāṇas.* It is said that the planets and stars move according to the breath (*prāṇa*) of these deities. Devī shines at the center of these deities; hence She is *Prāṇarūpiṇī.*

785. मार्ताण्ड भैरवाराध्या

Mārtāṇḍa bhairavārādhyā

She who is worshipped by Mārtāṇḍabhairava.

Mārtāṇḍabhairava is a *deva* residing between the twenty-second and the twenty-third walls of the *Śrīcakra. Lalita Stava Ratna* of Durvāsas (verse 100) describes him as residing there, "decked with a jewelled crown, and sporting with his wife Chāya who is the energy which supplies light to the eye." Since the power of eyesight arises from him, the name Chāya (reflection) is apt for his wife (Some texts say the location of Mārtāṇḍabhairava is between the thirty-second and thirty-third walls).

Tantracintāmaṇi recounts that Śiva incarnated as Mallāri or Mārtāṇḍabhairava to kill the demon Manimalla. The present *mantra* in this case, means that Devī is one who is worshipped by Śiva in that form.

Devī is worshipped by Mārtāṇḍa and Bhairava. Mārtāṇḍa is the sun. Bhairava means a *brahmacārin*. There is a group of Śakti worshippers known as Bhairavas, who believe it is possible to ascend to heaven with the earthly body intact. This indicates the extreme will power of such devotees.

Worshippers of the sun are sometimes called Bhairavas. Devī is also the object of their worship.

786. मन्त्रिणी न्यस्त राज्य धूः

Mantriṇī nyasta rājya dhūḥ

She who has entrusted Her regal responsibilities to Her mantriṇī *(minister).*

Devī has entrusted Her responsibilities of governing to Her minister, Śyāmala Devī.

Mantriṇī may also mean "in one who has *mantra*." In this sense, Devī is one who has entrusted Her responsibilities to the devotee who worships Her, using Her *mantra* with faith and devotion. Here the regal responsibility is the secret of *sādhana* that brings the worshipper closer to Devī.

The force that instills the desire in the *upāsak* to unite with Devī is called *mantriṇī*. That force is equanimity, which is an indispensable quality for governing. Thus, Devī is one who remains free of anxiety by entrusting Her duties of governance to Her ministers - Her devotees - who possess the required evenness of mind.

787. त्रिपुरेशी

Tripureśī

She who is the Goddess of Tripura.

Tripura is the *sarvāśaparipūraka cakra*, one of the nine *cakras* in the *Śrīcakra*. Devī is the presiding deity of that *cakra*.

The nine *cakras* contained in the *Śrīcakra* are: 1) *trailokyamohana*, 2) *sarvāśāparipūraka*, 3) *sarvasamkṣobhana*, 4) *sarvasaubhāgyadāyaka*,

5) *sarvārthasādhaka*, 6) *sarvarakṣākara*, 7) *sarvarogahara*, 8) *sarvasiddhiprada* and 9) *sarvānandamaya*. These names mean respectively, captivator of the three worlds, fulfiller of all desires, agitator of all, giver of all prosperity, bestower of all of life's goals, giver of all protection, remover of all ailments, giver of all *siddhis* and all-blissful.

788. जयत् सेना

Jayat senā

She who has an army which is accustomed only to victory.

Devī's army was victorious over Bhaṇḍāsura. It is an army that has never known defeat.

Also, the king Jayatsena was Devī's devotee. As She is not distinct from Her devotees, Devī Herself is called *Jayatsenā*.

789. निस्त्रैगुण्या

Nistraiguṇyā

She who is devoid of the three guṇas.

Māyā is made up of the three *guṇas*. Devī is beyond *Māyā* and thus transcends the *guṇas*. Man cannot transcend the *guṇas* as long as he has body consciousness. Without transcending the *guṇas* he will not be able to worship a power that is *nirguṇa* or free of all attributes. It will be possible for a *yogin* who has outgrown body sense. If someone bound by *samsāra* claims to worship a God who is formless, it is like claiming to swim in a waterless lake.

Devī is described as beyond the *guṇas* because She is pure, solid consciousness-bliss.

790. परापरा

Parāparā

She who is both parā *and* aparā.

Parā is superior, *aparā* is inferior. *Parā* is great, *aparā* is little. *Parā* is truth, *aparā* is myth. Devī is both of these opposites at once. While She is *aparā* to the *samsārin*, She is *parā* to the *yogin*.

Parā is far, *aparā* is near. Devī is, indeed, far and near at the same time. Everyone points to the heart and says, "I, I." The consciousness that is "I" is very near. But when we want to realize it directly, then how far it becomes!

Parā is knowledge of the Self (*jñāna*); *aparā* is the knowledge of the physical universe (*vijñāna*) (see *mantra* 551). All knowledge is, however, *Brahman*; thus, Devī is both *jñāna* and *vijñāna*.

Devī worship is also of three kinds: *parā*, *aparā* and *parāparā*. Meditation rooted in non-duality is *parāpūja*. Worship of *Śrīcakra* is *aparāpūja*. *Parāparāpūja* is the worship of various divine forms. *Yoginīhṛdaya* describes these modes of worship

Consciousness is also divided into two types, *parā* and *aparā*. The consciousness in the form of *parā*, *paśyantī* and *madhyama* is known as *parabodha* and the consciousness in the form *vaikharī* of the waking and dreaming states and the consciousness in the deep sleep state is known as *aparābodha*.

Homa (sacrifice to the fire) is also of two kinds, *parā* and *aparā*. *Parāhoma* is that which is performed in the mind, in the blaze of the power of *yoga*, without external fire or other materials of sacrifice. *Aparāhoma* is done externally with an actual fire. This itself is of two kinds, gross and subtle, the former aimed at the fire in the *mūlādhāra* and the latter at the fire of *prāṇa*.

Devī is in the form of *parāpara*, a four-syllabled *mantra*. This *mantra* is often chanted together with the fifteen-syllabled (*pañcadaśākṣari*) and the sixteen-syllabled (*ṣoḍaśākṣari*) *mantras*.

791. सत्य ज्ञानानन्द रूपा

Satya jñānānanda rūpā

She who is truth, knowledge and bliss.

Brahman is "Truth, Knowledge and Infinite Bliss." Devī is that *Brahman*.

This *mantra* is interpreted also as follows: *sati* + *ajña* + *anānanda* + *rūpa* meaning, "She who gives (*rūpa*) sorrow or pain (*anānanda*) to those who are ignorant (*ajña*) of true wisdom (*sati*)." Sati could also be Satīdevī, daughter of Dakṣa, who is another form of Devī. Then, She is one who gives pain to those who are ignorant of Her true form. It is clear that while *jñānis* get wisdom, the ignorant get only pain in this world. The *Gītā* (chapter 18) makes it clear that all the physical pleasures which appear sweet as nectar at first, turn out to be poison in the end.

792. सामरस्य परायणा

Sāmarasya parāyaṇā

She who is immersed in a state of steady wisdom.

Sāmarasa is the state of equanimity or steady wisdom (*sthitaprajña*), and *sāmarasya* pertains to that condition. This state is one in which the mind does not lose its balance in happiness or pain, in profit or loss, in victory or defeat. "He whose mind is not shaken by adversity, and who in prosperity does not pursue pleasures, who is free from attachment, fear and anger, is called a sage of steady wisdom." (*Gītā* II.56) Devī is one who is immersed in that state of steady wisdom. This state of equanimity is also a state of identity of Śiva and Śakti.

Devī is devoted to the enjoyment of the songs of *Sāmaveda* (*sāma* + *rasya* + *parāyaṇa*).

793. कपर्दिनी

Kapardinī

She who is the wife of Śiva.

Kapardin is Śiva, the one who has *kaparda* or matted hair.

The *Sūta Samhita* gives the meanings, "mother" and "praise" for the word *kaparda*. Hence *Kapardinī* is She who is the Mother Earth, or She who is the object of praise.

Kapardinī is the deity installed in the temple at Chagalāṇḍa, one of sixty-four sacred temples, according to *Devī Purāṇa*.

The *Viśvatīka* also gives the meaning of "cowdung cakes" for the word *kaparda*, and mentions the following story: When Śiva once took the form of Mailāra, Devī incarnated as Mahālasā, his wife, who wore a garland of cowdung cakes. Hence Devī was given the name *Kapardinī*.

794. कला माला

Kalā mālā

She who wears all sixty-four forms of art as a garland.

Devī is the inner luster of all the arts. Bhāskararāya also gives the meaning, "She who possesses (*lā*) the beauty (*kala*) of lightning (*mā*)." To the *upāsak*, the gift of Devī's *darśan* often comes as flashes of lightning.

795. काम धुक्

Kāma dhuk

She who fulfills all desires.

Devī fulfills the desires of Her devotees through the flow of the milk of Her grace, just as the celestial wish-fulfilling cow, Kāmadhenu.

796. काम रूपिणी

Kāma rūpiṇī

She who has a desirable form.

She who has the form of Kāmeśvara (Śiva) or of Kāma, the god of love.

She who can assume any form (*rūpa*) at will (*kāma*).

797. कला निधिः

Kalā nidhiḥ

She who is the treasurehouse of all arts.

How numerous indeed are the riches of art hidden in Devī, just as the wealth contained in a treasure buried underground!

Kalā can also mean *prāṇa*, the vital airs; Devī is the foundation for these.

Or, *kalānidhi* means the moon. The moon's disc is a place where Devī dwells. Individuals are sometimes called by the name of the place they inhabit; here She is called by the name of Her abode.

Kalā means the "body." Devī is the treasure that sustains it. *Kalā* also means brilliance; Devī is the abode of brilliance.

798. काव्य कला

Kāvya kalā

She who is the art of poetry.

A *kāvya* (poetic work) is of two kinds - that which is to be heard and that which is to be seen. A *kāvya* may be described as a work that is fit to be heard and seen. Devī is the embodiment of such poetry. When the most celebrated poets like Kālidāsa have attained their status through Her grace, what doubt is there that She is the abode of that art?

Kāvya may mean the sage Śukrācārya and *kalā* the *mṛtasanjīvanīvidyā*, the power to bring the dead back to life, the power to conquer death. Devī is then the embodiment of that particular power, meditated on and practiced by Śukrācārya.

799. रसज्ञा

Rasajñā

She who knows all the rasas.

Rasa is sentiment or emotion expressed in poetry. There are nine *rasas*: the erotic (*sṛṅgāra*, called the king of *rasas*), pathetic (*karuṇā*), heroic (*vīrya*), comic (*hāsya*), furious (*raudra*), terrible (*bhayānaka*), odious or disgusting (*bībhatsa*), marvelous (*adbhuta*) and quiescent (*śānta*). The ability to express any of these at appropriate times is innate in Devī.

"He is *rasa* itself," says the *Śruti*. *Brahman* is *rasa*, the very source of bliss. Devī who is not distinct from *Brahman*, is then the knower of the bliss of *Brahman*.

Rasa is taste or desire for something. Every living being has the greatest taste for life itself - and Devī is verily the basis for that taste.

Rasa is the sense of taste. There are six such tastes: sweet, sour, salty, pungent, astringent and bitter. Devī is the knower of all the tastes.

800. रस शेवधिः

Rasa śevadhiḥ

She who is the treasurehouse of rasa.

Here *rasa* should be understood to be the bliss of *Brahman*. Realizing that bliss is the ultimate goal of human life. Devī is the reservoir of that bliss. The *Brahmāṇḍa Purāṇa* says, "*Rasa* is the supreme *Brahman*, *rasa* is the supreme path, *rasa* is the giver of brightness to man; *rasa* is the seed, it is said. He is verily *rasa*. Having obtained *rasa*, one becomes blissful. On the authority of the scriptures, *rasa* is the vital breath."

Taittiriya Upaniṣad (II.7) declares: "He is *rasa* itself - the source of bliss. Having obtained this source of bliss, man becomes blessed."

Thus we complete the hundred names in the ninth *kalā* of the sun called *viśvakalā*.

801. पुष्टा

Puṣṭā

She who is always full of vigor, nourishment.

It is the sincere worship by devotees that nourishes Devī. The *Smṛti* concurs with this through the statement, "The *Brahman* is nourished by *brāhmaṇas*." The *Śruti* also makes it clear that "the long-living *Brahman* is given long life by *brāhmaṇas*." These statements assert that *Brahman* is well-nourished by the knowers of *Brahman*. This does not mean that *Brahman* was once weak and that the sages nourished It. When there are more *jñānis*, the tendencies based in *Brahman* get new life and grow. This is what is meant by nourishment of *Brahman*.

Devī is one who contains within Her all the thirty-six *tattvas* (categories), and constantly enjoys the nectar of *Brahman*. Hence She is *puṣṭā*, full of vigor and well-nourished.

802. पुरातना

Purātanā

She who is ancient.

As Devī was present at the start of creation, She is indeed ancient. Since the entire universe arose from Her, it is evident that She precedes everything.

803. पूज्या

Pūjyā

She who is worthy of worship by all.

She makes everyone Her attendant. Devī occupies the position of everyone's Guru. Therefore, She is worthy of worship in every way.

804. पुष्करा

Puṣkarā

She who is complete; She who gives nourishment to all.

Puṣkarā has several different meanings such as lotus, sky, water. Like the sky, Devī is all pervading, untainted and formless. Not only is the essence of water contained in Her, but She is also the source of the life giving power of water.

The deity at the sacred place *Puṣkara Tīrtha* is Puṣkarādevī.

805. पुष्करेक्षणा

Puṣkarekṣaṇā

She who has eyes like lotus petals.

There is a story in *Padma Purāṇa* concerning this name. It is said that *puṣkarā* is the name of the planetary conjunction when the sun is in the constellation of *Viśākha* and the moon is in *Kārttika*. There is then antagonism between the sun and the moon. Since Devī continues to look at them without blinking in order to avoid conflict, She received the name *Puṣkarekṣaṇā*.

Padma Purāṇa describes an image in which the universe is a lotus with its upward petals as the world of barbarians and downward petals as the world of demons and serpents. The earth is pictured as originating from the pericarp of that lotus, and is therefore known as *puṣkara*, lotus. This *mantra*, *Puṣkarekṣaṇā*, describes the Devī who remains with Her eyes fixed on the protection and well-being of the earth formed in this manner.

Puṣkara also means "a banyan tree." The *Purāṇas* describe Viṣṇu, at the time of the Great Dissolution, as an infant lying on a banyan leaf on the island of Puṣkara. There Viṣṇu Himself is referred to as Puṣkara. Since Devī beheld that infant with motherly affection, She became *Puṣkarekṣaṇā* (one with eyes on Puṣkara).

As said before, *puṣkara* also means "water." In this case, the *mantra* means that Devī is one who nurtures and protects four types of "waters" (*ap*), namely, *devas* (gods), men, *manes* (ancestors) and demons.

806. परम् ज्योतिः

Param jyotiḥ

She who is the Supreme Light.

Devī is indeed the "one who turns into darkness this sun with a thousand rays." Her brilliance is that of ten thousand suns rising at once. *Bṛhadāraṇyaka Upaniṣad* (IV.4.16) says, "Upon that Light of lights, the *devas* meditate for longevity."

Kaṭha Upaniṣad (II.ii.15) says, "The sun does not shine there, nor do the moon and the stars, nor does lightning shine, and much less this fire. When He shines, everything shines after Him; by His light, all these shine."

Paramjyoti is the name of an eight-syllabled *mantra* (described in *Dakṣināmūrtisamhita*). Devī can be thought of in the form of that *mantra*.

807. परम् धाम

Param dhāma

She who is the supreme abode.

Devī occupies the highest state. *Bhagavad Gītā* (XV.6) says that anyone reaching that state does not take birth again. "Nor does the sun shine there, nor the moon, nor fire; having gone there, they do not return; that is my supreme abode."

The *Śruti* describes this state as, "the supreme abode of Viṣṇu." (*Kaṭha Upaniṣad* I.ii.9) It is clear that Viṣṇu stands for *Brahman* here. *Kūrma Purāṇa* also describes this state: "My energy is Maheśvarī, Gauri, spotless, tranquil, the Truth, knowledge, eternal bliss, the supreme abode; so says the *Śruti*."

808. परमाणुः

Paramāṇuḥ

She who is the subtlest particle.

The statement in the *Śruti*, "subtler than the subtle," is very well-known. (*Kaṭha Upaniṣad*, I.ii.20) It means that Devī can be reached only through great effort.

Āṇu also means "*mantra*." Thus, the meaning, "She who is in the form of the most exalted *mantra*."

809. परात् परा

Parāt parā

She who is the most supreme of the supreme ones.

Higher than Brahmā, Viṣṇu and Maheśvara.

"*Para* refers to one day in the life of Brahmā, and half of it is *parārdhā*. Yet, for one who is subtler than the subtle and grosser than the gross, there is no day or night or year," says *Kālika Purāṇa*.

This and the previous *mantras* indicate Devī's nature that is subtler than the subtle and grosser than the gross.

810. पाश हस्ता

Pāśa hastā

She who holds a noose in Her hand.

The noose is the weapon in Devī's lower left hand. Her noose has been described under *mantra* 7, *Rāgasvarūpapāśāḍhyā*.

Devī is described as having four, eight or a thousand arms; this implies four directions, eight directions or the whole world, implying, sovereignty over everything.

811. पाश हन्त्री

Pāśa hantrī

She who destroys the bonds.

Devī is one who gives release from all *pāśas* or bondage. She is the one who cuts the bonds of time. She cuts all the bonds of *karma*, thus eliminating rebirth. It is Her grace that destroys the bonds of desire and other negative tendencies.

812. पर मन्त्र विभेदिनी

Para mantra vibhedinī

She who breaks the spell of the evil mantras *of the enemies.*

Devī protects Her devotees from the ill effects of all evil *mantras* and rites used against them by adversaries. *Para* here means "enemies."

Para may mean king. Devotees may be harmed by the powers of the rulers. Devī protects them from such harm.

She who divided the supreme *mantra*, the *pañcadaśi mantra.* Devī divided the *mantra* into twelve and gave the portions to the following twelve disciples: Manu, Sūrya, Candra, Kubera, Lopāmudrā, Agastya, Manmatha, Agni, Nandikeśvara, Subrahmanya, Śiva and Durvāsas.

813. मूर्ता

Mūrtā

She who has forms.

The entire universe in the *vivarta* form - the multitude of forms brought about by *Māyā* - is meant here. The concept of a divine form implies duality. The *ākāśa* perceived through sound, the air perceived through touch, the fire perceived through sight, the water perceived through taste and the earth perceived through smell are all Devī's forms. In the light of the statement in the *Śruti*, "All this, verily, is *Brahman*," all is Devī Herself.

A devotee once asked Amma, "If the Self is all-pervading, then shouldn't the life force be present even in a dead body?" Amma's reply was, "Just because a light bulb is burnt out or the fan stops working, we cannot conclude that the electricity is off. When you put down your hand-held fan, you stop feeling the air, but air does not cease to exist. When an inflated balloon bursts, the air that was in it does not cease to exist. In the same way, the Self is everywhere. The Lord is not absent anywhere. Death is just the destruction of the *upādhi*, the instrument; not the absence of the Self."

814. अमूर्ता

Amūrtā

She who has no definite form.

She who is formless. Actually, there is no contradiction here. One is the apparent reality; the other is the ultimate truth. Forms are apparent; the formless is the ultimate essence.

"The deluded despise Me clad in a human body, not knowing My higher nature as Lord of all beings," says Lord Kṛṣṇa in the *Gītā* (IX.11). His real essence is the cause of the whole universe, but the ignorant mistake Him for an ordinary being in human form.

"*Brahman* has two aspects, *mūrta* (with form), and *amūrta* (formless)." (*Bṛhadāraṇyaka Upaniṣad* II.iii.1) The form is the universe, and the formless is the Self. Also, the *Viṣṇu Purāṇa*, "That *Brahman* has two forms - *mūrta* and *amūrta*, perishable and imperishable; both are in all beings. The imperishable is the ever changeless *Brahman* (*kūṭastha*), while the perishable is the whole universe."

That which is perceived through the senses is gross or with form, and that which is imperceptible is subtle or formless. Devī is with form as the universe and formless as *Brahman*.

815. अनित्य तृप्ता

Anitya tṛptā

She who is satisfied even by our perishable offerings.

Devī is one who is pleased by our *pūjas* and sacrifices using perishable things. There is a well-known passage in the *Gītā* (IX.26): "Whoever offers Me with devotion a leaf, a flower or water, that offering by the pure-minded, made with love, I accept."

Devotion is the most important thing in worship. That is why a leaf or a flower or water becomes dear to Devī.

Alternately, She who is not pleased by a fixed *pūja* ritual. The modes of worship change with time and place. Those changes are pleasing to Devī.

The *mantra* may be interpreted as *aniti* + *atṛpta*. *Aniti* means "*jīvas*" (literally, *prāṇa* or vital breath) and *atṛpta* is "one who is not satisfied." She who is not satisfied just by living beings alone, according to Bhāskarācārya. The *Kaṭha Upaniṣad* (I.ii, 25) describes

Brahman thus: "For whom *brāhmaṇas* and *kṣatriyas* are but food, and even death itself a condiment, how can one know that *Ātman*?" Devī is all-devouring. Surrendering the vital breath alone is not enough to satisfy Her. How can one, without the proper inner transformation, know the Supreme in which all distinctions of class and creed vanish and in whom even death is swallowed up?

816. मुनि मानस हंसिका

Muni mānasa hamsikā

She who is the swan in the Mānasa lake of the minds of sages.

The Mānasa lake on Mount Kailāsa is supposed to be the abode of swans. In the epics, *Purāṇas* and poetic works of India, this lake has an important place. Devī sports at will in the hearts of the sages as the swans do in Mānasa lake.

Splitting this name as *muni* + *māna* +*sahamsika*, we get: She who dances wearing anklets, in celebration of the proud and dedicated life style of the sages. *Mana* is pride. *Sahamsika* is she who is wearing anklets or *hamsakas*, which are usually donned for dancing.

817. सत्य व्रता

Satya vratā

She who abides firmly in truth.

Abidance in truth (*satyam*) means words that match thought and deeds that match words. *Satya* is *Brahman* and *vrata* means dear. Those who abide in *Brahman* are dear to Her.

Saubhāgyabhāskara interprets *satya* as "that which yields results quickly." The *mantra* then means: "One who gives quick results to vows." The *Viṣṇu Bhāgavata* says that the Gopis who worshipped Devī with a firm vow to attain Kṛṣṇa had their wish fulfilled quickly.

Satya also means "refuge." Devī is one who observes a vow to give refuge to every living being. Śrī Rāma took the oath, "Whoever takes refuge in Me, to him I give protection; this is My vow."

If *satya* is given the meaning of bodily health, then the *mantra* means, "She who is intent on giving good health." *Śiva Sūtra* says, "Care of the body should be taken as a vow." The protection of this body, filled with the nectar of devotion to Śiva is, indeed, to be treated as a vow. Bhaṭṭotpala says, "May this body, nourished by nectar derived from Śakti, live long to enjoy the devotion to You!"

Devī is also hailed as *Satyavratā* because She was pleased by a *brāhmaṇa* named Satyavrata and blessed him. This story is told in the *Devī Bhāgavata*. Satyavrata was illiterate and very foolish. Once he was frightened by a boar and ran away repeating "ai, ai," the sound he heard from the mouth of the boar. Repeating this syllable which is a *mantra* of Devī, (although missing the final "m"), he became the wisest of the wise. The ever-compassionate Devī became pleased with him and made him the king of poets.

818. सत्य रूपा

Satya rūpa

She who is Truth itself.

Devī is the ultimate *Brahman* who shines as the Ultimate Truth at all times.

Devī is the embodiment of truth (satya). Wherever there is truth, there is Devī. "Truth and untruth are opposites; truth is protected by Śiva accompanied by Umā; untruth is destroyed by Him." (*Ṛgveda* 7.104.12)

819. सर्वान्तर्यामिनी

Sarvāntaryāminī

She who dwells inside all.

"This is thy self, which is within all and is immortal," says the *Bṛhadāraṇyaka Upaniṣad* (III.7.3). "This dwells in all and is the origin of all." (*Māṇḍukya Upaniṣad* 6) The *Śruti* also declares, "The one who is born in the form of all *devatas*, along with all the elements, and with Prāṇa (Hiraṇyagarbha), and who, entering into the heart, abides therein, he who knows that Aditi (the enjoyer of the universe), verily knows *Brahman* (the cause of all). This is verily that." (*Kaṭha Upaniṣad* II.1.7)

The *Smṛti* also says, "As She always knows the beginning and the end of all, and as She creates the being and the non-being (*sat* and *asat*), She is known as *Sarvā*."

Sarvāntaryāminī may also be interpreted as "She who directs (*yāmini*) the inner senses (*antah*) of all beings (*sarvā*).

Yāmini also means "night." Thus, the *mantra* may be taken to mean, "She who is night to the inner sense of all beings." Recalling the import of the following verse from the *Gītā* (II.69), "That which is night for all beings, in that the disciplined soul keeps awake; when all beings are awake, that is the night for the sage who sees." When all others are attracted by the glitter of sense objects, the sage is intent on understanding the Truth. He is awake to the nature of reality to which the unwise are asleep or indifferent.

820. सती

Satī

She who is reality, the Eternal Being.

Also, daughter of Dakṣa Prajāpati, the devoted wife of Paramaśiva, the embodiment of fidelity. Her husband was pleased because She made the name (Satī), given by Her father, true to its meaning (faithful) and He gave Her half of His body. Thus Śiva became Ardhanārīśvara. Pārvatī, the daughter of Himavat, is the reincarnation of Satī (see *mantras* 598 and 600).

821. ब्रह्माणी

Brahmāṇī

She who is the tail that is Brahman; *the support for all.*

Aṇi is a tail. This usually means the bottom or the end of the backbone and its continuation; it forms the support used by animals for sitting. The *Śruti* discusses the *ānandamaya kośa* (the bliss sheath), as made of five parts, the last of which is "the tail." This tail is the support for the universe and is *Brahman*. (*Taittiriya Upaniṣad* II.5) Devī is that *Brahman*, the support of all.

Devī gave life to Brahmā, the Creator, and is, therefore, known as *Brahmāṇī*, as mentioned in the *Devī Purāṇa*.

If Sadāśiva is considered indistinct from Brahmā, then Devī is *Brahmāṇī*, the wife of Brahmā.

822. ब्रह्मन्

Brahman

She who is Brahman.

The *Śruti* says, "*Brahman* is Truth, Knowledge and Infinity." Truth is the Pure Existence that is changeless with time. Real Knowledge is that which remains unchanged through the three divisions of time - past, present and future. The Ultimate Reality has no beginning or end, is not created and has no parts. That *Brahman* cannot be discussed. Its existence cannot be established by rules of inference. The sole proof is direct Realization. The essence of *Brahman* is to be experienced, just as the sweetness of honey or the fragrance of a flower. Devī is that Ultimate Being. "That knowledge is called *Brahman*, which annihilates duality, and is beyond words and is cognized only by the Self alone," according to *Viṣṇu Purāṇa*.

823. जननी

Jananī

She who is the Mother.

Devī is the mother of all - from Brahmā to the lowliest insect, the Mother of the Universe.

824. बहु रूपा

Bahu rūpā

She who has a multitude of forms.

Devī is of manifold forms, from the atom to the tallest mountain, from the glow worm to the sun. *Devī Bhāgavata* says, "As She is the Supreme Reality, She is formless; because Her nature is one of activity, She is also one who has many forms." Similarly, "Since She is everything movable and immovable, She is of countless forms," according to *Devī Purāṇa.*

This name is also interpreted as, "One who becomes one, two, sixteen and thirty-two." One is *Brahman.* Two means *Puruṣa* and *Prakṛti.* Sixteen stands for the vowels and thirty-two for the consonants; both these are, of course, essential in all affairs of the world. The number sixteen here may also refer to the sixteen daily deities.

Varāha Purāṇa says, "Raudrī, the *tāmasic* Śakti, is known as Cāmuṇḍā.There are nine *crores* of different Cāmuṇḍās. The *rājasic* Śakti, Vaiṣṇavī, who represents the universe, is in eighteen *crore* forms. The *sāttvic* Śakti of Brahma has an infinte number of forms. All these Śaktis are creations of Śiva; He is the Lord of all. Śiva is pleased with anyone who worships these Śaktis and with Him, the Śaktis are also pleased. There is no doubt in this."

Devī is celebrated as many-formed because She appeared in front of the eleven forms of Rudra in different forms that pleased each of them. *Devī Bhāgavata Purāṇa* celebrates the Devī who is of many names and forms as the "Lakṣmī who, through the manifestation of speech, shines like a dancer."

Bhāskarācārya also quotes *Varāha Purāṇa* to explain the meaning of this *mantra*: "The universe is seen to be manifold and She is everywhere. Thus, because of the multiplicity of Her forms, Śivā is known as *Bahurūpā.*"

825. बुधार्चिता

Budhārcitā

She who is worshipped by the wise.

Not only the wise, but virtuous men of other types worship Her as well, as described in the *Gītā* (VII.16): "Four kinds of virtuous men worship me, O Arjuna - the distressed, the seeker of knowledge, the seeker of wealth and the *jñāni* (the man of wisdom)."

A plain sheet of glass will not reflect the face; it has to be coated on one side to turn into a mirror. Similarly, just being born as a human being does not mean that one's thoughts will turn to God. One needs the *samskāra* earned in previous births. Only such a person can stay near the fire and ward off the cold. Others will keep a distance and suffer the cold.

826. प्रसवित्री

Prasavitrī

She who is Mother of the Universe.

One who gives birth to the cosmos. Bhāskararāya quotes from *Devī Purāṇa* to support this: "The Śakti from whom proceed all things, from Brahmā to the inanimate, the Devī from whom the whole universe from *mahat* down is born, we bow to that Mother of all. Since She gives birth to all living beings, She is known as Savitā."

827. प्रचण्डा

Pracaṇḍā

She who is full of awe-inspiring wrath.

Pracaṇḍā is the Devī who is about to kill Bhaṇḍāsura and his attendants.

One who has awe-inspiring attendants is also *Pracaṇḍā*. Air, water and fire are the fierce attendants. Devī's wrath is manifested through the wrath of natural forces.

Taittiriya Upaniṣad (II.8.1) says of *Brahman*, "Through fear of Him blows the wind. Through fear of Him rises the sun. Through fear of Him again Indra, fire and Death proceed to their respective duties."

"How can someone who has no anger and whom no one fears enforce righteousness?" asks Kāmandaka.

Pracaṇḍā is one who is especially fond of the *chaṇḍa* flower (the *śankha* flower). It is worth noting that this flower is an antidote to poison.

828. आज्ञा

Ājñā

She who is divine commandment Herself.

The *Vedas* are Her commandments; thus, She is of the nature of *Vedas*. The *Vedas* issue the command, like the Guru, "Speak the truth; tread the path of *dharma*!" There is no exception here. This commandment is firm.

The *Purāṇas* and epics instill in us the essence of the same commandment, as a friend does. Through stories of Hariṣcandra and Yudhiṣṭhira, the poems and plays impart the same commandment and awaken us as a beloved would.

Bhāskarācārya finds validity for this *mantra* in *Linga Purāṇa*, where Śiva says, "She is neither *prakṛti* (cause, Nature), nor *jīva* nor *vikṛti* (effect). She is the eternal commandment that emerged of old from My mouth."

This *mantra* may also be taken as *Jñā*. The word *jñā* means "Brahmā, a wise man, the planet mercury." According to the *Linga Purāṇa*, it is to be understood as, "One who enjoys the *guṇas*." The *Śvetāśvatāra Upaniṣad* (VI.2) says, " *Jñā* is the Lord of Time, possessor of *guṇas* and omniscient." The meaning is that Devī is the essence of the three *guṇas* and omniscient.

829. प्रतिष्ठा

Pratiṣṭhā

She who is the foundation.

The *Śruti* says, "She is the foundation of the whole universe." According to the *Brahma Gītā*, "This Consciousness, which is the Supreme, is the foundation of all things."

Pratiṣṭhā is the name of a meter with four syllables to a line, sixteen syllables in all. Devī is in the form of that meter.

A certain portion (*kalā*) of the water-element (*jalatattva*) is called *pratiṣṭha*. This *kalā* is said to give good health, long life and inspires the love of God. Devī is that power of inspiration.

Pratiṣṭhā also means "earth." There is also an implied meaning of fame. A poet who has gained *sthirapratiṣṭha* (solid fame) or *cirapratiṣṭha* (everlasting fame) is a common expression. Devī is both the Goddess Earth and the Goddess of fame.

830. प्रकटाकृतिः

Prakaṭākṛtiḥ

She who is manifested in the form of the universe.

Prakaṭayoginis are the deities of the first circle of the *Śrīcakra*. This *mantra* then means, "One who is manifested in the form of those *yoginis*."

This name may also be taken as *Aprakaṭākṛtiḥ* (unmanifested form). Then, the interpretation is that Devī is the Consciousness that exists unmanifested in this manifest universe. Bhāskarācārya quotes from the *Sūta Samhita*: "All beings know Him as "I," "I," yet because of *Māyā*, they do not recognize Him as Śiva."

Also, this *mantra* is sometimes interpreted as *ap* + *prakaṭākṛtiḥ*, meaning, "She who manifests in the form of the Water Element (*jalatattva*; *ap* is water)."

831. प्राणेश्वरी

Prāṇeśvarī

She who lords over the five prāṇas *and the senses.*

Prāṇa means the five vital breaths. "He is the *prāṇa* of *prāṇa* (breath of breath)," according to the *Śruti*.

Śaṅkarācārya, in the commentary on the *Brahma Sūtra*, has established that *prāṇa* indicates *Brahman*. Devī is thus the Īśvari who is *Brahman*. *Prāṇa* is *śakti* or energy. Devī is the ruler of all energies.

832. प्राण दात्री

Prāṇa dātrī

She who is the giver of life.

Devī is the giver of life to all the worlds. *Prāṇa* has several different meanings. They are all applicable here.

833. पञ्चाशत् पीठ रूपिणी

Pañcāśat pīṭha rūpiṇī

She who has fifty centers of worship.

Although *pañcāśat* means fifty, various *ācaryas* refer to fifty-one *pīṭhas*. In India, there were fifty-one famous centers of Śakti worship between Kāmarūpa and Chāyāchatra. Many of them still exist, although the names have changed. One possibility may be that Chāyāchatra is the state of Kerala. This conjecture is based on the fact that Kerala is the land where coconut trees abound, giving shade (*Chāyāchatra* means an umbrella that gives shade). Kāmarūpa to Chāyāchatra supposedly means from north to south.

Harṣadīkṣita interprets *pañcāśat* as fifty-one in the commentary on the first verse of *Śāradātilaka*. The works *Jñānārṇava* and *Yoginīhṛdaya* also mention fifty-one *pīṭhas*. Some commentators, however, insist that fifty-one is not the right number of Śakti *pīṭhas* and that in counting one *pīṭha* per letter of the alphabet, the letter *kṣa* need not be counted and that there are then only fifty letters to be counted giving fifty *pīṭhas*.

834. विश्रृङ्खला

Viśṛṅkhalā

She who is unfettered, free in every way.

Śṛṅkhala means "chain," *vi* means "lost or without." Here *karma* is the chain. Whether the chain is made of iron or gold, the bondage caused by it is painful. Bondage is bondage, even in a golden cage. The only difference is that the result of evil deeds may be an iron chain, while that of good deeds may be a golden chain. Merit and sin are both causes of bondage, and both lead to rebirth. All acts that are done according to commandments that are sanctions or prohibitions are for the ignorant, ("You may kill," implies a sanction, a form of *vidhi*, while "you should not kill," is prohibition, *niṣedha*). In other words, any act that is done with the result in view is rooted in ignorance. But any *karma* performed with no anxiety over its fruit becomes *yoga*. That does not cause bondage. That is why Lord Kṛṣṇa says in the *Gītā*, "I have no desire for the fruit of actions." It is thus, without any anxiety over the fruits of actions, that Devī busies Herself in the affairs of the universe. Therefore, She does not get entangled in the chains of *karma*.

This *mantra* is also interpreted as, "She who does not have even a girdle - one who is totally naked," since Devī is installed in many temples in that form.

835. विविक्तस्था

Viviktasthā

She who abides in secluded places.

Vivikta means secluded. It also means one who can discriminate between the Self and the non-Self - between the permanent and the transitory. Devī is one who dwells within such persons of wisdom.

836. वीरमाता

Vīramātā

She who is the Mother of the valiant; Mother to the best among the devotees.

Vīra also refers to Gaṇeśa. In the *Padma Purāṇa* Lord Śiva says, "This Vīra, O Devī, is always dear to my heart, he is the teacher of wonderful feats, he is worshipped by multitudes of Gaṇeśas."

837. वियत् प्रसूः

Viyat prasūḥ

She who is Mother to the ether.

Since *ākāśa* (ether) is considered to be the first element created, it is suggested here. The *mantra* truly means, "She who created all the elements in the universe." The *Śruti* says, "From which all these elements emerge." Also, "From *Ātman*, the ether is born." (*Taittiriya Upaniṣad* II.i)

838. मुकुन्दा

Mukundā

She who gives salvation.

As a giver of salvation, Viṣṇu is also *Mukunda. Tantrarāja* says that Devī gave joy to the Gopis in the form of Kṛṣṇa.

Mukunda is the name of a precious stone in the treasure of Kubera. Devī is considered to be in the form of that gem. All wealth stems from the Divine. Recall the words of the Gītā (X.41), "Whatever being is glorious, prosperous or strong, know that to be a part of My splendor."

839. मुक्ति निलया

Mukti nilayā

She who is the abode of salvation.

Devī is, indeed, the abode of the highest form of salvation. The five forms of salvation are *sālokya* (residence in the same world with the deity), *sārūpya* (sameness of form), *sāmīpya* (being near the deity), *sāyūjya* (intimate union with the deity) and *nirvāṇa* (eternal bliss, final emancipation from matter and reunion with the Self).

840. मूल विग्रह रूपिणी

Mūla vigraha rūpiṇī

She who is the root form of everything.

Since our minds based on the three *guṇas* cannot comprehend that formless power, we worship Devī in diverse forms and images. Of Her many forms, Rājarājeśvari is considered the root form (*mūlavigraha*). Other Śaktis such as Bala or Bagala all derived from that form. Thus, this *mantra* hails Devī as Rājarājeśvari.

841. भावज्ञा

Bhāvajñā

She who is the knower of all thoughts and sentiments.

Devī is one who knows all the internal secrets (*bhāvas*) of the devotee without being told.

Bhāva is given many meanings - existence, nature, thought, soul, birth, intelligence, wealth, compassion, sport, devotion and meditation. Devī is one who knows all of these. *Bhava* is *samsāra* and *bhāva* is something pertaining to *bhava*. Devī knows everything about those bound in *samsāra*.

Bhāva also means the six modifications that every living being goes through: birth, existence, growth, change, decay (disease) and death. Devī is one who knows all these well.

Bhava is Siva and *bhāva* is everything pertaining to Him; She who knows it is *Bhāvajñā*.

In philosophy, *bhāva* is *Brahman*, in poetry it is emotion and in grammar, it is a verbal root.

Mantras have six types of meanings (*arthas*). The six meanings are: *bhāvārtha*, *sampradāyārtha*, *garbhārtha*, *kaulārtha*, *sarvarahasyārtha* and *mahātattvārtha*. When it is said that Devī is *Bhāvajñā*, the knower of *bhāvārtha* (the obvious meaning or import), the implication is that She knows all these other meanings as well.

Bha means "light" and *va* means "going;" Devī is one who controls the motion of the sun, moon and other luminous bodies.

842. भव रोगघ्नी

Bhava rogaghnī

She who eradicates the diseases of the cycle of birth and death.

The *Rāmāyaṇa* says, "I see no other medicine than Śiva." And the *Śiva Purāṇa*, "Just as medicine is for diseases, so is Śiva the enemy of the sorrow of *samsāra*."

843. भव चक्र प्रवर्तिनी

Bhava cakra pravartinī

She who turns the wheel of the cycle of birth and death.

"Another birth, another death, and yet another time lying in the mother's womb." Thus the wheel of *samsāra* goes around through births and deaths. Devī is the one who turns this wheel.

Bhavacakra is the *anāhatacakra*. Also Bhava is Śiva and *bhavacakra* is Śiva's *cakra*. The *anāhatacakra* in the heart region is Śiva's abode and Devī is the one who activates or guides this *cakra*.

Having previously stated that the heart is Devī's abode, there may be confusion as to how it is now Śiva's abode. In truth, it is Śiva or Devī or *Brahman*. It is unity in diversity - the conjunction of all qualities.

Cakra means mind. *Bhavacakra* is Śiva's mind. Devī is one who plays with it. Kālidāsa's words may be recalled here: "And on Śiva's part, there is a little loss of composure." (*Kumārasambhava*)

Viṣṇu Purāṇa says (regarding mind as *cakra*), "Viṣṇu bears in His hand the mind, in the form of the *cakra*, which is constantly revolving and swifter than the wind."

844. छन्दः सारा

Chandaḥ sārā

She who is the essence of all the Vedas.

Chandas means the *Vedas*, meters like *gāyatri* and will or desire (*iccha*). Devī is the essence of all *Vedas*. Śrī Nārāyaṇa Guru salutes Her as the "bejeweled lamp of the four *Vedas*." *Chandas* also means unrestrained motion (of the mind). The implication here is that all motions of the mind should be directed towards the Supreme.

Sāra means essence, and strength or constancy. Devī is the embodiment of the constancy of will power (*icchāśakti*).

The essence of *chandas* or *Vedas* is said to be the fifteen-syllabled (*pañcadaśi*) *mantra* which is considered to be the essence of the *gāyatri mantra*. Devī is in the form of this *mantra*.

Fourteen methods have been promulgated for attaining knowledge. The *Vedas* are the most important and in them, the *gāyatri mantra* is the foremost element. This *mantra* has two forms, one that may be repeated by all and the other completely concealed. Even the *Veda Puruṣa* (*Veda* personified) mentions this only in symbolic terms such as *kāma*, *yoni* and *kamala*. (*Varivasyārahasya*)

845. शास्त्र सारा

Śāstra sārā

She who is the essence of all scriptures.

Śāstras (scriptures) are the *Vedas* and the *vedāngas* (auxiliaries to the *Vedas*). Bhagavān Vyāsa (codifier of the *Vedas*) says, "Gītā is the essence of all *śāstras*; Manu is the essence of all the *Vedas*; Gangā is the source of all holy waters; and Lord Hari is the essence of all Divine Beings." *Gītā* is the essence of all the *Upaniṣads* which contain the seed of all the *śāstras*.

"*Śāstra* is that which instructs men to act or to refrain from action." (Vācaspati Miśra)

846. मन्त्र सारा

Mantra sārā

She who is the essence of all mantras.

"Just as all the water that falls from the sky goes to the ocean, prostration to any deity goes to Keśava." Here we can think of the

Divine Mother in place of Keśava. All deities are indeed second to the Śakti that is Mother. Thus the essence of the *mantras* directed towards all deities is rooted in Her.

Mantra means the *Vedas*, that which is used in *Tantras* and also the sixty-four books about *mantras*.

847. तलोदरी

Talodarī

She who is slender-waisted.

One whose waist can be held within the palm of one hand. A slender waist is a sign of beauty according to the *sāmudrika śāstra.*

The name may also be taken as *atalodari*. In this case, Devī is in the Cosmic state (*virāṭ*) and *atala* (one of the fourteen worlds) is Her waist. The *mantra* thus means "One who is in the Cosmic form."

848. उदार कीर्तिः

Udāra kīrtiḥ

She who possesses exalted fame.

Instead of separating the syllables as *udāra +kīrti*, giving the above meaning, they can be separated as *ud +a +ara +kīrti*, which will give, "One whose worship quickly leads to exalted and all-pervading fame."

Ud signifies the golden person in the disc of the Sun. *Chāndogya Upaniṣad* (I.1. 6-7) says, "That Person, effulgent as gold, who is seen within the sun - His name is Ud." Bhāskarācārya gives the interpretation that Devī's worship gives the devotee fame that excels that of the Person in the Sun.

Udārakīrti is fame that is as glorious as the nectar of moonlight. Good fame is white as moonlight and ill fame is dark. The *mantra* means Devī is one whose fame is as white as the nectar that is moonlight and one who confers such fame.

She who dispels (*ud*) the influence of evil deities (*ara*) such as Maṅgala.

849. उद्दाम वैभवा

Uddāma vaibhavā

She whose prowess is unlimited.

The creation, preservation and dissolution are all part of Devī's glorious acts. Śaṅkarācārya points out that the glory displayed in the creation of the universe is unimaginable.

Uddama means "with untied rope." *Dāma* is a rope or that which limits. Thus, Devī is, "One whose might unties the rope of *samsāra*." She is the giver of Liberation.

850. वर्ण रूपिणी

Varṇa rūpiṇī

She who is in the form of the letters of the alphabet.

Even though we usually speak of fifty-one letters, there are "sixty-three or sixty-four letters in *Prākṛta* and *Sanskṛt* language together, as promulgated by Svayambhu Himself," according to Pānini.

Varṇa has many different meanings. The four castes (*cāturvarṇa*), different colors and graceful shape. All these must be viewed as Devī's manifestations. Seeing unity in this diversity is the ultimate goal of life.

851. जन्म मृत्यु जरा तप्त जन विश्रान्ति दायिनी

Janma mṛtyu jarā tapta jana viśrānti dāyinī

She who gives peace and repose to those who are afflicted by birth, death and decrepitude.

Peace from the sorrows of *samsāra* is, of course, *mokṣa* (Liberation). Thus the *mantra* means, "One who gives Liberation." Worldly life leads to sorrow. The more enjoyable life seems, the greater is the sorrow ultimately. Sorrow is greater at the loss of things which are dear to us. Only detachment will reduce that sorrow. *Vairāgya* (detachment) arises from lack of desires and passions.

The pinnacle of *vairāgya* is taking total refuge in Devī, and achieving the peace (*viśrānti*) referred to in this *mantra.*

852. सर्वोपनिषद् उद्घुष्टा

Sarvopaniṣad udghuṣṭā

She who is celebrated by all the Upaniṣads.

Upaniṣad is that which brings the self near to *Brahman* (*upa*) and destroys ignorance (*niṣat*).

The number of *Upaniṣads* is large - thought to be 1180 according to one calculation (1135 according to *Bhāgavata Purāṇa*). Each branch (*śākha*) of the *Vedas* is supposed to contain an *Upaniṣad*. *Ṛgveda* has 21, *Yajurveda* 109, *Sāmaveda* 1000 and *Atharvaveda* 5 or 50 *śākhas*, making the total 1135 or 1180. Most of these are now lost.

Ten of the *Upaniṣads* became more well-known through Śaṅkara's commentary on them. Those ten are: *Īśāvāsya*, *Kena*, *Kaṭha*, *Praṣna*, *Muṇḍaka*, *Māṇḍukya*, *Taittiriya*, *Aitareya*, *Chāndogya*, and *Bṛhadāraṇyaka*. The subject of all the *Upaniṣads* is the Self. Thus Devī is the subject proclaimed by all the *Upaniṣads*.

853. शान्त्यतीत कलात्मिका

Śāntyatīta kalātmikā

She who transcends the state of peace.

Peace (*śānti*) is the state of evenness of mind, free from anxiety. The state beyond that is total Liberation. It is called *śāntyatīta kalā* (the state beyond peace). The *Śaiva* scriptures describe this state of *parinirvāṇa* (absolute Liberation), Devī's inherent state.

854. गम्भीरा

Gambhīrā

She who is unfathomable.

Gambhīrā signifies a depth that cannot be described or fathomed. The *Śiva Sūtra* says, "Through meditation on the *mahāhrada* (the great depth) one experiences the power of the *mantra.*" The "great depth" is Devī, who is beyond all space and time and is omnipresent.

Taking *gambhīrā* to mean a place of great depth, the scriptures say that worship done in holy waters where the water is very deep gives special benefit.

Bhāskarācārya gives the following interpretation. *Gam* stands for *Gaṇapati*, *bhi* is fear and *rā* is that which drives out. Devī frees us from the fear of Gaṇeśa and other deities.

Here we should recall the various *pūjas* such as *Rāhupūja* and *Śanipūja* conducted in Amma's divine presence. To those who have been present, recalling that sweet experience will be heartening and reassuring.

855. गगनान्तःस्था

Gaganāntaḥsthā

She who resides in the ether, space.

Here "ether" refers to the space of the heart (*daharākāśa* - see *mantra* 609).

She is the Consciousness that dwells in the elemental ether; that is, She is the Supreme, the *Parākāśa Brahman.*

She is one who remains even at the time of the dissolution (*anta*) of the element ether. Of the five elements, the earth dissolves in water at that time, the water in fire, the fire in air, the air in ether and then the ether also dissolves. Devī remains strong even at that time.

According to *Tantraśāstra*, *gagana* stands for the syllable *ha.* The consonants *ya, va, ra,* and *la* are known as *antasthas* (in grammar). These five are also the *bīja* syllables representing the five elements. Devī is in the form of the five elements as represented by their *bīja* syllables.

856. गर्विता

Garvitā

She who is proud.

Here, the pride is in the creation of the universe.

"Thou art the act of creation, the creator and the myriad of things created; and Thou, O Lord, art also the materials for creation!" says the poet.

If creation is to take place, Devī Herself has to turn into creator and the act of creation. This urge for creation is *parāhanta*, the supreme ego. The question may arise how this transformation is possible. Eruttacchan says that he "cannot describe the bewilderment felt when seeing as two You who are One!"

Devī is naturally proud of Her great beauty which enabled Her to claim half the body of Lord Śiva Himself! Kālidāsa describes the condition of Śiva when He sees the exuberant beauty of Pārvatī who has come to attend Him during His *tapas*: "Hara, with His composure disturbed a little, as in the case of the ocean as the moon begins to rise, let His three eyes roam over Umā's face and Her lips as red as the *bimba* fruit." (*Kumārasambhava* III.67) Thus, Her indescribable beauty broke Śiva's *tapas* and won His attention.

857. गान लोलुपा

Gāna lolupā

She who delights in music.

There are four kinds of musical instruments: stringed instruments (*tata*), drums (*ānaddha*, bound with leather), metallic instruments like cymbals (*ghana*) and wind instruments like flute (*suṣira*, with holes).

Devī likes vocal music and also delights in the music played on all the instruments mentioned above. She is also fond of two types of songs from *Sāmaveda* - *sāma* and *gāndharva*.

858. कल्पना रहिता

Kalpanā rahitā

She who is free from imaginary attributes.

Kalpanā means command, form, similarity. The *mantra* means that Devī is unequalled, formless and not subject to anyone else's commands.

Kalpanā is a product of the imagination. The waves of the ocean of *saṁsāra* (which are the *jīvas*) are known as *kalpanā* (as they are imagined). Devī is free from those waves, *Kalpanārahitā*.

Kalpa means the time which passes until the dissolution of the universe. The *mantra* can be interpreted as "one who does what is beneficial (*hita*) to human beings (*nara*) until the time of dissolution."

Kalpa can also mean the dissolution of the universe. Then, Devī is one who does what is beneficial to souls at the time of the dissolution. Devī keeps within Her the subtle forms of all living beings in the form of *vāsanās*, and after dissolution, starts recreating everything as the beginning of a new age (*kalpa*). This cycle continues unabatedly. In the *Aṣṭhāvakra Gītā*, it is said, "In the infinite ocean of Consciousness that I am, the waves of living beings arise, beat against each other, play and return naturally to me; how astonishing!"

859. काष्ठा

Kāṣṭhā

She who dwells in the highest state (beyond which there is nothing).

Bhāskarācārya quotes from the *Sūta Samhita*, "Whether it be with form or without, real or unreal, the Supreme Śiva is the foundation for all the statements of *Vedānta*; it is the highest state (*parākāṣṭhā*)." The *Śruti* also says, "That is *kāṣṭhā*, the ultimate goal; that is the supreme way." (*Kaṭha Upaniṣad* I.iii.11)

Kāṣṭhā is that which pervades everything. Lord Kṛṣṇa declares in the *Gītā* (X.42), "I support this entire universe, pervading it with a single fraction of Myself." And *Liṅga Purāṇa* says that Devī is *Kāṣṭhā*, the wife of the Supreme Śiva who is in the form of *akāśā* known as Bhīma and who contains within Himself all living and non-living things.

Also, *Kāṣṭhā* is one who stands beyond the ocean of *samsāra*.

860. अकान्ता

Akāntā

She who ends all sins and sorrows.

Aka means sin and sorrow. Devī brings an end to all varieties of both. Sorrows of three types are meant here, those caused by oneself, those from the physical world, and those from divine forces (see *mantra* 397). They are all destroyed by Devī.

861. कान्तार्ध विग्रहा

Kāntārdha vigrahā

She who is half the body of Her husband.

The *ardhanārīśvara* is meant here, one who has taken half the body of Her husband or one who has taken half the body of His wife.

Bhāskarācārya takes *Kāntā* as indicating the letter *khā* (which comes after the letter *ka*) which means heaven. Devī is one who has heaven as part of Her body.

862. कार्य कारण निर्मुक्ता

Kārya kāraṇa nirmuktā

She who is free from the bond of cause and effect.

Everything in the universe is bound by the relation of cause and effect. However, Devī, who is the cause of all, does not have a cause. If She had a cause, it would be necessary to search for Her cause, and this chain of searches would continue without end. This state is technically known as *avyavastha* (unsettled).

Kārya means the categories of things starting with *mahat* and *kāraṇa* is the root cause, *mūlaprakṛti* (see *mantra* 397). The state of freedom from both of these means She is pure *Brahman*. The *Śvetāśvatāra Upaniṣad* (VI.8) makes this clear: "No effect or organ of His is known. There is not seen His equal or superior. His great power is declared (in the *Vedas*) to be of various kinds. His knowledge, strength and action are described as inherent in Him."

863. काम केलि तरङ्गिता

Kāma keli taraṅgitā

She who is overflowing with pleasure in the union with Kāmeśvara.

Devī is described as overjoyed, as an ocean with rising waves, in union with Kāmeśvara in the pericarp-chamber of the thousand-petaled lotus. The union of Śiva and Śakti has been described as *mahāmaithuna* - the great union.

864. कनत् कनक ताटङ्का

Kanat kanaka tāṭaṅkā

She who wears glittering gold ear ornaments.

In the portrayal of Devī in Her captivating female form, She is said to wear shining golden ear ornaments. In Her cosmic (*virāṭ*) form, the sun and the moon decorate Her ear. The rising full moon and the setting sun are both golden.

865. लीला विग्रह धारिणी

Līlā vigraha dhāriṇī

She who assumes various glorious forms as a sport.

This *mantra* is an answer to those who ask, "Does Devī, who is pure *Brahman*, need gold earrings and love to play?" All is only a sport of Devī. Why then this *līlā*?

Life is never totally matter-of-fact. If it were, it would be uninteresting and dry. Even the heart of Vālmīki, the sage rooted in restraint, melted when one member of a pair of love birds fell, killed by a hunter's arrow. And the result? One of the world's greatest epic poems, the *Rāmāyaṇa*.

When a flower blossoms, pollination is ultimately the only motive. The fragrance, the softness, the dazzling colors, the honey, all these are fabrications which cover the truth. They are untruths. That is pure sport - the *līlā* of the Maker of the Universe.

Devī's different *vigrahas* (forms) are the incarnations for the purpose of this *līlā*. *Yogavāsiṣṭha* says that the deity (*vigraha*) installed in the temple at Padmarāja is called Līlādevi. She is *Līlāvigrahadhāriṇī* in this sense also.

866. अजा

Ajā

She who has no birth.

The *Śruti* says, "The one unborn Being, She of red, white and black colors." (*Śvetāśvatāra Upaniṣad* IV.5) and the *Gītā* (II.20) adds, "He is not born, nor does He ever die." The *Mahābhārata* makes it clear, "I was not, am not and will not be born at any time. I am the *kṣetrajñā* (knower) of all beings; therefore, I am called *Ajā* (unborn)."

An end is certain for anything that is born. Devī who has no end has no beginning either. She is *Ajā*. "Unborn, eternal, unchangeable and primeval," the *Gītā* elaborates.

867. क्षय विनिर्मुक्ता

Kṣaya vinirmuktā

She who is free from decay.

Since Devī is not born, She has no decay (*kṣaya*).

The word *kṣaya* also means house. Bhāskarācārya explains that Devī saves from worldly sorrows even those (householders) who worship Her in their homes. A person who is fond of their home will leave it only when he finds another abode which is more pleasing. In place of this perishable physical body, Devī confers the permanent state of Liberation and thus makes Her devotee eternal.

868. मुग्धा

Mugdhā

She who is captivating in Her beauty.

Mugdhā is one who has a beauty that cannot be described.

Devī's lavish beauty has been celebrated by poets since *Vedic* times. Even today, persons of poetic genius are inspired to portray Her in new images. Śaṅkarācārya even calls his hymn to Devī by the name "*Saundarya Laharī*" which can be translated as "waves of beauty" or "intoxication of beauty." So unparalleled and ever fresh is Devī's beauty.

869. क्षिप्र प्रसादिनी

Kṣipra prasādinī

She who is quickly pleased.

A mother becomes easily drunk with joy by the sweet prattle and the playful gestures of her children. Likewise, Devī is pleased by even small offerings of untainted devotion.

"By worshipping other deities one gets salvation gradually, but by worshipping the Lord of Umā, one is liberated in the present birth itself," says *Saura Purāṇa*. The *Śiva Purāṇa* adds, "Even one who has a little faith will not have to go through a mother's womb after the third birth."

"Prayers, oblations and worship performed even without regularity in this birth will lead to salvation, at least in the next birth," says the *Tantrarāja*.

870. अन्तर् मुख समाराध्या

Antar mukha samārādhyā

She who is to be worshipped internally (by mental worship).

As one preceptor states, "One who picks the flowers of the mind and offers them to Maheśa need not do anything else." If unable to do that, "By offering wild flowers or uttering His names, *Māyā* will disappear."

This *mantra* makes clear the unique value of the *mānasa pūja* (mental worship) prescribed by Amma. If everything is created by the mind, how can mental worship fail to bear fruit?

Internal worship is the process that awakens the *Kuṇḍalinī*. The *Kuṇḍalinī* residing in the individual *jīva* is none other than Lalitāmbika. The process of awakening and guiding the *Kuṇḍalinī* to its union with Śiva in the *sahasrāra* and the astonishing changes brought about by it in the *upāsak's* body have been described earlier. Devī is *Antarmukhasamārādhyā* because She is worshipped by inward turning *yogins* through mental *upāsana.*

871. बहिर् मुख सुदुर्लभा

Bahir mukha sudurlabhā

She who is difficult to attain by those whose attention is directed outwards.

Physical science is devoted to the analysis of external objects. Spiritual light does not shine as a result of that analysis. How can one find a fish in a tree? One has to dive into the ocean. It is not enough to stand on the shore. One may cast a net from the shore and wait, but this brings only limited success. The returns will be greater if one braves the waves in a boat and casts a net. But Mother Ocean must also give her blessing! If not, the boat and the net and even one's life may be lost!

Only an ascetic who has tamed the five senses through restraint and discipline can see and enjoy the flashes of Devī's effulgence.

872. त्रयी

Trayī

She who is the three Vedas.

The three *Vedas*, *Ṛgveda*, *Yajurveda* and *Sāmaveda* are known as *trayi* (triple). Devī is the inner essence of these *Vedas*.

Sāma and *Ṛg Vedas* begin with the syllable *a*. *Yajurveda* begins with the syllable *I* (as in "give"). Combining the beginning syllables of *Ṛg* and *Yajus*, *a* + *i* according to the rules of grammar, we get the sound *e*. Adding this to the *a* of *Sāmaveda* results in *ai*. The sound *ai* is called *śucirūpa* in *Tantra*. This is the *bījākṣara* (seed syllable) in the *vāgbhava kūṭa* of the *pañcadaśi mantra*. Thus, by combining the first letters of the three *Vedas*, we get the meaning for the name Trayī, that Devī is in the form of Śuci, the *bīja* of *vāgbhava kūṭa*.

873. त्रिवर्ग निलया

Trivarga nilayā

She who is the abode of the threefold aims of human life.

The first three aims of life are *dharma* (righteousness), *artha* (wealth) and *kāma* (desires). These three together form a triad (*trivarga*) of which Devī is the abode (*nilaya*).

Trivarga can also be the three periods of time - past, present and future, or, the three sounds *a*, *u*, and *m* contained in the *praṇava* (Om).

874. त्रिस्था

Tristhā

She who resides in the three worlds.

The number three can signify many things. The triads mentioned in the previous *mantra* apply here - the three goals of life, the three divisions of time and the syllable *Om*. Other triads are the three worlds, the three *Vedas*, the Trinity of Brahmā, Viṣṇu and Śiva, the three Agnis (fire), the three stages of life (childhood, youth and old age), three forms of sins (occurring through thought, word and deed), the three ancestors in the form of day, night and twilight, the three *guṇas* and many others. Devī can be thought of as residing in all these.

875. त्रिपुर मालिनी

Tripura mālinī

She who is Tripuramālinī, *the Goddess of the* antardaśāra cakra *(the sixth* prākāra*)* *in the* Śrīcakra.

876. निरामया

Nirāmayā

She who is free from diseases of all kinds.

Not only Devī Herself, but also the devotees who worship Her with unswerving devotion become free of diseases through Her grace.

877. निरालम्बा

Nirālambā

She who depends on none.

Devī does not depend on anything, internal or external. Since She is the support for everything, She does not need any support.

878. स्वात्मारामा

Svātmārāmā

She who rejoices in Her own Self.

The Supreme Consciousness divided into two for the purpose of creation of the universe and became the pair, Śiva and Śakti. Thus the Supreme made Itself into a garden (*ārāma*) for the purpose of play. The universe is the pleasure garden of Śiva and Śakti. Devī, who is in the form of Śiva-Śakti, has thus made Her own Self the universe and sports in it.

She who sports in both *sva* and *ātma*, in both what is Hers (*prakṛti* or the universe) and in the Supreme Self. In this case, *ārāma* is the symbol of the perishable *prakṛti*.

879. सुधास्रुतिः

Sudhāsrutiḥ

She who is the source of nectar.

When the *Kuṇḍalinī* rises to the *sahasrāra* as a result of *sādhana*, it causes a flow of nectar from the moon there. This nectar cools the body of the *sādhak* and brings him bliss. This *mantra* makes it clear that Devī Herself is that flow of nectar.

According to *Jñānārṇava*, *sudhāsruti* is a form of meditation upon Devī.

880. संसार पङ्क निर्मग्न समुद्धरण पण्डिता

Samsāra paṅka nirmagna samuddharaṇa paṇḍitā

She who is skilled in raising those who are immersed in the mire of transmigratory life.

Samsāra is a mire of mud. The more one tries to get out of it, the deeper one sinks into it. Every step makes one slip into greater depths. *Samsārins* enjoy this mud puddle as if it were sandalwood paste. Within an instant, with one single experience, Devī can perform the marvel of uplifting those who are insatiably following a life of drink, dissipation and harm to others. Devī is called *paṇḍita*, an adept, (literally, one who knows the Self) because She knows the secret of raising their consciousness.

Amma's vow is this: "Mother will take your hand and lead you forward; She will remove the stinging handcuffs; She will give Her hand and show the way, so you don't slip into the fire of *samsāra*." What further assurance do we need in this life? Those who try it know that there is not a single empty word in this promise.

881. यज्ञ प्रिया

Yajña priyā

She who is fond of sacrifices and other rituals.

"*Yajña* is Viṣṇu," according to the *Śruti* (see *mantra* 769). Thus, the *mantra* means, She who is fond of Viṣṇu. She has the form of Viṣṇu (*mantra* 893) and in one manifestation, She is Viṣṇu's sister (*mantra* 280).

Yajña (sacrifice) is of five types: (1) *Brahmayajña*: the study of *Vedas*; (2) *Devayajña*: *agnihotra* and other *yāgas*. The *pūjas* for Rāhu, Śani, Kuja (Mars) and also the chanting of divine names fall into this category. These are directed at various *devas*; (3) *Manuṣyayajña*: sacrifice directed at men. The *Vedas* instruct that "The guest is God." Honoring and worshipping guests fall in this group; (4) *Pitṛyajña*: sacrifice for the ancestors; (5) *Bhūtayajña*: the feeding of animals, birds and insects (sacrifice directed at living beings). The practice and protection of these five forms of sacrifice are among the duties of a householder.

882. यज्ञ कर्त्री

Yajña kartrī

She who is the doer of sacrificial rites.

883. यजमान स्वरूपिणी

Yajamāna svarūpiṇī

She who is in the form of Yajamāna, *who directs sacrificial rites.*

Yajamāna is one of the eight forms of Śiva.

884. धर्माधारा

Dharmādhārā

She who is the support of the code for righteous living.

Dharma means "that which gives support." Devī is the support of that *dharma*. Bhāskarācārya quotes from *Samvarta Smṛti*, "In any country, the code of conduct that is handed down by tradition and is not contrary to the scriptures, is called *dharma*."

He who protects *dharma* is, in turn, protected by it. How is *dharma* protected? Leading a *dhārmic* (righteous) life is the way.

Splitting the *mantra* as *dharma* + *ā* (widely) + *dhāra* (stream), the meaning can be, "She who showers *dharma* everywhere."

885. धनाध्यक्षा

Dhanādhyakṣā

She who oversees wealth.

Dhanādhyakṣa is Kubera, the Lord of Wealth. Devī is called *Dhanādhyakṣā*, because there is no distinction between the worshipper and the worshipped.

886. धन धान्य विवर्धिनी

Dhana dhānya vivardhinī

She who increases wealth and harvests.

When there is an abundance of wealth, it is Devī's blessing. One who thinks that it is due to his own ability does not see the fall awaiting his next step. Devī's presence is seen where, along with the bounty of harvest, humility also flourishes.

887. विप्र प्रिया

Vipra priyā

She who is fond of the learned.

A *vipra* is a *jñāni*, a knower of the Self. This is the only meaning of *vipra* that will make the following celebrated statement meaningful: "The one truth is described by *vipras* in different ways." *Vipra* is commonly translated as a *brāhmaṇa*. But it is not a term that refers to the status acquired by one's birth; it is to be acquired by one's deeds.

"One is a *vipra* due to knowledge."

"A knower of *Brahman* is a *brāhmaṇa*."

"One is a *śūdra* by birth, but becomes a *brāhmaṇa* by actions."

The following questions deserve thought: "Does a *brāhmaṇa* know the imperishable *Brahman* without learning? Is he born with the mark on the forehead, the sacred thread or the tuft?"

888. विप्र रूपा

Vipra rūpā

She who is in the form of a knower of the Self.

Also, one who shapes knowers of the Self. It should be noted that this *mantra* describes Amma's true form.

889. विश्व भ्रमण कारिणी

Viśva bhramaṇa kāriṇī

She who makes the universe go around through Her power of illusion.

Bhramaṇa means both revolving and deluding. Both are apt here. Devī causes the great cosmic masses to revolve with the ease of a juggler. It is the same Devī who, hiding the true nature of the universe, causes confusion in the *samsārin* through the imposition of names and forms, as in the projection of the serpent in a rope. Why does She cause this illusion? For the maintenance of cosmic activity. One who has no illusion engages in no action, and thus the end of *samsāra*.

Viśva also means Viṣṇu (*Viśva* is the first name in the *Viṣṇu Sahasranāma*). Here Bhāskarācārya quotes a story from *Kālika Purāṇa*. Once, Viṣṇu, mounted on Garuḍa, was travelling through the sky. He saw the beautiful Kāmāmba Devī on the mountain called Nīlācala in the country of Kāmarūpa. She was Devī Herself. Viṣṇu continued the journey without paying respects to Her. She decided to teach Him a lesson. Within a few moments, Viṣṇu fell into the ocean. Hearing of this from Garuḍa, Lakṣmī became alarmed, and prayed to Devī. Pleased with this prayer, Devī rescued Viṣṇu from danger and showed Him to Lakṣmī. He praised Devī and returned to Vaikuṇṭha. Devī thus became the cause of Viṣṇu's confusion.

890. विश्व ग्रासा

Viśva grāsā

She who devours the universe.

The *Śruti* says, "That, to which returns the universe that exists."

That is the Devī who is none other than *Brahman*. The *Brahma Sūtras* also imply this: "It is the highest Self, since what is movable and what is immovable becomes Its food."

Recall the description in *Kaṭha Upaniṣad* (I.ii.25) which was quoted earlier: "For whom *brāhmaṇa* and *kṣatriya* are food and death itself is just a condiment."

891. विद्रुमाभा

Vidrumābhā

She who shines like coral (with Her red complexion).

Vidruma is coral. It can also mean the tree (*druma*) of knowledge (*vid*). Or, it is a special tree (*vi* + *druma*), the wish-fulfilling *kalpa* tree. Devī, who fulfills everyone's wish, shines like the wish-fulfilling tree.

892. वैष्णवी

Vaiṣṇavī

She who is in the form of Viṣṇu.

Devī is in the form of Viṣṇu or is the Mother of Viṣṇu. *Devī Purāṇa* gives the following definition of *Vaiṣṇavī*: "She is celebrated in song as *Vaiṣṇavī*, who wears the conch, disc and club, who is the Mother of Viṣṇu and the destroyer of foes and is in the form of Viṣṇu Himself."

893. विष्णु रूपिणी

Viṣṇu rūpiṇī

She who is in a form that extends over the whole universe.

In Her cosmic sport, Devī manifests in four different forms. Śrī Bhāskarācārya cites the following from *Lalitopākhyāna*, in which Viṣṇu says, "The original Śakti of Maheśa appears in four different forms: in Her normal or "enjoying" form (*bhogarūpiṇī*) as Bhavāni, in battle as Durgā, in anger as Kālī and as male in My own form."

In *Kūrma Purāṇa*, Śiva showed his Universal form to Mankanaka, and the latter enquired about the terrible, brilliant form by Śiva's side. Śiva replies, "She is my Supreme *Māyā* and the *Prakṛti* possessing the three *guṇas*. She is called the womb of the universe by the sages. She knows the universe and She bewilders the universe through *Māyā*. She is Nārāyaṇa."

894. अयोनिः

Ayoniḥ

She who is without origin.

Since She has no origin, She has no end. She who has no abode. She who has no limits.

If *a* is Viṣṇu and *yoni* is origin, She is the origin of Viṣṇu. Even the trinity of Brahmā, Viṣṇu and Śiva arise, exist and perish in Her.

895. योनि निलया

Yoni nilayā

She who is the seat of all origins.

"The one from whom all beings originate," says the *Śruti.* That Parāśakti is Devī. One who is the source even for the Original Cause, and the support for even the creator, Brahmā.

This *mantra* also means "She who dwells in the form of the *bindu* in the triangle in the *Śrīcakra.*"

896. कूटस्था

Kūṭasthā

She who remains unchanged like the anvil.

An anvil is a solid iron block on which heated metal objects are hammered into shape. It does not change even after hammering red hot iron pieces on it countless times. Similarly, Devī is the Supreme, the Eternal One who stays unmoved like the anvil, even when buffeted by worldly changes.

Kūṭa can be interpreted as ignorance (*ajñāna*). Then the *mantra* means that Devī stays shrouded by our ignorance. "Wisdom is enveloped by ignorance; thereby beings are deluded," says the *Gītā* (V.15).

Kūṭa also means mountain peak. Devī is as motionless as a mountain peak. Many of Devī's temples are on top of mountains.

Also, *kūṭa* is the world. Devī is one who keeps all the worlds fixed in Herself.

The *Tāntric* meaning is, "She who resides in the three *kūṭas* of the *pañcadaśi mantra.*" The other *Tāntric* meaning is that She dwells at the door (*kūṭa*) of the triangle in the *Śrīcakra.*

The *Viśvakośa* says *kūṭa* means machine, deception, zodiac, anvil, illusion, mountain peak, summit, insignificance, part of a plough, and gate of a city.

897. कुल रूपिणी

Kula rūpiṇī

She who is the deity of the Kaula *path.*

The various meanings of *kula* and the *Kaula* path have been discussed earlier under several *mantras*.

898. वीरगोष्ठी प्रिया

Vīragoṣṭhī priyā

She who is fond of the assembly of warriors.

Vīras need not be warriors. Scholars, leaders, rulers and poets can all be *vīras*. Since Devī is worshipped where any of these are assembled, She is particularly fond of such gatherings.

899. वीरा

Vīrā

She who is heroic.

One who has able offspring and a distinguished husband is called *Vīrā*. Devī is indeed unparalleled among *vīrās*, with offspring like Subrahmania, the warrior; Gaṇeśa, the remover of obstacles; Kāli, the slayer of Daruka and a husband like Śiva who consumed the most potent of poisons, burned the Tripura cities to ashes and is Himself death to the Lord of Death!

900. नैष्कर्म्या

Naiṣkarmyā

She who abstains from actions.

Lord Kṛṣṇa's words are recalled here: "I have nothing whatsoever to achieve in the three worlds, O Pārtha, nor is there anything to be obtained that has not been obtained, yet I am engaged in action." (*Gītā* III.22)

Devī, who does everything, expects no fruit from anything. The action done on one's own, without desiring any fruit, is called non-action (*akarma*) in the *Gītā*. All of Devī's actions are for the good of others. "Having abandoned attachment for the fruit of actions, ever content, depending on no one, he does nothing at all, though he is ever engaged in actions." (*Gītā* IV.20)

There is nothing that Devī needs to gain in the three worlds. There is nothing to be done. Still She is engaged in the acts of creation, preservation and destruction and in granting the desires of Her devotees. Since all actions done without the expectation of fruits are non-actions, Devī is called actionless, *Naiṣkarmyā*.

With this mantra ends the tenth *kalā* known as *bodhini*.

901. नाद रूपिणी

Nāda rūpiṇī

She who is in the form of the primal sound.

Devī is in the form of Nādabrahman, *Brahman*-as-sound.

Nāda is described in the *Svacchanda Tantra* on the basis of *praṇava*, the syllable *Om*. *Nāda* is at head of the *praṇava*.

The *anāhata cakra* in the heart is the position of *nāda*. On the basis of the five senses of sound, touch, sight, taste and smell, *nāda* is considered as made of five *tuṣṭis* (forms of elation). They have five obstacles (*vighnas*) also. They correspond to earthly wealth, its acquisition, guarding, spending and loss. The *sādhak* who overcomes these obstacles gains elation and progresses in the *upāsana* of Nādabrahman, will be able to realize Devī who is *Nādarūpinī*.

902. विज्ञान कलना

Vijñāna kalanā

She who realizes the knowledge of Brahman.

Here, *Vijñāna* is the knowledge of *Brahman* and *kalana* is one who realizes it or makes it one's own.

According to the *Kūrma Purāṇa*, *vijñāna* refers to the fourteen *vidyās* or branches of knowledge. These are the four *Vedas*, the six *Vedāngas* (auxiliaries to *Vedas*), law, *Purāṇas*, *mimāmsa* (philosophy) and logic. (There are other similar divisions of knowledge into systems.) Devī has realized the essence of all these, as She is the seat of all knowledge.

903. कल्या

Kalyā

She who is capable of creation.

This name can be understood as one who is proficient in the arts or possessor of creative abilities, or one who is the essence of the brightness of dawn.

Kalya has the dictionary meanings "creation, dawn, absence of disease, skillful person, auspicious speech and mead." Devī can be associated with each of these meanings.

904. विदग्धा

Vidagdhā

She who is expert in everything.

How marvelous is the expertise that Devī shows in the diversity of creation, in the dexterity of protection, in the manner of punishment!

905. बैन्दव आसना

Baindava āsanā

She who is seated in the Baindava cakra.

Baindava is the spot between the eyebrows. That is the position of the *ājñā cakra* and above it, the *sahasrāra*. The *bindumaṇḍala* in the *ājña cakra* is above the *Hākinī* Circle. The Śakti, Manonmani, dwells there.

Baindava cakra also refers to the *sarvānandamaya cakra* in the *Śrīcakra*. The *mantra* then says that Devī is one who dwells in that *cakra*.

Bhāskarācārya gives the following interpretation, by taking this *mantra* to be *abaindavāsana*, and splitting it as *ap* (water) + *aindava* (of the moon or moons, here referring to *jīvas*) + *āsana* (seat): "There is only a single moon, but it is reflected in many waters. Similarly, Devī is only one, but She is reflected in a multitude of *jīvas* brought about by conditioning."

906. तत्त्वाधिका

Tattvādhikā

She who transcends all cosmic categories

Tattvas are listed differently in different systems of philosophy. *Sāṅkhyas* adopt twenty-five *tattvas*. Thirty-six *tattvas* are generally recognized: the five elements, and their objects (sound, touch, sight, taste and smell), the five organs of knowledge, the five organs of action, the five *prāṇas* (vital airs: *prāṇa*, *apāṇa*, *vyāṇa*, *udāṇa*, and *samāṇa*), the five *upaprāṇas* (auxiliary airs: *nāga*, *kūrma*, *kṛkara*, *devadatta*, and *dhanañjaya*) and the six *cakras* (starting with *mūlādhāra*) making a total of thirty-six. These categories exist only until the time of dissolution. Devī transcends them and exists even beyond the dissolution.

The position and action of the ten *prāṇas*: *prāṇa* in the heart, *apāṇa* in the anus, *samāṇa* in the navel, *udāṇa* in the throat and *vyāṇa* throughout the body. *Nāga* acts in vomiting, *kūrma* in blinking of the eyes, *kṛkara* in causing hunger and *devadatta* in yawning. At death, *dhanañjaya* covers the body and remains for a while without leaving.

907. तत्त्व मयी

Tattva mayī

She who is Reality Itself or She who is Śiva Himself.

Tattva (reality) is of three kinds - *Ātmatattva*, *Vidyātattva* and *Śivatattva*. Devī is the essence of all these. Some consider *Turīyatattva* as the fourth. *Tattva* can be understood as *Brah-*

man, who is *Sat* - *Cit* - *Ānanda* (Existence - Consciousness - Bliss). *Ātmatattva* is *Sat*, *Vidyātattva* is *Cit* and *Śivatattva* is *Ānanda*. Thus, *Tattvamayī* is She who is *Satcitānanda*.

Ātmatattva is said to correspond to *Māyā*, *Vidyātattva* to Śiva and *Śivatattva* to Śakti. *Turīyatattva* is the combination of these three.

This *mantra* is also interpreted in terms of the states of *samādhi*. There are two kinds of *samādhi*: *samprajñāta* and *asamprajñāta*. The first kind is intense and quick in pace, whereas the second type is quiet and slow. *Jñānārṇava* describes these two types. The indications of *samprajñāta samādhi* are laughter, crying, hairs standing on end, trembling and perspiration. Those of *asamprajñāta samādhi* are fixity of eyes and of body, caused by the abidance of the mind in *Brahman*.

908. तत् त्वम् अर्थ स्वरूपिणी

Tat tvam artha svarūpiṇī

She who is the meaning of tat *(that) and* tvam *(thou)*.

Tat stands for *Brahman* and *tvam* for the *jīvātma*. These two are the same, declares the great statement from the *Upaniṣad*, "Tat tvam asi." Devī is in the form of that Self-knowledge. "*Jīva* is not distinct from *Brahman*," Ācārya Śaṅkara adds.

909. साम गान प्रिया

Sāma gāna priyā

She who is fond of the chanting of the Sāmaveda.

Splitting the name as *sāmaga* + *ana* + *priya*, we get "She who loves the singer of Sāma songs (*sāmaga*) as Her own *prāṇa* (*ana*)."

910. सोम्या

Somyā

She who is benign and gentle in nature; of a cool, gentle nature as the moon.

Somyā is that which belongs to the *somayāga*, the *soma* sacrifice.

Devī deserves the foremost position in this ceremony, and is therefore *Somyā*.

According to Bhāskarācārya, Soma is Śiva because He is with Umā (sa + Uma). Then, *Somyā* is one who belongs to Śiva, meaning Devī who is the union of Śiva and Śakti.

Soma also means camphor. Devī is like camphor in brightness, coolness and purity.

911. सदाशिव कुटुम्बिनी

Sadāśiva kuṭumbinī

She who is the wife of Sadāśiva.

This *mantra* may also be taken to mean "Always (*sadā*) blissful (Śivā) and with family (*kuṭumbini*)." She is *kuṭumbinī* (matron of the family) because the *śaktis* Śyāmalā, Śuddhavidyā and Aśvārūḍhā are all members of Her family. It has also been said that these *śaktis* are forms of Devī Herself.

912. सव्यापसव्य मार्गस्था

Savyāpasavya mārgasthā

She who occupies (or can be reached by) both the left and the right paths of worship.

The learned opinion is that there is also a central path. *Savya* (left) connotes the act of creation, *apasavya* (right) the process of dissolution and *mārga* the act of preservation. Thus Devī is the basis of all three processes.

The sun's course through the constellations during the year is divided into three *ayanas* or paths - north, south and middle, which correspond respectively to *savya, apasvya* and *mārga*. These connote the sun's passage to the north, to the south and in the region near the equator, each extending for four months. The present *mantra* then means that Devī occupies all three of these paths.

It is generally believed that death during the northern passage of the sun is desirable, yet this *mantra* makes it clear that for a true devotee of Devī there is no distinction. Such a devotee will merge with Her regardless of when death occurs.

The northern passage is called *jyotirmārga*, "the path of light" (the path of knowledge or the path of the *devas*). The southern passage is known as *dhūmamārga*, "the path of smoke." The former is said to be for *jñānis*, persons of knowledge, and the latter for worldly people.

The middle passage is called *dhruvamaṇḍala*, "the abode of Dhruva," or as the place of Viṣṇu. The course of the sun and the planets are said to be controlled from *dhruvamaṇḍala*. Devī resides here and directs all three paths. Thus She gained the name, *Savyāpasavyamārgasthā*.

It is common to consider only two divisions in a year, the northern and southern passages (*uttara* and *dakṣina ayanas*) each taking six months.

During each *ayana*, the sun passes through the region of nine stars or constellations, each divided into three groups known as *vīthīs* of three *nakṣatras* or constellations each. They are as follows:

Northern passage or Uttarāyana

Aśvinī, Kṛttikā, Bharaṇī:	Nāgavīthī
Rohiṇī, Ārdrā, Mṛgaśīras:	Gajavīthī
Puṣya, Āśleṣā, Punarvasu:	Airāvatīvīthī

Middle passage or Madhyamāyana

Makhā, Purva and Uttara Phalgunīs:	Ṛṣatīvīthī
Hasta, Citrā, Svātī:	Govīthī
Jyeṣṭhā, Viśākhā, Anūrādhā:	Jāradgavīvīthī

Southern passage or Dakṣiṇāyana

Mūla, Pūrva Uttara Āṣāḍha:	Ajavīthī
Śravaṇa, Dhaniṣṭhā, Śatabhiṣak:	Mṛgavīthī
Pūrva and Uttara Bhādrapada, Revatī:	Vaiśvānaravīthī

Also, *savya* connotes the *iḍā*; *apasavya*, the *piṅgalā* and *mārga*, the *suṣumnā*. Devī resides in these three *nāḍīs*.

913. सर्वापद् विनिवारिणी

Sarvāpad vinivāriṇī

She who removes all dangers.

In the *Kūrma Purāṇa*, Devī says, "I destroy by the light of wisdom the misfortunes of even mountainous size befalling those who take refuge in Me, worshipfully, forsaking all attachments, with compassion towards all beings, free of desire and anger, and with self-control, whether they are *sannyāsins*, *vānaprasthas*, *gṛhasthas* or *brahmachārins*."

In *Harivaṃśa*, Viṣṇu tells Devī, "You alone protect people from sorrows such as death, loss of wealth, the death of sons and other afflictions; in this there is no doubt." Brahmā praises Her in *Varāha Purāṇa*, "O Devī, for one who takes refuge in You, dangers and misfortunes do not arise."

Even Brahmā and others become the servants of one who remembers Devī.

The meaning of this *mantra* is to be appreciated from one's own experience. No one who constantly takes refuge in the Divine Mother can deny the truth of this *mantra*.

914. स्वस्था

Svasthā

She who abides in Herself; She who is free from all afflictions.

Brahman is that object from which there is nothing distinct or separate. *Brahman* abides in *Brahman*. That is why we say that Devī is *Svasthā*, abiding in Herself.

"Where does that *Brahman* abide? In Its own majesty," says the *Śruti*. (*Chāndogya Upaniṣad* VII.24.1)

Splitting the name as *su* + *astha*, the meaning becomes "She who has no fixed abode, but extends everywhere auspiciously."

915. स्वभाव मधुरा

Svabhāva madhurā

She who is sweet in Her inherent nature.

"She who, with Her presence (*svabhāva*), graces the city of Madhura." That is, "She who is in the form of the goddess Mīnākṣī of Madhura."

According to Bhāskarācārya, this name can be interpreted also as "She who bears the yoke of the wise." The meaning is that Devī, by Her power, becomes the yoke of the chariot of life of the wisest men. When the horses run forward, the yoke takes the chariot along to the goal. If the yoke breaks, the chariot breaks loose, and may even fall into a ditch.

Several additional interpretations have been given:

- She who is at the front of those who shed the light of the Self.
- She who is sweet to those who show absence of desire, anger and other negative qualities.
- She who gives (to Her devotees) the nectar that is naturally in Her.

916. धीरा

Dhīrā

She who is wise; She who gives wisdom.

Dhī is wisdom, knowledge of the Self; *ra* is one who possesses or one who gives. Thus, She who gives knowledge of the Self is *Dhīrā*. Īra is the daily deity of the tenth lunar day (*daśami*). *Dhīra* is Īra as the giver of wisdom. This *mantra* salutes Devī in the form of that deity.

"Only through the grace of God does one get a taste for non-duality," says Śaṅkara.

917. धीर समर्चिता

Dhīra samarcitā

She who is worshipped by the wise.

She who is worshipped for the sake of the bliss of the knowledge of the *Ātman*. The bliss of Self-knowledge makes everything else uninteresting, as recorded by those with experience. The secluded, serene, and non-dual bliss of the *Ātman* "far exceeds even the purest joy, untouched by a trace of sorrow or anxiety." If not, would those who are wise forsake everything else for it? "You may throw me into hell, or make me the Lord of all the worlds; whatever happens, I will not forsake Your Feet - that is certain!" says Kalyāṇacaraṇa.

918. चैतन्यार्घ्य समाराध्या

Caitanyārghya samārādhyā

She who is worshipped with consciousness as the oblation.

This is the worship of Devī not by using images or materials, but by invoking Her and the oblations in the mind.

Caitanya is the *bhuvaneśvarī mantra* and *arghya* is an offering during worship. Thus, one who is worshipped using the *bhuvaneśvarī mantra.*

919. चैतन्य कुसुम प्रिया

Caitanya kusuma priyā

She who is fond of the flower that is consciousness.

Worship of the formless is the subject of this *mantra.* Here, the flowers are the knowledge of the Supreme. It is the highest form of worship.

According to *Tāntric* experts, *caitanya* is the bliss called *Kuṇḍagolodbhava.* This is the bliss experienced when the *Kuṇḍalinī* enters the *Viśuddhi cakra.* Devī is fond of that *caitanya* flower.

Śaṅkarācārya says in *Saundarya Laharī* (verse 3) that, for those of low intellect, Devī is the flow of honey from a bouquet of *caitanya* flowers. This flow is the power of discrimination between the real and unreal. In saying "persons of low intellect," it is implied that even ordinary persons deserve to attain the bliss of *Brahman.* Hastāmalakācārya, Śaṅkara's own disciple, is an example.

The imagery of flowers is a way of giving form to formless ideas. Bhāskarācārya makes this clear with an example. The greatest form of worship is said to be that using eight kinds of flowers, non-injury, restraint of the senses, forbearance, compassion, wisdom, penance, truth and meditation (offering one's heart).

920. सदोदिता

Sadoditā

She who is ever shining.

One who has always risen in splendor (one who never sets). Or, one who always appears in virtuous individuals spreading the light of the Self.

921. सदातुष्टा

Sadātuṣṭā

She who is ever pleased.

She who is pleased with the virtuous. Devī is one who dwells happily in the company of virtuous individuals. Even wicked people turn virtuous in Her company. Thus it is clear that Devī is always in the company of good people.

922. तरुणादित्य पाटला

Taruṇāditya pāṭalā

She who is rosy like the morning sun.

Taruṇāditya is the young sun and *pāṭala* is rose-colored.

This is also interpreted as referring to the sun at midday. Thus Bhāskarācārya describes Devī as one who shines with a bright rosy color. One may feel that there is no red color in the sun at noon. The sun's light contains all colors, the red becoming evident at dawn and dusk. Red is always there. That is why Devī is described as having a combination of white and red colors as in the sun at noon.

Devī assumes different colors depending on the form in which the devotees worship Her. "When She confers salvation, She is peaceful and white in color. In controlling men, women and kings, She becomes rosy in color. In Her aspect of controlling wealth, She is yellow. In the act of killing, She assumes a black color; in acts of enmity, She is dark brown and in Her erotic aspect, She is rosy. Thus the ever-shining Devī is meditated upon in different colors according to different activities, according to the Smṛti."

923. दक्षिणादक्षिणाराध्या

Dakṣiṇādakṣiṇārādhyā

She who is adored by both right and left-handed worshippers.

Dakṣiṇa means capable men, and *adakṣiṇa*, those of low abilities. Devī is the object of worship by both types of people.

Lord Kṛṣṇa says, "Four kinds of *sukṛtins* (men of merit, virtuous men) worship Me, O Arjuna: the distressed, the seeker of knowledge, the seeker of wealth and the wise." (*Gītā* VII.16) The word *sukṛtin* is specially noteworthy. Not everyone will have the desire to worship Devī. Only the virtuous or meritorious men, falling into one of the categories mentioned, will seek refuge in Her. Among them there may be wise, able men and also incapable ones.

Here, Amma's advice seems very meaningful. She says, "Children, instead of praying for wealth, pray for devotion! If you get the king under your control, you get the whole treasury. Why then beg for little things?" That is the way of the wise.

Also, *dakṣiṇā* means offerings including wealth, and *dakṣiṇa* means wise men as above, and *ārādhya*, worshipped. Thus, Devī is one who is worshipped by the wise (Her best devotees) with various offerings.

Dakṣiṇas are *devas* and *adakṣiṇas* are *asuras*. Devī is worshipped by both groups.

Also, *dakṣiṇa* refers to the path of action (*karma mārga*) and *adakṣiṇa*, the path of knowledge (*jñānamārga*). Devī is worshipped through both these paths. The *mantra* can also mean that Devī is generous or lenient (*dakṣiṇa*) towards those devotees who are following the path of knowledge (*adakṣiṇas*). This is not to imply that worship through *jñāna* is superior to worship through *karma*. It is only meant that since the path of knowledge is harder, Devī may show more compassion towards those who follow it.

924. दर स्मेर मुखाम्बुजा

Dara smera mukhāmbujā

She whose lotus face holds a sweet smile.

Dara also means fear. In that case, the *mantra* means "She who smiles even when expected to feel fear." At the time of the final dissolution, even Brahmā and others are expected to experience fear. Devī keeps smiling even then.

Dara also means protection. When Her devotees need protection from danger, She is there with a smile on Her lotus face. What a sweet name this is! Only those who have experienced that kindness will know the sweetness of this name.

925. कौलिनी केवला

Kaulinī kevalā

She who is worshipped as pure Knowledge (Consciousness) by the spiritual aspirants following the Kaula *path.*

The name *Kaulinī* (*mantra* 94) means one who is worshipped by those following the *kaula* path. There Devī is worshipped with a form. The word *kevala* in the present *mantra*, on the other hand, connotes one who is Pure Knowledge, without attributes or name. Thus She is formless here. She is *Kaulinī* and *Kevalā* at the same time - with and without form. Worship with form and without form both reach Her equally.

According to some, this *mantra* is *Kālinīkevalā*. In that case, Devī is pure Time.

926. अनर्घ्य कैवल्य पद दायनी

Anarghya kaivalya pada dāyinī

She who confers the priceless fruit of Final Liberation.

Kaivalya has been described as the state beyond the *turīya* state.

927. स्तोत्र प्रिया

Stotra priyā

She who is fond of hymns in Her praise.

Stotra, (praise) is of six types. Salutation or prostration (*namaskāra*), blessing the deity whose power may have dwindled (*āśis*), praising the inner essence of the deity (*siddhāntokti*), praising the exploits of the deity (*parākrama*), praising the glories (*vibhūti*) and prayer (*prārthanā*). As examples, see the following *mantras* in the *Sahasranāma*: 63 (One who grants all wishes), 79 (describing Her exploits in the battle with Bhaṇḍa), 627 (Worshipped by the three worlds), 658 (describing Her as the combination of will, knowledge and action), 692 (Bestower of imperial dominion), 735 (Basis of the illusory universe), 928 (True object of praise) and 953 (Giver of happiness).

Stotra also means *Vedic mantra*. Devī is especially pleased by praises offered through the chanting of *mantras* from the *Vedas*.

928. स्तुति मती

Stuti matī

She who is the true object, the essence, of all praises.

How numerous are the praises that have been sung since *Vedic* times! And how many more are to come! This *mantra* makes clear that the true object or recipient of all those praises, sung in whatever language and aimed at whichever deity, is the primeval Supreme Śakti - Ādi Parāśakti Herself.

She is also one who bestows intelligence and knowledge on those who praise Her.

929. श्रुति संस्तुत वैभवा

Śruti samstuta vaibhavā

She whose glory is celebrated in the Śrutis.

Samstuta is known or experienced. Duśyanta says in *Śākuntala*: "The body moves forward, but the unknowing (*asamstuta*) heart goes backwards!" *Śrutisamstuta* implies that Devī's might and glory are comprehended only by the *Vedas*. As *Vedas* are four in number, the *mantra* may be interpreted as "One who has four known glories."

The four ways in which Devī's glory is manifested are: the Person in the heart (*Jīvapuruṣa*), the Person in the meter (*Chandaḥpuruṣa*), the Person in the *Vedas* (*Vedapuruṣa*) and the Great Person (*Mahāpuruṣa*). These four may be also understood as the *jīva*, the syllable *Om*, the *Vedas* and the *Virāṭ*.

The following four *śaktis* are also given as Devī's glories: patience (*kṣamāśakti*), knowledge (*jñānaśakti*), fixity (*pratiṣṭhāśakti*) and restraint (*nivṛttiśakti*).

930. मनस्विनी

Manasvinī

She who is well-known for Her mind.

The name *Manasvinī* should be carefully understood. Her mind is celebrated because it is not of the common mould. Everyone usually depends on the mind. In Devī's case, the mind depends on Her.

931. मानवती

Mānavatī

She who is high-minded; She who has great fame.

Māna also means measure and that which is immeasurable. When we talk about Devī's fame, it is immeasurable. When we take the meaning of measure, Devī is the one who measures and keeps score of fortunes and misfortunes.

932. महेशी

Maheśī

She who is the wife of Śiva.

Also, the great protector and one who is worshipped by great persons.

933. मङ्गलाकृतिः

Maṅgalākṛtiḥ

She who is of auspicious form.

One whose action (*kṛti*) is auspicious. Her action is the creation of the universe.

934. विश्व माता

Viśva mātā

She who is the Mother of the Universe.

Viśva is also Viṣṇu. She is the Mother of Viṣṇu. The origin of all three, Brahmā, Viṣṇu and Śiva, is from Devī.

935. जगद् धात्री

Jagad dhātrī

She who is the mother who protects and sustains the world.

"You are our Lord who gives us daily without fail, our food and clothes, protects us and makes us blessed!"

936. विशालाक्षी

Viśālākṣī

She who has large eyes.

This connotes the great beauty of Devī's eyes and also the fact that there is no place that Her eyes do not reach.

The Devī worshipped in Kāśi (Varanāsi) is Viśālākṣī.

937. विरागिणी

Virāgiṇī

She who is dispassionate.

One who has no desire for anything. Since Devī is not bound to anything, She is not particularly interested in anything. She is unattached.

938. प्रगल्भा

Pragalbhā

She who is skillful and confident.

The unerring ability shown in the acts of creation, preservation and destruction is implied here. How marvelous is the daring and skill shown in the creation of everything in the universe!

939. परमोदारा

Paramodārā

She who is supremely generous.

Devī is one who gives the ultimate bliss. This *mantra* can also imply that Devī is one who creates the ocean of *samsāra* everywhere.

Again, this name can be split from the previous one as *aparamodārā*, meaning She who is generous towards the poor or miserable. Such destitute people must surely deserve Her grace and She grants them all their wishes (*Aparama*: those who do not have the grace of Ramā, the goddess of wealth; poor; *udārā*: generous).

940. परा मोदा

Parā modā

She who is supremely joyful.

Āmoda is joy, fragrance and fame. Devī is one who possesses the ultimate in all of these. She is also the one who spreads supreme joy everywhere.

941. मनोमयी

Manomayī

She who is in the form of the mind.

The form of the mind is both manifest and unmanifest. Mind can be said to have and not to have a form.

"That Bhairava, Śiva, is Cidākāśa. His *spandaśakti*, His energy of motion, is Manomayi," says *Vāsiṣṭha Rāmāyaṇa.* The first pulsation of all the cosmic elements (*tattvas*) from the Earth to Śiva is known as *manomayi.* Devī is the primeval motion or pulsation of energy, *ādyaspanda.*

In view of the *mantra Manorūpekṣukodaṇḍā* (*mantra* 10), Devī is one who holds a weapon that is Her mind. She conquers and subjugates everyone with that weapon. The mind may be used as another term for *Brahman.*

942. व्योम केशी

Vyoma keśī

She who has the sky as Her hair.

The description of Devī as one who wears the crescent moon in Her hair is in keeping with this *mantra.* This applies to the hair of Śiva also. Śiva is therefore called Vyomakeśa. *Vyomakeśi* is Śiva's wife. *Vyomakeśī* is one who protects (*īśi*) even atoms (*vyomaka*). Devī is one who protects the atoms and also causes them to manifest in the many distinct forms and names.

This name also refers to the Cosmic (*virāṭ*) form, in which the ether element (*vyoma* or *ākāśa*) is Her hair.

943. विमानस्था

Vimānasthā

She who is seated in Her celestial chariot; She who journeys in Her celestial chariot along with the gods.

Vimānasthā also means one who resides in a special chariot consisting of light. The chariot of light indicates very high speeds. Devī, who travels in such a chariot, can give comfort and refuge to anyone in a fraction of an instant. Light travels 300,000 kilometers (or 186,000 miles) per second. It is hard to believe that the ancient sages of India had analyzed this speed of light long ago. There is a verse in the commentary of *Ṛgveda* by Sāyana: "O Lord Sun, salutations to You who travel 2202 *yojanas* in half an instant!" A calculation by Professor G. Krishnamurti of Madras puts this at a value almost identical to the modern value of the speed of light!

The chariot of light means a bright or radiant light. This indicates also the chariots *kiricakra ratha* and *geyacakra ratha* described in earlier *mantras*. Thus, the present *mantra* means that Devī travels in those radiant chariots.

The verse referred to here has another special meaning. The first three-quarters of the verse represents physical knowledge and the last, spiritual knowledge. It brings to mind that any physical knowledge can lead to a secure and peaceful life only if it is rooted in spiritual knowledge.

Vi indicates absence and *māna* is a measure. Then, *Vimānasthā* is one who dwells in the immeasurable, limitless *Brahman*.

Māna is *pramāna* or mode of proof. Devī's nature is knowledge. She is one who dwells in the form of knowledge in the *pramānas*, which are the various ways of arriving at knowledge, such as *pratyakṣa* (direct perception by the senses), *anumāna* (inference), *upamāna* (analogy), *arthapathi* (unavoidable inference from circumstance) and *anupalabdhi* (proof because the opposite is absent).

She is one who resides in the *Vedas* (*vimānas*). *Vimānas* may also refer to the fourteen *vidyās* or branches of knowledge. Devī is one who resides in them. The fourteen branches of knowledge are the four *Vedas*, the six auxiliaries to the *Vedas*, the *Purāṇas* taken together, *nyāya* (logical philosophy), *mīmamsa* (a system of philosophy) and the code of justice.

944. वज्रिणी

Vajriṇī

She who is the wife of Indra.

Indra is Vajri, as he possesses the weapon *vajra*, the thunderbolt. The Devī who is in the form of Indrāṇī, is the wife of Indra.

Devī is also one who bears the *vajra* weapon (see *mantra* 497) or one who wears ornaments studded with *vajra* (diamond).

Vajra also signifies *Brahman*. The *vajra* in the passage from the *Śruti*, "The great terrible uplifted *vajra*," indicates *Brahman*. (*Kaṭha Upaniṣad* II.iii.2) *Vajriṇī* is thus *Sakalabrahman*, *Brahman* with form.

945. वामकेश्वरी

Vāmakeśvarī

She who is the presiding deity of the Vamakeśvara Tantra.

Vāmakas are the worshippers of Śakti according to the *vāma* (left) path, as indicated earlier. *Vāmakeśvarī* is their goddess.

Vāmaka also means progenitor, the *Prajāpati*, the head of the race. *Vāmakeśvari* is, then, the deity of Dakṣa and other *Prajāpatis*.

946. पञ्चयज्ञप्रिया

Pañcayajña priyā

She who is fond of the five forms of sacrifices.

According to the *Vedas*, the five *yajñas* (sacrifices) are *Agnihotra*, *Darśapūrnamāsa*, *Cāturmāsya*, *Goyajña* and *Somayajña*. According to the *Smṛtis*: *Brahmayajña*, *Devayajña*, *Pitṛyajña*, *Manuśyayajña* and *Bhūtayajña*. Devī is one who likes *yajñas* and blesses the performers.

The lists according to the *Vedas* and the *Smṛtis* given above are the commonly accepted meanings, but there are several other lists of the five forms of *yajñas*. According to the *Pāñcarātrāgama*: *Abhigamana* (approaching God), *Upādāna* (collecting materials for worship), *Svādhyāya* (study of scriptures), *Ijyā* (worship) and *Yoga* (meditation). According to *Kaulāgama*: *Kevala*, *Yāmala*, *Miśra*, *Cakrayuk* and *Vīrasamgraha*. According to the *Bṛhattantrakaumudī*: *Āturī*, *Śautakī*, *Daurbodhī*, *Trāsī sādhanā* and *Bhāvinī*. Also, the five sacrifices have been defined as worshipping the moon, earth, sky, man and woman.

947. पञ्च प्रेत मञ्चाधि शायिनी

Pañca preta mañcādhi śāyinī

She who reclines on a couch made of the Five Corpses.

It has been mentioned previously that Devī's couch has Brahmā, Viṣṇu, Rudra and Īśvara as the four legs and Sadāśiva as the mattress (see *mantra* 58). *Tripurasundarī* rests on that couch. It is their deep meditation on Devī that makes these divinities motionless and corpselike. Bhāskarācārya quotes from *Bhairavāmala*: "On that great and auspicious couch, whose pillow is the great Īśāna, whose legs are Brahmā and others, and whose mattress is Sadāśiva, reclines the great *Tripurasundarī*, the Great Devī." Also Śaṅkara says in *Saundarya Laharī* (verse 92), "Brahmā, Viṣṇu, Rudra and Īśvara became the legs of Your couch and Sadāśiva became the pure white sheet."

948. पञ्चमी

Pañcamī

She who is the fifth.

After Brahmā, Viṣṇu, Rudra and Īśvara comes Sadāśiva the fifth, and the greatest; Devī is His wife and is, therefore, called *pañcamī*, the fifth.

Pañcamī may also be Vārāhi. Then, this *mantra* means that Devī is in the form of Vārāhi.

Pañcamī is *ānandabindu*, the fifth of five *bindus* in the body, which is bliss.

Pañcamī is said to represent the fifth state, the state beyond *turīya*, which has been previously described (see *mantra* 263).

949. पञ्च भूतेशी

Pañca bhūteśī

She who is the Goddess of the Five Elements.

Pañcabhūta means "things that originate from the five (elements)," and *īśi* is their goddess. The five things referred to here are five gems originating from the five elements: *indranīla* (a blue black gem) from the earth, *mauktika* (pearl) from water, *kaustubha* from fire, *vaiḍūrya* (lapis lazuli) from air, and *puṣparāga* (a red gem) from the sky. Devī wears an ornament decked with these gems called Vaijayantī.

There is a belief that wearing a chain or ring bearing gems similar to *indranīla* is auspicious.

950. पञ्च सङ्ख्योपचारिणी

Pañca saṅkhyopacāriṇī

She who is worshipped using five objects of worship.

The five objects are fragrance (sandalpaste), flower, incense, lamp and food.

951. शाश्वती

Śāśvatī

She who is Eternal.

Devī is called Eternal as She remains without change in the three periods of time. She is one who is worshipped eternally.

952. शाश्वतैश्वर्या

Śāśvataiśvaryā

She who holds eternal sovereignty.

Sometimes, this name is split from the previous *mantra* as *īśāśvataiśvarya*. It is then interpreted as *īśa* + *aśvata* + *aiśvaryā* giving the meaning, "She who holds dominion (*aiśvarya*) over

Brahmā and other divinities (*īśa*) putting them in the role of horses (*aśvatā*), as mounts or vehicles."

953. शर्मदा

Śarmadā

She who is the giver of happiness.

Devī gives happiness that is untouched by the afflictions or anxiety of danger.

954. शम्भु मोहिनी

Śambhu mohinī

She who deludes Śiva.

Śiva is the enemy of Kāma, the Lord of Desire. Devī's beauty is enough to spark desire even in that slayer of Kāma; not only external beauty, but internal as well. In order to describe Her internal beauty, Kālidāsa wrote the fifth chapter of *Kumārasambhava.*

955. धरा

Dharā

She who is Mother Earth.

She who is in the form of the earth element. She who is the support of all. Recall that the position of the earth element (*pṛthivī tattva*) is the *mūlādhāra*, which is the support of all. Just as the earth supports everything, Devī bears the cosmic bodies on Her finger tips, merely as a sport. Hence, She is *dharā*, one who carries.

According to *mantraśāstra*, this name means, Devī who is in the form of the syllable *la*. Bhāskarācārya quotes from *Jñānārṇava*: "The syllable *la* is the Goddess Earth, with mountains and forests, the essence of all the holy places of pilgrimage and blessed with fifty *Śaktipīṭhas*."

956. धर सुता

Dhara sutā

She who is the daughter of Dhara (Himavat); Pārvatī.

Dharasutā can also be Sītā.

957. धन्या

Dhanyā

She who possesses great wealth; also She who is extremely blessed.

Maṅgalā, Piṅgalā and Dhanyā are three *yoginīs* well-known in *jyotiṣa śāstra* (astrology).

Bhāskarācārya quotes from *Bhaviṣyottara Purāṇa*, describing the four kinds of thought that arise in persons nearing death: *ārta*, *raudra*, *dhanya* and *śukla*.

Ārta signifies thoughts concerning wealth, anxiety over house, wife, clothes and other possessions. In short, delusions due to *Māyā*. *Raudra* stands for thoughts concerning physical and mental wounds, torture and afflictions that have occurred. *Dhanya* is the meditation on the meaning of the *Upaniṣads* and the *Purāṇas*, which were previously learned. Finally, *śukla* is the one-pointed meditation on dispassion based in *yoga*, and the freedom from the temptation of the senses.

Those who die with *ārta* thoughts will be reborn in lower forms, as birds or animals. Those who die with *raudra* thoughts will be born in even lower forms, such as insects and worms. *Dhanya* meditation at the time of death leads to the world of *devas*. Those who die engaged in *śukla* meditation attain the Supreme State, without rebirth. Therefore, the wise one should fix his mind on the meditative path of *śukla*. The mind should be trained at least in the course of *dhanya* early in life. This path is not difficult. That is why Devī is called *Dhanyā*. Her form, celebrated as *Dhanyā*, can be easily fixed in the mind.

958. धर्मिणी

Dharmiṇī

She who is righteous.

The virtues that the great men of every age practice such as truth, forbearance, abidance in moral values and renunciation are given the name *dharma.* That *dharma* guides society on the right path. Devī abides in that *dharma.* "I am born in every age for the preservation of righteousness," is the divine vow. Devī is one who fulfills that vow.

959. धर्म वर्धिनी

Dharma vardhinī

She who promotes righteousness.

Dharma is not something that flows everywhere in society, though a society is never totally lacking in *dharma* either. Like the fire in the embers, it will be smoldering and from time to time, it will burst forth and burn brightly shedding warmth and light. *Vāmana Purāṇa* indicates that control of the senses, purity, auspiciousness and devotion are the *dharma* of Śiva, Devī and Sūrya (the Sun).

960. लोकातीता

Lokātītā

She who transcends the worlds.

Devī transcends all the worlds from the world of Indra to the world of Viṣṇu and resides in Mahākailāsa.

961. गुणातीता

Guṇātītā

She who transcends the guṇas.

The factor that controls the quality of an individual is the mix of the three *guṇas*. Recall the *sāttvic* Vibhīṣana, the *rājasic* Rāvana and the *tāmasic* Kumbhakarna, born as brothers. Devī remains beyond these *guṇas*. As long as the mind exists, it is not possible for man to transcend the *guṇas* completely, because the three *guṇas* are the inherent nature of the mind. It can conceive of only those things, which like itself, are made up of the *guṇas*.

962. सर्वातीता

Sarvātītā

She who transcends everything.

Devī stands beyond all the divine forms. It has been stated many times before that She is beyond even Brahmā, Viṣṇu and Śiva.

963. शमात्मिका

Śamātmikā

She who is of the nature of peace and bliss.

Śamātmikā is "one who is *śama* (peace, tranquility) and one whose essence is *śam*, (bliss)." Bliss is the innate nature of the Self and Devī is one who dwells in the Self.

This *mantra* can be understood in another sense. The universe is based in contradictions, in differences. For this very reason, conflict is its nature. Devī's form is this entire universe, yet the frictions and conflicts of the universe do not move Her. Bhagavān Kṛṣṇa makes it clear in the *Gītā* (II.70): "He attains peace, into whom all desires enter as waters enter the ocean which, filled from all sides, remains unaltered; but not he who hugs his desires." The ocean remains untainted by the inflow of impurities from all sides. Thus, he attains peace in whom the conflicts of desires do not create any agitation. That *śama* or peace is Devī's innate quality.

964. बन्धूक कुसुम प्रख्या

Bandhūka kusuma prakhyā

She who resembles the bandhūka *flower in beauty and grace.*

Bandhūka is a bright red flower. Recall the descriptions such as *Sindūrārunavigraha* and *Dādimīkusumaprabhā.*

965. बाला

Bālā

She who never forsakes the nature of a child.

The nature of a child is purity. "O Beloved, because You play like a child, You are called *Bālā* (little girl)," says *Tripurasiddhānta.* Devī is *Bālā* since She never gives up Her childlike play.

Bālā can also be a *kumāri,* a maiden. Kanyākumāri is a famous deity representing Devī. The *mantra* then implies that Devī is eternally in the form of a young maiden.

966. लीला विनोदिनी

Līlā vinodinī

She who delights in Her sport.

The wise say that the creation of the universe is a *līlā* (sport) for Devī; creation, preservation and destruction are all parts of Her sport and pastime.

Bhāskarācārya quotes a story from the *Yogavāsiṣṭha.* There was a king called Padmarāja. His wife, Līlā, was a great devotee of Devī. She prayed to Devī to bring her husband back to life when he met with an untimely death. Devī gave Her husband back to her and made her happy. Thus, She brought happiness to Līlā and is therefore known as *Līlāvinodinī.*

Lakṣmī has the name Līlā. Devī is called *Līlāvinodinī* because She amuses Lakṣmī.

967. सुमङ्गली

Sumaṅgalī

She who is eternally auspicious; She who never becomes a widow.

"Doing only commendable deeds, avoiding all contemptible deeds, is called *maṅgala* (auspiciousness) by the sages." One in whom such auspiciousness is present is *Sumaṅgalī.*

Maṅgala is a synonym for *Brahman.* Thus, Devī is none other than *Brahman.*

968. सुख करी

Sukha karī

She who gives happiness.

The reasons for happiness are physical and spiritual blessings. Devī is one who gives happiness to Her devotees through means based on *dharma* and justice.

969. सुवेषाढ्या

Suveṣāḍhyā

She who is very attractive in Her beautiful rich garments and ornaments.

The richness of attire is not in artificial glitter but in simplicity, purity, restraint and decency. The *mantra* means that Devī is one who is proud and graceful in Her auspicious attire and ornaments.

970. सुवासिनी

Suvāsinī

She who is ever auspiciously married.

Suvāsinī is one who is always attired in auspicious and beautiful clothes. Such clothes are not allowed for a widow by tradition.

Śrī Parameśvara's wife will never become a widow. Parameśvara here actually signifies *Brahman*. Devī, therefore, does not become a widow even at the time of the Great Dissolution, because *Brahman* is beyond time and never meets death.

971. सुवासिन्यर्चन प्रीता

Suvāsinyarcana prītā

She who is pleased by the worship performed by married women.

There are *Tāntric* rites in which married women (*sumaṅgalis*)are worshipped as Devī. Śrī Rāmakṛṣṇa has done such worship. This *mantra* may be interpreted as "She who is pleased by *Sumaṇgalī Pūja*."

972. आशोभना

Āśobhanā

She who is always radiant.

Śobhanā is synonymous with auspicious, prosperous and beautiful. Devī is indeed the embodiment of all these qualities.

973. शुद्ध मानसा

Śuddha mānasā

She who is of pure mind; one who purifies the minds of Her worshippers.

What is a pure mind? Lord Kṛṣṇa says in the *Gītā* (II.45), "The *Vedas* deal with the three *guṇas*. O Arjuna, free yourself from the three *guṇas*, from the pairs of opposites and ever remain in *sattva*, free from all thoughts of acquisition and preservation, and be established in the Self."

The ritualistic section of the *Vedas* deals with the three *guṇas* and the desire for the fruits, which always remains in the performance of such rituals. The true fulfillment in life is to become free from the pairs of opposites and abide in truth constantly. Turning the mind away from actions that are rooted in the three *guṇas*, and fixing it on the Self that is everlasting bliss, is true upliftment. Remaining in that state is true purity of mind. If there is a mind in that state, it is devoid of the three *guṇas* and is the essence of the Self. That state, reached by a long process of restraint and *sādhana*, is the final experience of the Self, the state of eternal abidance in Truth. Since Devī is constantly in that state, She is called *Śuddhamānasā*, pure minded.

974. बिन्दु तर्पण सन्तुष्टा

Bindu tarpaṇa santuṣṭā

She who is pleased by offerings to the Bindu.

Bindu refers to the *sarvānandamaya cakra* in the *Śrīcakra*. *Tarpaṇa* here means doing *pūja* and making offerings to the *cakra* according to prescribed rules.

Following the codes for honoring and serving others is important not only in human relations, but also in relation to the Divine. Amma often says, "Only the laziest will say, 'Observances are meaningless and I will never follow them.'" As said before, life is not an intellectual activity, but an emotional one. Naming a child, giving it solid food for the first time, celebrating its first birthday and other rituals, are a means of showing emotion. The child will grow without any of these, and usually does not demand them, yet they are important as rituals. Rituals are needed; it is improper rituals that need to be eliminated. Rituals are subject to time and circumstances. Wise men will correct unbecoming rituals from time to time. Devī is pleased at this.

Bindu also means intelligence. Devī is one who is pleased with the worship of wise men.

975. पूर्वजा

Pūrvajā

She who is ahead of everyone; first born.

"O Saumyā, this pure Sat (*Brahman*) is indeed that which existed at first," says the *Śruti*. It is the same *Brahman* who, as the original *Prakṛti* (*mūlaprakṛti*), continues the creative process. The name *Pūrvajā* means that *mūlaprakṛti*.

Pūrvajā also means the first pulsation of that primeval Śakti, or the first creation.

976. त्रिपुराम्बिका

Tripurāmbikā

She who is the Mother of the Tripuras *(Three Cities)*.

Tripura means the states of waking, dreaming and sleeping. Since Devī is the creator of these states, She is called Tripurāmbika. The three bodies, gross, subtle and causal are also known as Tripuras or "the three cities." Devī is Mother to them also. "The soul that plays in the three cities (*puras*)," says the *Śruti*, referring to the *jīva* that plays in the three bodies, gross, subtle and causal.

Śrīcakra has nine *cakras*, from *trailokyamohana* to *sarvānandamaya*, as previously described. Each *cakra* starts with a triangle. There are five triangles pointing downwards known as Śakti triangles (*Śaktikonas*) and four pointing upwards, known as Śiva triangles. From the *Śaktikonas* arise the five elements and from the *Śivakonas*, the four *tattvas*, *Māyā*, Śuddhavidyā, Maheśvara and Sadāśiva. The universe takes shape from these nine *tattvas*. Also, from the *Śaktikonas*, skin, blood, flesh, fat and bone arise. From *Sivakonas*, marrow, semen, life breath and *jīva* arise. Each triangle has a Tripura and each Tripura has a *mudrā*. The Tripuras are Tripura, Tripureśvari, Tripurasundarī, Tripuravāsini, Tripurāśri, Tripuramālini, Tripurāsiddhi, Tripurāmbika and Mahātripurasundarī. Tripurāmbika is the eighth deity among these. The present *mantra* states that Devī is in the form of that Śakti.

977. दश मुद्रा समाराध्या

Daśa mudrā samārādhyā

She who is worshipped by ten mudrās *(positions of the fingers and hands used in worship).*

Tāntric expert M.P. Pandit discusses *mudrās*: "*Mudrās* are the language in which a worshipper's body talks to the deity. The emotion of devotion in his heart is expressed through *mantras* and in body movements through *mudrās*. It is not enough to keep devotion in the heart; it should be expressed also. *Mudrās* are the offering of the soul through motions of fingers and other organs. They help self-surrender and give additional support for mental concentration. Each *mudrā* is filled with the deity's presence."

The following are the ten *mudrās*:

sarvasaṅkṣobhini (that which agitates all)

sarvavidrāvinī (that which drives everyone)

sarvākarṣini (that which attracts all)

sarvavaśaṅkari (that which brings all under control)

sarvonmādinī (that which deludes everyone)

sarvamahankuśa (that which inspires and awakens everyone)

sarvakhecari (that which causes travel in the sky - the experience of flight without wings sometimes comes to *sādhaks*)

sarvabīja (the seed of all)

sarvayoni (the origin of all; this *mudrā* is considered the most important, as it is the *mudrā* of the *Bindu*)

sarvatrikhaṇḍā: this last *mudrā* includes the *Śrīcakra* in its entirety. It is "celebrated as extending over the entire *cakrarāja*."

Pūjā Paddhati describes the *mudrās* in detail. Devī is one who is worshipped by all these ten *mudrās*.

978. त्रिपुराश्री वशंकरी

Tripurāśrī vaśaṅkarī

She for whom Tripurāśrī is under control.

As mentioned previously under *mantra* 976, among the *Tripuras*, the fifth one is Tripurāśrī. She dwells in the *sarvārdhasādhaka*, the fifth *cakra* of the *Śrīcakra*.

979. ज्ञान मुद्रा

Jñāna mudrā

She who is in the form of the jñānamudrā *(the finger pose of wisdom).*

This *mudrā* is also called *cinmudrā*. It is the *mudrā* in which one joins the tips of the thumb and the index finger, forming a circle, and keeping the other fingers straight. This *mudrā* can be seen in the pictures of various deities like Śrī Ayyappa.

This *mantra* also means "She who gives (*ra*) the bliss (*mud*) of knowledge (*jñāna*).

980. ज्ञान गम्या

Jñāna gamyā

She who is to be attained through the yoga of knowledge.

Śrī Bhāskarācārya quotes a passage from the *Kūrma Purāṇa* spoken by Devī: "My unconditioned form, which is Pure Consciousness, benevolence (auspiciousness or *śivam*), free of all limitations, infinite, immortal and supreme, is to be attained by wisdom alone. That Supreme Abode is attained only with difficulty. Those (wise persons) who think that knowledge is the best means, enter Me."

However firmly one fixes the knowledge of *Brahman* in one's mind, one does not experience *Brahman*, because of conditionings (limitations) - the limitations (*upādhis*) of the mind, of the sense organs, of the whole body. Only an intelligence that transcends the senses and becomes free of these limitations attains that experience.

981. ज्ञान ज्ञेय स्वरूपिणी

Jñāna jñeya svarūpiṇī

She who is both knowledge and the known.

"The mind has to be as still as the eye that remains, when, after counting one by one, there is nothing more to count."

Jñeya (that which is known) is what can be counted. After counting everything, nothing more countable remains, and only *jñāna* (knowledge itself), the "eye" that did the counting, remains.

The conditioned *jīva* (*samsārin*) is the one who is counting. When even the conditioning - the *upādhis* such as the body - has been counted, just the *jīva* which is *jñāna* remains. "*Jīva* is none other than *Brahman*," says Śaṅkara. Thus, this *mantra* means "She who is in the form of the Self and the non-Self."

982. योनि मुद्रा

Yoni mudrā

She who is in the form of the yonimudrā.

This is the ninth of the ten *mudrās* previously listed.

983. त्रिखण्डेशी

Trikhaṇḍeśī

She who is the ruler of the tenth mudrā, *the* trikhaṇḍa.

The three *khaṇḍas* (sections) referred to here are: the *soma-*, *surya-* and *agnikhaṇḍas* (the sections of the sun, moon and fire). These are the general sections of *mantras* and Devī is the presiding deity of them all. In particular, the three *kūṭas* or sections of the *pañcadaśi* (the fifteen syllabled *mantra*) are referred to here. Devī is, of course, the Goddess of that *mantra*.

984. त्रिगुणा

Triguṇā

She who is endowed with the three guṇas *of* sattva, rajas *and* tamas.

The earliest mention of the *guṇas* occurs in *Sāṅkhya* philosophy. Everything in nature is made up of the three *guṇas*. In varying degrees, these three are fused into all things. For this very reason, the Mother who is *prakṛti* (Nature) is called *Triguṇā*.

Bhāskarācārya quotes from the *Purāṇas* in support of this: "Devī, who is Yogeśvarī, by Her sport creates and destroys forms, appears in a multitude of forms, with many functions and many names. She is threefold in nature and is therefore called *Triguṇā*." (*Vāyu Purāṇa*) And, "I revere that eternal power which is the basis of the three *guṇas* and which resides in all beings." (*Viṣṇu Purāṇa*)

985. अम्बा

Ambā

She who is Mother of all beings; Mother of the Universe.

In *Tantra*, this name is referred to as *mantrajīva*, the soul of *mantras*. The three *guṇas* are the cause of energy, the forms of Śakti and the cosmos. Devī, Ambā, is the cause of the *guṇas* themselves.

986. त्रिकोणगा

Trikoṇagā

She who resides in the triangle.

The *yonicakra* of the *Śrīcakra* is meant here.

987. अनघा

Anaghā

She who is sinless.

Sin and merit (*pāpa* and *puṇya*) are the results of actions. Devī has no sin or merit, even though She is performing all manner of destruction (*nigraha*) and blessing (*anugraha*).

The *Gītā* (II.48) says, "Steadfast in *yoga*, perform your actions, O Dhananjaya, abandoning attachment, with an even mind in success and failure, for evenness of mind is called *yoga*." There is no sin or merit attached to actions based in *yoga*. That is why Devī is sinless.

988. अद्भुत चारित्रा

Adbhuta cāritrā

She whose deeds are marvelous.

The word *cāritrā* means both pertaining to *caritra* (history) and fidelity in marriage. Devī's history and Her fidelity both evoke wonder. The entire *Devī Purāṇa* is the portrayal of Her exploits. There is no need to look for a greater sign of Her faithfulness than the *ardhanārīśvara* concept, which is clarified by the name *Kāmeśajñātasaubhāgyamārdavorudvayānvitā* (*mantra* 39).

Bhāskarācārya also interprets this *mantra* as "She who protects from the results of natural upheavals like earthquakes, lightning and storms."

989. वाञ्छितार्थ प्रदायिनी

Vāñchitārtha pradāyinī

She who gives all the desired objects.

This includes both worldly and spiritual desires. Devī generously fulfills the desires of people in all four stages of life (*brahmacārya, gṛhastha, vānaprastha* and *sannyāsa*) including the ultimate goal of life desired by the *sannyāsi*.

990. अभ्यासातिशय ज्ञाता

Abhyāsātiśaya jñātā

She who is known only through the exceedingly strenuous practice of spiritual discipline.

Only through long and constant practice (*abhyāsātiśaya*) of all eight *yogic* paths (see *mantra* 254) is Devī to be realized (*jñāta*).

Or, She who, through constant practice (*abhyāsa*), becomes known exceedingly well (*atiśayajnāta*).

"She whose limbs are knowledge, whose body is all the *śāstras*, and whose abode is the heart, that Devī is to be seen by constant practice. She manifests through the union with the Self," says the *Brahmāṇḍa Purāṇa*.

991. षडध्वातीत रूपिणी

Ṣaḍadhvātīta rūpiṇī

She whose form transcends the six paths.

The six paths are words (*padadhva*), worlds (*bhuvanadhva*), letters (*varṇadhva*), the systems of philosophy (*tattvadhva*), the arts such as music (*kalādhva*) and the *mantras* like the *pañcadaśi* and *gayatrī* (*mantrādhva*). But Devī's real form is not what is invoked in any of these - it is beyond all these. After installing Bhavatārinī Devī in the Āśram temple, Amma said to Her children: "Today we have installed an image here. But my children, you shouldn't be seeing just this image, but the essential truth behind it." That essential truth is what is referred to as "beyond the six paths." The paths mentioned here are to be used for knowing Devī, but Her real nature is beyond all these.

Devotional paths are also said to be six in number: the paths of Śiva, Viṣṇu, Durga, Bhāskara (the sun), Gaṇapati and Indu (the Moon). *Kulārṇava* says that one who purifies the mind with the *mantras* belonging to these paths, obtains the knowledge of Kulā (Devī). However, this *mantra* implies that Devī's real essence lies beyond the reach of these devotional paths.

The six systems of philosophy are also paths to perceive the truth. Again, these systems form only the paths - Devī is the goal. Her essential nature (*svarūpa*) is beyond all these paths.

992. अव्याज करुणा मूर्तिः

Avyāja karuṇā mūrtiḥ

She who is pure compassion.

Devī is the embodiment of unalloyed grace and compassion. Mother is nothing but kindness. How easy it is for the children, who are deluded by the desire for worldly objects, to err in their paths. They don't even know that they have erred. Infinite, undiluted compassion is needed to condone all such mistakes. The constant distraction by children or their mistakes do not tarnish a mother's kindness at all. In fact, a mother shows greater love and compassion for a child who has lost its way. That is the real evidence of kindness.

993. अज्ञान ध्वान्त दीपिका

Ajñāna dhvānta dīpikā

She who is the bright lamp that dispels the darkness of ignorance.

This *mantra* represents Devī in the form of the Guru. The darkness of ignorance can be removed only by the light of knowledge. "*Gu* means darkness and *ru* is one who dispels it. Thus one who removes darkness is known as Guru," according to the sages. "Many prostrations to that Guru who opens the eyes that are blind due to ignorance with a needle coated with the ointment of knowledge!"

994. आबाल गोप विदिता

Ābāla gopa viditā

She who is known well by all, even by children and cowherds.

There is no one, from the greatest scholar to the idiot, who does not utter the word "Mother" from time to time. Devī is none other than Mother. The child who does not know anyone else will know its mother. Mother is known by all.

Bāla refers to Brahmā and Gopa to Sadāśiva; thus, Devī is known to all from Brahmā and Sadāśiva to the ignorant cowherd.

Bālagopa is Kṛṣṇa, the *Paramātman*. To Śrī Kṛṣṇa, who is a *pūrṇāvatāra*, a total manifestation of the Supreme Being, Devī is none other than His own Self. There is no one who does not know the self called "I." The only difference of opinion exists in who this "I" refers to. The meaning of this *mantra* is that all - from one who knows the "I" to be the same as *Brahman*, the primeval source of the universe, to one who takes the "I" to mean the *jīva* proud of its gross body - all know Devī well. She represents knowledge in all forms, from the gross to the subtle.

Also, *go* means knowledge or intelligence. *Gopa* is one who protects knowledge, a scholar. Devī is known by all, from children to the scholar. The only difference is in the nature of the knowledge, but that difference is not important. Devī's motherly love is equal for all, and all are proud that they know Her.

995. सर्वानुल्लङ्घ्य शासना

Sarvānullaṅghya śāsanā

She whose commands are not disobeyed by anyone.

Who can go counter to Mother's commands? From Brahmā to the lowliest insect, all are under Her sway. All the cosmic bodies dance to Her tune without the slightest departure.

All living things are like fish caught in a big net. It is just that they do not realize it until the net is hauled ashore. By then it is too late. We see in the net smaller fish caught in the mouths of big ones. The big fish swallows the smaller one without realizing that both are caught in the net! Both end up out of water, on the shore. That is the drama of life. Man is just like these fish. If he realizes that he is caught in the net, he can slip out and set himself free in the infinite ocean. But only one or two fish in a million manage to do so. Devī, though She is unyielding in Her edicts, will welcome them with the infinite waves that are Her hands.

Bhāskarācārya recalls verse 24 from *Saundarya Laharī* in this context. "Brahmā creates the world, Viṣṇu protects it, and Rudra destroys it. Īśa hides these three divinities within Himself and then hides His own body. And Sadāśiva receives Your command, issued through a quick movement of Your eyebrows, and gives His approval and blessing to Brahmā and the others in their tasks."

Should we discard this image as myth, take it to heart as devotion, or analyze it according to the rules of knowledge? It can only be decided in the light of one's experience.

996. श्रीचक्र राज निलया

Śrīcakra rāja nilayā

She who abides in Śrīcakra, *the King of* cakras.

Śrīcakra represents the union of Śiva and Śakti. With five Śakti *cakras* pointing downward and four Śiva *cakras* pointing upward, the *Śrīcakra* is the body of Śiva-Śakti. This King of all *cakras* is the abode of the Supreme Empress, the Parāśakti.

The Śakti *cakras* are *Trikoṇa, Ashṭakoṇa, Antardaśāra, Bahirdaśāra* and *Caturdaśāra*. The Śiva *cakras* are *Bindu, Aṣṭadala, Ṣoḍaśadala* and *Caturaśra. Srīcakra* is known by many names such as *Cakrarāja, Navayonicakra, Tricatvārimśatkoṇa* (containing forty-three triangles), *Viyatcakra* and *Matṛkacakra.*

997. श्रीमत् त्रिपुर सुन्दरी

Śrīmat tripura sundarī

She who is the divine Tripurasundarī Devī.

Tripura is Śiva; and *Tripurasundarī* is His wife.

Many meanings have been given for the word *Tripura.* They can be summarized as follows: The trinity of Brahmā-Viṣṇu-Maheśvara; the three sacrificial fires (*gārhapatya, āvāhaniya* and *dākṣiṇa*); the three powers of will, knowledge and action; the three worlds (earth, heaven and the netherworld); the *gāyatri* meter (as it has three lines to a verse); the three divine worlds of Kailāsa, Vaikuṇṭha and Satyaloka; the three *varṇas* or castes (*brāhmaṇa, kṣatriya* and *vaiśya*); the three *guṇas* and all such triads are known as *Tripura.*

Kālika Purāṇa explains *Tripura* in terms of the trinity of Brahmā, Viṣṇu and Rudra. "Maheśvara, in accordance with His own will, divided His body into three: the head became Brahmā's body with five faces, four arms and the white complexion of the pericarp of the lotus. The middle portion became the body of Viṣṇu, with one face, blue color, four arms holding the conch, disc, club and lotus. The lower portion became the body of Śiva, with five faces, the color of white clouds and bearing the crescent moon in His matted hair. Since Maheśvara transformed Himself into this trinity, He is known as Tripura." *Tripurasundarī* is the wife of that Tripura. She is the Śakti of the whole universe.

998. श्री शिवा

Śrī śivā

She who is the auspicious and divine Śivā.

She who is the wealth and auspiciousness of Lord Śiva. Numerous meanings of the word *Śrī* have been given, such as Lakṣmī, Sarasvatī, good fortune, wealth, victory and auspiciousness. All these meanings can be taken together with Śiva to interpret this *mantra*.

999. शिव शक्त्यैक्य रूपिणी

Śiva śaktyaikya rūpiṇī

She who is the union of Śiva and Śakti into one form.

The first creative impulse in the universe is desire. "Desire - it came first," says the *Śruti*. This desire is taken as the first stirring of the cosmic mind. *Tantra* calls it *Kāmakalā*. This name indicates the first motion of the eternal and indescribable primeval radiance; that light or *prakāśa* is called Paramaśiva and *Kāmakalā*, its motion, is called Parāśakti. The color of that light is white. And Kāma, as the mother of motion, is red in color. The shadow of the light is black. Thus there are the three *guṇas*, white (*sattva*), red (*rajas*) and black (*tamas*). They were not created, but existed always, as indicated by the *Śruti*, "One, unborn, the red-white-and-black."

Śiva is called *Prakāśa* while Śakti is called *Vimarśa*. *Vimarśa* can mean reflection and contemplation. The first change from darkness to light occurs through red as at dawn. That is how the first pulse of Śakti came to be known as red in color. The first impulse changes into *nāda* and its location is called *nādabindu*. Since everything is created from this *bindu*, it is called *parābindu*.

When *parābindu* turns towards the process of creation, it is called *Śabdabrahman* or *aparabindu*. It is here that Śiva and Śakti dwell as one - Śiva who is motionless and Śakti whose essence is motion. Recall the picture of Devī standing with Her feet planted on the chest of Śiva. One is inert and the other is full of vitality. Here is the great truth that inertness is contained in vitality and vitality in inertness.

Here there is the inert state of Śiva, the vital state of Śakti and the state in which They are united - thus the one Truth appears as three. This is known as *tripuṭi* or as the three *guṇas*. This is the secret meaning of the triangle. Thus we go from *vimarśa*, to *nāda*, to *parābindu*, to *trikoṇa* or *tripuṭi*.

Prakāśa and *vimarśa*, Śiva and Śakti thus unite into one. Devī is that union, the Parāśakti.

There is a *mantra* called *Hamsamantra* also known as *Śivaśaktyaikya mantra*. Thus Devī is one who is in the form of that *mantra*.

Śivaśakti may refer to the Śaktis of Śiva. The five *śaktis* are Dhūmāvati, Bhāsvati, Spandana, Vibhvī and Hlādani. Dhūmāvati is part of *pṛthvi*, the Earth; she veils. Bhāsvati is part of *Agni*, the fire; she reveals or assimilates. The ancient wisdom says, "The student is fire." How thoughtful! Power to assimilate is after all the requisite credential of a student. Spandana is part of *Vāyu*, the air. She stimulates the urge for strenuous effort. We salute the *Purāṇic* characters of Bhīma and Hanumān as sons of Vāyu. Even when everyone else succumbs to fatigue, those two are full of energy for action. Vibhvī is part of *ākāśa*, the ether; She pervades. Those who have a large measure of this quality in them are called *devas* or divine. Hlādani is part of *jala*, water. She nourishes and protects life, the race, the world.

The conjunction of these *śaktis* is connoted by the word *aikya*. Thus, the *mantra*, *Śivasaktyaikyarūpiṇī*, describes Devī as the collective form of Śiva's five *śaktis*.

1000. ललिताम्बिका

Lalitāmbikā

She who is the Divine Mother Lalitā.

She is *Lalitā* who is indescribably charming and graceful in Her attire, gait, words and look and the Mother (*Ambikā*) who nourishes and protects everything with sweet love. Thus She is *Lalitāmbikā*.

Śrī Bhāskarācārya recalls the description, "*Lalitā* is one who sports, transcending the worlds," given in *Padma Purāṇa*. There the term *Lalitā* refers to Devī who resides in the *Bindu* in *Śrīcakra*, transcending the rays of light from the surrounding deities. Bhāskarācārya goes on to describe *Lalitā* as one who is "endowed with the eight manly qualities of brilliance, playfulness, sweetness, depth, fixity, energy, grace and generosity." The term "manliness" (*pauruṣa*) is apt for women as well. *Puruṣa* is one who resides in the body that is called a *pura*, a city; the *jīva*, in other words. Man and woman cannot be said to have different kinds of *jīvas*; *jīva* is the same. Thus, *pauruṣa* is equally apt for man and woman. It is the quality of being human.

The *Lalitā* in front of Śiva is the amorous one full of erotic sentiments. *Lalitā* is one who is full of youth and beauty. She is the beautiful one with words and movements that provoke desire even in Śiva, the slayer of Kāma, the Lord of Desire.

Everything about Her is full of beauty and *lālitya*, playfulness. Her bow is made of sugarcane. Her arrows are flowers. The bowstring is made of black bees. Thus even Her weapons are graceful and enchanting! The name *Lalitā* is thus highly deserved.

Above all these, *Lalitāmbikā* is Devī's celebrated, sacred name which is true to Her full glory. Devī is always hailed as Ambikā, the Mother. The Mother who is *Lalitā*.

With this last mantra we complete the eleventh *kalā* of the sun known as *dhārani*.

In the first three names of the *Sahasranāma*, Devī is shown as responsible for creation, preservation and destruction. The fourth and fifth names have explained powers that are uncommon in other divinities but are inherent in Devī. From the sixth to the last names celebrate both Her manifested and unmanifested glories. And finally, Her true, holy name, Lalitāmbikā is revealed.

The sages prescribe that each name should be chanted with the syllable *Om* in front. There is usually an *Om* at the end also. Thus the hymn should be concluded with an OM.

MĀNASA PŪJA

By
Sri Sri Mata Amritanandamayi

(This is a description of a *mānasa pūja* - mental worship - that Ammachi conducted during the spiritual camp that She led from April 15 to 19, 1987 at the *Aśram* in Amritapuri, India)

"Children, everything should be done with concentration. One should not rush. *Sādhana* is the way to merge the *jīvātman* (individual soul) in the *Paramātman* (Supreme Soul). You should do this *arcana* with the utmost care.

"First of all, everyone should sit in the posture of their choice with the spine erect. Touch Mother Earth with both hands and pay respect to Her. She is the Devī who forgives whatever mistakes we make and showers Her compassion on us. Pray to her, 'O Mother, make me also as forgiving as You' and touch Mother Earth and touch your own forehead with both hands.

"Chant OM three times. There is this dirt of the ego in everyone. Imagine that all of that goes out as we chant. If there is someone to lead the chant, others can repeat after him.

"Children, repeat 'Mother! Mother!' in your mind and draw a triangle on the ground in front of you. Or you can just imagine a triangle. Put a dot (*bindu*) at the center of the triangle. Close your eyes, hold both your hands close to your hearts and picture in your mind a most beautiful form of the Devī. Call out 'O Mother, Mother' and enjoy Her beauty. Make sure to keep your eyes closed. When our eyes are open, we see thousands of objects in the world. When the eyes are open, we are forced to pay attention to everything. We won't get the absorption we need. Normally, don't we experience bliss when we close our eyes and sleep?

Enjoy the beauty of the Divine Mother, and pray, 'Mother..Mother..kindly merge into my mind! Mother, give me the right attitude so that all I enjoy is Your beauty.' Crying out thus, take Devī from your hearts and install Her at the center of the triangle in front of you.

"Some of you may be devotees of Kṛṣṇa or Ayyappa or other deities. Those children will not feel the same love for Devī that they feel for Kṛṣṇa or Ayyappa. Therefore, you may install your chosen deity in the triangle, because your mind is attached to that deity. Mother asked you to invoke Devī only because we are going to do *arcana* with the thousand names of Devī Lalitā. Whatever name we use, She will know that we are calling Her. Some children call their mother *chechi or akka* (elder sister), but the mother knows that they are calling her. She knows that it is just a habit of the child. In the same way, our Mother also does not mind whatever name we use in addressing Her. Those children who worship Kṛṣṇa or other deities can install their chosen deity in front of them, if they prefer.

"Try to do everything while seeing the Divine Mother clearly in front. 'Amma, I don't know meditation or *pūja* or anything. Forgive all my errors and accept this worship. It is said that You are one who forgives any mistake!'

"Children, God is the abode of compassion who accepts all our impurities and sins. Only He can take on the impurities in everyone. When the Ocean of Milk was churned, no one could accept the virulent poison that was produced; finally it was Śiva who accepted it. God is the principle that accepts all the impurities in us and cleanses us. Just as all germs are killed by a disinfectant lotion, all impurities are dispelled by *premabhakti* (devotion in the form of love).

"After praying like this, call out 'Amma! Amma!' with great love and touch Devi's feet. Do the *mānasa pūja* calling Her, 'Amma, Amma,' sobbing with love and devotion. There is no greater *mantra* than 'Amma.'

"Now we are going to bathe the Divine Mother. Imagine that you place a jar full of water in front of Devī for this. Imagine that you are washing Her with water taken in both hands. Call out to Her in your mind, 'Amma, Amma.' The Divine Mother really does not need to be bathed by us. This is all for purifying our minds. Mother does not say that we should not do other *pūja*, but *mānasa pūja* - mental worship - is the best. Children, you should really do everything with eyes closed. Then only you will get full concentration. There is no inside or outside in reality, but for us now, there is inside and outside.

"Pour the water on Devi's head in a stream, praying 'O Mother, give me the *darśan* of Your complete form!' Meanwhile keep that form continuously in mind. After that, imagine that you are holding a container of milk with both hands. Imagine that you are pouring the milk on Devi's head as *abhiṣeka* (bathing the deity) as you have seen done in temples. Now, imagine that you are pouring the *kalabham* (thick sandalwood paste) that is already prepared, on Devi's head in a stream. Next imagine pouring rose water on Her head. Imagine pouring this as you do when giving a bath to a child. You should lift your hand up and actually go through the motions of pouring the water on Mother. Without such acts, it is not possible to concentrate the mind that is running wild in the world of plurality. Only by imagining these things, we can take control of the mind at least for a little while. Picture in your mind the sandalwood paste being washed down as the rose water flows down from Devī's head.

"Children, everything should be done with concentration. There is no benefit otherwise. All this is being done for your spiritual upliftment and for the well-being and prosperity of the family. If your legs hurt, you can stand up and continue the *pūja*. Children, if you do not get concentration in the beginning, do not worry! You may get one second of concentration during a meditation lasting for one hour. In the beginning, that is all that is possible. But it is enough to make progress slowly. You cannot create a sculpture as soon as you begin to learn sculpting. That is why Mother talks about hymns, the thousand names and so on in the beginning. Only through such methods can we get the mind under control easily.

"Now imagine taking *bhasma* (sacred ash), and putting it on Devī's head in small portions. Imagine it falling all over Her body. Then imagine doing *abhiṣeka* again, thus washing all the sacred ash away.

"Touch Her feet and prostrate. You should feel your head touching Her feet. Now imagine that you are wiping the Mother's face and body with a cloth. Remember, we have installed in front of us the Mother of the Universe who protects us all.

"Now it is time to dress Her. Imagine taking a *sari* in a color that you like and draping it around Mother. You are used to dressing your children. Now do the same for the Divine Mother. So we have now put a new *sari* on Mother. Children, don't be thinking of home or your relatives now! We are doing the *pūja* after entrusting our home and our belongings in the hands of a good housekeeper - the Almighty! He will look after things without falling asleep! Children, you do not have to worry about any of that. Your mind should be completely here. Otherwise there is no use in all this. 'O Mother, our hearts are full of thorns and dirt. We have taken refuge in You trusting that You, who are the Mother of the Universe, will forgive all our mistakes! Only if You would come and stay in my heart, can I continue my journey, guided by Your light. Now I am not able to see the path because of the darkness! O Mother, come into my heart.'

"Now we decorate Mother. Let us put some fragrance on Her face and body. None of these is for Her. Mother Herself is the fragrance in everything. But we have to get Her in our minds. So we pretend all this!

"Now with your 'ring finger' put a saffron mark on Her forehead. Stand back and enjoy that beauty. Pray to Mother, 'Amma, Amma, stay in front of me! Don't go away.'

"Next, put gold anklets on Her feet and gold bangles on Her wrists. And earrings and other ornaments. Mother is always near us; it is just that we don't see Her. So either we ourselves turn into children, or we think of Her as a child. One way or the other, manage to make our minds pure!

"Now we take a beautiful crown and put it on Mother's head. Imagine taking a basket filled with flowers. All the while, cry out and pray to the Divine Mother, 'Amma, give me one-pointedness of mind. Amma, merge in me!'

"It is good to picture oneself as a child, for getting humility and modesty. We have to get rid of our sense of ego. Our great sages gave importance to humility even after Self-Realization. Only through humility we will grow. Humility does not mean becoming a slave to somebody. In fact, we become more cultured because of it. Humility is not a weakness. Only by pressing the button does the umbrella unfold. Only through humility our mind expands to include the whole world. Only through humility we become fit to receive God's grace. Doing *tapas* even for eons will not bring divine grace when the 'I' sense is still strong. And that grace is indispensable for cleansing the mind of desire, anger and other negative qualities.

"Pray to the Divine Mother, 'Amma! They say that You are the real Mother! But we can't see You! Are You hiding from us, after leaving us, Your babies, in this forest of ignorance? They say that You are nearby, but I can't see You! See

Mother, the wild animals are attacking me! The forest is on fire! Come running and take me in Your arms, Amma! Where is my Mother? They say that I have a Mother, but She is not to be seen. Everyone is hurting me. I don't make my mistakes knowingly. But the others are giving me pain. It is said that You alone will forgive all mistakes. Mother, please come running; I can't bear this any longer! If You come, I will gain strength. Take me and put me in Your lap, Mother! Only there I have freedom.' Sobbing like this, offer the flowers of your love on the Divine Mother's head. Shower them on Her head. Or imagine putting them on Her head in small handfuls. During all this, don't let anything else enter your mind. Keep seeing that face. Touch Her feet and prostrate, saying 'O Amma, please don't run away!' Now look and enjoy the beauty of Her form as a whole - Her face, the crown, the ear ornaments, Her lips, hair, Her *sari*, Her loving pose which is beckoning us, see it all in your mind. Mothers will beckon sulking children to them with their hand. Our Mother is calling us in the same way, to come near Her. Picture Her standing there ready to take us in Her arms. See Her clearly in front! We should have total surrender whatever we are doing. Our Mother has come with a boat to take us across. We have got on the boat, but we are still carrying our bag and crying. When asked 'Why are you crying', the reply is 'I can't bear this load!' We are not ready to put the burden down, that is why we are suffering. Surrender everything, only then Devī will accept us. We have to have total surrender. Otherwise it is like keeping the seeds in your waïst-band and asking the Lord to make them sprout and grow. They are not going to sprout because we do not have an attitude of surrender.

"We should have the attitude, 'This body, this house, none of these is mine. I have no ability to look after these. You take over and protect everything, Amma!'

"Children, you need not have any fear of having sinned or being ignorant. The Mother of the Universe will gladly accept anything that Her ignorant children do. She will not punish us. A mother will not show disgust and hold her nose when cleaning up the excreta of her little child. Similarly, if we err due to our ignorance, our Mother will not show any hatred.

"Now you should go ahead and embrace the Divine Mother in your mind. And pray: 'Mother, we don't know anything! Please forgive our mistakes! Pardon us! We are burning in a furnace. We are extending our hands in all directions for help. Save us, save us, Mother! Even those who are closest to us do not come to our aid, fearing that they will fall in. Is there a place where You are not present? Only You can save me. Amma, lift me up! I am struggling in the bondage of family. I have made countless mistakes thinking that this body is what lasts forever. Even now the mind does not let go of that. We held on to this thorny tree. Our hands are aching because of the thorns. We didn't foresee this; seeing the beauty of the flowers, we held on to this tree. Lift us up and heal our wounds! Mother, our minds have been taken over by a wild forest. Only Your sword can cut this growth away!

"'Mother, please don't disappear from our sight! These bodies of ours are made of desire and anger. You are pure love. We know you will not stay near us. There is the heat of pride and ignorance near us. Even then, kindly forgive us and stay near us, Amma!' Praying thus, embrace Mother with love.

"We cannot get animals to come near us by showing anger. Whether it is a dog or a cat or a bird, we have to offer it some food and coax it to come near. In the same way, without being bashful, without looking around, with a one-pointed mind, we must call Mother to come to us because we have not yet reached the state of total absorption. When we reach that stage, names and forms will no longer be needed. It is all right to quote Vedanta, but we have not yet reached the level of Vedanta. We say we are not the mind, we are not the intellect and so on. But wait till someone abuses us; we will go after him with a knife! When we sit for meditation, we don't get concentration even for a second. Therefore, we can focus our minds only through these methods.

"See that we are sitting in the lap of the Mother of the Universe. Indeed, that is where we are sitting! The universe is Her lap. If not, we would all have fallen long ago.

"When we are engaged in our family affairs, we cannot always contemplate on the fact that we are the embodiment of the Self. But we can think that the Lord or Devī is our protector. We always have the body sense. When we think of Devī this way, the shell of the ego will break due to our humility. There is no other way to break that. It is said that everything is the *ātman*. But we cannot understand that. The little baby's hand is cut. We say, 'O baby, don't cry, you are the *ātman*!' It is the same thing if someone now tells you that you are the *ātman*. The child knows the pain it is feeling. But when we think that we are really not the body, the pain is lessened a little. We don't need to think of non-duality and all beyond that. 'You are the river; we are the pond. There is dirt in us. Only through Your nearness we can become clean.' Only through thoughts like these we can dissolve our minds completely.

"Let us now sing a devotional song. Picture that the Divine Mother is dancing to our song and that we are also dancing with Her. Enjoy Mother's beauty as you dance. You should cry as you sing. A devotee's tears are the light of the world. The candle melts to brighten the light. A common man's tears are meaningless, because there is no benefit from them. There is only darkness. If you cry when the foot is cut, it does not heal. It only becomes infected. When a devotee cries, it is like dressing the wound with medicine and healing it. That is what we need. Crying for unreal things only causes ruin. The one who cries perishes and all the others perish too. But these tears are for what is eternal. This is the light of the world. This is never a weakness. These are tears that flow in the real presence of Devī. These are the tears of ecstasy that flow when the *jīvātman* touches the *Paramātman*.

"'O Lord, let there be prosperity for my family and peace in the world! Forget everyone's mistakes and forgive them! Give them the strength to know Your truth and live according to it! Give us prosperity and health and protect our family!' Praying this way, you children should join the singing of the hymn now.

Lalitā Lalitā Śrī Lalitā
Lalitā Lalitā Om Mātā!
Lalitā Lalitā Jayalalitā
Lalitā Lalitā Jaganmātā!

Vedavilāsini Śrī Lalitā
Viśvavimohini Śivalalitā
Mātā Bhavāni Śrī Lalitā
Mukti Pradāyini Śivalalitā

"If you are sleepy, stand up and do the *arcana*. Then you will be careful, because it will hurt when you fall down. Don't ever be a friend of sleep! Sleep is like a cat. However much you feed it, it will still steal some food. It is just waiting. It is just looking to see where it is comfortable, where the storeroom is. Don't let the mind wander in that direction. If it does, you have to beat it and drive it away from there. This will be possible only by trying for some time. If we fail in this, that will be the end! It will take our intellect also with it; we won't even know!

"Some people may not like this mental worship, without flowers or anything. But those who understand its meaning will like it. All other forms of worship come after *mānasa pūja*. What can we give the Almighty? Does the sun need a candle? God doesn't need anything. What we need is to get our hearts purified. If we try to put a coat of tin on a dirty pan, it will not stick. First we have to scrape all the dirt off. Paint will not stick to a wall that is dirty. First we have to remove the dirt. In the same way, only if we remove the dirt from our minds we can experience the presence of God.

"Tell the Divine Mother: 'O Mother of the Universe, kindly receive us in Your lap! Bring us up with care! You are eternal love. You are the one who stands by us in all the births. Only You can get us across this ocean of births and deaths! Take us into Your boat, O Amma! Please accept this ritual that we are going to perform! A father accepts both the little baby's 'cha' and the big boy's 'accha' (father) the same way. Kindly accept this too in the same manner! We can only say 'cha!' You know our language. Mother always knows the baby's language. We have no ability to utter Your names properly or to praise You or to appreciate who You are. Yet we want to chant Your name, like a baby. Kindly accept that and bless us with Your presence. We leave ourselves to Your will. If You forsake us, there is no one else to love us like You, to help us like You! You are the one who forgives a hundred mistakes that we make. The world, on the other hand, comes to destroy us when we make a single mistake even when we have done a hundred things right. Do not leave us, O Amma!' Pray to Mother like this.

"Now, imagine that you are lighting a lamp - the lamp of wisdom and unity. The fire to light it must come from the rubbing of your love for the Lord. Light the incense stick and wave it three times around Devī. Place some *tāmbula* (betel leaves and areca nut) on Mother's right side. Then we start the *arcana*. Learn to chant the *mantras* with an open heart. Offer each flower seeing Mother before you. Picture in your mind each flower falling at those divine feet. The real flower is the flower of the mind. That is what we need to give Her.

"There is a story. Once a brahmin priest worshipped the Lord with many different kinds of flowers. Then he asked, 'Lord! Do you want any other flower now? Are you satisfied now?' The priest was proud that he had done something big, that he had given the Lord everything. The Lord said, 'There is one more flower.' 'What flower is that,' asked the priest. '*Mānasa puṣpa* (mind-flower) ,' said the Lord. 'Where can I find that,' asks the priest. 'Right here,' says the Lord. He meant the flower that is the heart. Without knowing this, the priest wandered all over looking for *mānasa puṣpa*, all due to the lack of *sraddha* (attention). After running around for a long time, he came back exhausted and fell at the Lord's feet and said with great sadness, 'Lord, I could not get *mānasa puṣpa* anywhere; please be satisfied with this! I have only my heart to give you!' The Lord replied, 'This is the *mānasa puṣpa* I asked for! What I want is the flower of purity and love. Without that, even if you spend millions and do *pūja* for a hundred births, you will not get My presence for even a second. The attitude of surrender is the bridge that brings you close to Me. You have not put up that bridge. I am waiting near you for that.'

"Therefore, know who the Divine Mother is and do the worship with purity of heart. We are learning to talk openly to Devī. You are the river. We are the dirty gutter. Mother, please flow into us! Remove our dirt. Wipe out our ignorance! We should have the sense of surrender: 'Mother, You are the one who is capable of giving everything. We surrender everything to You!' We are just puppets in Her hands! 'We leave everything to Your will. We will get everything if we depend on You. If we depend on milk, we can get buttermilk and yogurt, butter, everything. But till now that is not what we did; we went after the buttermilk and the yogurt. We did not take refuge in milk. If we take refuge in You, we get the perishable and the Imperishable. We take refuge in the milk that is You. We did not do that till now.' We get everything when we depend on the Lord. 'We leave everything to You. These children of Yours want only peace of mind!'

"Now it is time to recite a hymn in praise of Devī. Children, when it is being recited, think as follows: 'Mother, we don't know anything. We don't know any *tantra* or *mantra*. We are just trying to call out to Amma. Mother, give us strength.' We should have the humble attitude that we are nothing. We should start the *arcana* with that feeling. The *arcana* should be done with concentration. Without that, all that you get from this is just fatigue. Time is wasted, too. The mind should stick to Mother totally. It should be merged with Devī who is nothing but the Supreme Self. When each name is chanted, picture that you are taking a beautiful white flower from your heart and placing it at Devī's feet. The white flower is a symbol of your pure heart. Everyone should do the *arcana* by actually offering the mental flowers with your hand. Only in such ways can we capture the mind. Get rid of your shyness, children! We are aiming for the eternal. All these external things are not going to last."

(A brahmacharin sings a verse starting with 'O Mother, I know neither your mantra..')

'O Mother, I know neither Your *mantra* nor Your *yantra*; I do not know any hymn in praise of You. I do not know how to call You or to meditate on You. Nor do I know any stories extolling Your greatness. I do not know the gestures to worship You. I do not know how to cry out for You. But Mother, I do know that following Your path is the sure way to end my sorrows!'

"After this, one person should recite the meditation verses for Lalita Devī and then the *Lalitā Sahasranāma*, name by name. After each name, the others should respond with 'Om Parāśaktyai Namaḥ' and do the *arcana* within their minds.

(Mother also chants the mantras loudly. The worship lasts for about one and a half hours.)

"Now imagine that you take some *pāyasam* (sweet pudding) in a vessel and place it in front of the triangle you drew. It is the *pāyasam* of love that you should offer to Mother, not any other kind. The sweetness of the rice, raw sugar and coconut in that *payasam* of love cannot be measured. Imagine scooping out the *payasam* and feeding it to Mother. Picture in your mind that She is eating it with great relish. Then imagine saying, 'O Amma, I don't have knowledge, I don't know the scriptures, the rituals, or *yoga* or *pūja*. Please protect me, Amma!'

"Now we will sing a hymn. Children, clap your hands to the rhythm and sing. Mother is standing in front a little above everything, transcending everything. The company of the Mother of the Universe is a great festival of joy. Children repeat the song with love. Every one should try to sing.

(Amma proceeds to sing the following three songs:)

Parāśaktī Param Jyotī
Parātpare Radhe Devī
Jaya Rādhe Jaya Rādhe
Rāsarāseśvari Priyā Priyā
Jaya Rādhe Jaya Rādhe
Rādhe Śyām Rādhe Śyām

Devī Devī Devī Jaganmohini
Chaṇḍikā Devī Chaṇḍamuṇḍahāriṇī
Chāmundeśvarī Ambike Devī
Samsāra Sāgaram Taranam Ceyyuvān
Nerāya Mārgam Kāttane Devī

Om Namah Śivaya Om Namah Śivaya

"Now we wave the camphor in front of Devī. We should in fact become the camphor. Imagine that you are taking the camphor, lighting it and waving it with concentration in front of the Divine Mother from head to foot and from foot to head. Then put it aside. As we do this, imagine that we ourselves are dissolving and merging with Mother. Then imagine that you are taking some flowers and after circling them around the burning camphor flame, offering them at the Divine Mother's feet.

"Now everyone should stand up, and imagine that you are circumambulating Devī three times, as you do in temples. Chant 'Amma.. Amma..' in your mind. Then prostrate.

"Now repeat the *ṣānti mantras* (peace invocations) that are about to be chanted. Join your palms and hold them close to the heart. Chant with attention and patience.

"If there is a madman next door, we are the ones who lose peace of mind. Therefore, we should first pray for a good environment. We should pray for goodness in others. We get the benefit of that. When we pick flowers for *pūja*, we are the ones who enjoy the fragrance first. Whether we wish for it or not, we will certainly get the benefits of selfless worship. We should wish for the good of the world. That will expand our minds.

"First, repeat OM three times.

Asato mā satgamaya
Tamaso mā jyotirgamaya
Mṛtyor mā amṛtamgamaya
Om śāntih śāntih śāntiḥ

Om sarveṣām svastir bhavatu
Sarveṣām śāntir bhavatu
Sarveṣām pūrṇam bhavatu
Sarveṣām maṇgalam bhavatu
Om śāntih śāntih śāntiḥ

Om pūrṇamadah pūrṇamidam
Pūrṇāt pūrṇam udachyate
Pūrṇasya pūrṇam ādāya
Pūrṇamevā vaśiṣyate
Om śāntih śāntih śāntiḥ

Om Śrī gurubhyo namaḥ
Hariḥ Om!"

"Now we should take Devī, whom we installed in the triangle, back into our hearts. Imagine taking Her with both hands and installing Her in the lotus of your heart, saying, 'Mother, please never forsake me! Always be with me!' You should imagine this with both hands pressed against your heart. Bend down and prostrate before the triangle. Then imagine wiping away the triangle. Meditate on Devi's form for a few seconds. Concentrate your mind on Devī. Crying 'Amma.. Amma..', focus attention on Mother's feet, then on Her lap, chest, neck, face, eyes, nose, lips, earrings, the gem-studded crown, Her hair. Thus enjoy that beauty by focussing on each part. Now focus attention on each part of Her body again, now from head to foot. Then prostrate, touching Mother's feet with your forehead.

"Children, you should plan to get together regularly once a month and do this *pūja*. Women can do it even during their monthly periods; take a bath, and sitting separately from others, make a triangle in front of you and do the *pūja*. Devī resides in our hearts, after all. There is no purity or impurity in Her world. But in this world, we have not advanced that far; therefore, sit apart; do not sit touching each other. We should set an example; otherwise, everyone will start making mistakes. You can do this *pūja* at home or anywhere.

"Śivane!"

BENEFITS OF THE ARCANA

"The *arcana* brings prosperity to the family and peace to the world. It will remove the effects of past mistakes. We will get the strength to understand Truth and live according to it. We will get long life and wealth. The atmosphere gets purified.

With the chanting of *Lalitā Sahasranāma*, the energy in every nerve of our body will be awakened. This *pūja* will eliminate all harm arising from the displeasure of ancestors or from evil spells from others. There is no need after this for you children to resort to special rites to ward off such evils, because the power that you gain by this one-pointed *pūja* is not achieved by any priest or *mantravādin* in a thousand years of worship. When we pray with open hearts, the effects of all evil spells vanish. You need not fear any more about such things. Of course there are some bad times in one's life; that is not from any evil spells cast by anybody. Do not be misled by these. Those who do this need not go for anything else. All evils will be removed."

Alphabetical Listing of the Names

NO.	NAME
994	Ābālagopaviditā
990	Abhyāsātiśayajñātā
285	Ābrahmakīṭajananī
554	Acintyarūpā
988	Adbhutacāritrā
615	Ādiśaktiḥ
649	Adṛśyā
553	Agragaṇyā
866	Ajā
663	Ajājaitrī
828	Ājñā
521	Ājñācakrābjanilayā
103	Ājñācakrāntarālasthā
993	Ajñānadhvāntadīpikā
860	Akāntā
489	Akṣamālādidharā
96	Akulā
537	Amatiḥ
985	Ambā
295	Ambikā
616	Ameyā
483	Amṛtādimahāśaktisamvṛtā
814	Amūrtā
296	Anādinidhanā
987	Anaghā
485	Anāhatābjanilayā
29	Anākalitasādriśyacibukaśrivirājitā
729	Ānandakalikā
926	Anarghyakaivalyapadadāyinī
50	Anavadyāṅgī
620	Anekakoṭibrahmāṇḍajananī
815	Anityatṛptā

517 Aṅkuśādipraharaṇā
669 Annadā
870 Antarmukhasamārādhyā
273 Anugrahadā
541 Anuttamā
642 Aparicchedyā
754 Aparṇā
413 Aprameyā
476 Āraktavarṇā
37 Aruṇāruṇakausumbhavastrabhāsvatkaṭītaṭī
15 Aṣṭamīcandravibhrājadalikasthalaśobhitā
662 Aṣṭamūrtiḥ
972 Āśobhanā
516 Asthisamsthitā
67 Aśvārūḍhādhiṣṭhitāśvakoṭikoṭibhirāvṛtā
508 Atigarvitā
617 Ātmā
583 Ātmavidyā
639 Avaradā
992 Avyājakaruṇāmūrtiḥ
398 Avyaktā
427 Ayī
894 Ayoniḥ
871 Bahirmukhasudurlabhā
824 Bahurūpā
905 Baindavāsanā
965 Bālā
677 Balipriyā
546 Bandhamocinī
964 Bandhūkakusumaprakhyā
511 Bandinyādisamanvitā
547 Barbarālakā
116 Bhadramūrtiḥ
115 Bhadrapriya
277 Bhagamālinī
715 Bhagārādhyā
279 Bhagavatī
276 Bhairavī
747 Bhaktacittakekighanāghanā

484	Ḍākinīsvarī
600	Dakṣayajñavināśinī
923	Dakṣiṇādakṣiṇārādhyā
725	Dakṣiṇāmūrtirūpiṇī
598	Dākṣāyaṇī
498	Ḍāmaryādibhirāvṛtā
488	Damṣṭrojvalā
608	Daṇḍanītisthā
602	Darahāsojjvalanmukhī
601	Darāndolitadīrghākṣī
924	Darasmeramukhāmbujā
977	Daśamudrasamārādhyā
581	Dayāmūrtiḥ
701	Deśakālāparicchinnā
5	Devakāryasamudyatā
64	Devarṣigaṇasanghātastūyamānātmavaibhavā
607	Deveśī
886	Dhanadhānyavivardhinī
885	Dhanādhyakṣā
957	Dhanyā
955	Dharā
956	Dharasutā
884	Dharmādhārā
255	Dharmādharmavivarjitā
959	Dharmavardhinī
958	Dharmiṇī
916	Dhīrā
917	Dhīrasamarcitā
446	Dhṛtiḥ
254	Dhyānadhyātṛdhyeyarūpā
641	Dhyānagamyā
695	Dīkṣitā
631	Divyagandhāḍhyā
621	Divyavigrahā
195	Doṣavarjitā
744	Daurbhāgyatūlavātūlā
650	Dṛśyarahitā
191	Duḥkhahantrī
194	Durācāraśamanī

526 Haridrānnaikarasikā
304 Heyopādeyavarjitā
595 Hṛdayasthā
303 Hṛdyā
302 Hrīmatī
301 Hrīmkarī
712 Ī
658 Iccāśaktijñānaśaktikriyāśaktisvarūpiṇī
594 Indradhanuṣprabhā
41 Indragopaparikṣiptasmaratūṇābhajaṅghikā
271 Īśvarī
418 Jaḍaśaktiḥ
419 Jaḍātmikā
935 Jagaddhātrī
257 Jāgariṇī
325 Jagatīkaṇḍā
378 Jālandharasthitā
823 Jananī
851 Janmamṛtyujarātaptajanaviśrāntidāyinī
766 Japāpuṣpanibhākṛtiḥ
745 Jarādhvāntaraviprabhā
377 Jayā
788 Jayatsenā
643 Jñānadā
980 Jñānagamyā
981 Jñānajñeyasvarūpiṇī
979 Jñānamudrā
644 Jñānavigrahā
71 Jvālāmālinikākṣiptavahniprākāramadhyagā
323 Kadambakusumapriyā
21 Kadambamañjarīkḷptakarṇapūramanoharā
330 Kādambarīpriyā
60 Kadambavanavāsinī
625 Kaivalyapadadāyinī
513 Kākinīrūpadhāriṇī
557 Kālahantrī
464 Kālakanṭhī
328 Kalālāpā
794 Kalāmālā

14	Kuruvindamaṇiśreṇīkanatkoṭīramaṇḍitā
436	Kuśalā
896	Kūṭasthā
740	Lajjā
503	Lākinyambāsvarūpiṇī
35	Lakṣyaromalatādhāratāsamunneyamadhyamā
1000	Lalitāmbikā
738	Lāsyapriyā
739	Layakarī
648	Līlākḷptabrahmāṇḍamaṇḍalā
865	Līlāvigraharūpiṇī
966	Līlāvinodinī
171	Lobhanāśinī
960	Lokātītā
664	Lokayātrāvidhāyinī
454	Lolākṣīkāmarūpiṇī
647	Lopāmudrārcitā
432	Madaghūrṇitaraktākṣī
159	Madanāśinī
433	Madapāṭalagaṇḍabhūḥ
431	Madaśālinī
717	Madhumatī
510	Madhuprītā
575	Mādhvīpānālasā
370	Madhyamā
222	Mahābalā
231	Mahābhairavapūjitā
219	Mahābhogā
223	Mahābuddhiḥ
237	Mahacatuḥṣaṣṭikoṭiyoginīgaṇasevitā
209	Mahādevī
78	Mahāgaṇeśanirbhinnavighnayantrapraharṣitā
752	Mahāgrāsā
220	Mahaiśvaryā
578	Mahākailāsanilayā
751	Mahākālī
233	Mahākāmeśamahiṣī
403	Mahākāmeśanayanakumudāhlādakaumudī
210	Mahālakṣmī

48 Mahālāvaṇyaśevadhiḥ
227 Mahāmantrā
215 Mahāmāyā
580 Mahanīyā
59 Mahāpadmāṭavīsamsthā
81 Mahāpāśupatāstragninirdagdhāsurasainikā
214 Mahāpātakanāśinī
571 Mahāpralayasākṣinī
213 Mahāpūjyā
218 Mahāratiḥ
212 Mahārūpā
109 Mahāsaktiḥ
217 Mahāśaktiḥ
582 Mahāsāmrājyaśālinī
229 Mahāsanā
753 Mahāśanā
216 Mahāsattvā
224 Mahāsiddhiḥ
226 Mahātantrā
774 Mahatī
234 Mahātripurasundarī
584 Mahāvidyā
493 Mahāvirendravaradā
221 Mahāvīryā
230 Mahāyāgakramārādhyā
228 Mahāyantrā
225 Mahāyogeśvareśvarī
932 Maheśī
232 Maheśvaramahākalpamahātāṇḍavasākṣiṇī
208 Māheśvarī
750 Maheśvarī
718 Mahī
570 Maitryādivāsanālabhyā
524 Majjāsamsthā
458 Malayācalavāsinī
455 Mālinī
165 Mamatāhantrī
500 Māmsaniṣṭhā
930 Manasvinī

931 Mānavatī
776 Mandārakusumapriyā
28 Mandasmitaprabhāpūramajjatkāmeśamānasā
933 Maṅgalākṛtiḥ
40 Māṇikyamakutākārajānudvayavirajitā
495 Maṇipūrābjanilayā
101 Maṇipūrāntaruditā
941 Manomayī
207 Manonmanī
10 Manorūpekṣukodaṇḍā
415 Manovācāmagocarā
846 Mantrasārā
786 Mantriṇīnyastarājyadhūḥ
75 Mantriṇyambāviracitaviṣangavadhatoṣitā
238 Manuvidyā
47 Marālīmandagamanā
785 Martāṇḍabhairavārādhyā
457 Mātā
445 Matiḥ
577 Mātṛkāvarṇarūpiṇī
576 Mattā
716 Māyā
538 Medhā
509 Medoniṣṭhā
775 Merunilayā
735 Mithyājagadadhiṣṭhānā
565 Mitrarūpiṇī
163 Mohanāśinī
562 Mohinī
564 Mṛḍānī
211 Mṛḍapriyā
561 Mṛgākṣī
579 Mṛṇālamṛdudorlatā
749 Mṛtyudārukuṭhārikā
181 Mṛtyumathanī
868 Mugdhā
519 Mugdaudanāsaktacittā
16 Mukhacandrakalaṅkābhamṛganābhiviśeṣakā
563 Mukhyā

736 Muktidā
839 Muktinilayā
737 Muktirūpiṇī
838 Mukundā
99 Mūlādhāraikanilayā
514 Mūlādhārāmbujārūḍhā
89 Mūlakūṭatrayakalebarā
88 Mūlamantrātmikā
397 Mūlaprakṛti
840 Mūlavigraharūpiṇī
816 Munimānasahamsikā
813 Mūrtā
34 Nabhyālavālaromālilatāphalakucadvayī
299 Nādarūpā
901 Nādarūpiṇī
900 Naiṣkarmyā
44 Nakhadīdhitisañchannanamajjanatamoguṇā
460 Naliṇī
732 Nāmapārāyaṇaprītā
300 Nāmarūpavivarjitā
450 Nandinī
733 Nandividyā
298 Nārāyaṇī
734 Naṭesvarī
19 Navacampakapuṣpābhanāsādaṇḍavirājitā
24 Navavidrumabimbaśrīnyakkāriradanachadā
287 Nijājñārūpanigamā
12 Nijāruṇaprabhāpūramajjadbrahmāṇḍamaṇḍalā
27 Nijasallāpamādhuryavinirbhartsitakacchapī
569 Nikhileśvarī
185 Nīlacikurā
177 Nirābādhā
132 Nirādhārā
156 Nīrāgā
161 Nirahaṅkārā
137 Nirākārā
138 Nirākulā
877 Nirālambā
876 Nirāmayā

133 Nirañjanā
151 Nirantarā
186 Nirapāyā
147 Nirāśrayā
187 Niratyayā
150 Niravadya
174 Nirbhavā
178 Nirbhedā
667 Nirdvaitā
139 Nirguṇā
155 Nirīśvarā
134 Nirlepā
170 Nirlobhā
158 Nirmadā
135 Nirmalā
164 Nirmamā
162 Nirmohā
180 Nirnāśā
154 Nirupādhiḥ
389 Nirupamā
143 Nirupaplavā
390 Nirvāṇasukhadāyinī
176 Nirvikalpā
145 Nirvikārā
160 Niṣcintā
140 Niṣkalā
153 Niṣkalaṅkā
142 Niṣkāmā
152 Niṣkāraṇā
182 Niṣkriyā
168 Niṣkrodha
166 Niṣpāpā
183 Niṣparigrahā
146 Niṣprapañcā
172 Nissamśayā
429 Niḥsīmamahimā
789 Nistraiguṇyā
184 Nistulā
136 Nityā

807 Paramdhāma
396 Parameśvarī
806 Paramjyotiḥ
940 Parāmodā
939 Paramodārā
573 Parāniṣṭhā
790 Parāparā
572 Parāśaktiḥ
809 Parātparā
246 Pārvatī
811 Pāśahantrī
810 Pāśahastā
482 Paśulokabhayankarī
354 Paśupāśavimocanī
368 Paśyantī
773 Pāṭalīkusumapriyā
619 Pāvanākṛtiḥ
480 Pāyasānnapriyā
593 Phālasthā
507 Pītavarṇā
394 Prabhārūpā
393 Prabhāvatī
827 Pracaṇḍā
938 Pragalbhā
574 Prajñānaghanarūpiṇī
261 Prājñātmikā
830 Prakaṭākṛtiḥ
783 Prāṇadā
832 Prāṇadātrī
784 Prāṇarūpiṇī
831 Prāṇeśvarī
826 Prasavitrī
395 Prasiddhā
610 Pratipanmukhyarākāntatithimaṇḍalapūjitā
829 Pratiṣṭhā
781 Pratyagrūpā
367 Pratyakcitīrūpa
730 Premarūpā
731 Priyaṅkarī

792 Sāmarasyaparāyaṇā
502 Samastabhaktasukhadā
963 Śamātmikā
98 Samayācāratatparā
97 Samayāntasthā
122 Śāmbhavī
954 Śambhumohinī
422 Sandhyā
268 Samhāriṇī
355 Samhṛtāśeṣapāṣaṇḍā
126 Śāṅkarī
66 Sampatkarīsamārūḍhasindhuravrajasevitā
710 Sampradāyeśvarī
692 Sāmrājyadāyinī
880 Samsārapaṅkanirmagnasamudharaṇapaṇḍitā
173 Samśayaghnī
726 Sanakādisamārādhyā
197 Sāndrakaruṇā
141 Śāntā
447 Śāntiḥ
131 Śāntimatī
853 Śāntyatītakalātmikā
129 Śaraccandranibhānanā
123 Śāradārādhyā
704 Sarasvatī
953 Śarmadā
125 Śarmadāyinī
51 Sarvābharaṇabhūṣitā
659 Sarvādhārā
702 Sarvagā
196 Sarvajñā
697 Sarvalokavaśaṅkarī
758 Sarvalokeśī
200 Sarvamaṅgalā
204 Sarvamantrasvarūpinī
203 Sarvamayī
703 Sarvamohinī
552 Sarvamṛtyunivāriṇī
124 Śarvāṇī

819 Sarvāntaryāminī
995 Sarvānullaṅghyaśāsanā
913 Sarvāpadvinivāriṇī
698 Sarvārthadātrī
49 Sarvāruṇā
199 Sarvaśaktimayī
206 Sarvatantrarūpā
724 Sarvatantreśī
962 Sarvātītā
532 Sarvatomukhī
529 Sarvavarṇopaśobhitā
263 Sarvāvasthāvivarjitā
645 Sarvavedāntasamvedyā
551 Sarvavyādhipraśamanī
205 Sarvayantrātmika
530 Sarvāyudhadharā
202 Sarveśvarī
708 Sarvopādhivinirmuktā
852 Sarvopaniṣadudghuṣṭā
533 Sarvaudanaprītacittā
705 Śāstramayī
845 Śāstrasārā
952 Śāśvataiśvaryā
951 Śāśvatī
700 Satcidānandarūpiṇī
820 Satī
130 Śātodarī
791 Satyajñānānandarūpā
646 Satyānandasvarūpiṇī
818 Satyarūpā
693 Satyasandhā
817 Satyavratā
699 Sāvitrī
912 Savyāpasavyamārgasthā
991 Ṣaḍadhvātītarūpiṇī
523 Ṣaḍānanā
386 Ṣaḍaṅgadevatāyuktā
108 Ṣaṭcakroparisamsthitā
387 Ṣāḍguṇyaparipūritā

473	Siddhamātā
472	Siddhavidyā
471	Siddheśvarī
632	Sindūratilakāñcitā
46	Śiñjānamaṇimañjīramaṇḍitasrīpadāmbujā
591	Śirasthitā
412	Śiṣṭapūjitā
411	Śiṣteṣṭā
53	Śivā
405	Śivadūtiḥ
727	Śivajñānapradāyinī
52	Śivakāmeśvarāṅkasthā
408	Śivaṅkarī
407	Śivamūrtiḥ
410	Śivaparā
409	Śivapriyā
406	Śivārādhyā
999	Śivaśaktyaikyarūpiṇī
540	Smṛtiḥ
492	Snigdhaudanapriyā
462	Śobhanā
683	Śobhanāsulabhāgatiḥ
910	Saumyā
2	Śri Mahārājñī
1	Śri Mātā
998	Śrī Śivā
996	Śrīcakrarājanilayā
392	Śrīkaṇṭhārdhaśarīriṇī
127	Śrīkarī
85	Śrīmadvāgbhavakūtaikasvarūpamukhapaṅkajā
56	Śrimannagaranāyikā
3	Śrimat Simhāsaneśvarī
997	Śrīmat Tripurasundarī
376	Śṛṅgārarasasampūrṇa
587	Śrīṣodaśākṣarīvidyā
264	Sṛṣṭikartrī
585	Śrīvidyā
539	Śrutiḥ
929	Śrutisamstutavaibhavā

289 Śrutisīmantasindūrīkṛtapādābjadhūlikā
36 Stanabhāradalanmadhyapaṭṭabandhavalitrayā
927 Stotrapriyā
928 Stutimatī
761 Subhagā
682 Śubhakarī
461 Subhruḥ
765 Śuddhā
973 Śuddhamānasā
25 Śuddhavidyāṅkurākāradvijapaṅktidvayojvalā
61 Sudhāsāgaramadhyasthā
106 Sudhāsārābhivarṣiṇī
879 Sudhāsrutiḥ
968 Sukhakarī
192 Sukhapradā
681 Sukhārādhyā
531 Śuklasamsthitā
522 Śuklavarṇā
467 Sūkṣmarūpiṇī
506 Śulādyāyudhasampannā
967 Sumaṅgalī
55 Sumerumadhyaśṛṅgasthā
459 Sumukhī
660 Supratiṣṭhā
260 Suptā
463 Suranāyikā
970 Suvāsinī
971 Suvāsinyarcanaprītā
969 Suveṣāḍhyā
915 Svabhāvamadhurā
536 Svadhā
54 Svādhīnavallabhā
504 Svādhiṣṭhānāmbujagatā
535 Svāhā
258 Svapantī
414 Svaprakāśā
764 Svargāpavargadā
638 Svarnagarbhā
914 Svasthā

448	Svastimatiḥ
723	Svatantrā
365	Svātmānandalavībhūtabrahmādyānandasantatiḥ
878	Svātmārāmā
486	Śyāmābhā
259	Taijasātmikā
847	Talodarī
559	Tāmbulapūritamukhī
361	Tamopahā
360	Tanumadhyā
359	Tāpasārādhyā
357	Tāpatrayāgnisantaptasamāhlādanacandrikā
20	Tārākāntitiraskārināsābharaṇabhāsurā
922	Taruṇādityapāṭalā
358	Taruṇī
425	Tat
22	Tāṭankayugalībhūtatapanoḍupamaṇḍalā
107	Taḍillatāsamaruciḥ
363	Tatpadalakṣyārthā
906	Tattvādhikā
908	Tattvamarthasvarupinī
907	Tattvamayī
424	Tattvāsanā
452	Tejovatī
270	Tirodhānakarī
872	Trayī
629	Tridaśeśvarī
984	Triguṇā
763	Triguṇātmikā
627	Trijagadvandyā
983	Trikhaṇḍeśī
986	Trikoṇagā
597	Trikoṇāntaradīpikā
588	Trikūṭā
477	Trilocanā
628	Trimurtiḥ
453	Trinayanā
626	Tripurā
875	Tripuramālinī

850 Varṇarūpiṇī
286 Varṇāśramavidhāyinī
333 Vāruṇīmadavihvalā
670 Vasudā
470 Vayovasthāvivarjitā
338 Vedajananī
335 Vedavedyā
652 Vedyavarjitā
904 Vidagdhā
337 Vidhātrī
891 Vidrumābhā
549 Vidyā
402 Vidyāvidyāsvarūpiṇī
451 Vighnanāśinī
346 Vijayā
253 Vijñānaghanarūpiṇī.
902 Vijñānakalanā
651 Vijñātrī
340 Vilāsinī
347 Vimalā
943 Vimānasthā
548 Vimarśarūpiṇī
336 Vindhyācalanivāsinī
887 Viprapriyā
888 Viprarūpā
899 Vīrā
778 Virāḍrūpā
937 Virāgiṇī
898 Vīragoṣṭhipriya
779 Virajā
836 Vīramātā
777 Vīrārādhyā
936 Viśālākṣī
102 Viṣṇugranthivibhedinī
339 Viṣṇumāyā
893 Viṣṇurūpiṇī
834 Viśṛnkhalā
475 Viśuddhicakranilayā
76 Viśukraprānaharanavārāhīvīryananditā

889 Viśvabhramaṇakāriṇī
759 Viśvadhāriṇī
334 Viśvādhikā
637 Viśvagarbhā
890 Viśvagrāsā
934 Viśvamātā
256 Viśvarūpā
384 Viśvasākṣiṇī
780 Viśvatomukhī
401 Vividhākārā
835 Viviktasthā
550 Viyadādijagatprasūḥ
837 Viyatprasūḥ
671 Vṛddhā
421 Vyāhṛtiḥ
399 Vyaktāvyaktasvarūpiṇī
400 Vyāpinī
942 Vyomakeśī
883 Yajamānasvarūpini
882 Yajñakartrī
881 Yajñapriyā
769 Yajñarūpā
534 Yākinyambāsvarūpiṇī
474 Yaśasvinī
654 Yogadā
656 Yogānandā
653 Yoginī
655 Yogyā
982 Yonimudrā
895 Yoninilayā
657 Yugandharā